COCKLESHELL
HEROES

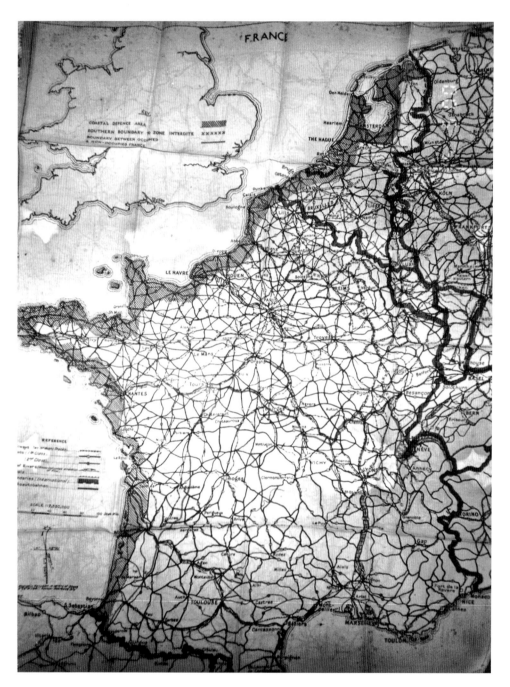

Laver's escape map.

COCKLESHELL
HEROES
THE FINAL WITNESS

QUENTIN REES

AMBERLEY

For the Homunculus

First published 2010

Amberley Publishing Plc
Cirencester Road, Chalford,
Stroud, Gloucestershire, GL6 8PE

www.amberley-books.com

British Library Cataloguing in Publication Data.
A catalogue record for this book is available from the British Library.

ISBN 978 1 84868 861 2

Typeset in 10pt on 12pt Adobe Caslon Pro.
Typesetting and Origination by Amberley Publishing.
Printed in the UK.

Contents

The results of the *Frankton* Raid.

Forewords

As the Royal Navy's senior serving submarine officer, I was delighted to accept Quentin Rees' invitation to provide the foreword for this book.

I recall a time when, as the Commanding Officer of Her Majesty's Submarine *Orpheus* in 1983, the boat visited Bordeaux for an operational stand-off. In common with most Royal Navy and Royal Marines personnel, I knew something of the Cockleshell Heroes and their exploits. It struck me, as I manoeuvred *Orpheus* through the tricky tidal waters of the Gironde, past the lush vineyards, that the freedoms we were to enjoy during that visit had been the result of considerable sacrifices 60 years earlier. To this day, the matchless courage and extraordinary motivation of the Royal Marines selected to undertake Operation *Frankton* remains inspirational. Theirs is a remarkable story in its own right, but the author goes further in shedding new light on the Operation.

His extensive research and thoughtful analysis reveals many new insights about the most outstanding commando raid of the War; not least the important enabling roles played by others, and the particular qualities of courage and leadership they demonstrated; those who conducted highly risky reconnaissance missions, who pushed untested prototype equipment to the limits, who risked their lives and those of their families to help the surviving Commandos make their escape from occupied France. All played their part in shortening the daunting odds against a successful mission.

There is much in this accomplished study to fascinate any reader. For me, the detailed account of the contribution made by the officers and ship's company of His Majesty's Submarine *Tuna*, under the command of Dickie Raikes, is especially compelling. It was Raikes who had the power to abort the mission if he believed that they had been detected, and to whom fell the responsibility for delivering the Royal Marines, undetected, at night, through a wall of mines and German patrol boats. You certainly need a sense of humour to take that on. The picture of Raikes that comes across is also one of a calmly determined man who knew his boat – and his men – inside out. These were characteristics typical of the many heroic submarine commanders of the Second World War, and which were no less in evidence during the Cold War. They are also, of course, common to the many other courageous leaders, not least the officer in charge of the Commandos, 'Blondie' Hasler. Both he and Raikes formed an effective partnership founded in mutual admiration. Both were born leaders, cast from the same mould – and, as the Nazis were to find to their cost, together they were a formidable foe.

Admiral Sir Mark Stanhope, GCB, OBE, ADC
First Sea Lord and Chief of Naval Staff

Quentin Rees has already proved himself to be the leading expert on British military canoes with his excellent book of 2008, *The Cockleshell Canoes*. There is no-one better, therefore, to write a major new work on the famous 'Cockleshell Heroes' raid on Bordeaux in December 1942. The details of this secret operation and its tragic aftermath have become garbled over the years and the author has spared no efforts in his attempts to set the record straight. I have been most impressed not only by Quentin's assiduous research skills and his capacity to track down obscure evidence from a wide range of sources but also by the enormous enthusiasm that lies at the heart of his historical endeavours. No stone has been left unturned and the result is as close to a complete and comprehensive analysis as is possible. It must replace all previous works on the subject as the standard account and it is a worthy monument to those who lost their lives in the events it so grippingly covers.

Eric Grove
Professor of Naval History
University of Salford

To many of the post-Second World War generation, the sight of José Ferrer and Anthony Newley paddling canoes in a darkened tank of water on a film set and their Royal Marine doubles braving the surf of the River Tagus was their first encounter with the 'Cockleshell Heroes' story. This 1955 film was quickly followed by the publication of Brigadier C. E. Lucas Phillips book of the same name, and between them brought the story of the 1942 Royal Marine canoe attack on German shipping moored in the French port of Bordeaux to the public attention.

The Royal Marines Boom Patrol Detachment was the unit responsible for this raid, and its commanding officer, Major George Herbert 'Blondie' Hasler, had connections with both the film and the book. He hated the title of both and walked away from his role as technical adviser for the former to try and set the matter right in the latter. 'Operation Frankton', as it was officially titled, had been lost to the war weary public awareness, and with its successful censorship and the fact that only Hasler and his canoeing partner Corporal Bill Sparks had survived the attack, it could have remained a small operation in the middle of a large war.

Hasler had drawn up his plans in July 1942, trained his volunteers from scratch and conducted the raid by December, then filed his operational report upon repatriation from Spain in April 1943. He would be embarrassed to be regarded a hero; his men were not even Commandos, although most would meet their fate as if they had been. Whilst the merits and lessons of the operation would occupy the general staff of Combined Operations and the Royal Marines, it was probably due to a junior officer within that staff that the story began to filter out. Lieutenant Wilfred Reginald Sendall was a 'Hostilities Only' officer commissioned from the ranks, who on completion of training at the 'Officer Cadet Training Unit' at Thurlestone, was appointed directly to the general staff. He had been a journalist for nine years with the *News Chronicle* (later absorbed into the *Daily Mail* in 1960) and obviously had an eye for a good story. Perhaps the first airing of the story appeared in the 1st February 1946 issue of Sir John Hammerton's part work 'The War Illustrated' where for sixpence you had a half page of narrative with an artist's impression of canoes launching from HM Submarine *Tuna*. By 1950 Sendall had left the Royal Marines as a Major, but had become the editor of *The Globe & Laurel*, the Corps Magazine, and in a whole page review of Sir Bruce Lockhart's book *The Marines Were There*, a paragraph was devoted to the operation that featured for four pages in the actual book. In 1951 the story expanded to a chapter in the fittingly titled *Now It Can Be Told* by James Gleeson & Tom Waldron. This all formed the backdrop to the full exposure of the mid-1950s, and came at a time when the Royal Marines were simultaneously fighting possible disbandment and morphing into a Commando amphibious force: the publicity was most welcome.

The story has since passed into Royal Marines mythology, especially amongst the SBS, but publicly apart from anniversary articles and ghost written memoirs of the late Bill Sparks, it has until recently stood still. The setting up of 'the Frankton trail', a national walk following the escape line of Hasler and Sparks from France to Spain, and a biography of Hasler has begun to draw some sources together, but what you are about to read puts these and new research under the microscope.

Since the publication of his work *The Cockleshell Canoes*, Quentin Rees has continued his detailed researches into this pioneering operation and has come up with new information some sixty-eight years after the event. He has also devoted considerable effort into recording information on all the people related to the operation as well as the events that form the story. His analysis of all aspects of the plan, conduct, and consequences of operation 'Frankton' will in some ways leave you, the reader, to be the final witness.

Matt Little
RM Museum Archivist & Librarian

We volunteered for a new unit known as the Royal Marine Boom Patrol Detachment in the July of 1942 and trained intensely under Major 'Blondie' Hasler, using canoes. Within six months, thirteen of us were embarked on the submarine *Tuna* on a top secret mission to occupied France. We were told there would be no RV with the submarine and we would have to make our own way back to England via neutral Spain.

We were to paddle 100 miles down to Bordeaux and place limpet mines along the sides of numerous German ships. I had been injured in training and was reserve man for Operation *Frankton* on the S/M *Tuna*. While the rest of the men prepared to leave the dubious comforts of the submarine, I helped bring the canoes up from the torpedo room and to launch them into the water. I was given letters by most of them for their relatives, as well as a letter from Hasler, which I delivered to the Adjutant in Plymouth on our return to Britain. One of the canoes was damaged as it was pulled through the torpedo room hatch and the two occupants were to remain aboard too. As the other ten men paddled off into the darkness, I did not know then that it would be the last I would ever see of eight of them. They were great lads and it was a pity our time together was so short.

Quentin Rees has spent a lot of time with me, questioning me, teasing every little thing I knew about the raid and my friends from me. He has researched the story intensively and has produced, for the very first time, a truly accurate and complete story of what happened to the rest of my unit on Operation *Frankton* even after these sixty-eight years. It is an epic work, and a credit to the memory and work of the men of the RMBPD who undertook this most famous mission. We were immortalised in the film, *Cockleshell Heroes*, and in a subsequent book, but these are a rather fictionalised accounts of the raid. It was really a suicide mission and it was doubtful any of us would survive. Major Hasler and Marine Bill Sparks did survive though and I think that was because of Hasler's cleverness, bravery and resourcefulness. He could even pass as a Frenchman, thanks to his moustache and hat. I thoroughly enjoyed reading this book, and it is an unbelievably fascinating and stunningly detailed tribute to my brave friends who died on the mission, and to the French people who assisted them and risked their lives in doing so.

N. Colley

I grew up aware that one of Mother's brothers was a hero of World War II – a 'Cockleshell Hero'. Mabel Siddall, née Sheard, was his youngest sister. Lucas Phillips' book about the raid stood on the shelf next to the Bible in our home in Plymouth. Mother went to the first showing of the film in Plymouth, at The Drake cinema in 1955 and then was invited in 1966 to the commemoration ceremonies in Bordeaux. The exploit started to take on a more significant part in my perception of the history of the Sheard family.

This interest was only increased by my spending two summer vacations from university working at the British Consulate-General in Bordeaux. But still my late uncle George – Corporal George Jellicoe Sheard RM – was only a face in faded sepia photographs. I spoke once on the telephone with Bill Sparks, who told me George had always been the life and soul of the team, with a ready wit – and certainly his beaming grin in the photos would seem to confirm this.

Thanks to his research and probing questions, Quentin Rees has done much to bring all the brave characters in Operation *Frankton* to life, while at the same time revealing much new information. On behalf of all the families, many of whom I have met, I thank him most sincerely.

Peter J. Siddall
Sussex, 2010

Quentin's commitment to writing this complete and detailed book about the *Frankton* Raid is greatly appreciated by our family. The level of research he has carried out and his way of writing represents an impressive achievement. His desire to cover every aspect of the story from start to finish is something we value greatly.

It is clear he cares very much about the men who were involved in the raid – including our uncle Lt John MacKinnon. All these men were tremendously brave and would have known how dangerous volunteering for hazardous service would be. They were highly motivated and, as Quentin writes, 'They were not anxious to die – just anxious to matter.'

With the thoroughness of his research it is evident that Quentin wanted the whole truth to be known; it is much more of a tribute to them and the others associated with the mission than has ever been attempted. It should prove to be of great interest to many people of all generations for a long time to come.

As a family we particularly relate to John (he was always known as Jacky to the family). His bravery and maturity for a young man of his age is truly inspiring. If 'Jack' had survived I am sure he would have been a wonderful uncle and it is tremendously sad that we were not able to be part of the continued life of this remarkable young man. The story of his life and the path he took and that of each of his friends can now be known to the world for the first time. We will remember him always.

Ken Simms on Behalf of the Family

For 90 years the Not Forgotten Association has tried very hard to make sure that as many surviving servicemen and women as possible receive a little relief in the form of entertainment or recreation. The Not Forgotten Association's aims are to bring a little lightness and brightness into the lives of those who have done so much for their country without thought for themselves. This publication, *Cockleshell Heroes - The Final Witness*, is proof, if ever it was needed, that there are kind, supportive people who continue to make sure that individuals who have served their country are remembered and are 'Not Forgotten'. Even after decades, the author has sought to bring the whole truth and story of these men who went to war in a conflict that should always be remembered. Quentin Rees has produced the ultimate tribute, a fine work of great detail which we are pleased to be associated with.

Think of Them
Think of Us …

the
Not Forgotten
association

4th Floor
2 Grosvenor Gardens
London, SW1W 0DH
020 7730 2400

Author's Note

Blondie Hasler was a prominent figure before, during and after the event of 1942. This account might seem unduly inclined towards him to the detriment of the other individuals who were a part of this story. However, it should be noted that considerably more is reported of the other players in this narrative than ever before, and there has been a concerted effort made to show how these many individuals played an equally vital role, without which none of the ten men would have returned home. It is believed that Hasler, as one of the two that did return, would have applauded this.

It cannot be stressed too often that, without the previously 'unknown' individuals, this celebration of the effort and bravery of 'The Cockleshell Heroes' would never have lived on. This continued fascination is due largely to the 1955 film of the same name, even though, in the words of the captain of HMS *Tuna*[1], 'the script was a mass of bollocks' and 'omitted many incidents, hazardous, amusing or merely commonplace', because 'they aren't good box office'. Without the film, the story may well have faded away; the black and white film is still broadcast today. Whatever evocative piece of music is used to dramatise war films or footage, nothing can distract from just how much of a dirty, filthy thing war actually is – however it is dressed up.

It is expected that people will always remember, and this is encouraged. In truth, as time passes, all that is likely to sustain a remembrance for some is the fascination of war. How anyone remembers is immaterial as long as they do. John Stuart Mill summed this up rather well when he wrote, 'War is an ugly thing but not the ugliest of things: the decayed and degraded state of moral and patriotic feeling which thinks nothing worth of war, is worse …'

By never forgetting, we can retain a gratitude of the time that very many gave, for they will never get that time back; it is not recoverable. 'Our time' is a precious resource, which is often not realised by the young; very many who have been involved with war know this to be the case – but they are older and wiser.

The amateur in all our dealings must often carry enthusiasm to the brink of madness in order to produce something of note. The motivation for writing this account was born from a realisation that there was too much inaccurate nonsense in circulation … and the publisher's challenge to do better. In truth, it did not require an expert to produce this work; all it required was an analytical mind and the will to succeed. The author is reminded that a great scientist[2] is reputed to have said that 'all radical development takes place in the teeth of opposition from the expert', which prompted Hasler to think that 'perhaps the most difficult thing to guard against, as you get older, is the danger of becoming an expert'[3].

Acknowledgements

In life, it is important to acknowledge those who have rendered support. The author, for his part, wishes to thank those who have helped in the delivery of this historical rendering of the efforts of the few:

Malcolm Cavan, OBE, Marilyn Bullivant and Richard Woolridge, Professor Eric Grove, Norman Colley, Peter Siddal, François Boisnier, Raymond Quick, DSM, Bridget Hasler, Bridget Legge, Isabella Rebecca MacKinnon, Judith Margaret Simms, Kenneth John Simms, Daniel McGonigle, George Hogg, Iris Walker, Kelvin Aylett, Tony Ward, Russel Mills, Mick Jones, Campbell McCutcheon, James Sparks, Gilly Sparks, Richard Mitchell, Elsie Ambler, Anthony Higgins, Frank Smith, George Davies, Ken Crisp, Carol Mayle, Sheila Bynham, Elizabeth Cook, Morris Andrews, Janet Lafferty (née Ewart), Brian Lafferty, Roger Grimes, Nicola Gale, Maureen Cummings, Stephen Jackson, Florence Bonneau, Dr Jolyon Young, Gary Bowden, Melanie Bowden, Phyllis Laver, Amelie Dubreuille, Sue Linsey, Eddie Ward, Jake Hensman, OBE, DL, Peter Cameron, MC, Michael Francis Hodder and Brian Christopher Mollan, Mike Jones, Paul J. Reid, Paul Siveyer, John Kenn.

Special thanks go to Matt Little for suffering the trauma of my research over many years and Nick Mifsud for his unwavering support over an even longer period.

It is through their kindness that the author has been able to tell this story in its entirety. As with most things of importance, it is the detail that matters.

Introduction

'It is said that if someone wants to ruin the truth all they have to do is stretch it ...'

It is always a good idea to re-examine what people have taken for granted as the truth. The correct level of research is the key to this kind of examination, and it is not until a deeper research is undertaken that the truth is often revealed.

The complete story surrounding Operation *Frankton* is a very human one. For decades, it has remained untold, hidden from three generations – until now. This work will unveil the true story, including the careful reporting of people's lives and their deaths. If a reliable narrative is required, this account should be trusted rather than any that has previously been offered.[1] Simply put, it is as accurate in its research, evidencing and reporting as it can be at this distance. This most exciting story of the 'Cockleshell Heroes' will remain one of the ties that forever bind two close neighbours.

In December 1942, ten of the thirteen supremely fit chosen men disembarked from HMS *Tuna*, a T-class submarine. Each pair was secured in their specialised 15-foot, two-man, collapsible, flat-bottomed, semi-rigid canoes as they were lowered on the specially designed hoist from the submarine on a bitterly cold, calm and clear evening. These men were guests of the submariners who had delivered them to the Bay of Biscay from a loch in Scotland. All the Royal Marines had spent eight days[2] in cramped and unfavourable conditions they were unused to. The event these men had volunteered for was a small-scale amphibious raid into the heart of occupied France. It was very likely that anyone who went on this raid would not return. The men who were chosen were not informed of their mission until they were ensconced in the submarine. There was to be no rendezvous or extraction; they were to fend for themselves. Once their mission was completed, they were to make their way on foot towards a specific village some 100 miles inland in order to try and make contact with a Resistance network. They had been supplied with money – but did not have any identity papers. Only one of their number could understand and speak the native tongue. The canoeists were to make their escape in pairs. They would be putting their freedom and their lives in the hands of the indigenous population, who were themselves living in fear of the German occupation forces.

The mission was to paddle by night in the specially and individually named canvas-covered Cockle canoes to the port of Bordeaux – unnoticed. The distance they were to cover amounted to 105 land miles, penetrating deep into the busy Gironde Estuary. It would eventually require extremes of endurance and skill over a sustained period of five nights. The days would be filled with the inability to move from cover, broken sleep and the winter cold. They existed only on the food and water they carried; it had all been measured quite precisely. The aim was to place Limpet mines on ships that were being used as blockade runners and to sink them where they berthed, in order to severely interrupt the exchange of goods and technology between the two Axis powers of Germany and Japan. Each Cockle carried eight Limpet mines. The total weight carried in each canoe was at its maximum – nearly 500 lb.

Within hours of leaving the submarine, one canoe went missing in the first of a series of severe tidal races. Shortly afterwards, another two men capsized in another tidal race and eventually had to be left to fend for themselves in the ice-cold water. The weather was so cold it froze the seawater on the cockpit covers. That first night, the remaining canoeists had paddled for eleven hours. By the second night, the attack canoes had been reduced to two; the third Cockle had made it through the turbulent waters but had gone missing, failing to rendezvous. The remaining four Cockle canoeists began their second night's paddle, traversing nearly a mile across the sticky, sandy mud flats pulling their fully loaded canoes. That second night of paddling had produced another 20 plus miles, the third night delivered only 15 nautical miles, and on the next night only 9 nautical miles. The commanding officer had decided to change the plan of attack from the 10th to the following night of 11 December, and due to a clear night sky and the moon not yet set, the planned time for launching for the final approach to target for the four Limpeteers was also delayed slightly. They set the time fuses at 2100 hrs before they launched together in the bad conditions of flat calm in order to make the appointment. The two Cockle canoes separated in order to target the blockade-running ships on either side of the Bassens-Bordeaux area. With great skill, they placed their fizzy packages, and then the exit strategy began. By chance, the two canoes met up briefly before they again separated. The Cockles were scuttled, and the long journey overland began. Only two men survived this excursion to a foreign field. It is written one should not sacrifice to the god of good luck (Isaiah 65:11, New Jerusalem Bible, 1985). Let us say that they were indeed fortunate to live to tell the tale. That fortune was made all the more certain by the efforts of men and women who have never been named before now.

In the words of Admiral of the Fleet the Lord Mountbatten, 'Of the many brave and dashing raids carried out by the men of Combined Operations Command, none was more courageous or imaginative than Operation *Frankton*.'[3] Sir Winston Churchill believed this mission shortened the war by six months.

This account of the *Frankton* Raid is one of a fine operation that, under the leadership of Major Herbert George Hasler, was carried out by a 'particularly brave party of men', which consisted of nine of the men of No. 1 section: 2nd Lt MacKinnon, Sgt Wallace, L/Cpls Sheard and Laver and Marines Moffatt, Mills, Sparks, Conway and Ewart. One canoe, crewed by Ellery and Fisher, failed to launch. Colley as reserve was not called upon. It should be realised that the men who were captured were given over to the security forces and most were interrogated adeptly. Those who worked on them knew that these commandos would be disposed of ('slaughtered'[4]) after interrogation; the ranks of the commandos did not[5]. There was a special dispensation from their Führer, and therefore any torture could be 'legally' used to extract information from any commando. During the escape route used, four men were captured. They had been assisted during this time by the French peoples. Due to the fact no French person was subsequently arrested, it is assumed that the worst that could be meted out by the interrogators was not used – but this is only an assumption.

In the Beginning

> We shall go on to the end, we shall fight in France, we shall fight on the seas and oceans, we shall fight with growing confidence and growing strength in the air, we shall defend our island, whatever the cost may be, we shall fight on the beaches, we shall fight on the landing grounds, we shall fight in the fields and in the streets, we shall fight in the hills; we shall never surrender …

Not a natural public speaker, but with a supreme command of the English language, this author of many speeches would often practise for hours. He delivered his words with the characteristic slight stammer and lisp that have only served to inspire and remind us of this historical giant.

Sir Winston Churchill is often referred to as one of if not the greatest orator of the twentieth century. The policy of 'no surrender' made through his speeches during the summer of 1940 helped make people feel they were not alone in the struggle against the Hitler ideology.

Behind his seemingly robust exterior, which successfully led the people of Britain and other nations away from the clutches of tyranny, lurked a disparate condition. He was fighting a battle on two fronts, one of which he was never destined to win.

Before Churchill's ascendancy to power, he witnessed and suffered many failures. Events such as his dismissal from the Admiralty after the Dardanelles disaster in the First World War only served to fuel his depressive periods, which tended to be intense and prolonged. Other episodes fitted the classic profile of serious unipolar or bipolar depression.

Had he been a stable and equable man, he could never have inspired the nation. In 1940 when all the odds were against Britain, a leader of sober judgement might well have concluded that we were finished.[6]

Churchill made frequent references to his depression, which he called his 'Black Dog'. These depressions began in his youth and came and went throughout his long and remarkable life.

In describing Churchill's mood swings, Lord Beaverbrook said that he was always either 'at the top of the wheel of confidence or at the bottom of an intense depression'. After the war, to escape his 'Black Dog', Churchill threw himself into writing his 'War Memoirs'. Towards the end of his life, he felt a failure due to world events such as the Cold War.

In another famous speech on Bastille Day 1940, Churchill said,

This is no war of chieftains or of princes, of dynasties or national ambition; it is a war of peoples and of causes. There are vast numbers, not only in this island but in every land, who will render faithful service in this war, *but whose names will never be known, whose deeds will never be recorded.* This is a War of the Unknown Warriors; but let all strive without failing in faith or in duty, and the dark curse of Hitler will be lifted from our age …

Even through his own struggle, Churchill's courage and strong, unwavering leadership guided people through the darkest days of the Second World War – he was the right kind of person at the right time. Within these pages is the true story about all the individuals who were in the right place at the right time. Each had their own 'struggle' but never gave up. They 'rendered faithful service' at a time when nations warred. They all served to bring about a finale that has allowed the memory of the few to endure.

In the process of bringing the single story of the *Frankton* Raid to the reader, it has always been the intention to give at least some history for each of the people that became a part of this epic struggle to survive against the odds. For some of these individuals, very little is known, as their bright young lives were cut short. Others have been well documented elsewhere, therefore only highlighted episodes are given.

This is the complete, integrated story of all the French and British people alike, inspired by testimonies that have remained silent. The personal thoughts and words showing the many twists and turns that have made this narrative an enduring one.

Without the ordinary French people risking there lives, and that of their children, the two 'Cockle' canoeists would never have returned; there would never have been a 'Final Witness' to the 'Cockleshell Heroes'.

A human tide of misery came rolling in over Europe in the wake of the occupying force of the German army. Britain's saving grace was the narrow waterway that the French call La Manche – 'the sleeve'. Britain's occupation was, at one time, possibly only a manoeuvre away – as with the channel, it was a 'narrow thing'. The French people suffered an occupation and a struggle that the British did not.[7] They existed in a sea of animosity and hatred; they were, to a large degree, 'pregnant with fear'. Simply thinking about how the French families existed at that time, some often near to starvation, yet feeding and giving clothing to the many Allied personnel on the run, is a lesson in the best of human nature. There are many tales of the risks taken by the helpers in this endeavour. Some escape-route helpers were imprisoned and tortured; others were presumably summarily executed for just being suspected or for the slightest of any number of other reasons, for they were never seen again. This introduction is not the place to fully convey the horrors meted out to those who dared to oppose the Nazi regime; however, it can be said, 'There was no 'why' in the concentration camps, only 'was'.'

The Resistance also played their part in the constant harassing of the German Forces and the consequential Liberation of France. Many members, friends and sympathisers of the Resistance who offered service to their country were cruelly dispatched, some through betrayal by their own countrymen, usually for money. Entire families were erased from the face of the earth. Contemplate for a moment how it is hoped you and your loved ones will be remembered … and for how long. Through the atrocities of man during the Second World War, millions have perished never to be remembered individually. Some 'names will never be known, whose deeds will never be recorded', but through those that are recorded, we are reminded of the 'Unknown Warriors'.

Each of us owes at least one moment of gratitude for the way in which all the good-hearted and valiant conducted themselves during a conflict that scarred so many people's lives. This is the author's moment of gratitude. Within these pages, there is a great need to 'place' people so as to show how they all became part of this particular story, or rather, noted episode in history.

This work has, in part, only been made possible by the existence of French, British and German documentation, some of which has only recently become available; of particular interest are the records in the German military archives at Freiburg. These also show what the German forces knew of the '*Frankton* Raid' from the captured men even at the time. It has also been necessary to delve into information contained in family records, operational reports, the previously published, third-party correspondence and, most importantly, oral history – the last voices – and then not to waver in the delivery for the sake of those that have given so very much. Instead of just a 'simple' story this comprehensive account illuminates the complexity of events.

Some of the correspondence between the parties concerned showed either great affection or love, but always a deep appreciation. It is hoped that this is evident within this narrative. The same feelings still exist: 'the English have remembered!'[8] The service rendered long ago has not been discarded but will be appreciated by the generations that follow. It is the author's belief that those who give something of themselves should not pass in life as forgotten souls.

This is a small tribute to the deeds of all the known warriors now recorded as part of this true story, along with their own individual paths that led them into the indelible part of history of the Cockleshell Heroes. It is their Final Witness!

1

THE *FRANKTON* RAID

CHAPTER 1

Of Mice and Men[1]

The so-called '*Frankton* Docket'[2] was at that time a single file of facts to do with attacks on the French Biscay ports, which contained an enormous amount of information, with the Port of Bordeaux featuring as a prominent target. A brief synopsis of this docket or file, which was simply given the name *Frankton*, reveals that the sections concerned highlighted twenty-six identified blockade runners and the nature of the cargoes, together with the most comprehensive and detailed accounts of the following subjects as of 5 October 1942: the number of ships under German control capable of making the voyage to the Far East; the targets within the Bordeaux area, which included the floating dock, two large dredgers[3] and the U-boat Shelter then under construction; the approaches to the targets; tides and tidal streams; defences; conditions for air attack; considerations for seaborne approach; the all-important method of attack (with the use of canoes, MFU, chariot and bombing). Indeed, a great deal of work had been done in order to sustain an outline plan, and even then it required the finer details and up-to-date intelligence once a course of action had been decided upon.

The original and rapidly produced outline plan was devised on 22 September 1942.[4] The '*Frankton* docket' had only been studied the day before! This initial plan was drawn up by Major Blondie Hasler as OC of the Royal Marines Boom Patrol Detachment (RMBPD) and Force Commander. The nature of the operational intent would be a Limpet attack on cargo vessels lying at Bordeaux Harbour in occupied France by *three* Mk 2 Cockles. The Cockle craft would use sail[5] where possible to assist in the passage-making and would move in company with the exception of the final approach. Each of the Limpets would be fused with time-delay and sympathetic fuses in order to ensure that they all exploded simultaneously. The force would be self-contained as far as food and water was concerned.

Six ranks of the RMBPD would be the attacking force with the intent to sink between ten and twenty of the cargo vessels lying up alongside the quay in Bordeaux Harbour. The timetable of events would last over five days, beginning no later than 2300 on day one with the carrying ship dropping the attacking force not more than five miles from the mouth of the estuary. The force would land by 0600 and go into concealment then resuming the passage by 2000. By 0600 the following day, again the force would lie up and resume at 2000. On day four, at approximately 0600, the attacking force would lie up at the advanced base position within ten miles of the targeted vessels, with the final approach commencing at 2000 of the same day. On day five, the final day, at no later than 0230, the withdrawal would commence to the advanced base with the Limpet mines placed on the targeted vessels exploding by 0600.

The escape plan was to either sink or destroy all remaining canoes and escape overland. The alternative was to return down the estuary on successive nights in order to rendezvous with the carrying ship no earlier than 0300 on the eighth day to a position not more than eight miles from the mouth of the estuary; although it was noted that this may well be impracticable in view of the probability of the programme being delayed by bad weather.

The requirements was that day four had to be within two days of the New Moon. The determined date that the RMBPD force could be ready with the necessary training and equipment was 7 November 1942.

Within Hasler's covering letter, he stated that there had 'not been a close study of the natural features of the locality or the defence measures which may be encountered'. He believed that the Cockle side of the operation (the term 'Cockle' was a code name used by the military for all canoes used during a certain time periods during the Second World War) had a good chance of success and hoped that 'the RMBPD may be allowed to carry it out'. He also wished to know if the intent of disembarking the canoes 'not more than five miles from the mouth of the river, in the dark, [was] practicable'.

This was the idea at least!

To think things were tickety-boo for Great Britain at the beginning of the war would be a mistake. The hazardous enterprise of the German invasion of Britain hesitated, at least until they had won the mastery of the air being denied by the skill and valour of Fighter Command. Following Dunkirk, the main armies of Germany and Britain were no longer in contact – a lull in land fighting in northern Europe came about. The Mediterranean became the new focus of attention. Then, at the most critical moment of Britain's recent history, the face of the German war machine turned towards the Russian front. This gave Britain and her allies a chance to regroup. The transition from defence to attack occurred, and building on that offensive continued to roll out. An opportunity to engage in another facet of war play began.

It would seem that Hitler took his eye off the ball, and instead of maintaining his goals with offensive action, he forgot the objective in hand. His failure time and time again to stick to a primary objective caused a breakdown in the German plans. In short, the principles of war had again been overlooked and his armies were stretched, therefore depleting the effectiveness of those forces.

It is evident that the British have always been, by both tradition and temperament, particularly suited to amphibious guerilla warfare. This is coupled with the national affinity for the sea and that of the chase. The aim was focused on the German infantry, which then guarded and oppressed those peoples they had conquered along the stolen coastlines of Europe.

It is said victory can only be won by offensive action: that is the great psychological principle. This offensive confers the initiative and with it liberty of action and the denial of it to the enemy. This then was one of the reasons for the many 'little actions'[6] by the 'special forces' of the day.

The Prime Mover

About one week after the evacuation of Dunkirk, Lieutenant-Colonel D. W. Clarke of the Royal Artillery was ordered to prepare a scheme for offensive operations using troops to be formed into special units. Independent companies were rapidly formed and sent to Norway to try and stem the German advance into the far north.

It is hardly surprising that these units, specifically chosen and trained for raiding, were unsuccessful in their first unsuitable deployment, but they were retained and formed into Special Service Battalions. These were in turn transformed into the Commandos, preserving their tactical use. These Special Service Troops were to be amphibious, learning to co-operate with the Royal Navy. Thus, Combined Training Centres were formed on the coasts of the United Kingdom in order to foster a link with the navy and provide training in joint methods of operation.

Admiral Sir Sydney Fremantle had been largely responsible for the 'Manual of Combined Operations', a pre-war document which contained the doctrine and policy that required participation of each of the services. This complete integration in the planning, experimentation, doctrine and action was in some quarters thought desirable but not possible, largely due to the fact that there had been no organisation to bring this to fruition. There had been some valuable work undertaken in developing certain craft but that was the extent of the co-operation. With Churchill's enthusiastic backing, the idea of 'Combined Operations' grew from an advisory role into a fully functioning entity first under Admiral of the Fleet Sir Roger Keyes and then Lord Mountbatten.

When Lord Louis Mountbatten relieved Keyes, he was forty-one years of age. He had been singled out by Churchill when at the diminutive rank of Captain in the Royal Navy due to his special qualities, which had impressed the prime minister.

On taking over on 27 October 1941, Mountbatten was promoted Commodore First Class and his title was changed to Chief of Combined Operations. Mountbatten was required by Churchill to 'mount a programme of raids of ever-increasing intensity with the invasion of France the main object'.

Mountbatten began to establish the most essential liaison between the Chiefs of Staff and the Ministries on whom the Combined Operations were dependent for weapons and everything else. Combined Operations took on an enhanced vitality as Lord Louis became CCO.

Through most of 1940 and 1941, due to a complex system of command, any raids from the UK were difficult to organise, with each Army Command responsible for raiding shores opposite their area in the UK and the navy having a final say on any seaborne raid. Red tape was a hindrance. This meant that the growing force of Commandos were forever on training exercises or simply standing by for operations that were cancelled before they were begun. Apart from operations by SOE, very few raids were ever accomplished. Mountbatten had the distinct ability of cutting through the red tape.

On 18 March 1942, the CCO's position changed, with Mountbatten being made Acting Vice-Admiral and Honorary Lieutenant General, Honorary Air Marshal with a seat on the Chiefs of Staff Committee, thus becoming one of the four military leaders in overall charge of higher direction of the war effort. This changed the fundamentals of development within Combined Operations and that enabled Mountbatten to order resources controlled by Churchill as the Minister of Defence.

Once approved by the Chief of Staff, a Force Commander was appointed and given responsibility of the detailed planning for the specific operation, together with the responsibility of co-ordinating army, navy and air force units. The required extra equipment or special materials were then sourced through the agency of the Headquarters Staff with the CCO responsible for obtaining final approval of the Force Commander's plan from the Chiefs of Staff Committee, of which Mountbatten was a member, the final seal of approval coming from the Naval Commander in Chief.

The men who volunteered for the highly dangerous task of raiding enemy-held strong points from the sea therefore enjoyed the title of Commandos. Britain's Mountbatten, wrote that on two occasions he had asked men to undertake even more hazardous small-scale raids than was usual. These men knew full well that great odds were stacked against them; often only one-tenth of a force would survive. Mountbatten himself was emotionally overcome by the courage shown.

The Commando 'Craft'

The co-operation that developed with the navy at the special coastal schools or Combined Training Centres became of great importance. The Commando training was tough – it had to be. The Commando not only had to be proficient in his use of the tools of his trade but also had to master his mind and body to instil self-reliance and confidence. Self-confidence sprang from the possession of confidence in those who led; it was discovered that the instructors are always better at the tasks at hand. One other thing was taught and that is to appreciate the full meaning and value of friendship in war. This will become more than evident as this story unfolds. The physical conditions of training were strenuous but well within the endurance of the young volunteers, who had passed a severe medical test. On reaching their Commando units, these individuals were already physically and morally hard men able to perform considerable feats of endurance. Certain individuals lived in billeted accommodation, receiving an allowance of 6s 8d[7] per day with which to keep themselves. Petty punishments were infrequent and were, as far as possible, avoided. Some of the craft that they were trained to handle were of curious and unexpected shapes. For the men that were accepted into the RMBPD, a new and most unexpected entry from the marine environment was to introduce itself to them – the Cockle.

'Red Indian Raids'

The year 1942 seemed to deliver one disaster after another for the Allied forces. As has been mentioned, one of 'sober judgement might well have concluded that we were finished'. There were, however, notable and heroic Commando actions that lit the darkness of the struggle, not only showing the spirit of the Special Service troops, but also playing an important part in the war.

For example, Operation *Chariot's* amphibious assault on St Nazaire with a superannuated destroyer was a 'large, weakly armed Force that had to make an undetected passage of over 400 miles to the scene of action at an average speed of 11½ knots through an area usually covered by enemy and air reconnaissance[8]; this was another action that was exploited by Allied propaganda.

Three Victoria Crosses were awarded for this action in which a total of sixty-eight officers and 329 ratings or other ranks were killed or missing out of the total complement of 108 officers and 515 ratings or other ranks. It was said of this that 'taking into consideration the extreme vulnerability of the coastal craft, neither losses in men nor material can be considered excessive for the results achieved'.[9]

This assault on St Nazaire, in early 1942, clearly determined the contribution that could be made by Combined Operations against an enemy base or target. The methodology used proved that a comparatively small force could assault and penetrate a heavily defended port (or fortified area) under the cover of darkness by the exploitation of the element of surprise. This type of action resulted in, as Churchill remarked, 'the dull, low, whining note of fear' from the German camp. They had to ensure their own forces were 'everywhere' and thus diluted its potency, sometimes making the crucial difference. No longer was there a safe harbour and each time Hitler was assured of this by his generals, each time they were surprised. This soon turned to anger and, with the out-flowing rage, Hitler issued his 'Führer Order Concerning Handling of Commandos' ('*Kommandobefehl*[10]) on 18 October 1942.

Certainly, within COHQ, Herr Hitler's infamous '*Kommandobefehl*' edict was discussed in great detail, along with the question of whether formation symbols for various raids and badges of rank should be worn. Indeed, some felt that raids should be conducted in civilian clothes given that, if commandos were apprehended, their fate would be the same as saboteurs. This arrangement of 'plain clothes' would facilitate escape and provide the lesser risk; logically, it was more sensible to have this 'advantage'. To Blondie Hasler, this attitude was terribly defeatist and he believed *his* men should operate in the uniform of a conventional military unit, and if their fate was to be caught, at least they would die a Royal Marine rather than suffer the ignominy of death as a spy. To this end, badges of rank were sewn onto the Cockle suits, as were the Royal Marines flashes above the Combined Operations badge[11]. In light of the distance they were required to cover and that most of the men were not French speakers, being in plain clothes would not, in all likelihood, have made very much difference.

Just twelve copies[12] of the *Kommandobefehl*[13] were issued, giving, perhaps, an indication that it was known that this order was in direct and deliberate violation of the laws of war. The order and its appendix 'was handled in such secrecy that it was handed down in written form to Generals only, by whom it could be passed on to the troops orally only and under special oath of secrecy'[14]. It was issued to 'commanders only and must not under any circumstances fall into the hands of the enemy' and was thus, possibly, unknown to masses of the Commando forces.

Führer Order Concerning
Handling of Commandos
18 October 1942
TOP SECRET
The Führer No. 003830/ 42 g. Kdos.
OKW/ WFSt
Führer HQ, 18 Oct. 1942
12 copies, 12th copy.

1. For some time our enemies have been using in their warfare methods which are outside the international Geneva Conventions. Especially brutal and treacherous is the behaviour of the so-called commandos, who, as is established, are partially recruited even from freed criminals in enemy countries. From captured orders it is divulged, that they are directed not only to shackle prisoners, but also to kill defenceless prisoners on the spot at the moment in which they believe that the latter as prisoners represent a burden in the further pursuit of their purposes or could otherwise be a hindrance. Finally, orders have been found in which the killing of prisoners has been demanded in principle.

2. For this reason it was already announced in an addendum to the Armed Forces report of 7 October 1942, that in the future, Germany, in the face of these sabotage troops of the British and their accomplices, will resort to the same procedure, i.e., that they will be ruthlessly mowed down by the German troops in combat, wherever they may appear.

3. I therefore order:
From now on all enemies on so-called Commando missions in Europe or Africa challenged by German troops, even if they are to all appearances soldiers in uniform or demolition troops, whether armed or unarmed, in battle or in flight, are to be slaughtered to the last man. It does not make any difference whether they are landed from ships and aeroplanes for their actions, or whether they are dropped by parachute. Even if these individuals, when found, should apparently be prepared to give themselves up, no pardon is to be granted them on principle. In each individual case full information is to be sent to the O. K. W. for publication in the Report of the Military Forces.

4. If individual members of such commandos, such as agents, saboteurs, etc., fall into the hands of the military forces by some other means, through the police in occupied territories for instance, they are to be handed over immediately to the SD.[15] Any imprisonment under military guard, in PW stockades for instance, etc., is strictly prohibited, even if this is only intended for a short time.

5. This order does not apply to the treatment of any enemy soldiers who, in the course of normal hostilities (large-scale offensive actions, landing operations and airborne operations), are captured in open battle or give themselves up. Nor does this order apply to enemy soldiers falling into our hands after battles at sea, or enemy soldiers trying to save their lives by parachute after battles.

6. I will hold responsible under Military Law, for failing to carry out this order, all commanders and officers who either have neglected their duty of instructing the troops about this order, or acted against this order where it was to be executed.

[signed] Adolf Hitler

Translation Of Document 498-Ps
Nazi Conspiracy and Aggression. Volume III. USGPO, Washington, 1946, pp. 416–417

The last paragraph shows how strong the pressure was to carry out this order. Nazi propaganda minister Joseph Goebbels spoke of the efforts made by the Commandos as 'Red Indian' raids. His analogy served only to enhance rather than diminish, as a closer acquaintance with the works of Fenimore Cooper would have revealed, what the Commandos were: stealthy, fierce and implacable.

The tight security that enveloped Britain was needed to ensure the spirit of the British people was not unduly and irreversibly eroded with the tide of detritus that was brought so close to our shores. It also was an important weapon to ensure the combined efforts of the services became an effective offensive force, thus ensuring success in the allied invasion of occupied territories.

Whilst the country pulled together under Churchill's leadership, the intelligence gathering and special operations were being planned, so too were all the ideas that came from the fine minds of commanders, designers and inventors. Our inventive genius was a tool yet to be fully sharpened.

This is what Churchill had wanted, and had encouraged.

The Organisation of COHQ

Combined Operations Command ('United We Conquer') was formed of officers and other ranks of the three fighting services. Its primary function was to provide training for amphibious warfare from small raids to large assaults. This endeavour made it possible for officers and men to execute those raids and successfully land on an enemy-held coast. Amphibious warfare, being a complicated business, has many aspects. From producing craft and weapons, the COC also created training centres in order to foster the spirit of co-operation within the three services, to give to each understanding of the other the services' methods and problems. Its growth, which was considerable in 1942, gained great momentum during 1943 and beyond.

The Chief of Staff of the Combined Operations Headquarters at Richmond Terrace, Whitehall, London, was Brigadier Godfrey Edward Wildman-Lushington, RM.

Such was the extravagance allowed the organisation that it was once remarked[16] that the motto of COHQ should be 'Regardless' – meaning regardless of effort, risk and cost.

Mountbatten 'rejoiced in the accusations' that his organisation was established on principles of eccentricity, saying of it that it was 'the only lunatic asylum in the world run by its own inmates'. Those that worked under Mountbatten found themselves with a sense of being in on something 'tremendously exciting, and tremendously important, but something – and here is the point – tremendously full of surprises'.[17] As far as Blondie Hasler was concerned, also in opposition to bureaucracy, COHQ was 'highly efficient [and] hyperactive'.[18]

From the headquarters, all the information was collated by talented and enthusiastic people from civilian specialists, an American contingent and the three British services. They then digested and formulated schemes, ideas and plots from their own groups. Some of these groups were the small inter-service 'syndicates' who prepared plans for the many operations abroad. Notably, the HQ also housed representatives of the Special Operations Executive. It was honeycombed with every branch of the services.

Other notables that played their part in this story were Captain the Hon. David Astor, who was part of the public relations staff; Chief Planning Co-ordinator, Colonel Robert Neville;

Head of Staff of Royal Marine planners was Lt-Col. Cyril Horton and Col. Antony Head, who was part of the Examination Committee along with Brigadier Wildman-Lushington as officer presiding.

Responsible for liaison with Whitehall, SOE and MI6 was Lieutenant-Commander G. P. L'Estrange, RNVR. Described by the captain of the submarine tasked with the delivery of the 'offspring' as a 'rather shadowy figure', L'Estrange was not only very fluent in French but was an expert in the requisite part of the French coast. He was a Royal Navy Reservist and had formerly been a rubber planter in Malaya. His liaison work[19] was of such quality that he was mentioned by Major Hasler in his report on the operation as deserving of a special distinction for his contribution to the success of the mission, saying he 'did the bulk of the detailed planning and personally prepared with great thoroughness and accuracy, the actual charts, tide tables, etc., used by the attacking force'. Indeed, he was one most intimately involved with the top-secret details, especially concerned with the escape and return of the force.[20]

There were two tasks: raids on the coast of German-occupied Europe and the preparation of its eventual invasion. Mountbatten supported Churchill's principle of raiding the enemy coastlines; 'a program of raids in ever increasing intensity'. Even though these enterprises seemed like pinpricks, they maintained the offensive spirit amongst the troops, which raised public morale and caused the Axis to deploy large forces to defend their positions against the amphibious threat.

Mountbatten had prepared and decided on a policy that 'small raids should be carried out on an average of once every two weeks'. The task of the Search Committee was 'to speed up the search for targets' and it was the Search Committee's obligation to devise and consider projects or raids submitted by others. The Examination Committee, after submission to Robert Neville, considered proposals put forward by the Search Committee. They then would approve any expeditions, passing on the details to the Council of COHQ (the Executive), the highest of the many committees. Once the project had been sanctioned by the Executive, it was given to a special group who would then prepare an outline plan on what methods could be employed. The Chiefs of Staff Committee could then decide on whether it should be approved.

The Eyes and Ears
The Bordeaux Problem

Prior to 1941, German merchant vessels had continued with their supply chain with relative impunity. In September 1940, Britain's Ministry of Economic Warfare (MEW) drew up a list that determined that certain supplies shipped to Germany constituted a hostile act, and then set about restricting access to sea routes leading to enemy ports. But these close blockades were not effective. The attempts to find shipping in the open oceans proved difficult; it also diverted resources from the defence of our coastlines. It was due to the intelligence gathering in and around Bordeaux by the French Resistance within the offices of river pilots, customs officials and other personnel that information on these shipping movements could be confirmed by RAF reconnaissance.

In a letter to Churchill, dated 9 May 1942, the Minister of Economic Warfare, Lord Selborne, wrote of the developing trade between Germany and Japan. He did so again, with more intelligence information, on 22 June, and again by 5 August, such was the urgency of the matter. In the August 'edition' of his warning of the trading partners, Lord Selborne says, 'Now Italy, too is planning to resuscitate her starved war industries with raw materials from the Far East.' Selborne also recognised that the most important task for aircraft operating over the sea was the destruction of submarines: 'I urge the importance of combining with that task the attack on blockade runners so that the defence of our own supply lines and the destruction of our enemies may proceed simultaneously.' In this letter, he ended saying,

'The importance of this traffic is no less today than when I wrote my previous Minutes. If immediate action could be taken it should not be too late.'

The well-equipped port of Bordeaux with its rail infrastructure to Germany, its protection by nature and from the heavily fortified positions of the German forces made it a boon for commercial traffic from the Far East. Lying in the Bay of Biscay, its very favourable position was protected by the 63-mile-long estuary.

Requisitioned or seized ships were equipped with 'hidden' weapons such as torpedo launchers and 150-mm guns. Each ship, of about 10,000 tons, had a speed of around 17 knots, allowing them to outrun British warships and submarines, hence the name 'blockade runners'. (On the whole, even with the many losses, the cargoes continued until July 1944.)

The merchant vessel movements in and out of German-occupied ports within Europe showed that they were receiving these fast blockade runners carrying cargo vital to the continued German war effort. Bordeaux was rapidly becoming the most important of these ports for the German maritime trade with the Far East.

There was hunger for raw materials such as animal and vegetable oils, pewter, molybdenum, kapok, jute, tin, tungsten, mercury, but most particularly latex. There were the inevitable signs of increased traffic and, during a twelve-month period of 1941–42, it was known that at least 25,000 tons of latex or crude rubber had passed through the port of Bordeaux and on into Germany and Italy. Whilst synthetic rubber was also being manufactured, this natural rubber was vital for products such as aircraft tyres. Lord Selborne and his team at the Ministry were also able to inform the Prime Minister's office that the cargo being shipped to Japan was believed to consist of prototypes of various weaponry such as that of radar as well as other equipment used in manufacture that the Japanese did not possess. The successful passage of a few ships would have benefits to the Japanese war effort out of all proportion to the size of cargoes carried.

There were, at that time, in both Far Eastern waters and occupied French ports, a sufficient number of suitable vessels to carry such cargo, and this would serve to sustain Germany's campaign in the following twelve months. Lord Selborne's Ministry of Economic Warfare knew of 'convincing proof' that both Germany and Japan were enhanced by the trade developments between the two countries. It was known at that time that there were eighteen ships able to outrun the blockade, which were either in the various Atlantic ports or en route. The intent by Lord Selborne was to obtain a decision for action from the War Cabinet as well as to encourage the General Staff to begin a study into the possible military options. Lord Selborne's proposition of attacking these ships had also passed through other channels, including the Examination Committee soon after his first letter in May.

Before Lord Selborne's third letter in September, the Search Committee, under the chairmanship of Commander J. H. Unwin, had already examined the appropriate courses of action that were available. It transpired that there were certain issues that both the Admiralty and the air force were not too happy about, both declining the invitation to participate in any separate or combined operation. For the RAF, the target of Bordeaux was within range for bombing, but to render pinpoint accuracy without causing a great deal of destruction and loss of life to French civilians, perhaps turning public opinion against the cause, was not thought to be any answer. The Foreign Minister and member of the War Cabinet Anthony Eden also made known his firm opposition to the bombing.[21]

Despite the blockade, the Admiralty could not promise to intercept every enemy ship, whose sailing dates were far from certain.[22] The task of intercepting a blockade runner was indeed fraught with difficulty as Admiralty documents show. One record reports that despite the Allied forces looking for just one blockade-running freighter inbound to occupied France, with a US carrier, three destroyers, also attacking it with eight Halifax bombers and a total of fifty-three Beaufighters and Mosquitoes, it still managed to safely reach the port of Bordeaux; her approach was shadowed by eleven German surface ships and up to thirteen U-boats. The process tied up much needed resources. Bordeaux port itself was too far within the fortified area for the Allies to even consider direct assault.

At the beginning of July, the Examination Committee had turned down a Combined Operation against the Port of Bordeaux. Under the title of 'operations to immobilize blockade runners at Bordeaux' the Search Committee – Commander Unwin; Wing Commander Homer; Majors Powell and Collins; and Capt. Hann – held a meeting on Monday 27 July 1942 at COHQ.

The Search Committee's decision was that the area was too large to bomb, a large number of bombers would be required to have any marked effect, and that patrolling by submarine would tie up too many craft, even with the very best of intelligence. Surprisingly, although no further action was undertaken, both a mission by SOE or Commando saboteurs landed by submarine and canoe was also mooted. In short, it was thought that any or a combination of these measures were the best options available. Submarine interference was carried out but was limited. There also were the badly laid mines, dropped by the RAF, at the mouth of the Gironde; which were to become a subject of contention in our story. It should be noted that there was a project (MFU concept[23]), which was begun in early 1942 and the original design was to an Admiralty requirement for an attack on Bordeaux in the November of that year. It was designed for carriage in a submarine but as this required considerable experimentation and alterations to the submarine, its method of deployment was altered and production was delayed. Had this option been available, it is likely that Hasler would have used it.

It should be noted that Head of Staff of Royal Marine planners, Lt-Col. Cyril Horton, had by mid-September almost decided that curtailing the blockade runners was a lost cause; that was until Horton had learnt that Hasler was nosing around for operations for his new team via the Chief Planning co-ordinator, Colonel Robert Neville. Meanwhile, the *Frankton* dossier or docket continued to be added to, and the COHQ were tasked with studying the problem. An attack by SOE agents had not been totally ruled out, but as with all things SOE, these details remained secret until many years after post-war Europe had rebuilt itself. Some interesting alleged sub-plot details are revealed within.

Oblivious to any activity under consideration by the SOE, the Chief of Combined Operations, Lord Louis Mountbatten, put Hasler's plan before the Joint Chiefs of Staff claiming it was 'the only plan which offers a good chance of success'. On the basis of Mountbatten's assurance that this was the only plan that might work the mission was approved on 3 November. This approval set in motion the detailed event about to be unveiled in the chapters beyond. It was just one event in many that provided a successful outcome.

CHAPTER 2
'A Ding-Dong Battle'

With the RMBPD being formed in July 1942 with two sections and an administrative team, Hasler's focus was to concentrate on the development of all types of small boat attack on enemy coasts and harbours. The new detachment had now to learn and become competent in many new skills and to attain a fitness level to match. The following months were difficult times, but it became apparent that Hasler knew they needed to be tested. He also knew that something needed to be done to ensure that the unit would not be overlooked. He started a search for operations that were suited to the unit's mode of warfare. Hasler discussed some schemes with Col. Robert Neville at COHQ having convinced him that his men were ready, despite saying 'providing it's not a job needing very good navigation or seamanship'.

In meticulous fashion, Hasler writes in his diary, '21st September 1942. 1024 train to London. a.m. Examining dockets on Frankton. p.m. Following up various other lines. Evening – seeing Neville re. *Frankton*. Slept RORC[1]. 22nd September 1942 wrote out outline proposals for *Frankton* and discussed them with Neville.' Once Hasler had read the '*Frankton* Docket' (see Appendix), he had become interested and had put up his outline plan of action, the focus was in the preparation of the actual operation itself, unbeknown to the rest of No. 1 section. Provisionally accepted by Flag Officer Submarines (FOS), the Examination Committee had passed these plans on 13 October with the revised outline plan completed on 29 October[2]. This showed that special training had commenced on 20 October and included boat practice, handling of Limpets, rehearsal from submarine, full-scale rehearsal on British estuary (if possible) and training for escape. Various things such as his work with the Boom Patrol Boat (BPB) and the canoe for their uses had progressed well, including the methodology of the crane arrangement and sling in order to launch the canoes from a submarine. The other major facet was the preparation and meetings for Exercise *Blanket*.

This is a short account of the immediate work up to an exercise which would be the prelude to the *Frankton* Raid itself. Hasler had been told that Mountbatten was not about to let him go on the operation. Hasler was simply too valuable to lose on a operation that was viewed by the CCO as very likely not to return any of the men safely back to the United Kingdom. In a heart-rending plea to be allowed to go on the mission, Hasler is recorded to have said to Colonel Neville, 'If they go without me, sir, and don't return, I shall never be able to face the others again.' He was right. This would have grated against his very character for the rest of his life. From this, the Colonel agreed to speak to Mountbatten. Not to leave it to chance, Hasler drafted a memo that would reach the COHQ in order for him to put his case in person. It read,

1. Operation is an important one, and appears to have a good chance of success. Main difficulty is a question of small boat seamanship and navigation on the part of the force commander. My second in command has only been using small boats for about four months and chances of success would be materially reduced if the most experienced officer available was not sent. 2. A failure would prejudice all future operations of this type. 3. In a new unit the OC can hardly gain

respect if he avoids going on the first operation. 4. If I am not allowed to go on this operation what type of operation will be permissible for me? The case of Major Stirling in Egypt is thought to be similar.[3]

Regardless, Hasler had forged ahead with training his men and buried his thoughts in the full expectation that he would indeed be allowed to lead the operation. It was on the cards that Hasler would *not* be allowed to participate. Hasler's only ally at the COHQ meeting was Col. Neville. Mountbatten queried whether Hasler should be allowed to go 'when there is little and, most probably, no chance of returning'. Hasler's last gambit was that future operations could only benefit from his first-hand experience. That is, of course, from the viewpoint that he never considered he would not return. Mountbatten canvassed the views of those assembled and, bar one exception, all believed that Hasler should be excluded from the raid; he was too important a cog in the ongoing operational needs. Mountbatten had listened to all the arguments against and looking straight at Hasler said, 'Much against my better judgement, I am going to let you go.' Perhaps it was the known fact that Mountbatten relished an operation that used ever more outrageous methods and delighted in the planning of them that swayed his ultimate judgement. Either way, Hasler recorded this event thus: '29 October p.m. chasing round details of *Frankton* and *Blanket*. 1700 – conference CCO, Haydon, Hussey, Selly, Neville, to decide if I should be allowed to go. Won after *a ding-dong battle*. Quick supper at club. 2115. Train to Glasgow- 3rd class sleeper.' Hasler arrived at Glasgow at 0745 on 30 October and his diary records, 'Bath in gent's lavatory. Breakfast at Central. 0945, train to Gourock. Steamer to Dunoon. Bus to Ardnadam. Arrived HMS *Forth* 1230. PM saw S3 [Ionides[4]] re object of visit. Fixed details of hoisting out apparatus. Fixing up various preliminary arrangements. Rang Neville. Planned instruction for No. 1 section. Evening, drinking with Bobby Lambert [a submarine officer].'

No. 1 section of the RMBPD was already en route to HMS *Forth* on Holy Loch on the afternoon of 30 October. Hasler's own diary records, '31st October. a.m. ferry to Gourock. 1053 No. 1 section arrive by train. 1230 Ferry to HMS *Forth*. 1445 Lorry arrived, stores came off in 1500 Ferry, p.m. troops stowing stores and unpacking Mk 2s up till 1830. Evening preparing lectures til 2320.'

At this stage, it is worthwhile explaining the nature of the canoes and that of the chosen method of getting them, the 'offspring', into the water. The standard method of delivery for the offspring was the floating-off technique whereby a canoe could be gently floated off the casing as the submarine trimmed down on low pressure. This method was only suitable for the relatively calm waters of the Mediterranean. The other method of delivery was to lower them, empty, over the side of the casing and then bring them into position to enable the crew member to use the forward hydroplanes as a platform from which to access the canoe. Both of these methods required the offspring to be lightly loaded and the latter required any stores to be passed down to the canoeists after they had boarded their little vessel.

The *Frankton* Operation involved taking a great deal of weighty equipment and required a swift transfer with the minimum of risk during this critical stage. It became obvious to every interested party that the operating conditions in the Atlantic were not going to be conducive to any method other than hoisting out the canoes over the side of a submarine, fully laden. The very nature of the Cockle Mk 2 lent itself to this kind of lifting technique, which is probably why Hasler thought it to be the answer. This new canoe, designed a year before by Fred Goatley, had great longitudinal strength, void of thin longitudinal members, and sported a flat bottom.

Given his background and keen mind, Hasler had designed a sling for the purpose which consisted of two wooden spreaders, themselves connected by two strips of broad but substantial webbing with a wire-lifting strop attached to each of the spreaders. The sling was first spread out on the submarine's casing. The canoe, loaded at this stage with the two end cargo bags only, was then placed onto the webbing by two of the casing crew. Having previously greased the hatches of the canoe, the other bags were then loaded, followed by the No. 1 and 2 of the canoe who then made fast the cockpit covers. With the two wire strops being brought together, the canoe could then be hoisted and, upon contact with the sea, the canoe floated off the webbing backwards out of the sling which would then be retrieved ready for repeating the operation *ad infinitum*.

Within the RMBPD War Diaries, it is found that Hasler had been hard at work solving certain problems with regard to the hoisting gear. An entry for 26 October 1942 says, 'Major Hasler experimented and tested new spring with quick release hook for launching Cockles Mk.2 from ships and submarines', with 'all ranks taking part in Major Hasler's launching experiments', which were repeated on 27 and 28 October at Portsmouth.

The only way this sling could be used was with a hoisting gear, and it is reported that the staff of the submarine base came up with a system using HM Submarine *Tuna*'s 4-inch gun. Resembling a rifle and its bayonet, the hoisting gear consisted of a steel girder which, when firmly double-clamped to the underside of the muzzle of the submarine's 4-inch gun, projected an adequate distance from the end of the muzzle. The girder could be fitted before leaving the base, as it did not conflict when firing the gun in anger. Shackled to the end of the girder was a rope, which provided the required manual hoisting power via a pulley system. Thus fixed, the ensemble could, using the training and elevation gear of the gun, be canted in the vertical and horizontal. It was hoped that with the weather state required, the necessary practice, and everything else coming together in the proposed window of opportunity, things would go swimmingly.

The programme of events during 31 October to 7 November are relayed in brief in order to show the process in working up to an operation. The need was to carry out advanced training with their craft and this involved No. 1 section moving up to HMS *Forth*, a depot ship, moored in a Scottish loch near Greenock, at the beginning of November 1942. This period began with a lecture by Hasler on future work and practising Limpet attacks from the Mk 2 Cockles. The next day, they practised hoisting out the canoes from the submarine and Limpet attacks.

On 3 November, the six canoes were hoisted out from HMS *Forth*, and at 1000, all the boats left for a long day trip up Loch Long 'in formation' with two boats fully ballasted. The men returned at 1630 having covered around thirteen miles, and as Hasler's own diary mentions, they were 'very exhausted'. The diaries show that during the morning of 4 November they prepared boats and stores, and at 1100, the hoist out began from HMS *Forth*. By 1330, they were practising hoisting out the canoes fully loaded from the minesweeper *Jan van Gelder* on the quarter davit. They then practised Limpet attacks on her side while she was underway at a speed of about 2 knots; this was intended to represent a tidal stream. Hasler's notes record repeating the Limpet attacks in the dark: '1900–2100 with southerly breeze and lop. Good value. 2330 return to *Forth*.'

On 5 November, they were instructed to paint the canoes and 'equipment' in camouflage colours to Hasler's specification. On 6 November, Capt. Stewart proceeded to *Jan van Gelder* to witness hoisting-out trials of the Cockle Mk 2 now fully loaded from a submarine. At

Artist's impression of the hoisting.

0740, No. 1 section, all ranks, now embarked for their first sea trials in submarine P339 (HMS *Taurus*), captained by Lt-Cdr Wingfield, and carried out experimental hoisting out under the lee of the Isle of Arran in heavy squalls. In such conditions, the first experimental practice of hoisting out the canoes on the gun-barrel extension occurred. Only Hasler's own diary records, 'Successful except for the bending of girder.' Meanwhile, *Jan van Gelder* was weatherbound at Rothesay and unable to make contact with the submarine due to the win blowing Force 6–7. The weather at Southsea was even worse, with the whole of No. 2 section failing to reach Wotton Creek on the IOW by canoe (the old Mk 1* types), as upon reaching a point just 1.5 miles west of Fort Spitbank, they were forced to turn back owing to the rough sea and wind at Force 5! That evening Hasler spent 'planning *Blanket* with MacKinnon. Cutting up maps and charts and drafting orders till 0045.'

The morning of 7 November proved useful, as the war diary records at 1000 'submarine rendezvous with *Jan van Gelder* at Rothesay'. Hasler's diary relates, 'hoist [with all stores] out under lee of land all 6 boats successful including one on the end of the gun barrel with P339 listed to starboard. Hoist into *Jan van Gelder* by ropes end and proceeded back to HMS *Forth* by 1230. Pack up all gear and leave at 1430 for Gourock. Stewart and self went ahead to Glasgow. Drank and dined, caught 2130 train South with two 1st Class sleepers.'

With Lt MacKinnon and No. 1 section arriving in London on the morning of 9 November, the crews were briefed for Exercise *Blanket*. Hasler had not told his team about the impending *Frankton* Operation.

CHAPTER 3

The Thames Fiasco

The morning of 14 November 1942 broke with Hasler in a dispirited and depressed mood, drowning his dismay with a glass of beer and a sandwich for breakfast in the all-ranks establishment of COHQ canteen in London. In this frame of mind, Hasler was now being canvassed about his recent 'jolly' and relayed the catalogue of disasters of Exercise *Blanket* to an interested party. Mountbatten looked Blondie in the eyes and with his noted wry smile replied with the unexpected and now legendary reported retort of 'Splendid! You must have learned a great deal, and you'll be able to avoid making the same mistakes on the operation!' No doubt Mountbatten knew, just as Churchill did, that it is our failures more than our successes that make us who we are.

It was not until after the war that any indication is found on paper as to Hasler's real thoughts about Exercise *Blanket*. In a private resume, it becomes evident what his original opinion was: 'No. 1 section start exercise in Thames Estuary from Margate to Deptford. *Complete failure.*'

The exercise had begun at 2015[1] on 10 November and finished at 0600 on 14 November. The intent was to proceed from Margate to Deptford and back with a force of six canoes in one formation, unobserved by the defences or the local inhabitants. This was to be conducted with all knowledge to the defending authorities. The route was from Margate along the North Kent coast to the Swale Estuary keeping within three miles of the shore, over the Swale Boom and via east and west Swale to the Medway, past the garrison point to the Thames, keeping inside Thames Boom and on up to Deptford, with the plan to lie up by day and move by night on the favourable tide returning to Boatship Wharf in Chatham Dockyard.

The aim was to test the possibility of small boats penetrating the defences of the Thames with six canoes in two divisions of three, with each division supposedly proceeding independently of the other. The code word was to be 'Blanket'. The distance set was to attempt to mirror that of the intended operation – some seventy miles.

The duration for *Blanket* was approximately five days. The defences were not required to make special searches for the canoes, but if observed and within hailing distance, they were to be hailed, 'Boat ahoy.' The canoe party would respond with 'Blanket' with the canoes ordered to land if possible. If any crew was forced to land by stress of weather whilst between Margate and Swale, they were instructed to remain below high-water mark until identified. If they had to land at any other time, they would be identified by the special pass that each man carried, and they then would be allowed to proceed without the canoes being searched or hindrance by other forces. Any reports or sightings of these 'insurgents' were to be made to C-in-C Nore Command by telephone in the form of 'Blanket' followed by the number of canoes sighted. The men in the canoes, if in distress, were to fire two red stars followed by SOS on a whistle at 15-second intervals, with all assistance by the defence forces rendered. All patrols, defences, police, Coast guards and Home Guards were warned about the exercise.

During early November 1942, No. 1 section, under Hasler's command, had carried out advanced training in the Mk 2 Cockles at HMS *Forth* and elsewhere until the afternoon of 7 November, when Hasler and Stewart had then left Glasgow for London, where they attended a meeting with Col. Neville, Lt-Cdr L'Estrange and Lt-Cdr Mowll about 'Blanket'. On 9 November, Hasler journeyed to Chatham, where he arranged accommodation for the section at the Royal Marine Barracks and then checked the final details of the exercise with Capt. Linzee, DCOS, Nore Command. Meanwhile, MacKinnon arrived in London in the morning of the 9th, and all met up at Margate where the crews were briefed about the exercise during 1715–1800. On 10 November, L'Estrange arrived at Chatham and discussed Operation *Frankton* with Hasler before Exercise *Blanket* began at 2015 when the lorry left in convoy.

It was a lot to ask – to get through unobserved – but so was *Frankton*. Both MacKinnon and Hasler had worked on the tide tables the previous evening until midnight, and on a misty, flat calm night, six camouflaged Cockle canoes began to be paddled out into the sea at Margate from the jetty. Norman Colley had recently injured himself and was given the job of ensuring all the equipment was where it should be and was in the lorry following them around.

The events of the exercise do not make good reading. Hasler's own diary records, '11 November 1942. 0330 Land at Sheppy. All teething troubles emerging fast. 1300 move two miles up the Swale. 1800 Proceed up Swale around to creek. 0200 Flat calm and misty. 12 November. Pleasant morning.'

As the first dawn had broken just hours into Exercise *Blanket*, Hasler and Sparks found they had lost the main party and that remained the case for the duration. Cpl George Jellicoe Sheard did not fare too well, having probably the worst experience, saying that he had lost formation and that he was under the impression that he had been following Hasler but realised 'Hasler' was in fact a seagull that he had been trying to advance towards until it had flown away. Sheard and partner ended up outside the exercise area and had gone down, not up, the Thames. MacKinnon also had a terrible start, having come independently out of the Swale on a northerly course, only to run aground on mudflats due to the fog. He had then lost his sense of direction, mistakenly taken a reciprocal bearing and only realised the mistake when he recognised a railway bridge that he had previously passed that same night. In all, it proved what seemed to be a bad omen with navigation being the biggest problem. All were feeling the strain of exhaustion. During the debrief and beyond, it was evident that Blondie Hasler was indeed a rabbit of negative euphoria[2], and he tried to put some cheer into himself that very evening. Hasler recorded, '0600 reached highest point, Blackwall Point. Picked up MacKinnon and three boats at Greenhithe and returned to Chatham, pm. Cleared up exercise at C-in C's. Evening to Wren's party with MacKinnon. Very weary.' The next morning, Hasler travelled from Chatham to COHQ to discuss Operation *Frankton* whilst MacKinnon and No. 1 section returned to Portsmouth.

The actual results were that all the canoes were challenged at least twice, owing to the vigilance of the defences and the clear weather conditions. It was said that it was proved that six canoes were too large a formation; with just one leader and to avoid confusion in case of unforeseen obstructions. One canoe was holed on the east Swale boom on the first night. Three canoes lost the formation on the second night, but met up by moving in daylight afterwards. The whole formation became dispersed in rough weather on the third night, and only two canoes succeeded in penetrating the Scar's Elbow Boom in darkness at 2400. One canoe got within two miles of Deptford and withdrew to Erith. The remainder failed to complete the approach, due largely to poor navigation and lack of stamina. Many valuable lessons were learnt on this exercise and were incorporated in the final training for the operation.

These results should be remembered when the narrative of the actual operation is read, as they will show some interesting parallels. Now the work up to the actual operation would intensify greatly; no sooner had they arrived back in Portsmouth than they were leaving again for HMS *Forth* in Holy Loch.

CHAPTER 4

A 'Blanket', a 'Hotel' Bed and the Spirit of 'Polish Grain'

The following evidenced account covers the time period from just prior to the thirteen Royal Marines taking their place on HM Submarine *Tuna*. It is derived from the various official reports given by the individuals who were a part of the submarine crew and the Commando raiding party at the time, as well as the unofficial papers and interviews given post war. Each had a different perspective due to the role they played. An allowance is made for any lapse in memory[1] that contradicts official or seemingly different accounts within British, French and German military documentation. Other information is derived from various diaries, both personal and official; including Blondie Hasler's own diary, which only omits the period of the operation itself, having left the diary with Norman Colley. The words from these individuals are interwoven into this narrative, much of which has never been related before now. In the author's opinion, there can be nothing better than reading a report from those who were actually there at the time. The precise dates and timings are used throughout to show the timetable of events as they rolled out in order to allow the reader a more vivid reconstruction. This also graphically depicts the risks that were evident in everyday life for the submariners, who were not volunteers for hazardous service.

Perhaps Blondie's summing up conveys just how much importance was placed upon the skilful delivery of the raiding party by *Tuna*'s Captain: 'Dick Raikes remains for me the very best type of British Naval Officer.'

Of the submarine crew, the accounts are from the captain of HMS *Tuna*, R. P. Raikes[2]; his first Lieutenant J. R. H. Bull[3]; the Navigator Sub-Lt G. J. Rowe[4]; CPO Telegraphist R. A. W. Quick[5]. The raiding party accounts are from the OC, Major H. G. Hasler[6]; his No. 2 in *Catfish*, W. E. Sparks[7]; the reserve of the raiding party, Norman Colley; with incidental information from Eric Fisher, No. 2 of canoe *Cachalot*.

The 'Off'

Although a complete failure, as Hasler viewed it[8], Exercise *Blanket* had served as an important and salutary lesson, which enabled him to improve on weaknesses before the main event. With this in mind, Hasler, knowing the timetable, began to step up matters ready for the departure day on 30 November. As intended, the detachment was scheduled to head for a base, which was tucked away in a secluded Scottish loch where the submarines could replenish their empty shelves from the depot ship, HMS *Forth*, and rearm with torpedoes and other ammunition for the next patrol.

Tuna's telegraphist Ray Quick tells us that 'when we returned from patrol[9] and after we had carried out the normal harbour routine, one half of the crew [was] given leave while the other half got the boat ready for sea. The engineers from depot ship HMS *Forth* completed any repairs that were needed. With the absent crew returned from leave we prepared to set off again on the next patrol.' For this crew, this patrol was 'entirely different'.

The MT driver, Marine F. J. Phelps, or 'Flash' as he was known by the lads, left Lumps Fort at Southsea in the Bedford truck and trundled along South Parade, into Clarendon Street past one of their locals, The Clarendon, and on to the pick-up. The lorry halted adjacent to their billet, No. 27, the White Heather Guest House of Worthing Road, a well-kept, semi-detached property. Within, each of the section had left their dress uniforms and other personal items awaiting them on their return; they thought this next jaunt would take about the same length of time as the last – the men had no idea it would be an actual operation.[10] They each said their goodbyes to their hosts as usual and with that they piled into the back of the lorry and, with smiling faces, waving cheerio to a young girl named Heather Powell, they headed for the Nissen huts.

On that day, 18 November, No. 1 section left Pompey[11] for London; for most, it was to be their last time of seeing White Heather, the Boom, their Nissen huts, Eastney, the canoe lake, the pubs and their own special long stretch of shingle beach that they had grown so used to. Capt. Stewart and Sub-Lt Ladbrooke departed for London along with Major Hasler and Lt-Cdr Allen to inspect *Larry*[12], a motor barge that was intended to be used as a parent vessel for motor boats (Boom Patrol speed boats being developed by Vospers and RMBPD) at Badgers Yard at Tower Bridge in London.

Meanwhile, Lt MacKinnon arrived at COHQ at 1500 and met up with Hasler ready for a final meeting at the War Office, where they received an hour's instruction in the POW No. 3 Code, a signal that could be used via the Resistance movement or if taken prisoner[13] – a secret but simple communication message meant for Military Intelligence. A noted individual at the briefing was another Royal Marine officer named Major Ronnie G. Sillars[14].

An interesting and previously unreported journey during the afternoon of Wednesday 18 November is recalled by Norman Colley, our reserve for Operation *Frankton*. With the arrival in London of No. 1 section, Norman remembered that another cloak and dagger operation now began. Three taxis with blacked-out windows arrived in a secluded section of the COHQ and all of the section took their seats; they did not know where they were going. They were delivered to a photographer's studio somewhere near and each had their photograph taken.[15] They had to wait a while to ensure that the photographs were satisfactory, and then they were taken back to COHQ in the same blacked-out taxis.

Previously, none of them had any inkling of any actual operation, and this is borne out by references made in letters. One such letter from Ty Cpl Laver talked about the 'cursed luck' of not being able to attend his brother's wedding but still held on to the possibility of making

Hasler, November 1942.

it; even though he knew they were going to be busy on another 'trip', he was 'sure they would get leave' afterwards. But this was the point at which the men realised that things were about to become more serious.

On 19 November, Hasler and all his 'gang' proceeded to Glasgow and then Gourock on the 0945 train and the 1230 ferry to HMS *Forth*. With the stores arriving by lorry at Gourock, the men began the evening transferring them on board the depot ship. Finding all the cabin accommodation taken on HMS *Forth*, the entire detachment was found lodgings aboard an Indian merchant ship, the *Al Rawdah*, moored nearby. This 'hotel ship', as it became known, was luxurious as compared with the sleeping arrangements they had been used to. Hasler's evening was spent 'planning programme till 0015'.

The training in the wilds of Scotland, as compared with the balmy south coast, was the tonic to stir them on, even though to many 'it always seemed to be near freezing point' with some never feeling quite so cold before. In comparison, it was still summer at Southsea! The next day, 20 November, the section was building and examining the canoes, arranging repairs and unpacking stores on the superstructure of HMS *Forth*. Hasler then took them on a trip across to Ardnadam in Holy Loch for a short forced march over the hills. This was followed by an 'interlude for instruction on the .45 Colt and silent Sten gun'[16]. They returned to their base and spent the evening cleaning the guns followed by a lecture on the Cockle suit and escape box. A mini celebration party for David Gabriel Moffatt's twenty-second birthday was held later that evening on *Al Rawdah*. On the morning of 21 November, Cpl Laver woke knowing that his elder brother, Jack, was getting married that very day at Barnet Church without him as his best man; he couldn't even telephone him to wish him good luck.[17] For Laver and the group, the day began with an amphibious landing, another cross-country march and another evening of lectures on the fitting of a .45 Colt holster, the commando dagger[18], and fusing Limpets. So it was that matters moved on and picked up in pace, convincing the men of No. 1 section that something was afoot. It seems that speculation had grown and they began to think of Norway as the destination.

There was plenty of canoeing in the lochs, and swimming was bearable, if a tad colder than the daily dips at Southsea. After all, these were toughened marines who had reached their peak, with Hasler intent on keeping it that way by continued daily exercise. Along with the exercise came the unrelenting hard graft. With no 'drinks down at the local', or for that matter anywhere to go, the only option was to use the mountains for recreational purposes, even though they were doing the same thing during 'normal day work'.

They fused the Limpets and dropped them on the sea bed the morning of 22 November and, in the evening in the chilled valley, practised single-paddle drill with 'approaches' and 'hull work'. Whilst Hasler and MacKinnon spent the evening making out an equipment list until 0400, another birthday was an excuse for a wee dram as Norman Colley became twenty-two.

As 23 November dawned back in Southsea, two new officers joined the RMBPD in Pompey, which brought the new establishment up to strength; their first canoe outing along the Boom was at hand. No such light duties for No. 1 section as, following on from a morning of navigational training with sectional charts, the entire contingent in six canoes embarked on an old coaster, reported to be a minesweeper, a Dutch ship named *Jan van Gelder*. They proceeded to the upper reaches of Loch Long. Between 1500 and 1730, they practised dummy attacks on this Dutch lady – the Limpeteers gently caressing her with their fiendishly sticky Limpets, aided by the hand-held magnetic holdfast. This was accomplished with their quarry doing 1–2½ knots both with and against them. The process was repeated at 1930 and 2130 in the darkness, but doing with-tide runs only. They returned to the depot ship at 2330 ready for the next day of lectures on navigational charts, preparing stores, overhauling the canoes and paddles followed by speed building /un-building exercises and fusing Limpets.

On the same day, back in Southsea, the two new officers had their first paddle in the north-east Force 1 wind on a misty and cloudy day that sported a sea temperature of 48 degrees. Some of No. 1 section at this time were thinking how inviting it would be getting up to no good and enjoying the night life of 'off duty' in Portsmouth; but all shared an ever-increasing sense of intent and purpose. They became keen for action due to the small telltale signs that something big was afoot. Rumours about the *Tirpitz* floated on the air. If they had thought about it, they would have realised that their Limpets would not have made a dent in that ship's amour-plated exterior.

Submarine *Tuna* had meanwhile undergone a series of degaussing[19] operations, unusual in that they occurred three times in succession over as many days; a fact that had not gone unnoticed by the crew. Capt. Dickie Raikes commented post war, 'They removed pretty well all the electricity out of us.'

Capt. J. D. Stewart arrived at HMS *Forth* on 25 November with additional stores, and as normal, the detachment had their usual sorting and preparing stores with Hasler instructing on the fusing of Limpets. The instruction was a series of lectures in order to learn its complexities, including how it was assembled. With the emphasis centred on the Limpet, it required every operation of the process completed to perfection, with the ultimate goal of ensuring the Limpets exploded exactly as desired. The object was characteristic for a special force, and they viewed it as another 'toy'; with the mines lying between the legs,[20] there was an element of contempt for their 'little packages'.

During the evening of the same day, Hasler went aboard *Tuna*, now alongside HMS *Forth*, and met First Lt 'Johnnie' Bull, who, along with Dickie Raikes, had only just been told by the Captain HMC Ionides (S)3, of HMS *Forth*, to prepare for a special operation and to embark a party of thirteen marines led by Major Hasler and his second in command, Lt MacKinnon. Once Hasler had explained certain matters, two things now occupied Lt Bull – time and space.

The sheer quantity of stores made the operation very difficult, as he had to find space for them, as well as the six 15-foot canoes sewn up in their uncoloured canvas sheaths. Lt Bull soon found out that the collapsed depth of the canoes would be no more than 7 inches[21], making them very stackable; but in the confines of the submarine much rearranging had to be done. The navigation officer, Sub-Lt Gordon James Rowe, said in a post-war anecdote, 'Johnnie Bull had a hectic couple of days, I noticed, arranging accommodation, involving offloading some of the spare torpedoes.'

The methodology of launching the canoes had been decided on before, so there was no discussion about using the floating-off method, which only left Lt Bull the effort of rigging up the hoisting-out technique. So it was that Lt 'Johnnie' Bull, Second Coxswain Harry 'Shakem' Fright and his casing crew rigged the 4-inch Mk 12 gun as a makeshift crane. Only Dickie Raikes, as No. 1 on HMS *Talisman*[22], had any experience of offloading canoes, and by a strange coincidence, that too was a delivery of two insurgents[23] to the Gironde Estuary; one of the first examples of an operation using the sub/canoe/floating-off combination.

HMS *Tuna* alongside the depot ship HMS *Forth*.

16 September 1942, aerial recon.

Aerial recon photographs of the
Gironde Estuary showing (top) the
islands and (below) path of the paddle
over great length into Bordeaux.

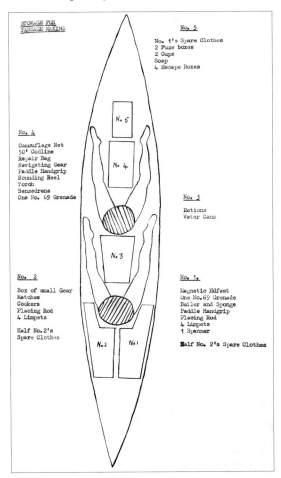

The positioning of cargo
for the passage-making.

By 26 November, Commander L'Estrange had arrived. He supplied the escape instructions and all the relevant information and advice on the escape. With the latest topographical and geographic data, Hasler pored over the aerial photographs of the Gironde Estuary, enabling him to select the daytime hides needed. As was his way, Hasler took very many notes on tides, terrain, ship dispositions and enemy defences and factored in the meteorological information. Hasler now had all the maps and necessary papers for the men. As for the men, they were busy packing, re-packing and checking the equipment.

To allow the reader to fully understand the equipment and stores carried by each of the canoes on the operation, the following detailed list is related. The five cargo bags contained[24] three pairs of double paddles of the Mk 2 type (elliptical blades); Mk 2 Handgrips; repair bag; bailer and sponge; P8 compass and corrector; escape kit; whiting line; pencil with paper and chart; magnetic holder; Codline; sounding reel; log pads including tide tables; dim reading torch with spare bulbs and batteries; protractors; camouflage net; waterproof watch; WT matches; tin of camouflage cream; two No.69 grenades; eight six-magnet Limpets; two ampoule boxes; Limpet spanners and two placing rods; compact rations for two men for five days; five cans containing half a gallon of water each; one box of Benzedrine tablets; water-sterilising sets; two 1st field dressing sets; one Iodine bottle; two packets of toilet paper; two Morphia syringes; five Hexamine cookers; five pint dixie; one tin of foot powder; WT ditty box; one tin each of cough lozenges and laxative pills.

In addition to the .45 Colt automatic pistol and fighting knife for each man, there was one silent Sten 9 mm carried by both Hasler and MacKinnon. Each man also had spare clothing and certain accessories that were within the bags, namely one pair each of short pants, felt-soled boots with spare laces and socks, woollen gloves, twenty cigarettes and an extra box of matches, razor and blades, handkerchief, towel, toothpaste and brush, seawater soap, rollneck sweater, and one shaving brush between two men. In all, the total weight carried was thought to be in excess of the intended gross safe carrying weight of 480 lb.

The evening of 26 November was set aside for compass deviation adjusting with the fully laden canoes. Lt Bull had also been busy, with the hoisting-gear mechanism. The startling simplicity, as related by 'Johnnie' Bull,[25] 'was to adapt the 4-in gun as a sort of makeshift crane'. The special slings for the canoes were designed by Hasler and then supplied to 'Johnnie' Bull in order that the whole ensemble could be worked up.

The next day, 27 November, brought together Commander L'Estrange, Blondie Hasler, Capt. Stewart and the officers of HMS *Forth*; they convened for a conference about the forthcoming operation. Meanwhile, the men prepared for another day of unpacking the stores they had already packed many times before and fitting the cargo bags inside the canoes, followed by compass checking. This was accomplished with the added assistance of the navigation officer from the depot ship. In order to determine any compass deviation, the canoes were loaded as operational and 'swung' with a compass corrector taking out any error. For the men, the rest of the day was given to shore leave, for just one night, as ordered by Hasler, who believed, rightly, that it would do them all good.

Whilst Blondie's idea of enjoyable relaxation from the constant readiness for the operation was a hill climb on the Isle of Bute with Stewart, others in the group had their own plans. Lt MacKinnon and Marine Ewart took the opportunity to visit their respective families in Glasgow, just a few miles away, on 27 November. 'Bobby' Ewart had on previous occasions brought home others including Conway and Sparks, but on this occasion he visited alone. Bobby's brother, the then-eleven-year-old George Ewart, remembers one particular moment during that evening well: 'He came home on his own that time. Bert hugged mother and said, I won't see you for a while.' Nothing was mentioned about the impending event to their respective families; they themselves only knew something was afoot. Indeed, Lt MacKinnon did not even let on that he was just a few miles away training.

It should be highlighted that Blondie liked a drink – beer at breakfast was not unusual – and although the polite decline was initially made, the night of the 27th and the morning of the 28th was a milestone even for him; and as such is worthwhile relating. As his diary revealed, his 'evening – drinking in *Al Rawdah* with the Poles' would result in one drink, literally, too many. Following the hike on the hills, then dinner, the intention was to get an early night. However, they were joined by a couple of Polish officers, who convinced the RM officers that 'just one glass of port – to help you sleep' would not do any harm. Rather than order the mess port, the Polish officers fetched a bottle from their cabin. It was not long after they had consumed the concoction that both Hasler and Stewart began to feel quite odd. On attempting to head to his bed, Stewart got up, wobbled and had to lean against the bulkhead. Both did actually make it to their bunks, but Marine Todd[26] remarked that they 'looked funny', and both of these officers knew it. The drink was homemade Polish grain spirit[27] and had a kick that Hasler would never forget. Had the Poles not been such staunch allies, it could have been thought they were infiltrators sent to nobble the operation!

Stewart's head was still spinning when he attended parade early morning of 28 November. Stewart's state was noticed by Sgt Wallace, who, when reporting the 'parade correct', quipped something about Stewart having white chalk covering his entire face. Stewart just looked at Wallace with resignation; the critique was very accurate. That same morning with Storeman Marine W. J. H. Drew's help, No. 1 section continued to do work with the operational stores; there could be no mistakes. Each store item needed a precise place within each cargo bag, each cargo bag needed to be sewn up and stowed in the set place allotted for the trip. Whilst distribution was an important facet, so too was knowing where every individual item was, so they could retrieve anything instantly from the canoe cockpit covering. The evening was given over to 'make and mend'.

Whilst it is not possible to determine exactly when the painting of the canoe names took place, a recollection by Bill Sparks and reports from the German archives at Freiburg do give an indication. Bill remembered that one morning they boarded HMS *Forth* and were instructed on

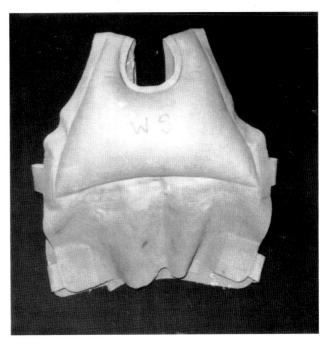

Bill Sparks' 'Reliant' life jacket
as used on the raid. Note his
hand-painted initials.

how to camouflage their Cockle canoes by means of drawing lines with chalk together with advice on the colours that should be used. Following this lesson by a colonel, they duly painted the canoes 'battleship grey' with the flexible paint. It was at this point that the names of the canoes were painted on in small letters on the bows.[28] It can be established from the German interrogation records[29] that the names were painted on the canvas in blue paint[30] on the port side and then over-painted with the two-tone camouflage colours a few days before embarkation in Scotland. The comment by Hasler in the war diaries that he left them 'touching up the camouflage' also gives this some weight. It is this information that gives an indication as to the day this was done, and the author suggests that the day in question was 28 November. It is probable that this was also the time when the life jackets were personalised by each man with their own hand-painted initials.

Leaving the section packing stores, checking equipment and 'touching up the camouflage on the canoes' and 'painting cockle suits', Blondie, sporting possibly the worst hangover of his life, met Dickie Raikes aboard *Tuna*. A mutual admiration began between these two talented, determined and perfection-orientated guys; they remained friends throughout their lives.

Dickie Raikes had by now received his 'Operation *Frankton* Orders' of 26 November and his 'Sailing Orders', which had been prepared immediately before. Telegraphist Ray Quick had replied as required with the acknowledgment signal quoting 'HLS 218 received'. With these orders, Raikes and Hasler's discussions centred on getting to the position best suited, from both points of view, for disembarkation. The details of both these sets of orders are related below, as they give an insight into the requirements and decisions that would have to be made by Dickie Raikes in order to launch the raiding party.

Also on the 28th, Sub-Lt Gordon James Rowe[31] made his way to HMS *Tuna*. The fore hatch of the submarine was open and, clutching his charts, he handed himself down at the ladder into the torpedo stowage compartment and turned aft to the control room. As he passed the Wardroom, Dickie Raikes called to him, saying, 'Pilot! I want you to meet Major Hasler. He's coming with us on the next patrol.' Rowe observed what most others did of Blondie: an outdoor type, tall, sandy-haired and moustached, and a Royal Marine officer. After the formal handshake, Christian names were exchanged, with Hasler using his 'Blondie' nickname, as was the form.

At that stage, all Sub-Lt Rowe knew, care of Hasler, was that they 'were planning an exercise in a few days'. Hasler explained that there would be a lieutenant and eleven men with him. None of Dickie's crew knew about the planned operation.

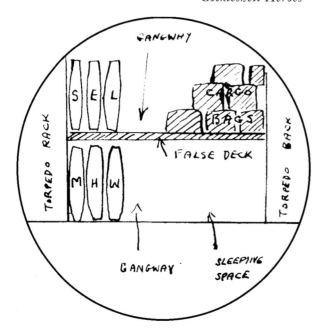

Hasler's original drawing of equipment stowed for passage. The canoes are unbuilt and facing forward.

Early morning of Sunday 29th, Hasler and Sparks went to *Forth* with cargo bags, and compass deviation was checked with *Forth*'s navigator. The evening had been spent packing the operational clothes after the badges of rank and recognition had been sewn on the Cockle suits. Around late morning, a reported meeting between Captain Ionides, Dickie Raikes, Rowe, Commander L'Estrange and Blondie Hasler took place; this is likely to have been to do with the final up-to-date Intelligence reports and weather information. Additionally, L'Estrange supplied a complete set of sectional charts of the estuary for each canoe, as well as the safe areas for lying up, and ensured Hasler had the requisite currency for his men. No doubt it was at this time that Hasler and Raikes were wished well for the operation they had been chosen to undertake. As they were very alike, their minds were running over all the details in tandem. This meeting was soon followed by a 'test lift with *Catfish* loaded'. Hasler's diary continues, 'Loading stores and boats in *Tuna*. Finishing sewing badges on cockle suits. Painting operational clothes. Evening. Discussions with L'Estrange, Jock and packing up papers until 2330.' Blondie packed his personal items and sundry papers and left certain items with Capt. Stewart along with notations on the jobs that required attention during his absence. Hasler did not believe in anything other than a positive outcome to the operation.

It was suggested that time was taken to 'write a letter home', and on the evening of the 29th, some were occupied doing just that. Some of the men thought they had no reason to write, having done so days before, indeed Lt MacKinnon had only just visited his mother a couple of days before.

The stores had been loaded into the torpedo room of HMS *Tuna*, along with the canoes, stacked in precise order. The entire area resembled a well-packed Pickford's removal vehicle; every cubic metre of space was utilised to its maximum potential. This economy of space was evident throughout the submarine. Without being too technical, the submarine was similar to an underground train coach, and apart from the arch, which was far more pronounced, the only real amount of headroom was in the control room, the centre of the submariners' universe. The control room was directly below the conning tower where there were two periscopes, the hydroplane wheels and the valves that flooded or 'blew' the tanks. Here resides the piece of kit colloquially referred to as the 'fruit machine', so called because, when used for its purpose in torpedo attacks, it gave all the correct 'symbols'.

The Patrol Orders for HM Submarine *Tuna* arrived on 29 November 1942 and acknowledgment of receipt by signal was 'HLP 29 received'. The route outwards as ordered by FOS 2244A/27 and the special instructions are given later.

For the 'Method of Execution' of the orders, they gave, amongst other things, the place and time of departure, which was 180 degrees 10 miles off Wolf Rock on Wednesday 2 December at 1800. It also stated that bombing restrictions were in place whilst on passage and when in position on the French coast. The route homebound was 'will be signalled', which meant that, following the successful disembarkation of the raiding party, the submarine would steam to the appropriate position by 13 December at the latest to receive instructions.

Charge Document for Operation *Frankton* – Orders to Submarine

These orders were received from the Office of the Admiral (Submarines), Northways, London, on 26 November (SM 04316/395) and show the information and objective for HMS *Tuna* during the operation. It contained appendices that dealt with the meteorological data as well as information and intelligence pertinent to *Tuna* for the operation, which included a trace of the RAF mines. It gave the 'Outline of the Operation' and stated that the 'Object of the Submarine' was

> to disembark the special military landing party in a position in which they can proceed in their 'cockles' to the mouth of the Gironde estuary approaching from the southwestward. The whole operation [was] to be so conducted that the disembarkation [was] to be undetected by the enemy.

The 'Method of Execution': the preliminary training was to take place in the Clyde area under the direction of Dickie Raikes with 'the operation not to be proceeded with unless the standard of training meets his requirements'.

It highlighted that, 'whilst desirable for as many cockles to be disembarked as possible', it was realised that during the journey some of the crews of the canoes may become unfit or at the time of disembarkation the weather might prevent some of the cockles actually taking part. 'The actual number of the crews taking part [was] entirely at [Captain Raikes'] discretion after consultation with [Hasler].'

In the report, it was considered that the accuracy of the positioning of the mines was 'within 1 mile'. As a result of this, '*Tuna* [was] *on no account to proceed within the dotted line* [as] shown on the tracing'. The first possible night of the disembarkation was 5/6 December with the last possible night being 12/13 December.

The cancellation of the operation was at the order of Admiral (S) or Dickie Raikes, if by reason of unsuitable weather, enemy surface or air forces there were unforeseen risks to the submarine, or by Hasler, as the Military Force commander, if, in his opinion, 'it [became] clearly apparent that the enemy position is such that the military task cannot be accomplished without seriously prejudic[ing] the safety of his force'. Orders for *Tuna* on passage to the operation were that '*Tuna* may attack at all times, should enemy forces be encountered. And if such an attack was considered prejudicial to the operation said operation was cancelled and *Tuna* to withdraw to predetermined point'. The amount of secret and confidential matter was reduced to a minimum and withdrawal from the operation was to be no later than 12/13 December, withdrawing to a vicinity of 44 degrees N, 5 degrees W.

The orders were to be destroyed after completion, i.e., post 12/13 November and certificates of destruction to be forwarded to Adm(S). There were reports of an RDF station in the vicinity of Soulac capable of picking up surface ships within a 15- to 25-mile range with other RDF stations north of Gironde. There were also heavy and medium coastal batteries at Royan and heavy batteries at Arcachon.

Sailing Orders and *Crescent*

These were prepared on 28 November 1942 and were for HMS *Tuna* and *White Bear*. The orders were to be destroyed when complied with; i.e., after passing Wolf Rock. The port of departure was in the vicinity of Gourock Head, Clyde, on 30 November at 2200 proceeding according to Fleet notice to north and east of Lundy Island, then 2 miles off Trevose head and on to 180 degrees, 10 miles off Wolf Rock by Wednesday 2 December at 1800. At this time, all chart folios, bar three operational ones, were to be transferred to *White Bear*. *White Bear* would depart and head to Falmouth and await instructions, and *Tuna* would continue on her way to the French coast. Fighter co-operation was arranged for the whole passage, code-named *Crescent*. Special instructions were that particular attention was to be paid to the accuracy of navigation when proceeding within positions on given routes and to passing through the positions ordered.

In order for the reader to better understand the 'abilities' of a T-class submarine, and that of the journey undertaken from Holy Loch to the Gironde, it should be noted that HMS *Tuna*'s speed underwater was only 8 knots flat out for an hour and a half or 2 knots for twenty hours, whilst on the surface her speed was 13 or 14 knots.[32] In British waters during the day and night, *Tuna* would proceed on the surface under escort from *White Bear*. This 'large raking motor yacht with handsome lines' was one of the most distinctive of the time.[33] At 318 feet (96.9 m) with a draft of 16 feet and 1,647 gross tons, she had a reported speed of 19 knots (4,000 bhp). Originally named *Iolanda* when built in 1908, she spent some time in St Petersburg around the First World War, then was registered in New York during the 1930s. She was hired by the Royal Navy in 1939,[34] being part of the 3rd Flotilla and used as a submarine target and armed inshore escort vessel out of Scotland; she was latterly purchased and used as a survey ship going under the name *Lexamine*. During this period of conversion, all her fittings were moved and stored at Camper & Nicholson's yard at Gosport (including the well-carved, clothed female figurehead). Postwar, this figurehead was acquired by a London dealer and allegedly eventually mounted outside a restaurant in Seattle, Washington! Capt. Dickie Raikes said of the *White Bear*, 'It was a millionaire's private yacht … the last lap of luxury that was used as escort in home waters' and its like was needed 'because the RAF were so very trigger happy in those days'. This comment was coloured, no doubt, by having been bombed by the RAF twice during the war.

Iolanda. (J&C McCutcheon Collection)

Monday 30 November 1942

During the previous evening, 'while it was still dark[35] the ship's company (HMS *Tuna*) went into 'Harbour Stations' and the Commandos came aboard – bringing with them, in pairs[36], long packages which slid down the fore hatch with the men'. On this Monday morning, the men of No. 1 section again rose early and were ferried over to HMS *Forth* and then onto *Tuna*. They had no idea this was the 'real thing'; it seemed like it was just an enhanced exercise. In the RMBPD War Diary, it was stated, 'All records of *Frankton* are kept by CCO and no further details will be given in this diary.' The last reference to the event was simply 'No. 1 section embark for *Frankton*'.

In place of the 'reload' torpedoes removed by Lt Bull and his crew were the six canoes secured within the fore ends[37], each on their robust sides within their canvas sheaths awaiting attention. 'The torpedoes *Tuna* carried were about as long as the canoes, but the canoes were obviously wider. *Tuna* did not carry its full complement of torpedoes, as there was no room for the torpedoes and canoes.'[38] Every other nook and cranny was used for the pre-packed, sealed cargo and personal bags. Once aboard, the marines went below, and it is reported that both Capt. Stewart and Lt-Cdr L'Estrange came on board to say their goodbyes to them. Again, we rely on Hasler's diary to show the events of 30 November 1942: 'a.m. to Forth with personal gear and papers. Embarked *Tuna*. 1030 said goodbye to Jock and L'Estrange. Sailed.' As HMS *Tuna* prepared to slip her moorings from beside the grey hulk of HMS *Forth*, the Royal Marines turned out and in single file stood at ease on the after casing until Hasler brought them to attention as the coxswain's pipe released its tune in salute to the mother ship.

As the long, black hull slinked away under main motors at 1030, the familiar eyes of Lt-Cdr L'Estrange, Capt. Stewart and Capt. Ionides bid them farewell from the high reaches of HMS *Forth*. Below were two other interested parties: MOA Marine Todd and Storeman 'Willy' Drew, who had also ferried over for the occasion. They waved goodbye. With the coxswain's pipe now sounding 'Carry On', the 'Royals' were then dismissed, and they went below decks. Stewart and L'Estrange left for COHQ in London on 1 December, and Stewart had a meeting to discuss the future training and administration of the RMBPD.

The officers and crew of *Tuna* went about their normal duties. Meanwhile, Blondie brought his men together in the forward torpedo space, and amongst the stacked canoes and cargo bags, they grouped together like sardines in a can or, as Bill Sparks put it, 'inside … a cigar-shaped coffin'. He was not the only one that did not like the confines of the submarine. Normally shared by four 'reload' torpedoes in their racks along with ratings, this compartment, situated right forward, was about twenty-five feet long; it now had a false floor and contained thirteen very fit outdoor types and their kit.

In the five months of training, the party had learnt everything they needed to know except where and when they were to make use of it; they were about to be educated. Hasler's diary records, '1130 explained outline plan to men.' He had erected a blackboard and standing beside it he began his short diatribe. 'Right Lads, this is the real thing,' he said and turned the blackboard over to reveal his previously chalked drawing of a map of the Gironde Estuary. His explanation grew in information and intensity. Spellbound, they gradually learnt about the plan. He told them of the target and the methodology of getting there. This was of course all new stuff to the men; some were surprised yet relieved that the operation was in France and not Norway. Sparks remembered thinking that at least the water would be warmer down there in the south … it was an illusion he was to hold for only a short time.

The raid contained two cardinal problems: how to cover over 100 land miles[39] of a busy and well-patrolled river undetected and, having done so, how to withdraw. The first part was with hard and continuous paddling by night and perfect concealment by day; the second was not so easily accomplished. The men still sat motionless and captivated as he told them of the problems they needed to overcome in order to get to the port of Bordeaux. After this onslaught of information, Hasler, as all good orators do, paused and asked if there were any questions. Sgt Mike Wallace threw a log into the fire; all the men looked at him as he said,

'How do we get back, sir?' Instantly, all eyes focused on Hasler, awaiting his reply. Hasler then explained the reasons for not being able to use the submarine to retreat and the fact that there would be a need to get as far away from Bordeaux as possible – independently. They were informed that the escape route was being dealt with by French Resistance and the route would be overland from France to Spain and then home.

Eric Fisher is noted to have said, 'The more we heard, the more we were surprised.' That was true of everyone. For the time being, that was all the information he was going to impart regarding the escape plan. He emphasised that each canoe had to withdraw separately, regardless, and that the land route had to be travelled in pairs only. He advised that 'one man's peril must not jeopardize the operation', and this he meant without exception. None of the team were prepared for this challenge; it slowly began to sink in, and each tentatively looked at the other. Hasler, always having the ability to size up the situation, paused and became more serious in his inflexion, adding, 'If anyone feels that this operation is too much for him, I want him to say so now. No one will think any worse of him.' He paused again, looked around and saw some with long faces, but then the slightly bowed heads rose and they grinned at each other. Hasler proffered, 'After all, it's a good deal less dangerous than a bayonet charge.' And how right he was. Another chirp from Sgt Wallace entered the momentary vacuum: 'If I get captured I'm going to declare myself neutral – because I'm Irish!' For one second, Hasler thought to himself that this ruse could be an option for him as well, which caused his moustache to raise up at the ends as he grinned widely in response. The next question from one of the men was about the language barrier. Hasler told them all that there would be a few nights of learning a few French phrases. It was at that moment that Lt MacKinnon smiled lightly as he caught Hasler's eye and realised the reason for Blondie's 'French speaking only' on three evenings each week when they were staying at 9 Spencer Road prior to the operation.

Hasler then produced a large-scale map and briefing began again. He explained that Bordeaux lay on the River Garonne, 16 miles south of the point where that river and the Dordogne meet to form the Gironde; it was this waterway that they would be negotiating. Further words of wisdom were offered by Hasler to do with the happenstance of being approached by a hostile craft. He told them the first option would be that of evasive action, and if certain to be seen due to proximity, they should stop paddling and adopt the lowest position. Then, if the craft came alongside, grenades should be used prior to boarding the enemy craft. He told them never to take offensive action unless they were compelled to do so. He emphasised that the job was to get through. On land, concealment first, then, if discovered by enemy forces, the use of the knife to kill silently and then hide the body ensuring it was below the high-water mark. There were instructions for every eventuality, including what to do if they came into contact with the French peoples. This was Hasler's way – pearls that flew in the face of convention. These men were intelligent; give them all the details of the difficulties and they, as Royal Marines, would rise to the challenge – the very spirit of the Corps.

The feeling amongst the men at the time can be best described by Marine Eric Fisher, No. 2 in canoe *Cachalot*: 'The morale was really something and had to be seen to be believed. We all had tremendous faith in the Major and would have followed him anywhere … someone might raise a query about the escape plan, but old Stripey Wallace at once had a few words to say and everything was all right again. We were going to have a smack at Jerry and he wouldn't know what had hit him. Everyone was in fine shape and rarin' to go.'

After the realisation of what was to come, some wrote further letters home. Lt MacKinnon wrote a letter dated this day, but even this did not give any indication of the danger he was to face. All Jack mentioned to his parents was that he wanted to confirm that they would not hear from him for a number of weeks; not to worry about not getting any letters and 'I will carry on watching crossing the road.'

The Preliminary Period at Scalpsie Bay

Whilst *Tuna* slowly made her way down the Firth of Clyde in a southerly direction to Inchmarnock Water, Hasler had called the men together for the first part of the plan of events; 'at the same time Dickie Raikes had told [Lt Bull] and the 'trugs'[40] what was involved'[41]. At 1200 they had reached Helensburgh Bay and, with her 'trials complete', at 1250 *Tuna* proceeded to Inchmarnock Water passing 'gate outward' by 1345. *Tuna*'s 'course was altered[42] to bring [them] to a lonely stretch of coast, a secluded bay on the Argyllshire coast, [they] went to Diving Stations'. 'After catching trim [they] cruised at periscope depth for an hour or so; presumably to allow the Marines to become accustomed to the conditions. Then the exercise began.'[43]

Until this publication, the true position of this inaugural event has only been alluded to. In fact, at 1519,[44] the submarine came to a stop at Scalpsie Bay[45] on the Isle of Bute. 'The Captain stopped both engines [surfaced] and ordered the fore hatch to be opened. Then came the order to 'Shakem' and the crew, "away canoes".'[46] Should anyone living in the vicinity of Scalpsie Bay have seen a submarine and a bunch of men with canoes, they would have been the first and last civilians to have seen the 'Cockleshell Heroes' rehearsing for their famous raid. This full dress rehearsal was the last one for the marines and the first one for the crew of the *Tuna*. Much was at risk should the submarine be discovered on the surface during the disembarkation of the canoes. As they say, 'the devil is in the detail', and it takes much more research before one is able to determine the actual facts during this period.

Lt Bull's recollection of these events is quite brief: 'We stopped and did a full scale dress rehearsal which showed we could get all the canoes away in half an hour flat. It also proved the efficiency of the gun/crane we had rigged up. When the canoes had been re-embarked we set off for the Bay of Biscay diving by day after we cleared the English coast.' This very succinct version of events belies the complexity of the efforts during this crucial piece of training. Little more is given from the different perspective of Pilot Rowe, who refers to 'a drill prepared beforehand'. 'The Marines made ready their folboats[47] … in the fore ends and we surfaced. Time and time again, getting better at each effort, the men and their folboats were, one at a time, raced up to the upper casing through the fore-hatch which was re-secured after each pair and their boat were up. *Tuna* then dived and surfaced many times … [to] simulate operational conditions, and then we sailed south.'

Dickie Raikes reported that the whole rehearsal was completed about three times, in one interview he said, 'Our first practice run took about one hour forty minutes.' Within the *Tuna*'s log, we can be assured that at 1519[48] on Monday 30 November, Raikes ordered *Tuna*'s engines stopped and they 'commenced exercises'.

HMS *Tuna*'s log then reports that following the trials, finishing at 2000, they were still at Scalpsie Bay. With this it can be determined that the canoe exercises took no more than five hours, after which they then 'sailed for the Bay of Biscay'. Raikes says in the patrol report of Operation *Frankton*, 'Preliminary trials in Inchmarnock clearly showed that it was unlikely the whole operation would take less than an hour to complete without damage to the boats. Thirty minutes to assemble the boats. Forty-five minutes to disassemble boats.'

The authority on the event at Scalpsie Bay is that of Hasler via his personal diary. He tells us a little more, writing, '1530–1930 two trial hoist outs in Inchmarnock. Time for night hoist out, starting on top of casing. 31 mins for five boats. Wind force 4. Damaged *Coalfish* getting out and *Cuttlefish*'s compass getting in. Evening inspecting and drying out boats in turn, then unbuilding and stowing.'

Previous trials in the methodology of launching the canoes had proved that it was possible, with the Hasler-designed slings and the development of the use of the 4-inch gun and girder, to dispense with the floating-off method of launching the offspring. What remained was to ensure that the specially positioned canoes and stores would add to the swift departure needed. It should be noted that the canoes had a specific stacking, loading, positioning and 'upping' order. They also had a specific 'ready to be launched' order. The ultimate dual purpose of this was, firstly, to ensure that the two division leaders, Hasler and MacKinnon, would already be in the water to take charge, and secondly, should Raikes have to abort the launching of the canoes and dive, those already launched could proceed with the operation.

It should be reiterated that Hasler was extremely good at getting every detail crystal clear on paper and in every segment of the operation from inception to delivery. Much of this meticulous attention is shown in the reports and sketches by Hasler and drawn on here.

The identification names on the canoes had been over-painted, so there had to be a way for each crew to identify their own craft so as to ensure the correct order during 'upping' and launch; it is believed this was accomplished by means of the single letter, which was painted on both the canoe canvas sheath and the canoe itself. The letters used were the first letter of the surnames of the No. 1 in each canoe thus: *Catfish* – **H**, *Crayfish* – **L**, *Conger* – **S**, *Cuttlefish* – **M**, *Coalfish* – **W**, *Cachalot* – **E**. The identification markings were essential for the correct disembarkation order and could well have been temporary. An indication that this was the case is found within Hasler's own report under 'Disembarkation Drill'.[49]

4 Hours Before Timed Opening of Hatch

The crew would each build their own boats one by one (this actual operation took two men less than sixty seconds and was achieved using the interior struts, two each side and one at each end). They then inflated the buoyancy bags and fitted them into the bow and stern reaches of the canoe, along with the paddles, Nos 4 and 5 bags and compasses. They then greased the round cover hatches used for accessing the building struts at each end of the canoe and secure with the wooden fixings. They had to then ensure that both breakwaters were in the down position, then stow canoes in ready-to-use position. Part of their operational clothing was now worn. The raiding party were then instructed to eat and drink, which would give them the energy at the appropriate time, and offer an opportunity for any necessary evacuation, before donning the complete set of operational clothing followed by applying the camouflage face cream.

HMS *Tuna's* 4-inch gun. (Raikes Archive)

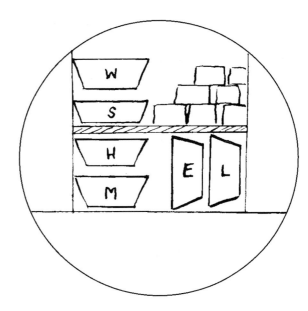

Canoes built stowed ready for
disembarkation four hours before
(facing forward).

30 Minutes Before Timed Opening of Hatch

The hoisting-out drill was resumed and on the opening of the fore hatch, the slings went out first, then the crews would take the canoes up and stow them on deck ensuring that they kept the bows to starboard. This was done in strict order, thus ensuring Hasler's and MacKinnon's canoes were first into the water. Under the supervision of Lt MacKinnon, the Deck Party would follow on with the Sten guns along with Nos 1, 2 and 3 bags. During the approach run of the submarine, bags 1, 2 and 3 were loaded and bags 1, 2 and 4 were slit open. The cover was then done up and crew would get into the canoe. At the beginning of the hoisting-out sequence, the ensconce crew would get out and remove No. 3 bag without unbuttoning its cover and, keeping the canoe aft, move the canoe into next vacant place. The No. 3 bag would then be brought over as far as the waiting position. Crew would then remove their gloves and carry the canoe into the slings, making sure the front of the slings were level with the front of the cockpit and the spreaders at equal height each side. No. 3 bag was put in and canoe crew would get in, leaving putting on gloves until after the hoist out.

The individual crews would form into the prescribed division within their allotted place in the assembly positions, facing the bow and in the lee of the submarine, which was either the port or starboard side. The last canoe in the water would get ready for a sixty-minute run and would give a blast on the whistle to commence.

The recollection of this stage of progression can be related from another viewpoint, that of Telegraphist Quick. He recalled that 'although the operation was carried out with success, apparently the Major considered it was not done quickly enough so the canoes were brought inboard with the crews and the hatch closed; *crane and all*. Why, as 'Shakem' said afterwards, we did not know, [until] we realised what it was all about. The crane was a vital part of this operation, having to be dismantled after the canoes were waterborne [with] *Tuna* having to get away speedily … so the practice was repeated a couple more times … until the Major's opinion was that it could not be bettered. The 'crane' was dismantled, with the marines and canoes below in the fore ends, and the hatch was closed. With the Captain ordering engines restarted and the Escort vessel advised by signal, which I duly sent, away we went down the Irish Sea.'

Marine Norman Colley, who would have been MacKinnon's No. 2 on the *Frankton* Raid if it had not been for an untimely recreational injury (which ultimately saved his life), volunteered and had been picked to be the reserve man.

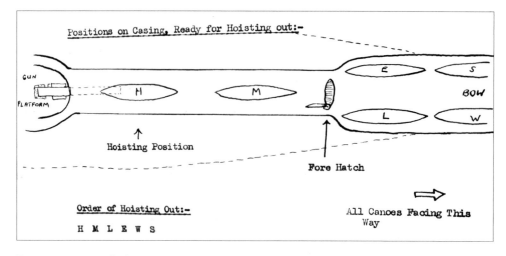

Positions on casing for hoisting out. Note the position of the gun platform.

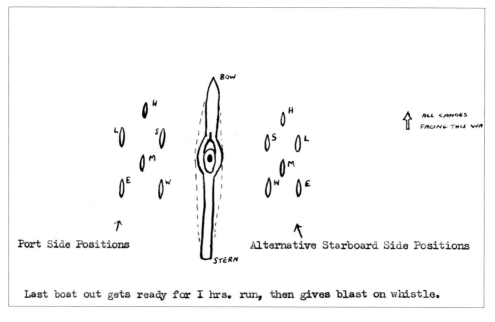

Positions in the water; canoe E did not launch.

For the thirteen Royal Marines, these special operation trials would be the very last time they would get to be on deck, breathing the wholesome fresh air and feeling the crisp free-flowing wind on their faces. For these men, the unnatural thing was being restricted and cooped up in a metal box for the next seven days – almost to the hour. They had become accustomed to the daily high-end training in barely five months of belonging to this very special Detachment of Boom Patrollers. Now their exercise was limited to simple muscle toning, but even that was restricted due to the need to conserve air. The recreational periods were mostly occupied by playing cards and board games like 'uckers', drinking and eating very good food in the very cramped conditions never before experienced … after the initial passage in rough weather that is.

The 'White Bear' from Campbeltown

The route taken by HMS *Tuna* has until now been largely unknown, the submarine simply arriving at the destination after the passage. This new snapshot brings a brief but intimate insight into that journey for the crew of HMS *Tuna* and the thirteen guests.

With the signal sent to their escort HMS *White Bear* by Telegraphist Quick, *Tuna* sailed on her main engines, proceeding at an average surface speed of 10 knots in a southerly direction from the proving ground of the secluded Scalpsie Bay. As recorded by Lt Johnny Bull, at 2235 on the 30th, HMS *Tuna*'s rendezvous with *White Bear* occurred in the vicinity of Gourock Head.[50] The green shores of Bute with the rocky outcrops were being left behind, swinging past Little Cumbrae Island, the steep shores of Arran with the summit of Goat Fell, they steamed down the Firth of Clyde.

Tuna and *White Bear* passed the Clyde Light Vessel abeam at 0253 on 1 December, with most of Hasler's men asleep on the torpedo room floor. Meanwhile, Dickie Raikes' cabin was occupied by Hasler. Lt Bull had relinquished his bed to Lt MacKinnon, whilst Sgt Wallace was being accommodated by the Petty Officers.

When the marines awoke their senses were beginning to be affected by the 'smell' of the submarine; however, before things became even more unpalatable, they enjoyed a very good and hearty breakfast as prepared by the resident gypsy: Joe, the ship's chef. The chef cooked for the entire company, all of which had to be accommodated in relays as messes had not the room to seat much more than a handful comfortably at a sitting. Most just took their meals when and where they could due to the shift system. The marine officers took their meals in the wardroom, with the rest of the gang accommodated by the respective messes.

By 0835, the lookout had sighted Chicken Rock Lighthouse,[51] and by 0958, it was well behind them. Meantime the marines' education began with Lt MacKinnon teaching them the No. 3 Code for the first, but not the last, time. The byproduct of the instruction for every aspect of the operation was that it would distract from the claustrophobia that some were beginning to suffer from. It wasn't until midday that weather gave a portent of things to come and a squall blew up and then dissipated; it was enough to send some to the 'heads'. *Tuna* made her way further down south, and at 1703, a fix was taken with Bardsey Lighthouse just ten miles away; by 1818 that too was behind them.

After things had calmed down slightly and whilst some were enjoying the evening meal and a relatively early night, by just gone 2000 the south-west wind had got up a Force 5 and the submarine began to roll heavily. On the surface, she pitched and dived in the heaving seas during that night's passage; even those used to it commented. Lt Bull remembered that the 'weather was foul and there was much sea-sickness particularly amongst the marines which took the edge off their training'. Ray Quick sported the comment, which seems to sum it all up, 'as usual the weather was pretty gloomy, although we were used to it, because wherever we went poor old *Tuna* seemed doomed to run into heavy seas much to our sorrow'.

Whilst a few of *Tuna*'s crew succumbed, the 'sorrow' was felt much more by most of the 'Royals' in this narrow steel drum, making these supremely fit young men feel dizzy and numb. The overbearing and unfamiliar smells coupled with the seemingly never-ending rocking made, in Hasler's own words, 'everyone except NCOs pretty useless. Self continuing planning till 0145'.[52] With the air quite foul, when the seasickness finished, the bouts of claustrophobia continued. In modern parlance, they must have been stir-crazy by the time the disembarking day arrived. Hasler's diary tells us that he 'slept all day between meals' in a rolling *Tuna* down the Irish Sea. By 2115, all the party were having to restow all the equipment and re-check their kit due to the washing machine effect. (On 1 December 1942, in Lyon, France, a mother was visiting her son to see how he was getting on with certain tasks she had given him, little did they know they both would become involved in this little operation … but more of that in a later chapter.)

The journey progressed and the Smalls Lighthouse appeared 9½ miles away at 2248 and was abeam to port by 0019 on Wednesday 2 December. At 0346, the St Goven Light Vessel was spotted. Passing north and east of Lundy Island in the Bristol Channel, *Tuna*'s watch noted the 325-foot-high rocky outcrop of Hartland point on the north-western tip of the Devon coast to port at 0712. The midweek morning had dawned and the wind abated somewhat by 0800 only to kick again throwing a westerly Force 4 directly at them by 1200 having passed two miles off Trevose Head, abeam, and altered course to 245 degrees. All this while, *White Bear* was consorting with them. With an average speed of 9 knots, *Tuna* was just 5½ miles from Longships Lighthouse[53] at 1433 and at 1500 she commenced her first zig-zag followed by a new zig-zag at 1613 and took her fix on Wolf Rock Lighthouse, which was 7½ miles away, at 1700.

Before *Tuna* proceeded independently at 1710, Dickie Raikes complied with the order 'to transfer all folios [bar three] to *White Bear* before they [separated]'. At 1800, *Tuna* dived for an hour and travelled 4½ nm before surfacing at 1857 to commence a zig-zag course. Hasler reports that at 1500 he 'turned out troops and began to go through bags, restowing and sewing up again ... lecturing troops, who had by now recovered'.

After leaving Wolf Rock[54] some 8 miles south-west of Lands End[55], *Tuna* remained dived by day commencing 3 December at 0740, so as to remain undetected, until surfacing at 1900 at just under 3½ knots for 40.9 nm. On this day, back at Southsea, the 'Training Section' of new officers and other ranks began their time in the RMBPD with an introductory talk by Capt. Stewart, followed by PE, a swim off the shingle beach, drill and lessons with the Mk 1* canoe (lessons 1 and 2). Aboard *Tuna*, Hasler was 'lecturing troops all day – examining photos of approach. Instructions for escape'.

It should be noted that the Mk 2 canoes were not on a production footing until 16 January 1943. Hasler had taken the very first non-production models of the Mk 2 canoe on the *Frankton* Raid.

The *Frankton* Patrol

The estuary of the Gironde is wide and long and leads to one of the largest cities in France, Bordeaux, and then on to the Garonne and Dordogne rivers. Just inside the mouth of the estuary, there are two good harbours: Royan and Port Bloc. The estuary is known to be dangerous to enter in heavy weather, swell and conditions of poor visibility. Within, there is some fifty-five miles of tidal river and both the tidal and river currents are 'very strong and do not always follow the expected direction, especially at the mouth' of this sandbank-infested estuary. Some of the sandbanks change position during winter storms, making the constant variations difficult to chart for this pilot.

The routine of the submarine whilst on patrol had to be adhered to, and the marines began to realise the format – all the energetic work was saved for the times they were surfaced. When submerged, everyone took things easy, encouraging as much sleep as possible, thus keeping bodies still and conserving air. Day became night to suit the routine. As soon as they had left the escort, instead of supper it was breakfast. Following breakfast, at around 1800, the diesel engines were started after surfacing in order to charge the batteries. With the flow of air to the diesel engines via the conning tower the submarine's interior took on a more pleasant atmosphere.

Friday 4 December 1942

The next stage of the trip is recorded with the aid of Pilot Gordon Rowe, who relates that, 'With a last running-fix on the Wolf Rock lighthouse we set course for the Bay of Biscay. Diving by day and speeding on the surface at night on the diesel engines, we made first for Ushant and then for south of the bay. The weather wasn't bad at all and the bay didn't measure up to its reputation. German [extensive] mine fields obliged us to shape course well out to sea but we made our landfall and crept along the coast. The depth of water kept us at periscope level during the day and at night we moved but little on the surface while charging batteries.'

Lt 'Johnnie' Bull related that 'it was impossible to get any sun or star sights on passage so the Captain decided to head for a point some twenty miles south of the river entrance and work his way up the coast in a northerly direction whilst endeavouring to establish a really accurate position'.

The marines woke and things were getting better in the health department. For Marine Ewart, his day was brighter than the others; it was his twenty-first birthday. He was given a little more 'breakfast' and spoilt by the others. He did reflect on how much he missed the young Heather Powell; she no doubt was thinking of him, hoping he was safe and longing for his return. But the lads were not about to let Robert Ewart's special moment go without some form of small celebration. Hasler's mind was elsewhere. His diary reads, 'Lecturing troops all day. Subjects – the attack. Resume of complete orders. Evening. Working out detailed time tables for the attack and first nights passage. As a result asked *Tuna* to make night of 6th Dec the first possible night.'

Tuna duly dived at 0735 on 4 December and surfaced at 1847 taking up various courses to avoid the fishing vessels. Dickie Raikes' recollections are contained in his 'pseudo night order book' that he wrote up after the war. Within is revealed that 'on 4 December we surfaced at 1900 [log book records 1847]'. Dickie Raikes' intentions were 'to go in and get a good land fix for tomorrow (5th), but Blondie had asked for an extra day, so we patrolled well off the coast that night, clear of the magnetic mines sown all over the place by RAF'. An amusing anecdote centres around Marine Conway, who noted a change of odour in the submarine after surfacing. It is reported that he asked a question of an older hand on the submarine: 'What's that funny smell?' The reply was, 'That, son, is air! Whilst it was 'normal' for the submariners, it was quite odd for the marines who had been subjected to the conditions within. The only respite from the sweaty woollen clothing and life below was on the surface when the hatches were opened at night and 'the big mist was swept out of the sub all the way through – it was like being in a fog until it all cleared,' remembered Norman Colley. 'We then could breathe fresh air.'

Our marines were finding life in a 'cigar-shaped coffin' quite strange; this foreign world was offset by the warmth and companionship of *Tuna's* crew. The atmosphere was literally warm and stuffy! The smell of diesel oil permeated the boat and everyone's person; their clothes smelt. It brings a new meaning to Fuel for Life by Diesel, eau de toilette for men.

The marines found that it was only possible to use the toilet at certain times, and with permission, as the waste was discharged directly into the sea rather than into a holding tank. Hot meals were not available when the boat was submerged in the daytime due to the galley using too much battery power. There were three watches and only bunks for two-thirds of the men. The marines found that they too were subjected to 'saving air' as much as the off-duty men. A strange life, thought the marines. It was about this time that Hasler had instructed his men to write any letters to loved ones, and this is when Marine Ewart wrote his heartfelt letter to Heather Powell, somewhere in the Ocean twixt France and the UK. Hasler collected the letters and held them until packaging them up with his own letter addressed to the Commandant at Plymouth barracks and giving them over to Marine Colley, the reserve on the operation.

Saturday 5 December 1942

Whilst surfaced during the dark period, 0027 brought the night alarm, which was not relaxed until 0143. Meantime, they had heard aircraft in the vicinity. *Tuna* then commenced a zig-zag followed by the dive before dawn which broke at 0726; this brought about another incident of note. Signalman Smart found himself on the sick list care of his captain! Dickie Raikes and Smart were on the bridge, and during the descent into *Tuna* from the bridge Raikes attempted to pass an Aldis lamp, or signal lantern, but dropped it on Smart's head, causing a gash and a shout that startled all close by. It was some time before Smart could actually see the very apologetic captain. The *Book of the Prophet* caught the story and headlined it – 'Ivory Dome' was then adopted by all from that day onwards.

After they were submerged, they spotted two trawlers with painted white hulls and black superstructure at 0905, both flying a yellow flag. This and other fishing vessels caused them to make various alterations, and at 1240, the sub went deep. At 1850, they surfaced and continued avoiding the fishing vessels until nearly midnight.

In his notes, Dickie Raikes gives away a more amusing slant on this period: 'We were then a few miles off the French coast and about fifteen miles south of the entrance to the Gironde. I remember that night vividly as we spent the whole of it dodging through a positive wall of fishing boats. My notes say that there were seldom less than ten of them in sight at a time, most of them had lights, which made it easier. Our track chart was like a snake's honeymoon.'[56]

With *Tuna* the furthest south she was ever going to be at 44 degrees 59 minutes N; Pilot Rowe also commented, 'The sea there is heavy with plankton which gives off a luminosity, lighting up the bow wave and giving the look-outs impressions of unexpected light which they dutifully reported to the officer of the watch every few minutes. True the skipper had some tense moments weaving through a huge fishing fleet but we were not detected. Visual fixes through the periscope upon recognising landmarks were difficult owing to the flat calm and the presence of aircraft but our position was established and we sailed up the French coast. My first view of Biarritz was from 30 ft submerged.'

Tuna steered closer inshore but weather was bad enough to postpone for twenty-four hours.

Lt Bull tells us, 'After 5 days on passage we went ahead and made landfall and turned up north. The visibility was very poor and it soon became apparent that it was going to be very difficult to get an accurate fix as there was a myriad of houses and churches on the land which were impossible to connect with objects on the chart.' Hasler's diary for this day tells us, 'a.m. troops stand off. Self and MacKinnon continue working on attack time table and study photos. p.m. Lecturing troops on timing of first night, and of attack. Evening – MacKinnon lectured troops on coastal features around 2nd lying up place – Then spent evening writing fair copy of orders and studying advanced bases.'

Sunday 6 December 1942

The morning broke; the sea was flat calm along with a slight swell.

Indeed, all the day suffered from the light winds starting with a WNW Force 1 at 0400 backing to a Force 2 ESE by 0000 that night. Another problem that was encountered, as remarked on by Dickie Raikes, was the 'inexplicable density layers changing … you could be in perfect trim at 30 ft one minute and the next – wham! You'd gone down deep. We hit the bottom several times at periscope depth at about 38 ft – making periscope work particularly difficult.'

Lt 'Johnnie' Bull informs us that, 'after trying all day to get the required fix, the Captain was forced to say to Major Hasler the whole thing would have to be postponed till the next day and we would retire from the coast during the night and try and get a star fix in the morning dawn. The importance of this accurate fix cannot be overemphasised because, due to a typical lack of inter-service co-operation, the RAF had laid a minefield very near where we were planning to disembark the canoes and in any case we could not rely on the RAF's stated position [of the minefield]. The Captain and Hasler were obviously most concerned about this but took great pains to conceal their misgivings.'

Post war, Dickie Raikes said of the situation, referring to his notes on the subject, 'Rather nice expression I put here: "Landmarks do not exist or have been moved by the Germans and the charts are as much good as a midwifery course to a rabbit" – I thought that was rather nice!' He was referring to the lack of accurate mapping by the RAF of the mines, which he made reference to in his report, but with slightly less colourful words.

Hasler did comment to Dickie at the time, 'If I am reading your trace correctly those mines are right in the spot I'm asking you to disembark us,' to which a slight grin was perceived on the face of Dickie Raikes as he replied in the affirmative, adding, 'It's going to be very tricky!'

Ray Quick's take on the situation, as always, had an ounce of humour attached, saying of Sub-Lt Gordon Rowe at this time, 'The poor navigator was fed up with the Captain getting on at him, as well as me making disparaging remarks about his capabilities in the daily magazine, *Book of the Prophet*. It wasn't really fair, still, he would get his own back on me when I could not read the signals he required.'

The last part of the day is related by Lt Bull: 'There were, at the same time and had been present the day before, a large number of fishing boats and we had to use the periscope with tremendous care to avoid being sighted and reported to the Germans. There were also a large number of German aircraft flying around and we had to take care to avoid being seen by them.' In these calm conditions, aircraft noise carried a long distance. The activity on the Sunday had begun at 0558 with a night alarm; a darkened ship had been sighted and resulted in various courses and speeds used. By 0634, the night alarm had been relaxed with the vessel identified as a fishing schooner under sail. At 0720, *Tuna* dived at position 44 degrees 59 minutes N by 1 degree 55 minutes W and the flurry of fishing vessels appeared as if ordered at 0800 together with one Arado float plane flying past to starboard at 0929.

Dickie's notes again connect the period: 'We dived before dawn on Sunday the sixth and spent the first four hours slipping through the fishing fleet until we made landfall about 1300. We were quite unable to distinguish a single landmark through the periscope during the day. That meant we had to postpone the operation again.' Things quietened down until 1617 when one Blohm & Voss was sighted.

With both the master of the submarine and the military force commander face to face in the control room, quite late in the afternoon Raikes had told Hasler the situation; both understood each other. Borne from exasperation not frustration, Blondie's personal diary makes mention of the agreed twenty-four-hour delay was one with a 'slight reaction [from] both sides'. Blondie's men had completed as perfected the 'four hours before timed opening of hatch' sequence and were stood down much to the men's dismay; only buoyed up by a comment regarding being able to again enjoy the usual excellent breakfast prepared by 'Gypsy Joe', instead of the compact rations. Unpacking and re-stacking commenced. That day had started with the marines in very high spirits and joke telling; they had prepared themselves for the off.

Dickie Raikes' intended plan was to get close to the coast south of the mouth of the Gironde, some twenty nautical miles, then with a certain fix, approach the southern edge of the minefield. This reading from the stars in the last hour of darkness, before morning and the inevitable submerging, would have given an accurate location for the following afternoon's landmarks. This fix had been scuppered in the main by the heavy mist and by *Tuna* being bothered by the fishing vessels. If the vessels had spotted the periscope, they could have alerted the shore, resulting in attack by air in the relative shallows of the waters.

In his official report, he wrote, 'The night of the 6th/7th proved impossible, as I was completely unable to establish my position with sufficient certainty and it was imperative to be dead accurate. This was unfortunate as conditions were quite perfect; a nice mist coming immediately after dark.'

By 1900, *Tuna* broke the oily, dead-calm surface again to take a look at the pitch darkness ready for that night's patrol. Blondie joined Dickie on the casing and looking into the inking blackness said, 'It's a damned shame it's exactly what we wanted.' The submariner felt a twinge of guilt and apologized, adding encouragingly, 'I hope we will be able to do something tomorrow. We'll see if we can get a decent astro-fix before the morning.'

HMS *Tuna*'s log for 7 December 1942 begins, '0000; stopped; ESE wind force 2, with a barometric pressure steady at 1009mb.' They had proceeded on main motors from 0105, first port side, stopping at 0200, to restart at 0309, stopping again at 0324 with fishing vessels sighted. The main engines were started at 0457. They dived at 0700. The log shows that there was a great deal of intense air activity by Bf 110s, Bf 109s, Arados, Ju 88s, Dornier 18s throughout the day. It is known that there was an aerodrome nearby,

The all-important Cordouan Lighthouse.

and even Raikes believed that the aircraft were 'just patrolling, I'm sure they weren't looking for me.' Dickie Raikes spent the whole of the day working northwards along the coast and finally obtained an accurate fix at 1345 at position 45 degrees 22.5 feet N by 1 degree 14.1 feet W. Further fixes were taken approximately every thirty minutes until 1735. Raikes' previous experience in the area proved useful, as he explained: '[I] got a lucky confirmation fix by catching sight of Cordouan light which I recognised from [HMS] *Talisman* in 1940.'

Lt Bull explains, 'We duly spent the night well off the coast and, getting a good fix by starlight at dawn, renewed our reconnaissance of the coast. Finally getting a sight of the [white Cordouan] lighthouse at the mouth of the Gironde and fixing by bearing and range as we knew the height of the lighthouse and could estimate the range accurately by observing the angle subtended by the lighthouse using the high power periscope.'

Clearly the viewpoint from Pilot Rowe was focused on noticing 'navigation', as he is recorded as saying, 'The morning was beautiful, a brilliant sunny day with only a lop breaking in the surface of the sea. At periscope depth we circled around in wide curves well away from the shipping channel (the RAF had sown a field of magnetic mines at the mouth of the river) but near enough to register the lighthouse and the German boom defence vessel. Needless to say great care was employed in using the periscope but Blondie was afforded much use in preparation for the launch of the operation [for] that night.'

Indeed, that night was to be *the* night. Dickie Raikes had told Hasler, 'I should be able to put you off tonight, right where you asked – if these damned patrol boats keep out of the way, and if we don't get blown up by one of those RAF mines.' That evening, after mealtime, Dickie also told him about the patrol trawler, or 'Chasseur'[57], that had been observed at 1800, explaining that it was patrolling a line about 130–310 degrees which meant that the course ran through the intended disembarkation point.

In Dickie's own words, 'The added complication was that a German patrol boat came out from the Gironde and hung about in almost exactly the position that we had chosen ... I then moved the disembarkation point to inside the minefield, about 3 miles off the coast, which had the added advantage that [the raiding party] had the tide behind them. But it brought us much closer to the RDF Station, which was likely to cramp our withdrawal; however the weather forecast was too good and Hasler was very keen to get away tonight.' It should be pointed out that within the charge document for Operation *Frankton*, the Orders to Submarine stated that *Tuna* was on no account to proceed within the dotted line showing the positioning of the mines. Given that it was considered that the accuracy of the positioning of the mines was actually correct 'within 1 mile', it can only be assumed that he obeyed the order not to enter the 'dotted line' demarcation but in effect had to disobey the intent as he clearly did enter the minefield[58]; although his own report merely says, 'Disembarked close to the coast and near the RAF's badly laid mines.'

Raikes' own operational report was 'a poke in the eye' for the RAF, as he stated quite clearly that 'I don't think those mines could have been laid in a more embarrassing position, as they seemed to interfere with every possible plan of action from the very start. They might have been anywhere.'

Are You Happy To Go?

The original idea[59] had been to surface at a certain position on 6/7 December, assemble the canoes on the fore casing at full buoyancy then trim down and approach the Gironde to disembark in 45 minutes. The positioning at that time had been thought the best compromise from both Raikes' and Hasler's viewpoint. Now, due to being unable to establish his position, Dickie Raikes' plan entailed getting four miles off the coast (closer), to the 'evident delight' of Hasler, yet only ten miles from the RDF station, then bringing *Tuna* to full buoyancy and doing the whole operation in one, cutting out the low buoyancy approach. This plan of action gave the raiding party a 'fair tide for an extra hour'.

In his official report, he made no reference to rabbits, this time saying only, 'This plan quite evidently required extreme accuracy in navigation even allowing for the rather touching faith of the authorities in the accuracy of the positions given by the RAF – a faith which I did not share'. His notes tell us, 'We dived at 0700 on Monday the seventh, we were only about six miles off the coast, but even so it was not until *c.* 1400 that day that we were able to establish our position with absolute certainty. This may sound strange, but it must be remembered that the periscope could only be used very sparingly because of air patrols and that the Germans were busy altering the face of the coast with huge anti-invasion defences which were not shown on the charts.'

As he said after the war, 'It brought us "uncomfortably close" to the newly constructed Radar station, which was likely to cramp our withdrawal. But we carried out the whole operation in full view of that patrol boat at a range of 5,000 yards. I was sure that our lookout would be infinitely better than theirs because we knew what we were watching and I'm quite sure they never saw us.'

During the entire passage, Hasler and MacKinnon had been instructing and educating the men on every detail of the mission; apart from the times when they were ailing due to the unfamiliar conditions. They knew precisely where every item in the canoe was to be located in an instant. They knew intimately the launching order and procedure of their canoes. Each knew their place at any given moment.

There were two Divisions each with three canoes. 'A' Division was headed by **H**asler with his No. 2 Sparks in *Catfish*; **L**aver and his No. 2 Mills in *Crayfish*; **S**heard and his No. 2 Moffatt in *Conger*. 'B' Division was led by **M**acKinnon and his No. 2 Conway in *Cuttlefish*; **W**allace and his No. 2 Ewart in *Coalfish*; **E**llery (the only No. 1 who was not an NCO) and his No. 2 Fisher in *Cachalot*.

Each canoe had been given their intended target areas within the Bordeaux Harbour basin: *Catfish* and *Cuttlefish* were to attack the shipping on the west bank of Bordeaux; *Crayfish* and

Coalfish were to head for shipping on the east bank; *Conger* and *Cachalot* targeting Bassens' north and south quays.

In order to establish for the reader the exact intent of the operation as well as some of the other information, as laid down by Blondie, the following additions are taken from his Summary of Verbal Orders.

Frequent question and answer revision had been given verbally to the raiding party with regard to the detailed information of enemy dispositions, targets and approach routes as extracted from intelligence summaries, charts, maps and air photographs.

The proposed intent was to sink the twelve largest ships, excluding tankers, lying in the Bassens-Bordeaux area. Following the drill for disembarkation but before hoisting, the captain was to give a last-minute estimate of the magnetic bearing and distance of the headland 2¼ miles NNE of Pointe de la Négade, which would then be set on their compass grids. The summary assumed a starting point about 9½ miles 259 degrees from Pointe de la Négade, where the German searchlight battery was situated.

It was stated that the force would enter the estuary and proceed towards Bordeaux in stages, necessitating lying up by day and travelling by night on the flood tide. On the first convenient night, the attack would be delivered with Limpets at high water slack, after which the force would withdraw down the estuary on the ebb as far as possible. At low water slack, the crews would land on the east bank then scuttle the canoes and equipment before escaping overland via Spain to the UK. Before entering the estuary, once a point 1 mile from the shore had been reached, the canoes were to follow the coast to a point one mile due north of Pte De Grave, and at this point, the CO would decide on which side of the estuary would be taken for the first lying-up place by each division. At some stage during that first night's passage, the Force Commander would give the final instructions to 'B' Division, which would have been three canoes, to proceed independently under its own CO (nominally MacKinnon) for the remainder of the operation.

Whilst both divisions were together, the formation within 'A' Division was the arrowhead followed by 'B' Division in another arrowhead. When the leading canoe stopped, 'B' Division would close and each canoe would go alongside the canoe ahead. The passage would only take place in darkness, and no attempt would be made to move in daylight or in foggy weather; the canoes should keep out of the buoyed channel without moving close to the coast. Whenever they were laid up, there had to be a concealed sentry on duty at all times for each group of canoes. They had been issued with sectional charts showing safe and danger areas throughout the route, and due to the many eyes that could be watching, everyone was ordered to keep under total cover without movement during daylight hours, stretching their limbs whenever possible after dark. The last lying-up place would be treated as the advanced base and would be as near to the target area as possible. It would be from this position that the fusing of the Limpets would be completed and from that time onwards, the cargo bags would be restowed, the breakwaters would be folded by their hinged brackets and compasses unshipped and stowed below to ensure the luminous markings could not be seen by lookouts while the Limpets were being placed.

Hasler also told them they might have to act on their own initiative. He added, 'If any canoe gets into difficulty and gives the SOS only canoes of its own division will assist. Any canoe that gets swamped and cannot be bailed out will be scuttled and the crew left to swim for it with their No. 5 bags, unless it appears safe to try to get the canoe and crew ashore.'

The objectives of each canoe were as follows:

a. Primary. Two Limpets on each of the four largest merchant ships (excluding tankers) in their target areas. The two Limpets are to be placed 5 feet below the waterline in the following positions:

'A' Division Canoes. On the upstream end of each ship, one Limpet just short of amidships and the other between there and the upstream end of the ship.

'B' Division Canoes. On the downstream end of each ship, one Limpet just short of amidships and the other between there and the downstream end of the ship.

In addition, *Catfish* and *Cuttlefish* would carry one cable cutter and one wire cutter each to be placed during the withdrawal on any vessel lying in the stream and if of sufficient size these two canoes would reserve a pair of Limpets each for said ship. (The wire and cable cutter devices were developed by Hasler with the development centre of Combined Operations and were small explosive charges for fixing to cables and mooring wires of the mined vessels so as the ensure the vessels would be drifting in the channel as the Limpets exploded, thus adding more difficulty to the salvage operation that would ensue.)

b. Secondary. (These were only to be attacked if it was impossible to get the full quota of primaries.) In order of choice: 1. Large Tanker in the target area (two Limpets from each canoe all between midships and the stern. 2. Any smaller vessel (except submarines) in the target area (one Limpet from each canoe). 'A' Division canoes on the upstream end and 'B' Division canoes on the downstream end. 3. Any vessel that was not in the target area which may be encountered during the withdrawal down to and including dumb lighters.

Of the security, the instructions were that all charts covering the areas north of Blaye should be destroyed or concealed, whilst lying up during daylight hours, as soon as that area had been passed. Air photographs should be destroyed or concealed at the advanced base with all remaining charts and papers scuttled along with the canoe with the exception of the escape gear. In order to aid every man, each had his own plastic box, 'the escape box', about 6 x 2 inches, which had a miscellany of the essentials a man could not be seen without! It was so well known that this would be a sign to the French peoples of who they were dealing with. The standard escape box was only a part of a complete escape set and was not intended to make a man independent, but to help him exist on the land for seven to fourteen days. The standard type had a compass which could be used without opening the box. The compass had to be jiggled to make it swing freely. The compass itself was only accurate to 15 degrees either way and being very small had to be kept a long way clear of all magnetic material. There were a number of tiny luminous compasses just smaller in size than that of a man's fingernail. The compasses became useless when wet, hence the need for extras; two more were secreted in the clothing. Within the box was a rubber water bottle (the neck of which was not watertight), Horlicks tablets, a tube of Nestlé's sweetened milk, chewing gum, emergency chocolate, adhesive tape (which could be used to reseal the box if necessary), matches, and Benzedrine and Halazone (water purification) tablets. They also had a silk handkerchief with the map of France printed on it, a 'book' of matches printed with the manufacturer's name and the well-known 'V' sign (for Victory), and a pair of felt-soled boots which were to be used instead of the gym shoes and thin-soled waders.

Of the withdrawal, the canoes were to proceed downstream on the ebb with caution, avoiding the ship channel and the middle ground banks, keeping well out from the shore. At low water slack, they were to select a suitable landing place, land their two bags of escape equipment, then destroy the reserve buoyancy in the canoe and scuttle it with all the remaining equipment. They were then to proceed independently in pairs according to the escape instructions. Upon reaching the British Consul in Spain, he was to be informed that the party consisted of Combined Operations personnel escaped from a raid but make no further mention of any other details.

As for the actions to be taken in case of emergencies, should the submarine be surprised on the surface with any of the canoes out on the casing, the fore hatch would be immediately closed. Crews on deck would inflate their life jackets, load the canoes, get in and fasten the covers. If the submarine should dive, they were to endeavour to float clear and proceed independently with the operation, or if ordered by the captain from the bridge, the crews should withdraw via the conning tower hatch having first destroyed the reserve buoyancy of the canoe. Once clear of the submarine, any canoe that lost the remainder of its formation should take the prescribed action to rejoin; if this should fail, the crew should continue on the operation independently.

To this end, we can take some information from the testimony of the thirteenth man, picked as reserve for the raid, Norman Colley. He informs us, 'The skipper of HMS *Tuna* told us that if E-Boats approached, the sub would dive, possibly leaving individuals to swim

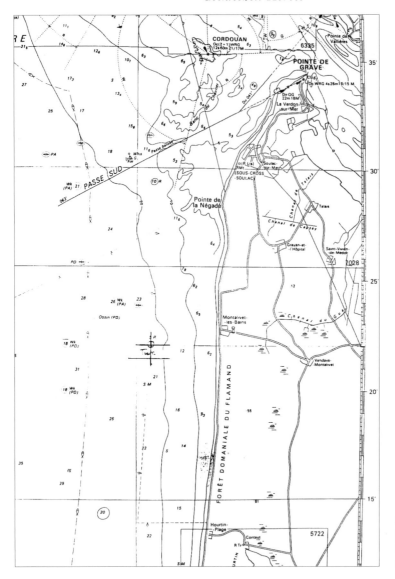

A chart with the
position of *Tuna*
at disembarkation
marked by a cross.

for it.' Thus the raiding party were supremely ready for the next phase, poised to 'Up' the 'offspring' to the casing of the Submarine that had 'contained them' since 30 November.

Hasler's diary entry, scrawled quickly in pencil at that time, simply reports, '*Tuna* [was] right inshore trying to obtain a fix. Succeeded about lunch time. Self slept most of the morning and afternoon. 1700 final talk to troops 1745, supper. All set for disembarking.' Blondie Hasler's last entry for that day was recorded the following year, it reads simply, '7th December – 2nd April 43. Away from UK on operation *Frankton*.'

Four hours before the timed opening of the fore hatch at 1515, they had built up the canoes and made ready for disembarkation and inflated and positioned the buoyancy bags in the bow and stern of the canoes. They had eaten and for the second time during the passage were sporting the black camouflage cream which prompted *Tuna*'s captain to call them 'black-faced villains'.

We learn from Lt Bull of the following few tense minutes, 'The Captain watched the trawler very carefully for some time and finally said to Hasler that if he wanted to go ahead they were unlikely to be seen as we would be in a trimmed down state on the surface. Finally, the Captain asked Hasler if he wanted to proceed and receiving a "yes" to his query gave me the order to surface which I did at once at position 45 degree 21 minutes 8N by 1 degree 14 minutes 1W.'

HMS *Tuna* surfaced with intent; the time was precisely 1917. Before the casing had met the crisp night air, Dickie Raikes was on the bridge duly setting aside his dark-red goggles[60] and focused the huge pattern 1900A binoculars on the enemy patrol trawler that he had been monitoring whilst submerged. He was quickly followed by the rest of the team of watch keepers.

Sub-Lt Rowe recalls the moment: 'First Lt and I went to the bridge along with two seaman lookouts. [The Captain said,] "Pilot, get up on the periscope standards and keep your eyes skinned." Pilot Rowe climbed the rung ladder aft of the rear standard and sat on top. 'This brought me about 15 feet higher than the other eyes with consequently a further horizon. From that position I could see the boom defence vessel showing faint signal lights but otherwise my binoculars found nothing to report. The port lookout reported in a quite voice, "Object bearing Red Nine-O sir, distant," meaning the patrol boat.' The observation was acknowledged by the captain, knowing it to be about 5,000 yards to seaward. A determined lookout continued. The order to stop both engines was given at 1919.

Hasler was in the wardroom, his blond mustache greased with the camouflage cream, as ready as his men, awaiting word from the captain; he noted the engines went silent. The quiet wait ended with 'Major Hasler to the Bridge', via the voice pipe. Within seconds, Hasler had climbed the conning tower ladder and was standing beside Raikes.

'Beastly clear', Raikes said, as he looked up at the star-studded cloudless night. He mentioned the patrol boat, adding nonchalantly, 'Looks all right for your launching … do you want to start?'

Blondie's eyes cast their gaze on the eastward horizon to the dark French coastline; feeling the crisp night air on his blackened cheek, he took a huge breath of the sweet, cold, yet invigorating air. The surfeit of oxygen now made him feel dizzy and euphoric. He turned to Raikes and made the decision that would propel these men into the history books … 'Yes.' Dickie Raikes' simple response into the voice pipe was 'Up canoes'.

With that, and at the same time, Lt Bull 'established that the Captain and Hasler were safely on the Bridge. I [then] went forward to supervise getting the canoes up onto the casing.' The fore hatch opened and the shadowy figures of the hoisting party emerged, deftly assembling the necessary apparatus.[61]

In post-war notes, Dickie Raikes makes mention of the discussion and appointment between himself and Hasler to do with meeting up again upon Hasler's return. It is believed that Hasler suggested that Dickie Raikes should book a table at the Savoy for 1 April. (The suggestion of this place and date should be noted for later on in the story.)

In the final farewell, Blondie Hasler turned to Dickie Raikes and said, 'Thanks for everything you have done on our behalf, its time to get along.' Dickie Raikes held out his hand, smiled and replied, 'The very best of luck to you all.' Hasler smiled thinly, took Raikes' hand in a firm grip and said thank you. Their last word to each other was 'Goodbye'.

As MacKinnon supervised at the foot of the fore hatch, the canoes began to be manoeuvred by the marines and assisted by the sailors, all in the correct order. First out was canoe 'W' then followed by 'S', 'E', 'L', 'H' and 'M', all of which were dutifully positioned on the casing.

The Cockle Mk 2 is an extremely robust animal when folded flat, but when erected, the canvas hull, between the floor and the gunwale of the canoe became vulnerable. The canoe had great longitudinal strength; the hull material was an early rubberised canvas, and although extremely strong[62], a small amount of care needed to be exercised when negotiating the route from the torpedo room to the casing via the torpedo hatch with these in the built-up state. This operation entailed upping the canoe semi-loaded through the hatch at an angle of about 45 degrees.

This 'upping' of the canoes did not fully go to plan, as reported by Lt Bull: 'Unfortunately one of them got badly damaged and I called Hasler down from the bridge to have a look; he immediately said the canoe and its crew were to return to the UK with us. On hearing this, one of the canoe's crew burst into tears [Fisher], without realising that this order was subsequently going to save his life.' Indeed, Raikes himself recorded, 'The two Marines were devastated.' Ellery's expression at that time could be described as being sullenly repressed. Oddly, Colley, the reserve man, noticed that whilst Fisher did break down and cry, Ellery seemed passively resigned to events, 'unmoved'.

Canoe 'E' was Ellery's and Fisher's. Theirs was the third canoe to be brought up to the casing and had its set position on the casing ready for hoisting, which, in their case, did not take place. All the other three canoes bypassed *Cachalot*, one at a time, and were made ready for hoisting out. *Cachalot* was returned to the torpedo room and stored until they returned to port. Marine Norman Colley was out on the casing helping to load the canoes with the kit, including Limpets. The kit that needed to be loaded included two cans of drinking water, Nos 1, 2 and 3 bags and the two silenced Sten guns, which were to accompany Hasler and MacKinnon (one per division). Norman's own testimony of this time sheds a little more light, 'I was in charge of the launch party bringing the canoes up one by one via the torpedo loading hatch, loading them with stores, slinging under the gun crane extension and launching to the leeward side.' By the time hoisting out commenced, each of the canoe crew had a seagull mew whistle around their neck and were wearing their inflated, personalised, tan-coloured 'Reliant' life jackets.

The first canoe was put in the slings and Hasler and Sparks took their seats in *Catfish*. The first of five canoes was lifted away from the casing and hoisted out into the calm seas of the Bay of Biscay and the lee of the submarine. Dickie Raikes reflected, 'When the first boat was in the slings searchlights suddenly started sweeping the sea from Pointe de la Negade and all down the coast, but there was no light opposite us. There was an uncomfortable feeling that this reception may have been due to the RDF Station plotting us and this feeling was strengthened by the fact that the trawler was evidently closing.'

The process of hoisting out the canoes is described by Pilot Rowe: 'The submarine was not blown up to full buoyancy. The fore hatch opened and up came the first canoe and two men, fleet of foot but silent. They brought their small craft aft beneath the muzzle of our four-inch gun [with its appendage] which, like the jib of a crane, protruded beyond the bridge structure. To the muzzle of the gun the 1st Lt and the Cox hurriedly affixed a sling which the former had made of such length that the barrel of the gun depressed the cradle rested on the casing and the marines could lay their canoe in it and then get in. Slowly the gun was elevated as *Tuna* was flooded a little deeper; the gun was traversed to starboard carrying the manned canoe and when it was at right angles to the sub the gun was again depressed enabling the marines to paddle away and lay off waiting. Using low pressure air blowers to keep the noise down, the Captain brought *Tuna* partially up again and the routine was repeated four times further.' *Catfish* gently firmed up and floated away from the straps. Next was MacKinnon and Conway's turn to disembark in *Cuttlefish* followed by the remaining three canoes.

It was around this time that Hasler had found out about the unofficial items bequeathed by the kind-hearted submariners: a quantity of chocolates and small bottles of rum. As Dickie Raikes remembered, his sailors had given the men of Hasler's party 'huge quantities of chocolate and this annoyed Blondie intensely because they were very definitely limited to the weight they could carry and he did not discover it until they were in the canoes and were away ... he was furious, absolutely furious.' It is reported that whilst Hasler blamed his own men for accepting the gifts, he said nothing, correctly believing it was not the time or place.

As *Coalfish* was being lowered from *Tuna*'s casing, it has been mentioned that Sgt Wallace remarked as he pointed to the number N94 on the conning tower and in thick Irish tongue, 'See that boys, nine and four make thirteen ... we'll need all the luck that's going on this spree.'

Colley, Ellery and Fisher had said their goodbyes to their comrades in arms as each canoe was dispatched. Eric Fisher's last words to David Moffatt were 'Hurry up back and I'll have a pint waiting for you at the Granada'.

'A' Division was formed up headed by *Catfish* and astern was 'B' Division led by *Cuttlefish*, both in the prescribed arrowhead. For the remaining three marines, they would have to endure another week without seeing daylight or getting out in the night air.

In the words of Lt Bull, 'The disembarkation proceeded smoothly without further incident and, wearing their green waterproof clothes, the marines set off after [the] customary farewells.' Pilot Rowe also reported, 'When all afloat, the commandos in camouflage canoes, uniforms and faces mustered together and splitting into two parties set off.'

Within HMS *Tuna*'s Log the following is reported on the events until *Tuna*'s departure: '1930[63] … Commenced Operation; 2003 … Operation Complete; Proceeded M/M course 200 degrees; 2010 … both M/Engines; 2016 … course 205.'

The last notation of events is from Pilot Rowe: 'Clear the bridge ordered the skipper and the lookouts disappeared below. I came down from the numbing periscope standard watch and we turned south to retrace our passage. I landed on the bridge deck with the searchlights probing the surface from the river's mouth.'

According to *Tuna*'s log, the operation of disembarkation had taken just thirty-three minutes, and as Raikes remarked for his report, 'I consider now this time was remarkably fast, and reflects great credit on Lt Bull and his upper deck hands. He added after the war, 'During the whole operation searchlight activity was intense but we were never actually caught in a beam. The keenness shown by the marines was an inspiration and it is hoped very much to have a reunion with them.'

On an extremely cold and bitter evening, the Royal Marines were ready, poised for the command to paddle. They left behind the smell of diesel oil that had invaded their every waking hour. Hasler had placed most emphasis on the importance of the mission, saying that nothing should prevent at least some of them getting through to their targets. With that in their mind, they fixed focus and paddled in earnest for the first time in seven days. The five canoes were paddled away in the moonless sky on a heading of 035 degrees, towards the mouth of the Gironde. They ached mightily from lack of exercise … but the muscle memory would return as they got into the rhythm. The submarine steered away, first on her electric main motors and then when further away on her diesel engines.

Telegraphist Quick recalls, 'Johnnie Bull's crew dismantled the crane and [we] sped away to the south and west. Later that night upon surfacing we sent a signal to HQ saying that the launch had been successful, which ended my small part in this terrific operation.' This simple signal that Ray Quick sent was 'operation *Frankton* completed. 2100/7, showing exactly what time and date this was sent.

British Sabotage Squad Finished Off in Combat

A very low profile was maintained for the next forty-eight hours in order to ensure there was no link with the raiding party. HMS *Tuna*'s Log shows that the next few days (until 11 December) were spent on routine patrol in a new area, avoiding the fishing vessels by taking up various courses during the surface periods at night. The diving, surfacing and zig-zagging all continued at the requisite times.

On Tuesday 8 December 1942, the Commander-in-Chief Submarines, Admiral Sir Max Horton, was taking late afternoon tea at his desk at the Admiralty. He was brought news that a message had been received from HMS *Tuna* telling of the completion of the operation. It was immediately passed it on to COHQ at Richmond Terrace for the attention of Vice-Admiral Lord Mountbatten.

The log shows where they were on 9 December 1942 at 1833: in the deeper waters off the Gironde area, having just surfaced at position 45 degrees 35.5 N by 3 degrees 46 W. Ray Quick furnishes us with more information on the days leading up to their next port of call following on from the disembarkation of the raiding party. 'We then were recalled to the UK, cheering us up no end, until a couple of days later a further message came [in] to go back and continue patrolling. When on surfacing one evening, a signal addressed to us turned out to be the recall and telling us to rendezvous with an escort somewhere off the Lizard Head and from there to proceed to Devonport. The crew was delighted with the news, especially Willie [Stabb] and I because it was only an hour's bus ride to our homes [Paignton]. All went according to plan although Johnnie Bull would not believe that my bearing of South Bishop Light was correct. This [error] was due to a slipped cursor in the D/F on the previous patrol that neither I or anyone else could have suspected at the time; (they did make a new one near the end of our stay in the dockyard).'

This interlude was also reported on by Lt Bull: '[The] passage home was be-devilled by poor visibility and lack of sights. Approaching the English Coast without a single sight I climbed to the top of the periscope standards and sat there with a sextant for about five hours and finally got a sun/moon fix on a poor horizon. I rushed below and worked this out and as soon as I had finished, shouted to Dick Raikes to alter course to the westward or we would pile up on the rocks. This he did and after a short while we heard the sound of the Lizard foghorn and shortly after saw the lighthouse itself so we were able to get a fix to see us safely into Falmouth from where we went to Devonport to have the first ever submarine Radar fitted.' This fact is borne out by the captain: 'We were badly popped by a heavy and very cold sea' rounding Ushant, this 'pretty filthy weather almost forcing [them] ashore' at the Lizard Peninsula in Cornwall.

Our last recollection of the trip to the Bay of Biscay is reserved for our friend Ray Quick, who tells us, 'The escort duly left us as we passed the breakwater and we made our way past Drake's Island and up the Hamoaze[64] and alongside the wall in Devonport dockyard. I then went to the bridge and looked at the scene. It was more battered by air attacks than it had been when I left it four years earlier.' Flying above was their Jolly Roger with its skull and cross bones and the distinguishing mark of each kill.

When the marines were aboard, Dickie Raikes had rested on the narrow settee in the wardroom, simply closing his eyes, all the while being constantly alert. He had given over his cabin to Hasler. This was no hardship, as even the crew knew from experience that regardless of where the captain was resting he had the uncanny ability to suddenly materialise should anything require his intervention or attention. This kind of constant alertness has a price, which is related at a later stage.

At the same sort of time as *Tuna* was progressing towards the Lizard Peninsula in Cornwall, the senior Staff Officer of the Royal Marine Planners at COHQ in London, Lt-Col. Cyril Horton, sampled the crisp evening air as he took his regular walk into the streets of Whitehall to buy an evening paper. As he stood on the pavement near the news vendor, he scanned his copy in the usual fashion before folding it and proceeding on his way. The chill of the night air was replaced with the sensation of anxiety as his eyes caught the Stop Press margin on the back page reporting on an official radio announcement of 10 December from the German High Command.

> On December 8th a small British sabotage squad was engaged at the mouth of the Gironde River and finished off in combat.

In France, the news had also reached the newspapers by 11 December and was reported on the front page of *La Petite Gironde*. As expected for a local area paper, it was slightly more comprehensive in its headline and coverage, but it carried the same unwelcome news,

> 8 December. A small British force, planning to carry out acts of sabotage, was spotted in the Gironde estuary and, following a brief fight, was wiped out.

13 December 1942, Plymouth

The last log for HMS *Tuna* during the patrol period of 30 November 1942 to 13 December 1942 reads, '13 Dec. Secured to D Buoy, Plymouth Sound'. As was usual for the crew of HMS *Tuna*, shore leave was available for a certain section and it is likely this number was greater than usual as a minor fitting out was required for the new radar equipment, which took about three weeks. Of the Red, Blue and White watches two of the three enjoyed the time ashore. Dickie Raikes met up with his wife and took his well-earned break at the Moorland Links Hotel at Yelverton, near Plymouth. Meanwhile, Willie Stabb and Ray Quick hot-footed it home to Paignton, just 25 miles away.

Most reports, including some from officers such as Raikes, Bull and Rowe, only mention twelve Royal Marines embarking on HMS *Tuna*. A probable cause of this is that, as all submariners seemed to be superstitious, this thirteenth man was referred to as the 'twelfth man' and was the reserve on the operation. The reserve, Marine Norman Colley, very ready to take his place on the raid, played his part and was entrusted by Hasler to ensure documents and letters were passed on.

Of our three returning Royal Marines, Ellery, Fisher and Colley, the only contemporary report available is from Norman Colley. With the disembarkation at Plymouth, Norman, remembered, 'It was absolutely marvellous getting ashore, as the only time we had been on deck and outside was when we were launching the canoes.' Norman 'leisurely walked into the Stonehouse barracks, enjoying [his] newfound freedom and clean air, without a cap, unshaven, in dirty, smelly, grease-covered rig and an oily sweater, carrying six letters[65] written by the lads to their next of kin.' Challenged at the gate by the guards, he identified himself with name, rank and number and told them of his business; they wondered 'if I was real'. Whilst he was waiting, the guards looked quizzically at this strange individual whom they kept some distance from due to the odour. He was then escorted to the Adjutant's office and duly reported and presented a sealed letter from Blondie Hasler. Within was a request from Hasler to provide sustenance, new uniforms, kit and accommodation for his men. Norman had already given back Ellery and Fisher's letters; Norman had not thought to write one himself and admitted that had he been called upon he would have had to scribble something in great haste. One letter from Robert Ewart is known to have been written on the submarine and was especially entrusted to 'the care of Norman'.

Meanwhile, Ellery and Fisher remained with *Cachalot* and the stowage bags before being sent for and along with their kit they were transported to the barracks. The Adjutant duly arranged for the three men to have the first long hot shower in two weeks; their last was on the depot ship HMS *Forth*. They were then clothed, fed and given good beds for the night in the barracks. Having slept on the floor of the torpedo room in their sleeping bags, the barrack room beds felt so soft that they could not get to sleep on them, so they put the mattresses on the floor; being segregated from all other human contact, there was no one around tell them they could not.

14 December, Portsmouth

A lorry, driven by 'Flash' Phelps, had been dispatched from Portsmouth and followed the single-carriageway coastal route via the New Forest, through the centre of every town including Dorchester and Exeter down to Plymouth. The three marines, canoe *Cachalot*, and the bags were duly picked up and the journey was retraced, delivering all to the familiar surroundings of Southsea by the evening. *Cachalot* was temporarily put in the boathouse (one of the two Nissen huts at Lumps Fort) and was eventually returned to the manufacturers[66] for repair, where it remained until the 1980s. Within the RMBPD War Diaries, an entry for this date reads, 'Three ranks rejoined the unit from *Frankton*.'

In general terms, the segregation continued and they were not allowed to mix with the other lads from No. 2 section, so they played snooker and billiards for two or three weeks before joining up with the rest of the men and continuing training. Normality came to pass after a short while as they returned to 'digs' at White Heather. They were forbidden to talk about *Frankton*, and other members of RMBPD were forbidden to ask about it.

15 December

The RMBPD War Diary carries this entry: 'Capt. Stewart with one rank who had returned from *Frankton* proceeded to COHQ to see Lt-Cdr L'Estrange.'

As the No. 1 in *Cachalot*, it is assumed that Marine Ellery was the individual taken, and this does seem the most likely. It is also presumed that this was to ascertain precise details of events for COHQ taken from the most senior of those who returned.

After a few months following the raid, Fisher moved in with No. 2 section, as he knew some of the other men there; no doubt, this was also due to the fact that Ellery had since disappeared and that Fisher and Norman Colley had been asked to leave by Mrs Powell. When Sparks returned, he, along with Fisher and Colley, were eventually absorbed into No. 2 section.

CHAPTER 5
'It Was A Beastly Clear Night'[1]

In order to provide this part of the account, much of the information is taken from the two survivor accounts. Only a small amount of detailed oral history was available from Bill Sparks before he passed away. Apart from the official reports, any information that clearly suffers due to a lapse in memory is adjusted. The most accurate reporting is only available by actually quoting from the early accounts of the two individuals who returned, namely Sparks and Hasler, but more importantly the latter, who, it has to be remembered, compiled the entire official report on his return by 8 April 1943. Given that this was only a few days after he actually arrived in the UK, it is a remarkable feat of memory retention, containing the most incredible amount of detail, some of which has never been revealed before. By reading material quoted from these individuals, the reader becomes aware of the origin and validity of the words written and can be assured of the accuracy. This chapter of the story deals solely with the advancement to target without distraction.

Indeed, it was exceedingly beastly, clear and bitterly cold. The black-faced villains wearing their personalised, tan-coloured life jackets slowly faded into the inky blackness of the night with the rhythmic message of their paddling slicing into the black sea water. As the electric main motors purred away, it caused some of the men to glance astern and see their home for the last eight days, the black hulk of HMS *Tuna*, being consumed by the darkness. Hasler did not look back; his focus was the future. The time recorded was 2003[2].

Night One (7/8 December)

Flagship of the oddest of all small flotillas was Hasler's craft and, as he was CO and mastermind of the operation, the raiding party followed *Catfish*, proceeding in one arrowhead formation steering 035 degrees magnetic.[3] Astern was the depleted 'B' Division, led by Lt MacKinnon in *Cuttlefish*, without his original No. 2 man, Colley.

Marine Norman Colley was one of the twelve original men picked to go on the *Frankton* Raid. Something that has never been revealed until now is that during the work-up sports training session, a metatarsal injury sent Norman to hospital and his place in the team was taken by 'Jim' Conway, who also completed Exercise *Blanket*; Norman was on this exercise but in the truck following them around and helping out. A hospital visit by Lt MacKinnon had secured Norman his place as reserve man for the operation itself 'so long as I would forgo sick leave' remembered Norman. A series of events thus spared Norman's life.

Even though the hospitality of the submarine mess was an outstandingly wonderful experience, life below the waves was different, too different for some. Now every one of the raiding party was out of familiar territory, some felt the loneliness descending after being 'abandoned' right on the enemy's doorstep. They knew they would not be meeting up with the submariners again. The surprise and shock[4] felt by some after they had been told of the lack of any pick-up following the raid was resurfacing. Within the submarine, these supremely fit men had spent a whole week in cramped surroundings which were completely different to their 'hotel ship'. They also had been told to exert themselves as little as possible in order to conserve the very precious air within when submerged.

This mood of anxiety and fear of the unknown initially felt now gave way to what can only be described as 'a wild surge of exhilaration'. All of the party were now experiencing positive light-headed euphoria. They had begun to paddle and that had increased their heart rate, which required more oxygen to their muscles. After the humid atmosphere in the submarine, the cold night air was the elixir of the moment; the sudden increase in the supply of pure air has the effect of making one drunk. However, the arms, shoulders and torso muscles ached badly. For Sergeant Mike Wallace this caused him to vomit a number of times even during the first hour.

Thus, in the cloudless sky, and in Hasler's own words, 'Weather oily calm with a low ground swell from the south-west', the ten headed off towards the mouth of the Gironde and the Pointe de Grave; the northernmost tip of the Médoc Peninsula, which marks the northern end of the sandy Landes coastline. A slight haze enveloped the landmass. The offshore Cordouan lighthouse and island lies seven kilometres off the point with a second lighthouse on the shore at the Pointe de Grave.

The Biscay sea lifted the heavily laden canoes slightly as they rode low through the turgid waters, allowing the wavelets to break over the cockpits. The No. 2 in each canoe was taking spray from the paddles of their respective leaders, the salt water stinging their eyes. Each of the men paddled without a word; each becoming damp with sweat. The flotilla remained close enough to adhere to any hand signals, which were now the primary method of communication. An hour into the paddle, Hasler put the palm of his hand on the top of his head; the signal for rafting up each holding on to the cockpit coamings. This was to become the first of their hourly rest periods with only biscuits or sweets to sustain a high-calorie-burning workout. After the first raft up and rest, they resumed their paddle with things becoming easier on the muscles by the stroke.

In tandem, each dipped their paddles; for more than 3½ hours, they had crafted their way through the darkness with Hasler having to adjust his direction with the aid of the North Star. All were sweating under the green rubber jackets, despite the cold. The only thing that could be heard was the splash of the paddles and the hiss of the water along the canoes' sides. Sparks had the job of bailing out on the hour due to an annoying leak, and occasionally someone 'taking it easy' for a few strokes broke the rhythm of the paddles' drip and swing, but no one spoke. Apart from that all was well. At around 2345 there was a ground swell, which was building up into some steepish rollers over the shallows; by 2350, Hasler's determination of the situation was realised as they passed over the sandbank. Hasler later made mention in his report that, had they been a little further ashore, the rollers would have proved dangerous for the canoe.

It is worthwhile relating exactly what Hasler wrote of this period.

> The full force of the flood tide now began to be felt and [the] course was altered further eastwards to follow the line of the coast, now clearly visible about 1½ miles away. Shortly afterward the sound of broken water ahead indicated a tide race. This came as an unpleasant surprise, not having been apparent from the chart or the Sailing Directions. Owing to the strength of the stream there was no chance of avoiding this race which proved quite severe for such a small craft, comparable with those at Start Point [in Devon].

It was at this point he stopped and raised his arm, the four Cockles behind glided up to *Catfish*. Sparks described the moment he first heard the 'steady sound distant but distinct like the miniature roaring in a sea shell held against the ear' and then 'over the Major's broad back came the sight of a white froth ahead'. Knowing full well that the nearest his men had come to experiencing this would have been during rough water drill, Hasler got the canoes rafted up and in a calm manner told them what to expect, reassuring them and urged, 'Don't be afraid of it. Use your drill for rough weather and we'll ride through. Muster on the other side.'

The sound became a roar. Now with the flood tide at four knots, and in line each plundered into the fray having secured fast the cockpit covers. Sparks followed suit as Hasler 'arched his back, bent forward, his double paddle poised tensely'. Through the turmoil, the canoes trembled beneath them, they could feel the fierce waters trying to grasp their legs through the thin, flat plywood bottom of the canoe. The bow and stern of each canoe suffered the same rigours, lifting and plummeting off the 4-foot-high white-water waves as they body balanced, allowing their paddles to flail at will, driving ever forward to the safety of the calm waters beyond. The best way of describing the scene would be that it was reminiscent of a mixture of riding a mechanical bucking bronco and the action the shoulders and arms make when successfully riding a camel at a gallop!

In his report, Hasler confided, 'The Cockle Mk 2 proved quite able to weather it provided it was kept head into the waves and cockpit cover securely fastened.' Sparks said of it that it was a 'timeless ten minutes 'till soaked and shaken we were through'. But the event proved disastrous for one of the five craft, as Hasler and Sparks, being the first to have been churned out of the cauldron, found out as they turned about to watch the others emerge.

Out of the unpleasant baptism, they watched as first *Crayfish* then *Conger* and *Cuttlefish* came through the hazard with each one of the crew cold to the bone, completely soaked and a little disorientated. The darkness did not reveal *Coalfish*, Wallace or Ewart. The Force turned back to look for *Coalfish*, but without success, Sparks sounded his seagull mew but received no answer to his calls. Unable to paddle against the fast-running tidal race, they began to be swept away, stern first. The orders were that 'one man's peril must not jeopardize the operation' and no exception was to be made.

The judgement call seems harsh but time was of the essence and Hasler wrote later he thought it possible that 'they had not capsized, but had turned further inshore on finding themselves separated'. Sparks confirmed that 'the old man waited for ten minutes' and did more than he should have, but all for nothing. Hasler simply wrote, 'Nothing further was heard of this boat.'[5]

The orders had been that, should they become separated, any canoe should press home the attack independently or, given untimely events, hide up for four days before making good the escape plan.

They could wait no longer, resigning themselves to the fact that the night had swallowed *Coalfish* and its crew. Now moving very fast in the 6-knot tide, the four craft paddled on. It was now past midnight, and they knew that the fast tide would soon be slackening. The expected patrol boat was anchored some five miles upstream. It was essential to pass it on a running tide and while dawn was still some hours away. The tide race had half filled the canoes and, after a short pause for bailing, *Catfish* led the way up river, hugging the west bank. The paddles were worked in order to return warmth to the weary limbs. Frost coated the canvas-covered cockpit, and breath condensed. The stars blinking in the cold night sky. They wondered where the patrol boat would be anchored, if it would be lit up and if they would be able to craftily slip past or have to alter course. The rhythmic cadence of the well-executed strokes brought a regular splash of spray from the No. 1's paddles, speaking as it hit the taut canvas around the waist. The visible landmark in the form of an outline came into view it – the Pointe de Grave lighthouse; they knew it was the entrance to the estuary.

The familiar roar returned, heralding another dangerous obstacle. Hasler alerted all with a hushed but gruff 'Look out!' Apprehension and caution followed, but almost without warning, *Catfish* and the other canoes were suddenly plunged into more rapids. The torturous torrent of white water was worse than previously. Nearly 5 feet in height, the white water descended on the tiny craft, which buckled and pitched again and again in the boiling waters, crashing down from all angles yet again. As the crews boxed with the wildly swinging watercourse, the Cockle bucked and twisted; all the while, they tried to maintain balance. In another moment, the thin three-ply flat bottom of the canoe twisting as it went. Some felt sure they would not make it, but as suddenly as the trauma had arrived the calm waters prevailed.

These sabotage canoe crews were indeed grateful for their long, dreary training days. *Catfish* rushed through with *Crayfish* following seconds later, then *Cuttlefish* joined the raft, each holding onto the other. Breathlessly, they awaited the last canoe. Moments passed, and a cry and splash echoed out. *Conger* had capsized. The race spat out the capsized canoe with the crew members clinging onto *Conger* as they gasped for breath while they coughed up the icy sea water.

The joy of seeing the two men was immense but short-lived as the realisation of the predicament sank in to all. Hasler already knew what the most obvious course of action was likely to be. Both Sheard and Moffatt were suffering even at this early stage. The warmth of their bodies was being quickly sapped by the sudden introduction to the icy waters; the automatic responses had rapidly come into play, and their bodies trembled in shock as their lips turned a dark shade of blue.

Swiftly, Hasler told Sparks to try and turn *Conger* over. An attempt was made, but due to the fact it was full of water, it was an impossible task. Hasler had determined and made all aware that 'any canoe that gets swamped and cannot be bailed out will be scuttled and the crew left to swim for it with their No. 5 bags, unless it appears safe to try to get the canoe and crew ashore.' This was a fully laden, flat-bottomed canoe; even with the buoyancy bags in bow and stern it was not about to co-operate. The futility of the action was enhanced in the knowledge that any bailing out would have been scuppered by the waves washing into the cockpit. The only other way of bailing out the canoe would have been to beach it on a shoreline and risk being seen by the German defence force.

The waterborne men held on dearly to the canoes. The softly spoken order was given to scuttle the capsized *Conger*. Both Lt MacKinnon and Sparks took their clasp knifes and began to slash the canvas sides of the canoe and pierce the buoyancy chambers by the same strokes. After a great effort and much lunging with the knife, *Conger* began to sink at 0200 on 8 December 1942.

The rescuing canoes were the only lifeline for the two who were hanging on for dear life; efforts were now channelled to getting Sheard and Moffatt to the beach. However, time was of the essence. Hasler was the one who had prepared the summary of verbal orders, and although internally tormented by the decision he was to make, he knew the mission must not be put in jeopardy; logically, there was only one course of action. The very strong tidal flow was carrying the party into the narrows between the mainland and Cordouan Island.

Hasler determined that to leave them far from shore in the open water would give them no chance at all. The painfully slow struggle of progress to the west shore began. With Sheard holding on to the stern of *Catfish* and Moffatt grasping on to the stern of *Cuttlefish* both canoes were barely making one knot due to the drag of the towed bodies. At that precise moment, about 0200, the full strength of the 250,000 worth of candlepower from the lighthouse had just been switched on; as usual, Hasler nonchalantly described the moment, saying it 'lit up the scene quite brilliantly for a time', until about 0400. Hasler's understatement of the situation in his report revealed only that 'an effort was made to tow the crew somewhat further inshore'.

A third and 'less violent' three-foot breaking tidal race was now navigated with complete acceptance of this terrifying ordeal in the darkness by Sheard and Moffatt. Both the hangers-on made it through still grasping the canoes.

As the three canoes reached the middle of the passage, it became more apparent that they were more exposed than ever before, the tide now played them a winning hand as it carried them all round the Pointe de Grave and into the Gironde proper. Although it was only an hour since they had been picked up, to Sheard and Moffatt it must have felt longer, and both were now trembling uncontrollably and clearly very weak.

With the knowledge of the imminent turning tide threatening to push them all out into the bay, Hasler now ordered the canoes to raft up. They had been paddling for some 6½ hours and were very tired. It was now 0300. Knowing that the odds were not in their favour and that he was having to abandon them for the sake of the mission, Hasler tried to sound almost upbeat to try to stop them losing heart. He turned to the helpless, grey-faced bodies that had been in the water for a full hour and softly said to Sheard, 'I'm sorry, but this is as close to the beach as we dare go; you must swim for it. It's no distance. I wish I could take you further, but if we are all caught the operation will be at an end, and none of us want that. Get yourselves ashore and make your way overland as best you can.' Sheard's last croaking words to Hasler were 'It's alright, sir, we understand; thanks for bringing us so far.'

They would be lucky to make it to shore, and Hasler knew it. With that, the two reached up with their waterlogged blue woollen mittens, shook hands with each crew member and wished their canoeing comrades 'Good Luck'. Corporal Laver's hand grasped Sheard's firmly as he stuffed 'a small flask' of Pusser's Rum[6], which the crew of the submarine had bequeathed them, into the inside of Sheard's still fully inflated life jacket. 'Drink that to us when you get ashore; we'll see you in Pompey.'

Blondie regretting his earlier anger when he found out about the contraband. He knew the alcohol might well save their lives in these cold waters. Hasler remained silent until the two men let go of the craft that had supported them. As they did, he looked down at them and said, 'God bless you both' – without looking back, the three crews melted away into the darkness away from George and David. The shoreline was but a hundred metres away.

The heartfelt pain must have been immense for each of the party that paddled away from George Jellicoe Sheard and David Gabriel Moffatt. Sparks thought that Hasler's heart must have been particularly heavy. He believed he had heard Hasler sobbing as he turned the team north and paddled furiously hard up river. Hasler's subsequent opinion was that under any other sea conditions, it was unlikely that *any* of the canoes would have got through the race.

The failing tide was hard going and the darkness was less opaque by this time, and that meant dawn was approaching with the patrol boat ahead. Within thirty minutes, a grey shape the size of a sloop could be seen just fifty yards ahead at the expected spot, with a blue light burning at the bow. The three canoes surged on across the current to make for the open channel, avoiding the Le Verdon jetty with its blue light burning; this had been visible about four miles away. Intelligence had warned to expect a patrol boat at the mouth of the estuary.

Hasler reported the state of play as he saw it:

> This incident wasted so much time that it was impossible to attempt to reach the east bank of the Gironde that night. Also, the remaining three boats were by now closer inshore than had been intended, and the strength of the tide compelled [us] to pass between the Mole at Le Verdon and a line of three or four anchored vessels[7] lying about ¾ mile north east of it. These vessels appeared to be of the French 'Chasseur' type of the Gironde 'Hafenschutzflotille'. In order to get through this defile unobserved, it was necessary to change to single paddles and proceed with caution, and the three boats separated to a distance of several hundred yards to lessen the chance of being seen.

The estuary was three miles wide, and there was little time before the incoming tide race and the darkness disappeared. The gap between the jetty and the patrol boats was just seventy yards. Pressed for time, Hasler, in a whispered conference, elected not to waste more time taking the longer but safer route but decided on the shortest route between the ships and the jetty. This was risky, there were bound to be sentries on duty. They broke the paddles in half at the brass ferrules and in the lowest possible position and in absolute silence dipped the oval blades deep and steady into the water. The order was *Catfish* first, then *Crayfish* and, if no alarm, then *Cuttlefish*. All stealth and speed was exercised; only the dripping noise from the paddles could be discerned. *Catfish* raced past the first ship and, as they came abreast of the second Chasseur, a lamp blinked from deck only thirty yards from them; a signalman calling to the jetty. Hearts beating faster, not daring to look, throats dry with fear of being seen, the sweat took the bitter taste of the camouflage cream into the mouth. As the hairs on the back of their necks stood to attention, they waited for a shot that never came. They wondered how it was possible that they had not been spotted. They passed the jetty, and *Catfish* made it to

Le Môle d'Escale du Verdon in 1942. (J&C McCutcheon Collection)

Le Môle d'Escale du Verdon post war.

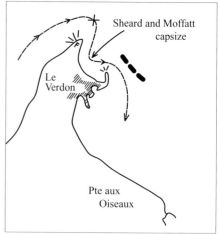

Sheard and Moffatt
capsize

Le
Verdon

Pte aux
Oiseaux

Aerial view showing the course that would
have had to be negotiated around the jetty
and a map showing the point at which
Sheard and Moffatt capsized.

the third ship; if the sentry had looked, he would have seen the black outline of the canoe
from his position onshore. With the last ship clear behind them, *Catfish* carried on fifty yards
more, stopped, turned, and the canoe was held against the tide.

Soon the outline of *Crayfish* loomed near, and Laver gave the 'thumbs up'. A few more
minutes passed; just visible were the patrol boats but no sign of *Cuttlefish* anywhere between
the jetty and the Chasseurs. As they waited, they each took turns working their freezing
fingers to life through the saturated blue woollen mittens as the other kept them stationary
in the current, their breath condensing in the ice-cold morning air. The light broke out again
and with it a shout and an answered challenge from the jetty followed by a fleeting moment
of silence and more shouting that carried on the still air.

With no more signals from the ship, no more noises, they all listened for an indication of
an approaching canoe. None came. The gull mew cry was given with no response. Again they
heralded with no reply. It was now before 0600 and they had little time to waste. All seemed
to be suffering from both mental and physical exhaustion, but they, as the elite, would push
on and ignore the pain.

Hasler was later to write in his report, still not knowing the fate of *Cuttlefish*,

> On getting clear of this danger, it was found that the third boat … had lost the formation.
> Nothing further was seen of this boat, but there is no reason to suppose that it met with any
> mishap at this stage, since it was in perfectly good shape and no alarm could have been raised by
> the enemy without it being audible to the other two boats on such a still night. The remaining
> two boats proceeded on a course of 196 magnetic and picked up the west bank of the estuary near
> Chenal de Talais, turning south eastwards in order to continue up as far as possible. At about
> 0630 on [8 December] the first attempt was made to land, but it was found that there was a line
> of half submerged stakes on a shingle bank running along the shore about one cable from the
> beach, and the ground swell breaking over these obstructions made it impossible to negotiate
> them in safety.

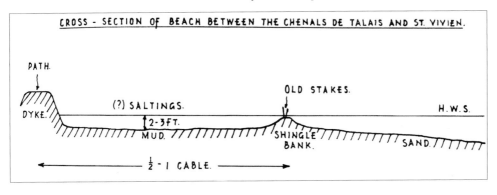

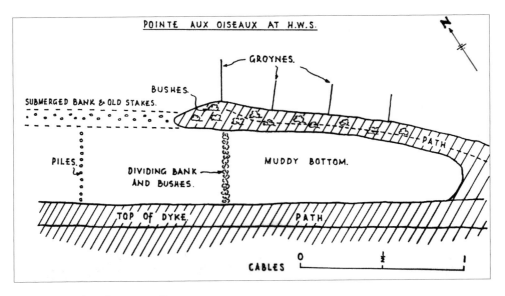

Plan of the hide at Pointe aux Oiseaux.

It is believed that these stakes formed the outer wall of saltings and were not placed for defensive purposes. The canoes continued along the coast for some time without finding any possible landing place, and it was only as daylight was breaking that they were able to get ashore on a small sandy promontory near the place known only to Hasler as Pointe aux Oiseaux.

'Tea time at the Reid's'[8]

Due to the effluxion of time, further detailed information of this stage in the proceedings has come to light and is related as separate from Hasler's report of these immediate events.

The river on the west bank of the Gironde was shallow and muddy with either picket fences or dykes which bordered the shoreline and prevented access. On a number of occasions that they did find access, the team had to withdraw because of the lack of cover. It was just before daybreak that Hasler found a narrow channel that led inland. Sparks related that 'the Major quickly jumped out of the canoe to reconnoiter the land beyond'. The rest of the party remained in the canoes, and reappearing from the twilight, Hasler signalled the all clear and the canoes were dragged through the mud and beached in the reeds above the high-water mark and then 'concealed as well as possible with the camouflage nets' behind a hedge of Tamarisk. They were in agony, having covered some 23 nautical miles[9] during the eleven hours of nearly constant paddling and fear. The wiry frame of Sparks had 'never felt so mentally and physically exhausted', and he was not alone. Each of the marines was bone-chillingly cold, cramped and soaked with perspiration.

0745–2330, 8 December

The traditional cup of tea was the first thing they wanted but a hive of activity started to descend on them at about 0830 as they observed a miscellany of water craft emerge to their right. The chattering of women laden with kitchenware and children proceeded from a single-file pathway worn from the regular use of this ritual they were witnessing. Hasler's personal description is reported thus:

> A considerable number [about 30, ranging from 16-foot pulling and sailing boats to 30-ft motor boats] of small fishing vessels had begun to issue from the Chenal de St Vivien on the first of the ebb, and now headed towards our beach, at the same time about six women appeared, walking towards us along the shore. We took cover as well we could, but it became hopeless when a number of the boats landed on the beach and the fishermen began to light a camp fire and make preparations for breakfast within a few yards of us.

The following passages are brought together care of a lady by the name of Jeanne Baudray. She knew well the Ardouin and Chaussat fishing families and was with them when they came into contact with the four commando canoeists. It is due to her testimony[10] that this new piece of information can be related. Whilst the whole village seemed to know of the 'event', the information was subsequently held within the hamlet.

Hasler and company had found themselves close to a small creek with the hamlet of Saint-Vivien-de-Médoc nearby; with French fishermen servicing the shellfish beds with their 'Calups'; boats with pointed prows around 3 to 4 metres in length. Hasler and his men lay under the camouflage net watching the locals who were chattering and laughing as they came towards the raiding party from the rear of the fishing boats that were scraping on the beach in front of them. The noise of the women and the shouted greetings of the men grew louder but then came an abrupt silence with furtive glances out the corners of their eyes – the Cockle canoeists had been seen.

Hasler ordered his men to keep him covered, unbuckled his pistol and approached the group, holding his hand out in welcome and addressing them in French, saying, 'Good morning'. In equal measure, the assembled locals looked alarmed, concerned and frightened on seeing this tall man with black and green streaked camouflage and unshaven face sporting a flowing moustache. The thing that failed to convince them of the validity of what they were being told was probably that Blondie, in his schoolboy French, was speaking with a German accent. Whilst the other three who were still under cover did not understand at that time what was being said, they observed the mannerisms that led them to think that Blondie was having difficulty in making them believe the story he was telling them, which was, 'We are English soldiers, your friends, and we ask you not to tell anyone that you have seen us.'

Hasler himself explains the following scene that played out during the interview. 'Some of the party seemed quite unconvinced and declared that we were Germans, but [I] pointed out that in any case it would be to their advantage to say nothing to anybody on the subject'.

One of the men seemed to understand and took the lead, and all the others in the group kept quiet. He told Hasler, 'If you want to hide, carry on upstream a further 200 metres and get into the next mouth of a small river. It doesn't lead anywhere. The canal where we are now is the Gua Canal and leads to the port of St Vivien. It's used by other French fishermen, and the Germans have a building site near here. As for your safety, I'll tell the other fishermen and it's obvious we won't say anything to others, but I can promise nothing.'[11]

With that, Hasler thanked them and before it became too light, he had the two canoes neatly tucked up in bed under the camouflage nets at the location that had been recommended, believed to be the Chenal Neuf. The fisherman who helped them secure a safer hiding place was Yves Ardouin, an oyster fisherman. The other party was that of Family Chaussat. This was the simple act of assistance that could have met with severe consequence for the families. Indeed, had the Germans found out, the game would have been up for our Cockle canoeists within the first few days of the operation.

Now, at last, the commandos could have a cup of tea, and with their special burner that sat over a paraffin fuel block, they 'brewed up' by the reeds. They then ate their compact ration packs, so called due to most things being 'compressed'; from meat and fruit to cheese. The hard biscuits were no match for the hot tea flavoured with real sugar and powdered milk. Once they had consumed the food, they took their places in the canoes again. With the cargo bags removed, the men stretched from bow to stern, one man's head level with the other's chest. They too became 'compressed'. The raiding party took turns sleeping after having had their breakfast, with Hasler taking the first watch. Although Sparks was due to relieve him within the hour, dear Blondie let him sleep for four hours before shaking him out of a deep sleep. There is an amusing anecdote worthy of mention at this juncture. Still bitterly cold, Sparks retrieved his flask of Pusser's Rum secreted since the departure from the submarine. This action caught the all-seeing eye of Hasler, who apparently, despite being so partial to alcohol with his breakfast and knowing well of the contraband, glared at his No. 2 as Sparks took a swig. Hasler just held out his hand and said, 'After you.' Sparks passed him the flask and Hasler took down a good mouthful.

Yves Ardouin returned in the early afternoon proffering wine, bread and a big smile, the latter making the marines feel more easy about the situation. He stayed for a short while, understanding that they needed to sleep. This, however, was not realised by others and did not prevent yet a further visit. Later that afternoon, the sentry on duty roused Hasler from sleep with news of an approaching body of returning women. Hasler, seeing that they were hesitant about approaching, made the first move. As Sparks related, the women, who had also brought some food, stayed for about forty minutes. After stories from one of the two women about her husband being a prisoner in Germany, a moment of jollity as she tried to catch Hasler out, they parted company having consumed chocolate and cigarettes, still without any promises of silence on their part. They did, however, tell Hasler about German soldiers working on the new defence work nearby. One of the women was Jeanne. She was only nineteen years of age, but she subsequently urged all to ensure the secret of the meeting was retained in the village.

Hasler, in his report, omitting the fact that he noted that one of the two women was young and attractive[12], wrote, 'At about 1600 some women returned for a further chat, but as we were otherwise undisturbed it seemed it was as if they had followed our instructions.'

The day was short but cold and passed without further alarm. The silence and thoughts were distracted by few aircraft flying high overhead. Although their daily bodily functions were awkward given the limited space at the hiding-up places, they washed and shaved each day, each even having a toothbrush. The nocturnal urination was either left for the hourly rest stops or, if necessary, completed ad hoc with the aid of their bailing-out bowls.

River traffic was sparse and there was no suspicious movement on the flat wet landscape beyond the estuary. The sounds from the working Germans were noted. They were reassured that the French people had not betrayed them and were content to snatch sleep before the cold woke them again. There were several things that needed to be attended to before the sun set; a small leak in *Catfish* that Sparks fixed, oiling and cleaning weaponry, consulting the air photos for the journey ahead and destroying them once studied. The intent was to cover some 22 nautical miles[13] in order to make up for lost time as well as to find a good hiding place well before next morning, with only six hours of a fair tide to aid them. With the sun setting, they brewed tea and Hasler briefed them on the next stage.

The next event is not reported on by Hasler but is related elsewhere. As dusk began to fall, someone alerted them to 'troops'. Each of the other three saw what he had – some fifty figures that appeared to be heading their way. The Sten gun was cocked and their Colts were drawn. A column of grey shapes was advancing from the west, silently fading, then emerging in the grimy light; at 100 yards away, Mills said, 'The French have talked.'

Sparks, for one, drew his commando knife and stuck it in the ground by his left hand. Lavers looked at Sparks and grinned. Dissolving and taking shape again, the grey silhouettes came on. Sparks whispered, 'I think they have halted.' Hasler put down his Sten gun and looked through his glasses. After a long scrutiny, he gave a low laugh. The boys thought he had 'flipped his lid' as he got to his feet. The three looked up at him aghast. 'Relax, boys, stand down, our Jerries are a lot of invasion stakes.' Their hearts were pumping with the surge of adrenaline. Hasler quietly explained to them that such imagination was part of the psychology of being tired and on edge. He suggested some more sleep.

Night Two (2300, 8 December – 0730, 9 December) Lower Estuary

Next came the difficult task of getting the canoes to the water, as Hasler explains:

> It was not possible to resume the passage until the flood stream began to run at 2330, and as this was low-water springs it was necessary to man-handle the boats over nearly ¾ mile of sandy mud before we could launch them. The method employed was to drag the boats by their painters, fully loaded, which was only possible owing to the flat bottom and strong construction of the Cockle Mk 2[14]. Getting the boats clear of the shore was difficult owing to the large areas of outlying sand banks on which the ground swell was running in the form of small breaking rollers which had to be met head on, but eventually we got clear and out into the shipping channel. Navigation was easy, as the port-hand buoys were all showing a dim flashing blue light, and we kept about one cable to the north-east of them. [The] weather was flat calm, no cloud, visibility good but with haze over both shores.

Ever one for an understatement, Hasler's report of this element of the game is better understood by noting the level of 'difficulty' as witnessed by his No. 2:

> In thigh-deep mud we dragged the canoes down to the channel. It was extremely hard going, each of us sweating profusely by the time we had reached the water. The sound of squelching mud, feet dragging through slime echoed down river. Once launched we scrambled into the cockpits taking the mud with us into the canoes.

The pace up the river was very fast. Hasler knew that they had a short window of opportunity before the tide would turn. As usual, they rested on the hour during the six-hour paddle, to ensure the muscles did not get strained beyond their limits. No vessels were seen underway. The automatic, robotic fashion of their paddling belied their status of alert. Sparks was passed a Benzedrine tablet and Hasler took one for himself, furnishing Laver and Mills with the same when they showed signs of exhaustion.

0730–1845, 9 December, east bank opposite Trompeloup

By the time dawn was about to break on 9 December, Hasler reports,

> Continuing on the same course we picked up the east bank just north of the Portes de Calonges, and followed it about one mile offshore until the approach of daylight made it necessary to lie up. At this time it became suddenly extremely cold, so much so that the splashes of salt water were freezing on the cockpit covers.

Exhausted, they had achieved the aim, having covered the 22 nautical miles; they were ready for their canoes! Hasler continues,

> We were fortunate in finding a suitable field at the first attempt and got the boats against a thick hedge with the nets over them. There was a farm house about 300 yards away but we were undisturbed during daylight in spite of the arrival of a herd of cows in our field. During the day we discarded certain stores which were no longer of much value as we got into more inland waters. The plan for the following night [10th] was complicated by the fact that during darkness we would only have three hours of flood tide at the beginning of the night, then six hours of ebb followed by a further three hours of flood by daybreak. This entailed an intermediate lying up place and it was decided to use a site codenamed 'Desert Island'.
>
> That evening, the twilight weather was still flat calm, no cloud, visibility excellent. In order to catch as much of the tide as possible we started somewhat earlier than was prudent and were seen silhouetted against the western sky as we launched the boats by a Frenchman from the nearby farm who came to investigate. We repeated our story of the day before and he seemed quite convinced by it and was rather upset when we declined to go up to his house for a drink.

A little more detail of this meeting and the day is available and worth recording. They had made their way along the Saintonge passage, a quieter place than the main channel, having left the Saint-Louis Bank to starboard, passing the original hideout near the Port of Callonges at the outlet of a channel coming from Saint-Ciers-sur-Gironde, some three miles to the east. The low hills in the region of Blaye are planted with vines, which descend to the river's edge. Situated on a rocky outcrop which dominates the river is the 'Citadel of Blaye', surrounded below by the fields and isolated farmsteads. Hasler had studied the maps of the area and knew some of the names: La Conseillère, La Procureuse and La Présidente.

Finding a well-appointed dry ditch at the outlet of a stream, it gave them ideal shelter between two thick hedges, which were at right angles to the river with frozen fields on either side. From their position, they could see the floating dock at Pauillac with a steam cargo ship beside. They had decided to abandon stores that could lighten the load, given the task ahead; the Sten guns were dispensed with. They had begun the rest period by having a brew of tea followed by the ration pack food, then took catnaps. They were startled awake by a German plane, which flew so low they could actually make out the pilot in the cockpit; this made them a little wary, as there

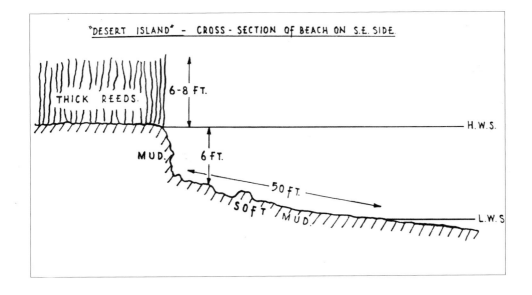

was additional activity throughout the day. Whilst they had not been spotted by their low-flying aviator, the barking of dogs and the approach of a farmer soon brought them the contact they could have done without. At about 1730, they decided to launch at half flood whilst it was still not dark. In the course of this, they were spotted by a Frenchman, who approached them intrigued and without fear. As was the form, Hasler engaged him with the 'we are English Commandos, we ask you as a good Frenchman not to say anything to anyone about us' routine.

While the others were trying to gauge the mood of things in order to lend swift assistance, Hasler kept his inscrutable countenance yet warmed to the farmer's smiling and open face. The Frenchman seemed like a good sort, quiet, open and affable, yet naive in his ways. He was instantly convinced he was dealing with the real thing and pressed the group to accept his hospitality saying, 'It's cold! Come up to the house and have a glass of wine. It'll do you all good!' Hasler politely declined the Frenchman's kind invitation for them all to accompany him to the farmhouse for 'drinks', but seeing the man's evident dismay upon being rejected, Hasler relented, saying, 'Perhaps after the war'. The retort was quite amazingly, 'The next time you are passing, don't forget to pay me a visit. I assure you, I will say nothing. Bonne chance, monsieur!' This kind Frenchman was Monsieur Alibert Decombes, who was the tenant farmer at La Présidente, Braud et Saint Louis, Gironde.

Night Three (1900, 9 December – 0730, 10 December) Upper Estuary

To assist, the area is now described in order to provide names for the route used by the party. As the two canoes came away from the eastern shore, they left the islands of Patiras to starboard and Bouchaud to port. These are the start of a chain that extends upstream towards the Bec d'Ambès. The southern end of Bouchaud is called Île Nouvelle. Then comes Fort Paté, which is opposite the fort at Blaye. These are followed on by Île Verte and Île Cazeau at the entrance to the River Garonne.

We continue the story of the passage of the raiding party with Hasler's assistance. The weather remained flat calm with good visibility.

> The course now lay between two islands and as the waters got more restricted we were uncomfortably conscious of the amount of noise which the boats made when being paddled at cruising speed. At one time a motor boat started up nearby and we lay in a clump of reeds until it had gone, but there was no other sign of life either ashore or afloat and we soon got going again as before. The 'Desert Island' [the island of Bouchaud, opposite St Julien, possibly also known as Île de Patiras] proved to be covered in thick reeds six or seven feet high with occasional trees, but the landing was difficult owing to the vertical mud banks on which the reeds, for the most part, were almost impenetrable without using a knife. Very dry, they made a loud crackling noise if trodden down. For this reason landing was difficult. After many attempts, at 2045, we found a place where we could get ashore and where the boats could safely be left to dry out as the tide fell. [They had accomplished only 15 nautical miles.]
>
> At 0200 on 10th December we got under way again to catch the first of the flood, but we were ¾ of an hour too early and had to wait for the ebb to stop. We then proceeded across the ship channel and entered the shallow passage to the west of the Ile Verte. We saw no sign of life in this area, but as the passage was narrow we made ourselves as inconspicuous as possible by using single paddles and keeping right in close to the shores of the island which are covered in tall reeds. By 0630 we were approaching the southern end of the Ile de Cazeau and began to look for a lying up place on the island. The banks were similar to those of Desert Island and it was only after considerable difficulty that we got ashore near a small pier about ¾ mile from the southern tip of Ile de Cazeau.
>
> It had wooden decking in a very bad state of repair. A quick reconnaissance of the area disclosed what appeared to be a light Ack-Ack position about 40 yards away, in view of which

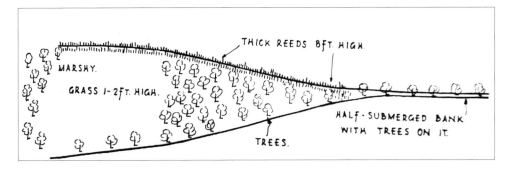

we again embarked and proceeded further south. The situation was now getting rather urgent owing to the approach of daylight, and we finally put ashore at 0730 (10th December) on the extreme southern tip of the island where we had no very good cover but placed the two boats in the middle of a marshy field in long grass with the nets over them. We were not observed at all in this position, although a man and his dog came within one hundred yards of us and at one time a herd of cattle came and stood around in a circle looking at us.

Hasler, due to the nature of his reporting, neglects to tell us about the fact that the party spent the day in a nervous and physically drained condition. The day was cold and filled with fine drizzle. The added discomfort was that they could not go to the toilet, smoke or cook and they were caked in mud. With the reconnaissance planes flying low, they had no option but to remain as still as possible in their semi-recumbent position within the canoes, only able to urinate in a tin can which was emptied over the gunwales. The situation was both dangerous and one of great anxiety. The cows faced them in a circle 'chewing the cud and poked their runny noses against the net' thus pinpointing a target for the spotter planes. These bovine intruders completed this ritual twice during their daily trip on the island. Hasler remarked of the bovine pointers that 'they have an unpleasant habit of standing in a circle around any suspicious object they encounter'.

Hasler had intended to carry out the attack on the night of the 10th and the morning of 11 December. In his own words, the crucial report of the events shows that they 'had not got high enough up the river to enable this to be done with any chance of withdrawing in darkness afterwards. It was therefore decided to move up to an advanced base close to the target area on the night 10/11th and to carry out the attack early on the night 11/12th.'

Night Four (1900–2330 10 December) Lower Garonne

They had already spent twelve hours sitting in the canoes, so paddling again was viewed as a relaxing option, despite the fact that they had to first lower the canoes down the very steep and muddy banks. The canoes were launched at 1845 on 10 December. Once ensconced, they viewed the weather they had to paddle in as a positive thing, it being 'cloudy with occasional rain and a moderate southerly breeze'. They left the Gironde and entered the Garonne where Bordeaux was their next port of call.

With Blondie Hasler and Bill Sparks in *Catfish*, and *Crayfish* being crewed by Laver and Mills, the two canoes were paddled for the first two nautical miles up the centre of the River Garonne, then they split the paddles, stowing one half, and proceeding with the single paddle, they followed close along the western bank, which, apart from an occasional miniature creek, was lined thick with reeds eight feet in height. Defences or sentries were evident and no craft were seen.

Night Four and Day Five (2300, 10 December – 2115, 11 December) Garonne West Bank, opposite Bassens South

Rounding a bend in the river, they saw two large ships and the industrious efforts all lit by floodlights. Quoting directly from Hasler's reporting, 'After an uneventful passage we passed underneath the pontoon pier opposite Bassens South and found a small gap in the reeds into which we were able to force the boats at about 2300. As soon as the tide began to ebb, the boats dried (the canoes grounded on the mud) out and we made ourselves comfortable for the night' within tall reeds which were about seven or eight feet high.'

The cover was so good that they felt confident enough to make some tea, which warmed them. Just nine nautical miles had been paddled that session. This saved energy would prove a useful reserve for the night of attack.

As the daylight increased its reach, they not only found that they had been extremely fortunate in their lying-up place, it being quite inaccessible and well concealed, but that it also afforded them an opportunity to observe the traffic on the river by standing up in the canoe. This vantage point gave them sight of what the Limpets were to become intimately attached to: the merchant ships the *Alabama* and the *Portland*, which were just over half a mile away at Bassens South. There was much activity from the populace around this very busy waterway bordered by housing. This was the hustle and bustle of everyday life in an occupied territory. The men felt the senses become heightened; they had been away from this kind of mass contact for very many days. Shipping passed them constantly. They felt like naughty schoolboys playing truant from school, hiding from authority as they poked their tongue out at it. But if they got this 'jolly' wrong … it would not end in the headmaster's office!

During the day, they stretched out in the canoes feeling quite safe in their little hideout. For the last time, they had their meal and slept in the wonderful and cleverly constructed Cockle canoe. They talked in whispers and even smoked. The day passed with only a little rain. There they sat or lay in Mr Goatley's canoes. Meantime, back in England another of Mr Goatley's collapsible inventions, the 8-ton load carrier, was undergoing final trials off Hayling Island with truck and Ack-Ack guns loaded.

'During the day we re-arranged the stowage of the boats so as to have all the escape equipment in two bags, and in the evening we completed the fusing of the Limpets. A nine-hour setting was used on the time delay,' reported Hasler. Sparks gives us a little more of the detail when he says, 'We took the Limpet mines from beneath our legs and began the delicate job of fusing them … we were told to fit orange ampoules … time enough for us to make our getaway. Whilst we armed the sixteen Limpets, Blondie watched over us like a

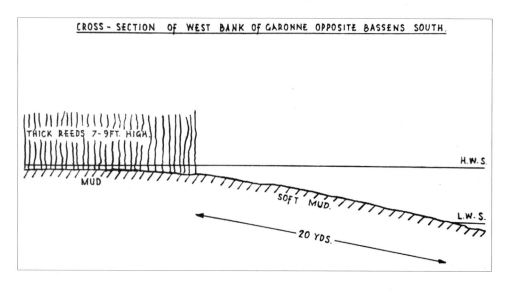

hawk. He then took the 60-in[15] (1,465 mm, folded 395 mm) placing rod and made sure that it engaged and disengaged each mine. After that he took us through our instructions one more time.' The stowage and positioning of the 'cargo' as carried during 'the passage-making' versus 'stowage for the attack' shows the kind of fine detail that Hasler required and implemented.

The process of fusing the Limpets had been done so very many times, they had listened and learned from the lectures, they had practised. There was great emphasis placed on this skill. With Hasler overseeing the process in the daylight[16], before the attack, each man took one pair of Limpets from between his knees and separated them apart. In the reeds on that evening for the next hour and a bit, Hasler, Sparks, Laver and Mills ensured this part of the job was done by the book. And the book said,

1. Take one pair of Limpets. Remove one A.C. Delay cap. Lute the threads. Place required ampoule in, point down, replace cap. Use cloth to screw up taut with the fingers.
2. Put a cross on the original scratch mark on the fuse [showing it was ready for starting].
3. Untie the securing string of the safety pin. Open points.
4. Repeat for other A.C. Delay.
5. Turn over, remove rubber cap, small split pin, and collar from sympathetic fuse. Place soluble plug in place (after removing wrapper). Replace collar and small split pin. Check it is right in, clear of the sleeve. Open its points. Remove the 2 ft of sailmaker. Replace cap. Remove sailmaker from safety pin.
6. Test placing rod in each Limpet, to see it goes in freely. Extend placing rod. [from folded size of 15½ inches 395 mm to fully extended length of 58¾ inches 1,465 mm]

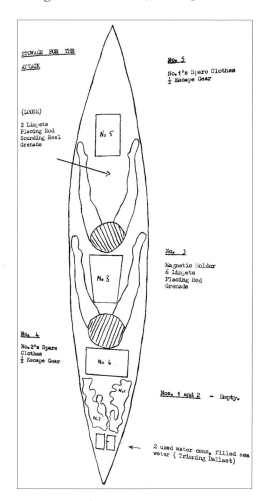

The stowage and positioning of the 'cargo' as carried during 'the passage-making' versus 'stowage for the attack' shows the fine detail that Hasler required and implemented.

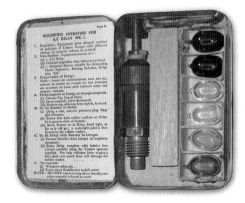

AC delay and different timing ampoules.

Limpet placing rod.

7. And at a given number of hours before Limpets are required to explode, remove safety pins from A.C. Delays. Screw spindles down as far as they will go. Alongside take each Limpet, remove the rubber cap, and the safety pin from the sympathetic fuse. Keep the pins.

Once this process was completed, it only remained to offer the last caress to any shape they chose. The compasses were hidden away to keep the luminous dials from the view of any eye that had an elevated position to the canoe. They each painted their faces and were ready for the word, and in Hasler's words,

> The weather unfortunately cleared up in the evening and by twilight it was once again flat calm with a clear sky and good visibility. Owing to the fact that the moon did not set until 2132, I considered it essential to delay leaving our lying up place until 2110, which was about 30 minutes later than would have been desirable from a tide point of view. At 2100 the time fuses were started.

Night Five (2115–2345, 11 December) Port of Bordeaux, west bank

The liquid acetone from the orange-coloured ampoule began to bleed at the same moment the requisite sound of the broken glass was heard. In each canoe, eight Limpets were fused and ready.

> The plan of attack was as follows:
> *Catfish*: To proceed along the western bank to the docks on the west side of the river at Bordeaux.
> *Crayfish*: To proceed along the east bank of the river to the docks on the east side at Bordeaux, but if no suitable targets could be found to return and attack the two ships at Bassens South which we had been studying during the day. Both boats left the lying up place at 2115 and separated for their respective attacks.

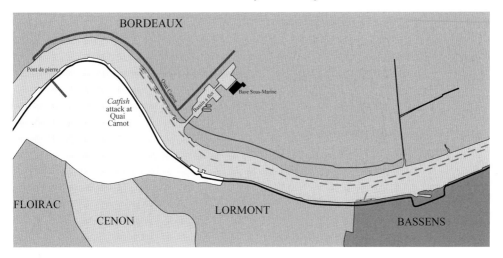

Districts of the Bordeaux Harbour area.

Aerial recon overdrawn by Hasler with the route paddled by *Catfish* to Quai Carnot.

There was no wind, clouds or rain – it was clear and frosty. Before they parted company with faces blackened, Hasler told Laver, 'Corporal, when the job has been done, you and Mills must make your own way back. We cannot travel together.' They shook hands and wished each other 'good luck'. Sparks wrote, 'I was especially sorry to say goodbye to Bill Mills, who had been my close friend for these past months.' Sparks is recorded promising to him, 'I'll get the first round when we return to Southsea.' They covered their heads with the camouflaged hoods and, with their blackened faces, ventured forth.

Watched by Hasler and Sparks, *Crayfish* slipped first, then glided away with the flood tide carrying them towards Bordeaux; the forthcoming area was lit up like a city centre on steroids. *Catfish* followed on to find the tide also towed them along on their side of the river;

they then took to the middle of the stream in order to benefit from the dark area. Within an hour and a half of paddling, *Catfish* came around a long bend in the Garonne. The cluster lamps lit the area brightly including the waters they were floating on. This area was a hive of industry; German and French voices, music, welding, laughing, loading and the maintenance of the night shift workers. Hasler takes up the story:

> *Catfish* got up past the entrance to the basins without difficulty, except it was necessary to keep about a cable[17] offshore owing to a good many lights on the shore, particularly around the lock gates.
>
> Owing to the necessity for a late start it was not possible to examine more than half the length of the target area before the tide began to ebb and it became impossible to proceed further in silence.

Hasler knew they could not reach the rest of the bevy of beauties upstream that needed caressing that night. Several ships were now awaiting attention in the immediate area. They inspected the targets as they silently tripped by. From the diminutive Cockle at water level, they viewed the giant monoliths that were lined up along the Quai Carnot as far as the Quai des Chartrons. Five were moored. The first two vessels were a tanker followed by a medium-size cargo vessel. Hasler purposely passed these ships to get up to a third, which was clearly one of the blockade runners, alongside which was moored a petrol tanker. Since mining these presented some problems, Hasler decided to keep them until last. So it was the next ship which the team attacked first: a freighter of at least 7,000 tonnes. She was in relative darkness, which made the operation less dangerous. Now was the moment to carry out for real the procedures which had been practised *ad infinitum*. Unknown to those remaining Royal Marines attending to their targets, two of their kind had been extracted from their prison cells and had just started on a forced journey to a sand pit.

Hasler took the honours first, and whilst Sparks attached his magnetic holder to the side of the ship, he reached for his first Limpet, attached it to the 5-foot placing rod[18], lowered it into the water as far as he could reach then closed the Limpet to the hull. Feeling the mine clamp itself on, he detached the rod. Sparks released his magnetic holder. The process was repeated amidships; this time it was Sparks' turn. Then a third mine on the stern end. *Catfish* glided towards the next victim, which was a cargo ship obscured by a minesweeper[19] (which was a small frigate-sized ship known as a *Sperrbrecher*[20] or 'Pathmaker'). Advancing on the minesweeper, after being drenched in the condenser outfall spray from their previous quarry, they easily located the engine room.

Sparks fixed two Limpets a few yards from each other whilst in motion and swung out away from this ship's side. Sparks remembered the hobnailed boots of a sentry who they thought had seen them,

> who shone a torch on us. Fortunately, we were able to get back close to the ship's side and drift along with the tide without making any movement. The sentry followed us along the deck, shining his torch down on us at intervals, but evidently unable to make up his mind as to what we actually were, owing to the efficiency of the camouflage scheme. We were able to get in a position under the bow of the ship where he could no longer see us.[21]

Hasler had passed Sparks the holdfast making the 'hold on' signal and with deft aplomb had attached the device almost silently.

> After waiting there for about five minutes everything went quiet, so we resumed our course down stream. The attack on the second merchant ship was rather spoilt by the presence of the tanker alongside her, and the fact that the tide was now running so strongly that I considered it unsafe to get in between the bows of the two ships; this forced us to attack the stern end only.

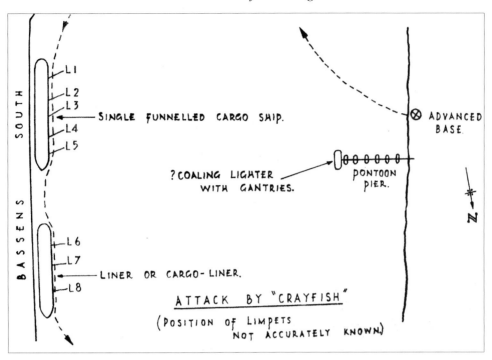

Attack by *Crayfish*. One of Hasler's original set of drawings showing the attack by *Crayfish* and Limpet placing on the single-funnelled cargo ship *Alabama* and the cargo ship *Portland* on Bassens South Quay.

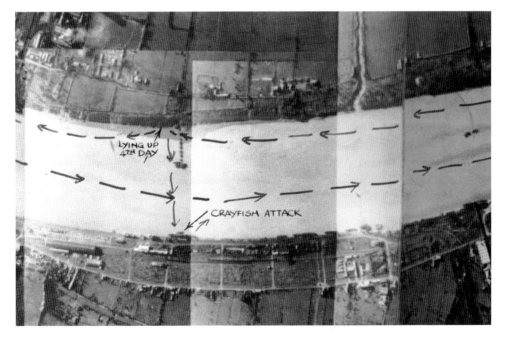

Aerial recon overdrawn by Hasler with the course of canoe *Crayfish*, attack and lying-up place on the fourth day.

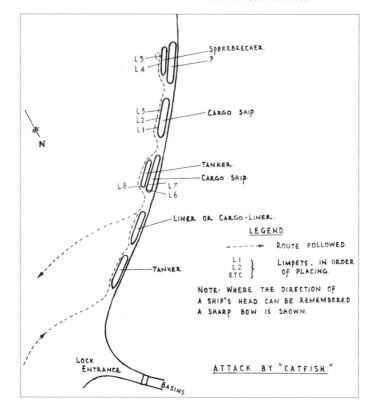

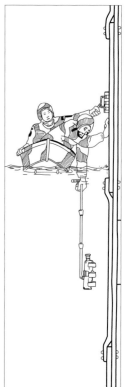

From top: *Sperrbrecher* named *Schwanheim* (Limpets 4 and 5); cargo ship named *Tannenfels* (Limpets 1, 2 and 3); tanker named *Python* (Limpet 8); cargo ship named *Dresden* (Limpets 6 and 7). Only eight Limpets were available to use. The two lower ships were bypassed for the other vessels.

This reported section of events by Hasler belies the fact that a near disaster almost occurred. They had positioned themselves between the bows so as to attack the two ships moored alongside each other: a cargo ship and a tanker. At some stage of the game, the influence of the tide began forcing the two ships' hulls together and with Hasler first to realise what was happening, he tried to prevent the Cockle being crushed and pushed against each monolithic hull with his hands. Sparks followed suit and both behaved in a manner not dissimilar to that of the Herculean figure of Samson who used his tremendous strength to bring down the two central temple pillars. It was probable that the yawing abated due to the swell of the tide changing rather than either of our heroes' efforts, but it is reported that Hasler remarked of the incident post-war, saying, 'I felt like Atlas holding up the world.' Sparks also remembered the incident, saying, 'I thought I was going to die.' Either way, the result was that they managed to push the canoe backwards out of harm's way.

It should be noted that if a skeleton-based canoe with longitudinal members had been used, especially that of the only other type of canoe then available (Mk 1*), then the hull of the canoe would unquestionably have been crushed, terminally compromising its structural integrity. It was only the extremely tough construction design of the Mk 2 that could have afforded enough compressive strength within its structure.

With all their might, they now back-paddled against the swift-flowing tidal force, rounded the tankers' bows, drifted towards the stern end of the cargo ship and stuck two Limpets as far apart as was possible, thus leaving their last for the tanker. The relief was beginning to be palpable. The senses kicked in with the sudden realisation that the only effort needed now was to paddle away, but not before Hasler turned to his faithful No. 2 and offered him his hand, which was accepted as warmly as it was given. The broad, black, smiling faces said it all. It was euphoria and to hell with the consequences.

Indeed, Hasler is recorded as saying, 'I felt as though I owned the river and my respect for the enemy gave way to contempt.' Whilst in his report he casually mentions,

> In order to reach the Blaye area by low water slack, it was necessary to abandon much of our former caution and proceed in mid-stream using double paddles, and although we must have been clearly visible and audible at least 200 yards away, we did not see any further signs of life.

The ebbing tide urged them away with every paddle blade and they surged downstream faster than they had ever done. The Cockle was now a very different and lively creature, responsive, agile, without the terminal weight of their sticky friends.

Lower Garonne, passage west of Île de Nord, and channel west of Blaye, 0015–0600, 12 December

The scene at Bassens South was passed with the habitation and the familiar reeded areas. *Crayfish* proceeded downstream, close under the west bank, to Labarde (opposite the Île de Cazeau). They took a break and the world changed to a calm and very pleasant silence. Hasler found it difficult to be pessimistic or to worry amid the tranquillity. The two heard a noise: 'It sounded like a Mississippi stern wheeler at full speed, but we knew what it was and we laughed out loud.' The noise abruptly terminated as the 'paddle steamer' poised before releasing a tentative gull mew and was received by a full belly laugh from Hasler. *Crayfish* rafted up with *Catfish* and the four were merry on the heady fumes of success and reunion. Much congratulation was given by each to all but most especially from Hasler to his men. He was elated, and after congratulating Laver and Mills, he turned abaft, saying, 'And well done Sparks'. Blondie Hasler, their commanding officer, had said, 'You have all done wonderfully, and I am really proud of you.' That meant the world to these men, and it uplifted them to a level never experienced before.

The official report gave nothing of the jollity or camaraderie, saying only,

> Whilst having a short rest in mid-stream near the south end of the Ile de Cazeau [Labarde] we were rejoined by *Crayfish* who was also on her way back, having completed her attack. This meeting was purely by chance, but it was decided to continue in company until the end of the withdrawal. Corporal Laver reported that he had proceeded some distance along the east bank at Bordeaux without encountering any targets, and that as the ebb tide had then turned against him he returned and attacked the two ships previously seen at Bassens South, placing five Limpets on the large cargo ships and three on the smaller cargo liner, he had not seen any sentries or patrols during this attack.

The two boats sped from that meeting point in line ahead along the west bank to Fort Medor, crossing over the shipping channel after recognising the northern point of the Île Verte, passing between the Île Nouvelle and the Île Paté (Fort Paté). They continued for a further mile before the flood tide started to play its weary sport with them.

Hasler's last words to Laver were, 'Well, Corporal, this is where we have to separate. You are about a mile north of Blaye. Go straight ashore here and carry out your escape instructions. I shall land about a quarter of a mile further north. Goodbye, both of you and thank you for everything you have done. Keep on as you have been doing and we will be meeting again in Pompey in a few weeks time; good luck to you.' One last time across the gunwales they shook hands, but not before Sparks would remind them, 'See you in the 'Granada'; we'll keep a couple of pints for you!' The crew of *Crayfish* took one look at their dark-skinned companion and could not help getting involved with the smile and the well-spaced teeth within. One last laugh was had before they

Bordeaux. Looking towards Quai Carnot.

Bordeaux basins, adjacent Quai Carnot.

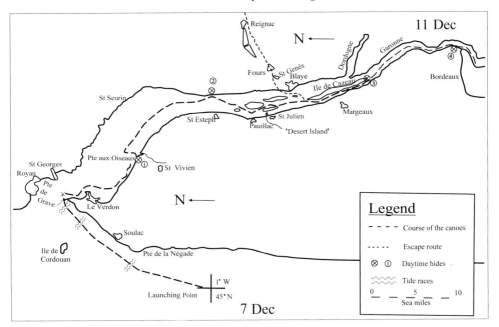

1 = 0745–2330 8 December, Pte aux Oiseaux
2 = 0730–1845 9 December, Port des Callonges
3 = 1900 9 December – 0730 10 December, Ile de Cazeau
4 = 2300 10 December – 2115 11 December, Bassens Pontoon Pier
Escape route begins = 0015–0600 12 December, Blaye

separated at 0600 on 12 December 'and both Cockles proceeded to land independently about ¼ mile apart'. Uncharacteristically, Blondie Hasler afforded himself a last look at the canoe and company within. He realised a loss; his 'children' were now all grown up, and it pained him that the world awaited their arrival. Not for the first time was his heart beating heavy – and as rough and ready as Bill Sparks was, he felt every beat with him. Sparks thought of his brother Benny and the promise he had made to himself long ago.[22]

That night they had paddled some 22 nautical miles. The official line reported, '*Catfish* landed without any difficulty in a fairly deserted area, and having disembarked the escape equipment the boat was scuttled by destroying the buoyancy bags and pushing it out into the stream in a sinking condition.'

During 12 December, the border guard service, or Grenzschutzdienst, had been sent out on patrol following the explosive situation at the docks and had discovered two canoes downstream from Blaye which had been sliced open in order for them to sink; unfortunately, the low tide had not quite concealed them.

On 21 December 1942, the Department of Naval Intelligence (DNI) reported the receipt of a secret message that read, 'The merchant ships *Dresden* and *Alabama* and three others were damaged by mysterious explosions on December 12th. Two of the ships at Bassens and three at Bacalan. The damage can be repaired.'

On 8 April 1943, following Blondie Hasler's return, he began to compile his detailed report as the Military Force Commander of Operation *Frankton*.[23] Within his own report is the admission that, at the time of writing, it suffered from being incomplete due to certain information which was lacking and was a narrative of events as witnessed by him or reported to him by the other members of the assault force during the operation. It also 'lacked from the knowledge of the results achieved' on the targets and the fate of two of the boats and four of the boats' crews. The events leading to the disembarkation of the canoes from HMS *Tuna* were not reported on due to the fact that Commander Raikes had already given his account. Hasler's report deals clinically with the departure from *Tuna*.

By 31 December 1942, the RMBPD War Diaries carry the event entry 'posted missing *frankton*'. On 29 April 1943, Mountbatten was moved to write of *Frankton*, 'This brilliant little operation carried through with great determination and courage is a good example of the successful use of 'Limpeteers'.'

CHAPTER 6
The Four Noble Truths

The information contained within this narrative of these Royal Marines has originated, and been compiled from the captured German documents of the High Command of the Wehrmacht, the Kriegsmarine, now within the German Naval Archives. French people sympathetic to the Allied cause at the time were another source of supplementary information. Local archive information from historians has also been used. This information, which has only been available in recent years, has been taken from statements made by various individuals who were witnesses at the requisite period. All the verbal recollections and statements made are taken as true and honest. As all this information is of great importance, it is delivered in an almost clinical form, and wherever possible, this is shown with inverted commas. Small minor contradictions were found, but with a modicum of common sense and further research, these were usually resolved satisfactorily. Some material could be thought to be contentious, although not to report a necessary sworn statement made would be a failure of due diligence.

The only caveat within is that from the original document translations some words could well be inaccurately reported[1]; indeed, not all translations were made by any one individual.

The Unreported Path

Exactly what happened to eight of the ten Royal Marines that ventured out on the *Frankton* Raid has never truly been told; there is a great need to relate the fine detail of the events. Here is the first ever detailed narrative of the last days of the first Cockleshell Heroes to be executed under the new 'Hitler Commando Order'

Sgt Samuel Wallace, Marine Robert Ewart and *Coalfish*

The Saint-Nicolas Rocks, the first tidal race that the Cockleshell canoeists had encountered on the Médoc Peninsula, had proved too much for Sgt Samuel Wallace and Marine Robert Ewart in *Coalfish*. It might have been a momentary mistake or just a series of waves that would have proved too difficult for anyone. Either way, they lost the argument with the surging waves of white water. Fortunately, the design of the cockpit, one of the few parts of the Cockle to have been jointly designed by Goatley and Hasler[2], proved its worth and released the men on request. As they lay in the water hanging on to the hull of the inverted canoe, the turbulent waters slowly subsided. They knew they would not be able to right this specialist canoe. The open-top waders had instantly filled with the icy salt water and had become detached by the force at the waist-fixing points. They were only held on by the laces of the rope-soled shoes. The clothes became sodden, but the Reliant life jackets, each sporting their own hand-painted initials, kept their heads above the water. They knew that they must get to the shore regardless of the distance or the cold would take them. They barely made it! Avoiding hypothermia, they lay on the shoreline exhausted, in an area of the unoccupied Le Verdon battery.

Recovering, the waders and life jacket were removed. They had swum the short distance ashore at Pointe de Grave and, as far as it is possible to reconstruct the events, had walked in an exhausted state from the lighthouse[3], to the lit building[4], a 'bungalow' or a small single-storey dwelling, believed to be occupied by the Luftwaffe, to give themselves up[5]. This was a medical unit in a room of the German AA detachment, Battalion Soulac (German Air Force (GAF), Ferry Flak Division 595), which occupied the Bordeaux-Médoc Sector and guarded the Fahren Flotilla (ferry boats) across the mouth of the Gironde. The 'arrest' of Wallace and Ewart is uncertain, as Vice-Admiral Johannes Bachmann's[6] War Diary gives this timing as 0615 on Tuesday 8 December 1942; other timings are from Operations Section HQ 708th Division report giving 0600. Yet another report shows 0545 and another as 0530, as well as yet another for 0630. Regardless, all reports confirm that the marines were in uniform.

Even taking the earliest quoted time, Wallace and Ewart must have been hiding for a couple of hours before deciding to make tracks. Unwittingly, their path did not lead them to the hoped-for friendly Frenchman[7] in his single-storey dwelling but one infested by the very individuals they sought to avoid. They were in no state to put up any resistance and simply raised their hands when they were confronted by an equally perplexed and surprised German soldier. This soldier, if the statement below is to be believed, at least in part, was of the Medical Corps.[8] He apparently started to shout at them, which brought more soldiers, one of whom was an NCO, who had his pistol drawn and took control.[9]

It is reported[10] that 'they reached a small barracks which was marked with the Red Cross and in which were located the hospital room and the doctor. The British soldiers were trembling with cold, knocked on the barracks and were admitted by a soldier of the Medical Corps. They were immediately taken before the Medical Officer, reported their mishap and wanted to be taken prisoner.'

They were[11] 'treated well'[12], received clothes, blankets and an opportunity to sleep. They were plainly recognisable by their uniforms as members of the enemy forces and were supposed to have declared repeatedly (in English), 'We are fighting soldiers.' Another separate report mentions that Wallace and Ewart 'reported at sick bay of G.A.F. Ferry flak at 0630 at Pointe de Grave lighthouse stating that they were shipwrecked English sailors'.

Sea Defence Commandant Gascony informed Counter Intelligence Unit (GIS) Station in Bordeaux at about 0800 on receipt of information from GAF Flak. During this time, Wallace had spun a story about them being shipwrecked sailors from a warship that had been torpedoed during the night. Some of the reported information could be due to the seeds of the plausible stories entered into by Sgt Wallace. It is known that both men remained together as they slept in those early hours after being arrested.

The surgeon of the Ferry Flak stated that 'the prisoners – their faces painted green – arrived soaked through'. Footprints discovered led one to conclude that landing was made off Pointe de Grave at low water. They wore 'British uniforms, without headgear, consisting of a type of twill trousers and blouson, similar to a camouflage shirt. On their sleeves are rank and insignia, and the wording 'Royal Navy', plus badges for mixed enterprises, army, navy, air force [Combined Operations badges].'[13] Indeed, the full ensemble was described later by Interrogator Harstick: canvas shoes with rubber soles, heavy linen trousers, military shirt, pullover, and scarf, rubber protective and camouflage clothing with black irregular camouflage patches on a green background; on their arm they were wearing the 'Combined Operations' badge (anchor, gun, propeller) rank badge and shoulder flash with 'Royal Marines'. The blue woollen caps and mitts were lost.

According to a deposition[14], Capt. Max Gebauer[15] was deputising in Royan during December 1942 for Senior Naval Officer Inshore (SNOIS) Gascogny, and on the evening of 7 December, Vice-Admiral Bachmann arrived at Gebauer's HQ in order to attend practice firing of the batteries on the Gironde Estuary on 8 and 9 December. On the morning of 8 December, at about 0800, shortly before their departure for Le Verdon on the Pointe de

Grave, the officer commanding the Royan harbour defence flotilla (HDF), Lt Wild, rang Gebauer and reported that two Englishmen (members of the British Navy) had been seized … Lt Wild was told he should bring them before Bachmann and Gebauer after they had inspected the crews of the vessels of the HDF lying at Pointe de Grave. Whilst Gebauer relates in his March 1948 deposition that 'the two men arrived in a collapsible boat from a submarine [with it] lying in heavy surf and a rising tide and could not be reached', the timing of this canoe sighting was 0800; these details are not related in his June 1948 deposition. Gebauer ordered the OC of HDF to salvage the collapsible canoe with its contents at the next low water. The HDF reported that on account of the sea running, salvage was out of the question, as the canoe had 'gone to pieces in the surf' with only single parts of it together with bits of equipment being salved.

During the course of 8 December, the following items were found: detailed maps[16] of the Gironde upstream as far as Bordeaux, several cans of fresh water, non-perishable provisions, automatic pistols with silencers, ammunition, an aerial map of Bordeaux dated November 1942, one dagger, one hand grenade (the Germans noted that it was the same type carried by Commandos at St Nazaire), one magnetic holder, one tube containing dark face paint, rubber boat (canoe), etc.

Gebauer ordered that 'the two British soldiers be kept in custody until he arrived at Le Verdon at about 0900 with Admiral Bachmann'. Gebauer further relates that 'when we arrived at Le Verdon the two Englishmen were brought before us; this happened on the road near the quarters of the officer commanding the HDF. An interrogation was not carried out there as the Admiral and I had agreed to leave this to the Counter Intelligence Section in Bordeaux.'

Bachmann decided he would 'settle this matter himself' and, after returning to Nantes, gave orders on the morning of 10 December to clerk PO Gustav Schulz 'to search the files for the Führer order concerning commando troops'. He was assisted in doing so by Wilhelm de Vries[17]. It is intimated that they did find this order; it is probable that this was not one of the only twelve copies of the actual Führer order but some form of paper being passed down which related the same details. Bachmann personally then contacted Navy Group West to 'obtain a decision as to whether it was justifiable to shoot the commando men at once without interrogating first'.

Wallace and Ewart were eventually handed over by the AA unit to the harbour control unit at Royan, 'not the Harbourmaster'. Once on the other side of the estuary, Wallace and Ewart were secured in the old fort. They were handed over to the HDF in the afternoon.

Bachmann ordered the immediate interrogation of the two prisoners by GIS[18] Station in Bordeaux. It was then reported to Bachmann that the GIS had refused due to protocol; as the men were 'shipwrecked English sailors', transfer to naval prisoners camp Fallingbostel was necessary. Bachmann then gave orders that the Officer in Charge of the GIS Station should go to Le Verdon immediately to examine the prisoners. At around 1800, the GIS officer arrived from Bordeaux. Bachmann then told Lt-Cdr Helmut Harstick,[19] (III)M, about his wishes concerning the interrogation. Bachmann had already told Harstick[20] that, after the interrogation had taken place, he would then 'give orders for the prisoners to be shot on account of attempted sabotage'.

At about 2330, Harstick telephoned Bachmann saying that 'the interrogations had produced important results' and requested 'a postponement of the order to shoot'. Harstick also reported that whilst the 'prisoner from Glasgow refused to make any statement, an Irishman had only told them that the two alone were lowered from a submarine which had left England fourteen days before and their task was to sink ships in the Gironde'. Regardless, Bachmann refused to withdraw the order but was then telephoned by a Captain Koenig[21] from Paris, who told Bachmann it was considered more important to defer the shooting. On receiving confirmation, Bachmann gave orders for the postponement 'and for the continuation of the interrogations on the following morning [9 December]'. 'Under the pretext of the preservation of life and the assurance of good treatment', every effort was made to obtain specific 'information of importance to Operational Control before shooting'.

Bachmann and Gebauer then returned to Royan, Bachmann staying at a guest house in Royan; Gebauer's HQ was outside Royan.

Before the execution, Harstick had found out the following information[22] from Wallace and/or Ewart[23]: the names, places and dates of birth of both Royal Marines; training and time attended[24] on the 'special course run by Combined Operations at Portsmouth; that the unit consisted of thirty men in two sections with each section kept apart while on duty, meeting only on Sundays and church parades; The fact that they were billeted, first in barracks then in private houses with board and lodging paid for by the RN; That Cpt. Stewart and a Sub Lt were the instructors as well as a Sergeant and several corporals, with the remainder of the soldiers only being either English, Scottish or Irish. The training consisting mainly of sport, duties aboard ship, navigation and weapon training together with Limpet mine instruction.' Other information given was the fact that, during training, men taking part in the course were continually drafted and others joined the course. 'No details were given with regard to the tasks of those drafted with the prisoners stating that they did not see the drafted persons again. Within the last two weeks both men were ordered aboard sub P49 at Portsmouth without them knowing the reason or task. Once embarked, the submarine cruised for about two weeks until 8 December and at the beginning of December, only Wallace was told about the task which was to proceed up stream on the Gironde and attempt to damage any German vessel with 2 Limpet mines provided, paddling by night hiding by day under the camouflage provide.' Interrogator Harstick also learnt that Wallace had been given a note 'which contained several French words and sentences which could be handed to French people to read' and 'Ewart had learnt several words such as "Je suis anglais" and "echapper".'

The German's had found only two Limpet mines with the holders attached and knew of the workings, a magnetic holder including the strop, but were again lied to by Wallace, who gave the description of the old Mk 1* canoe that they had used in early training; 'a wooden boat covered in heavy camouflaged canvas'. Also of interest were the Red, Yellow and Green maps of the coastline which caused Harstick to remark of them, 'the markings are very exact and suggest that the English[25] are well informed with regard to coastal fortifications.'

Interestingly, the German interrogator learnt that they were not Commandos, but in spite of that, they expected to be shot on being arrested in Germany; that the men's superiors did not mention this to them, but rumours to that effect were circulating amongst those taking part in the course.

Here we can see that the interrogator had presented the pieces of equipment the Germans had recovered, which Wallace then, very cleverly, it has to be said, created a believable story around, in order to maintain the integrity of the men still afloat and that of the intended targets. Hasler would have been extremely proud of Wallace's ingenuity. Indeed, at least until the explosions happened, Harstick had bought into the 'Words of Wallace'.

In the afternoon of 9 December, Wallace and Ewart were transferred from the HDF to the fort at Royan on Bachmann's orders. During the day, Bachmann and Gebauer attended practice firing of the batteries on the North Bank, during which Bachmann was in communication with his HQ at Nantes. Also, during the afternoon of the 9th, a teleprinter message was received by Gebauer saying that the interrogation was to be continued by Sonderführer[26] Heinz Corssen[27], from Dulag Nord in Wilhelmshaven, at the Counter Intelligence Unit in Bordeaux (GIS) on his arrival on 11 December and the execution was to be postponed until then. For some reason, Corssen was recalled by Navy Group West[28] when he was at Oldenburg railway station at the beginning of his journey. He was then told to report to the HQ of FOIC in Paris. (Corssen never did interrogate Wallace and Ewart but subsequently interrogated MacKinnon, Conway, Laver and Mills at Bordeaux.)

Harstick records, 'In accordance with orders received by telephone from [Gebauer] the interrogation was broken off in the afternoon of 9 December and the entire research handed over to the Security – Special Detachment – Bordeaux.' On the evening of the 9th, a teleprinter message arrived from Navy Group West saying that 'the prisoners were to be handed over to the SD (*Sicherheitsdienst*; Special Detachment) in accordance with paragraph 4 of the Führer Order and that measures pursuant to this order were to be carried out by 1100 on 10 December'. Gebauer gave orders to the Commander of the fort at Royan that an officer of 284 Naval Artillery Unit was to hand over the prisoners to the SD and that a request was forwarded to the SD for them to collect Wallace and Ewart from the Fort at Royan.

According to a report from the Sea Defence Commandant, Gascogne, Wallace and Ewart were actually handed over, with the material found on the beach, to the Security Service, the *Sicherheitsdienst* or SD (the security department of the SS) by the German Navy at 0415 on 10 December.

By 9 December, Bachmann had returned from his visit to Royan and had arrived back at his HQ at Nantes. He received a telephone call at 1015 on 10 December from SS Obersturmführer Dr Julius Schmidt[29] requesting a postponement of the shooting as the interrogation had not been concluded.

In the afternoon of 10 December, Gebauer received a telephone call from FOIC HQ asking about the completion of the shooting. Gebauer then rang the SD in Bordeaux to elicit the details. Gebauer learnt that 'the SD had applied through official channels to the Führer's HQ for a three-day postponement of the shooting', since it was expected that Wallace and Ewart would make future statements; Gebauer had learnt nothing about the interrogation but passed on the fact of the postponement to FOIC by teleprinter. The General Staff at the Führer's HQ were not prepared to sustain the wrath of Hitler by granting an extension to interrogate, and it is apparent that they denied the request for the three-day postponement by the SD in Bordeaux in order for them to pursue their investigations. To this end, the SD made a telephone call to Capt. Ernst Kühnemann's[30] office; it was to no avail, and the trend for carrying out the shooting as soon as possible was decided upon. Kühnemann had informed Lt Theodor Prahm[31] that he would be away and that he could not be reached during the evening of 10 December (the author surmises that this might have been contrived in order not to be held responsible for the impending execution).

The following detailed information is related verbatim in its entirety for the sake of accuracy.[32] Prahm reveals that 'at about 1930 or 2000 the CPO Otto Reckstadt of the HQ company (NOIC) reported by telephone to me that the SD had applied to him for an execution detail. As I already knew Admiral Bachmann's order for execution the request for an execution detail appeared to me to be completely normal and was in accordance with this order.' At about 2200, Dr Luther[33], nominally the head of the SD in Bordeaux, i.e., Commander, rang Prahm and demanded to speak to Kühnemann. Prahm attempted to contact him, but to no avail. Prahm relates,

[Luther] asked me to come to see him at once in an urgent matter … he was in the town with a convoy which he could not possibly leave. He then sent me a car, which brought me to the Place de Tourny[34]. Here [Luther] informed me that he required my presence at the execution, in accordance with orders of the two English prisoners.

When I refused this, he showed me an order that execution had to be carried out by the Navy, and at the same time produced a certificate[35], which gave him authority over all of the Armed Forces. The execution detail of the HQ defence platoon was already waiting there in the truck.

The two prisoners were waiting in a big car under guard of SD men. [Luther] would not accept my repeated refusal and my demand that he should have the execution carried out by his own men and pointed out that execution by the Navy had been expressly ordered. He explained that as he was in charge of the operation he bore the responsibility. He insisted on haste, as he had to report completion to one of the highest headquarters by 2300 or 2400. I then was forced to comply with his request as I already knew Admiral Bachmann's order and as the head of the SD had the necessary authority and in addition bore the responsibility for the action. I joined [Luther] in his car and the column moved off (one truck with the execution squad consisting of one PO and sixteen ratings, one big car with the two prisoners and three or four members of the SD as guard, a further car with [Luther], his driver and me).

We drove first to the submarine base where we fetched a naval surgeon, as the harbour surgeon had not been available. When I asked whether a priest was coming [Luther] replied that a priest had been with the two prisoners for the whole of the afternoon. He also said that the death sentence had been read out to the prisoners before their departure.

The column then drove into a wood, which lay, as far as I recollect (and it was difficult to see where we were going at night), to the north-east of the town, approximately 5–10 km outside the town. As far as I can recollect the SD already had two coffins put ready on the edge of the wood. These coffins were taken along by the lorry to the place of execution. The place of execution itself was a sand-pit of which served to stop the bullets.

The SD men dug in two posts, which were lying there. The prisoners were tied to the posts; this was the first time I saw the prisoners. The two cars were then placed in such a position that the beams of the lamps fell upon the prisoners. I placed the sixteen men into two rows, the front row kneeling, gave each group its target and gave the order to fire.

Immediately after, I ordered the squad to turn about and march off. The surgeon went to the men who had been shot, while at the same time two SD men, who had already drawn their pistols, fired several shots into the backs of the neck of the victims. The surgeon then established that death had taken place. The SD men placed the dead bodies in the coffins and loaded these on the truck. As it appeared to me and to my men too as irreverent to get into the lorry with the coffins, and therefore we went on foot up to the road to the edge of the wood. The truck also came up there, after the two coffins had been placed in a building, which was also at the edge of the wood. I then drove back into the town in the truck with my men. On the next morning I reported what had happened to the NOIC[36]. He told me that the matter was in order and that I acted correctly.

Given the fact that by at least 2300 the convoy had begun to make its way to the execution destination said to be only around 10 km north-east of Bordeaux and that the executions had taken place at 0300, it has to be wondered what had been happening in the intervening hours. It would seem that the burial detail took place during the early hours, probably nearby to where the shooting took place. It is possible that to avoid the bodies being found the witness, Prahm, had deliberately falsified his statement. Given the time that passed, it could be that the travelling distance involved was greater than that mentioned.

There is no mention of whether blindfolds were offered or used, but it is believed that they had been taken from the prison blindfolded and bound with their hands behind their back. Prahm had only extracted some relatively unimportant information after the soft interrogation, and he then carried out the 'special task'. Although the detail had departed at 2200, they were still not back by 0450. Gebauer said, 'I received the report from NOIC at 0945 that the shooting had been carried out at 0300 on 11 December.'

One of the last remarks from Bachmann in his war diary is, 'The operation was particularly favoured by the weather conditions and the dark night.' A notation was made in green pencil saying, 'Security Service should have done this. Phone F.O.I.C. in future cases.'

It was concluded that 'as the execution of saboteurs is a matter for the Security Service (Gestapo), it is ordered that in future cases delinquents are to be handed over to the Security Service to be shot'.

These two Royal Marines had been told they were going to be executed in the early afternoon of 10 December. They had awaited their death, each in their own prison cell, for some eight hours before they were bound and taken by the SD into the night air and bundled into a car. Then the journey was halted and they waited at least half an hour for their chief executioner with the odious SD guards sat beside them.

In all, these men had been kept bound for five long hours in transit before they were shot. At least our two marines were not separated any longer but sat together, the elder man offering the moral support to the younger marine. Sergeant Samuel Wallace and Marine Robert Ewart suffered an undeserved mental torture and a death that should never have been.

German officers at FOIC HQ, having looked through the interrogation reports, had found that these 'had been carried out most ineptly'. In other words, not enough information had been extracted due to the ease of the interrogation method used.

At the time of this execution, Hasler, Sparks, Laver and Mills were among the reeds awaiting their time to attack the shipping at Bordeaux. Sgt Wallace and Ewart would not have known about the delay in the plan of attack. They must have hoped the mission had already been successful. They no doubt died believing it was. Given the character of the senior man, it is very likely that Sgt Wallace would have reassured Robert Ewart with uplifting words even to the end; the true blue Royal Marine. It is very likely that Ewart's last thoughts would have been for his sweetheart in Southsea, the teenager Heather Powell.[37]

The Bordeaux Case

Some readers are bound to question what happened to those Germans that were part of the deeds mentioned. It is neither the purpose nor appropriate for the author to relate the fate of those Germans wrapped up in this indictable War Crime. Suffice it to say that the work of the Allied forces to bring to justice those responsible for the crimes against humanity began well before Germany's formal surrender on 7 May 1945.

It should be noted, however, that it was easy to show how evil the regime was, but individual evidencing was far more difficult. Certain decisions had to be made on the basis of likelihood of a successful conviction, no different from in today's society. At the Nuremberg Tribunal, the British Assistant Prosecutor, Mr G. D. Roberts, quoted from an official German report when he introduced the list of British soldiers, sailors and marines shot under the 'Führer Order'. He said, 'This is cold-blooded murder of brave men.'

The narrative of the 'The Bordeaux Case' is largely taken from the investigation by Major E. A. Barkworth of the SAS War Crimes Investigation Team and deals with the information to do with the German decision making. It is worthwhile relating in order for the reader to be appraised of the inner workings of the Nazi regime. Some of the information shown has already been dealt with in the detail of the main narrative. This only concerns the lives of the two individuals mentioned who were terminated under Hitler's '*Kommandobefehl*'.

Following their swim ashore at Pointe de Grave, Wallace and Ewart were handed over to the harbour control unit at Royan, and Vice-Admiral Johannes Bachmann[38], who was at the HQ of SNOIS Gascony in Royan, was informed on 8 December. Bachmann gave orders to the Counter Intelligence Section in Bordeaux (CIS/B) to interrogate the two prisoners. The CIS, having its own chain of command, at first refused to comply with the order on the basis that the two men were shipwrecked sailors and that no interrogation was allowed before they arrived at the Naval POW camp at Fallingbostel. With some justification, Bachmann insisted CIS carried out his orders. Lt-Cdr Harstick[39] of CIS/B reported to Bachmann in Le Verdon. Bachmann mentioned points on which he wished the prisoners to be interrogated and informed Harstick that, when the interrogation was over, he would give order for the two prisoners to be shot, should the suspicion that they were engaged on sabotage be confirmed. The Vice-Admiral's war diary shows that he telephoned Admiral Marschall, C-in-C Navy Group West, at 1730 and informed him of the incident with the call being confirmed by a signal which Bachmann sent off at 2015; the signal was drafted by Bachmann's artillery officer (A2) Hortschansky then corrected by Bachmann before he signed it. The signal read, 'I have ordered immediate execution at conclusion of interrogation (if present facts confirmed) on account of attempted sabotage.'

Received, presumably, by the staff officer on duty in the operations office, it is recorded that some 'understandable flap' was in evidence from the senior commanders: Admiral Wilhelm Marschall[40], Admiral Wilhelm Meisel[41], Captain Bernhard Viehweger[42] and Capt. Henno Lucan[43], and Commander Hans Joachim Lange[44]. This was no doubt due to the level of importance the safety of the blockade runners held.

Commander Lange's own statement shows that he requested Marschall to telephone WFSt, the Armed Forces Operational Staff, a part of the Führer's HQ, to endeavour to obtain at least a postponement of the execution of the two prisoners. With Marschall unwilling to make the call himself, it was left to Meisel to telephone. With both the Chief of Staff and Deputy, General Alfred Jodl and General Walter Warlimont[45], at the cinema with Hitler, it was Col. Werner Von Tippelskirch[46] who answered the call with 'a cold-blooded attitude'. The result of the conversation was that Tippelskirch ordered that the prisoners should be interrogated as soon as possible using any method before they were shot.

The Navy Group West officers now did three things. Lange telephoned a Captain Pheiffer[47] of Counter Intelligence HQ in Paris and asked if his organisation had any good methods of extorting confessions such as laughing pills, light projectors, or by any kind of drugs which would make a man ready to confess. Lange was somewhat rebuked by Pheiffer, who in no uncertain terms told Lange that they did not possess these drugs, and even if they had, they should not use them.

Next a signal was sent to Bachmann's HQ in Nantes, thus showing that the intention to shoot the prisoners had been accepted, saying that they should, 'with no methods barred, also using the subterfuge of sparing their lives and assurance of good treatment try to obtain before execution following information of operational importance'.

The third step taken by Marschall's HQ was to make a report to the SKL (the Naval Operations Staff of the German Admiralty). Bachmann's war diary reads, 'Group West orders interrogation of prisoners … postponement of the execution until interrogation finished. The two prisoners were handed over to the SD in Bordeaux. Accomplishment to be reported to Navy Group West and to Admiralty by 1100 – 10 December 1942.' The word 'accomplishment' means the carrying out of the commando order.

At 1820 on 10 December, the SD Bordeaux had applied for three days' grace to the WFSt. Later that evening (SS Stubaf.) Commander Dr Luther of SD Bordeaux first telephoned to his HQ Company of the NOIC Bordeaux and demanded an execution squad and then again to Lt Theodor Prahm[48], the Adjutant of the NOIC.

It is recorded that the execution of Sgt Samuel Wallace and Marine Robert Ewart was carried out in a sandpit outside Bordeaux. The naval detail, under the orders of Bachmann, consisted of Prahm, one PO and sixteen ratings. In addition, Dr Luther of the SD and certain other men of his unit were present. The bodies were placed in coffins and, according to a report from the Red Cross, were later buried 'in the POW cemetery in Bordeaux'. It is believed that another officer, SS Ostuf. Friedrich Wilhelm Dohse, who was Head of Section 4 (officer i/c) of the SD in Bordeaux, also by virtue of his appointment and character, was probably connected with the arrangements for the execution.

Bachmann was the author of the order pursuant to the Commando Order but the killing of these two men was ensured and hastened by the direct order of Warlimont and Tippelskirch. Admiral Marschall and certain members of his staff accepted Bachmann's intention of shooting the prisoners of war and, on receipt of instructions from Warlimont and Tippelskirch, passed the orders to Bachmann on what to do before the prisoners were shot. Tippelskirch raised, and Marschall's staff elaborated on, the suggestion that 'no methods should be barred in interrogating the prisoners'.

Lt-Col. Nightingale subsequently traced all the members of the raiding party up to the time of their death and had established that no such POW cemetery existed, and it was suggested that the bodies may have been buried in the German military cemetery, also in Bordeaux.

The conclusion reached by the investigative authority is worth reporting. This was viewed as a classic example of the working of the Commando Order and gives the full picture from the Führer, surrounded by his staff of cynical toadies, down through the various formations to the simple and obedient members of the execution squad.

> The contemplation of a crime of violence is often less sickening than the dissection of the moral attitude that inspired it. Here, then we are faced with the spectacle of Senior Staff Officers, some of them gently born and bred as Christians, without the moral courage to stand up to the Führer's vicious and sadistic bombast. Or even taking the way out, so easy in the German army, of requesting a posting to a combatant unit, bullying lower formations in a servile imitation of their Master's manner, refusing to listen to the protests of humanity, conscience or reason and exerting all weight of their authority and position to extort the immediate execution of prisoners, captured in war. A peculiar exoneration might be sought in the light-hearted partiality of higher formations for rapid and frequent returns to any paper investment they make. Nothing can excuse the keenness with which certain individuals expended time and energy (for which they might have found more profitable application) in pestering lower formations, until they were able to present themselves before their Führer for a pat on the back, with the satisfactory sensation of

a job well done; for, after all, if killing there had to be, it was done by others, less well connected, probably less religious and not upon the Staff. They themselves had no share in the dirty work. They only used the Staff Officer's weapon; they only murdered by telephone.

This is just one of the many war crimes perpetrated by the Nazi regime against the legitimate soldiers of the day and as such helps the reader to fully comprehend and help highlight the many other unreported incidents that were a product of this Commando Order.

It has been stated elsewhere as undoubted fact that Sgt Wallace and Mne Ewart were imprisoned and/or executed at the bunker in the grounds of Château Magnol in Blanquefort – this is simply untrue; they never set foot there. Despite a French website stating that the chateau was the place of execution, it should be noted, lest the reader be misled, that the bullet holes, still evident in the cemented end of the bunker, have no association with either man[49] as has been claimed. The château, even though on the *Frankton* trail, has no connection with these two marines bar that of any remembrance.

'The *Sicherheitsdienst*'

A/Ty. Cpl. Albert Friedrich Laver, Marine William Henri Mills and '*Crayfish*'

This is the first ever detailed narrative of the four Royal Marines that were intercepted by a betrayal and taken into the clutches of the *Sicherheitsdienst* (SD).[50]

Corporal Albert Friedrich Laver and Marine William Henri Mills piloted *Crayfish* and delivered their cargo of Limpets to the shipping at Bassens. They had accidentally met up with *Catfish*, parted company for the independent escape and subsequently disappeared into the reeds along the riverbank on 12 December 1942. Hasler's last placing for them was 'seen landing about 2 miles N.W. of Blaye at 0700 … in good shape and all set to make their way by land independently to the Ruffec district near Angouleme.' (Sparks and Hasler moved along much the same route having to take evasive action to avoid arrest.)

The escape briefing given by MI9 included the following: 'When starting on the overland escape, get well clear of the river (say ten miles), moving by night and in uniform. Then try to contact friendly farmers or peasants, borrow civilian clothes, hide uniform and weapons, and proceed by day.'

Due to the receding tide, Laver and Mills waded almost waist deep in the sticky soft silt and then unloaded bags Nos 4 and 5 (containing the spare clothes, boots and the escape equipment for both men, maps of the locale, the remaining two days' compact rations and half a gallon of fresh water). Laver crawled back to *Crayfish* in order to scuttle her. The canoe was pushed into the stream of the river half-submerged. Despite the effort, involving the slicing of a knife through the faithful Cockle to puncture the flotation bags, this well-constructed craft never completely sank. The Germans subsequently found and recovered canoe *Crayfish*.

Laver and Mills assessed their situation ashore; all the training came into play. This was the point to all their training; the ability to use your own initiative and wits. Their next task was to find a hideout before the next dawn and make good the escape plan. The thin-soled waders had provided some respite from the mud but they were still caked in it. They ditched their gym shoes and waders. Donning the soft-soled boots, they felt lighter. After not having walked any distance for very many days, the sensation was odd and somewhat painful. Dawn was soon to be on them.

An interview during March 2004[51] shines new light onto the beginning of the escape route for Laver and Mills. We know from Hasler that the *Crayfish* crew had been 'seen landing about 2 miles N.W. of Blaye at 0700 and they were heading in a north-east direction'. As her name suggests, 'with dignity', Madame Solange Gacis wrote a heartfelt letter, in 2002, to her two children and grandchildren. In essence, this was to apologise for accusing her children of an act of thievery during 1942. With great pride, she also explained to them how her husband Pierre Gacis had, unbeknown to her, sought to protect his wife and children from death through deportation.

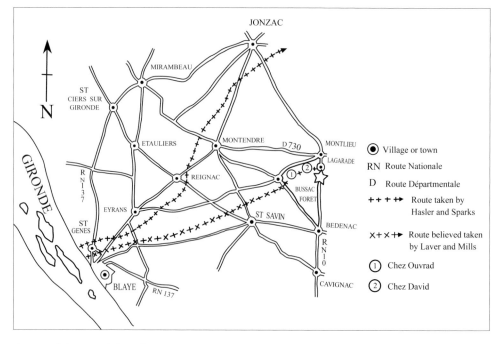

A map of the route believed to have been taken by Laver and Mills. The star shows the point at which the two men were stopped and handed over to the Germans.

It has to be remembered that this was occupied France, and if anything was seen that was in any way connected with the potential interference of the German forces, it was kept close to heart. For the most part, France, and the rest of the continent, was 'pregnant with fear'. So it was that Pierre Gacis had kept a secret until after the liberation of that region, and even then, Pierre had only told her that he had helped some British soldiers during the war. He still failed to tell her about the Cabane and the gift of the rabbit pie he made the soldiers! It was not until she read a newspaper article that told of some British military equipment that had been dug up in the 'Cabane Fumebas' that she made the connection between the soldiers and the missing rabbit pie. This in turn prompted her apology to her children, whom she had severely scolded in 1942, via letter. She was of course extremely proud to tell her family of their father's heroism and kindness to two unknown foreigners.

Laver and Mills had landed near some fishing cabins that perch out into the Gironde via short pier-like structures; small sheds on stilts. By the time they had kitted up, it was well past 0730. Laver and Mills had taken a reading with one of the tiny luminous compasses they had been issued with and started on their journey using the nearby tracks. From the flood plane area, they slipped over a main route, now the D255, and across the cultivated land – the daylight was imminent. They needed cover until darkness returned on 12 December. They chose a very small hut seemingly in the depth of the countryside. It was a tiny space, no bigger than an old tool shed – for that is exactly what 'Cabane Fumebas' was!

A young man by the name of Olivier Bernard was out in the 'wild places' hunting with his catapult, not far inland from the River Gironde. Nosing around the structure, he stumbled upon the two 'intruders' inside. The two marines managed to indicate their need for food and the fact they would do no harm to the young man. Bernard walked back to the village of Fours and reported his meeting with our two 'cockle pilots' to a true patriot, Monsieur Pierre Gacis. What his wife, Madame Solange Gacis, did not know was that her quite wonderful husband had taken the pre-prepared rabbit pie from their pantry, which had been made to feed the whole family, and delivered it to our two tool shed hideouts without telling his wife anything about the affair. Pierre's reasoning being that what they did not know they could not speak of;

thus the secret was kept to protect the family. At the time, Solange had been convinced that the children had taken it and dealt with them appropriately. With the realisation of the great care and love shown by her husband, she was able to tell the story even to her grandchildren. For that single act by Pierre, they all could have been deported and that could have ended in death. Just another brave act of defiance. It is mentioned now, and will be mentioned again, there was fear, fear of not knowing who was friend and who was enemy, even within a small village.

Now well fed, our pair of intrepid marines launched out into the night air of 12 December having rested their unexercised legs. Soon, they were striding at the 'Southsea Stroll'[52] rate, imagining themselves back with 'Stripey' Wallace on the Southsea Esplanade; this soon infused warmth within mind and body. Their route now took them north-east crossing the main arterial route that is now the A10 somewhere between Reignac and Saint-Savin through an uninhabited wooded area, hiding up during the day of 13 December. On the night of the 13th, it was Laver's decision to continue on in a north-easterly direction, heading across the route now known as N10, ghosting the road to their left. So far, they had avoided farms and contact with the local populace. It is guessed that their route took them between Collardeau and Fradon using the tracks within the vales and wooded areas. In due course, they came across an isolated small dwelling.

It showed no signs of life and its door was unlocked. Laver and Mills entered the building and searched the larder cupboard for food. To their delight, they found a small amount of stale bread, cold meat, milk and some wine. Eagerly devouring the food and wine, the pair rested before leaving the property with the morning light intending to find another hideout elsewhere. They had not secured any change of clothing as they tracked over the uninhabited countryside; this would be their downfall. As they walked, unbeknown to the pair, they were being viewed by two farmworkers.

The following is only available due to information that was furnished in spring of 2000[53] from one Raymond Furet, a teenager in 1942. His testimony gives us the link mentioned above. He related,

> The farm is situated in the commune of Orignolles and is called Chez Ouvrard; I inherited it. It used to belong to my parents, who lived in the neighbouring hamlet of Clérac. At that time I was fourteen years old. Because I didn't want to stay on at school, my parents punished me by forcing me to take care of the land at Chez Ouvrard. So I used to go there every morning at eight until nightfall. The house was left unoccupied at night, with the door unlocked. On that morning I was surprised to find that the larder cupboard was empty and that whoever had been there had eaten and drunk the contents. There was seldom anyone around that isolated spot. But whoever they were had left on the table a note on a piece of paper, written in English.

This was a thank-you note from Laver, something he perhaps should never have done, but without which the time before their arrest would never have been known of. Raymond had shown it to his father. He related, 'My father hurried to burn it, for fear of having problems with the Germans.'

The next positive evidence is given in a deposition by a warrant officer of the Gendarmerie who commanded the Montlieu La Garde brigade in the Charente Maritime region. Warrant Officer Georges Rieupeyrout states that at about 1700 on 14 December[54] 1942, he was informed by a resident of the village of Chez-David[55], Monsieur Gagnerot, that 'two British parachutists he had just met on the road in the vicinity of his home had asked him for rest and shelter and that he had directed them into an abandoned house' saying that it would be safe for them during the night. Gagnerot, in order to ensure Rieupeyrout arrested the men, told him that he should 'do his duty'. In order to placate Gagnerot and hopefully avoid delivering the men to almost certain death, Georges Rieupeyrout's response was that he would 'do what was necessary when my staff come back from duty', telling Gagnerot to 'go home' and that, if he were required, he would be called for.

With that, Gendarme Georges Rieupeyrout 'immediately asked a civilian in the neighbourhood to go to the scene so as to request the parachutists to leave the spot before my arrival'. The civilian in question was a Monsieur Gaujean who duly cycled to the spot, but

Monsieur Gaujean failed in his quest to warn Laver and Mills, as he could not find them. In fact, the two Limpeteers had been given shelter at a farm named Chez David, which was just two kilometres from Chez Ouvrard; they had 'hidden themselves in a storage barn under a heap of hay' and, exhausted, had fallen asleep.

Georges Rieupeyrout had to be careful, as Gagnerot, 'a whole hearted collaborator, [was] in constant touch with his immediate superior', Grollier in Montlieu, the chief quisling of the RNP party[56], who was the instigator of various denunciations in that area. It should be noted that within Georges Rieupeyrout's statement (and confirmed elsewhere) is the fact that 'the denouncer Gagnerot, a member of RNP, a known collaborator, was arrested on the day of liberation and I took him along with some other suspects to the command post of the Maquis at Reignac where he was shot'.

Before Georges Rieupeyrout undertook any search for the marines, he noticed that Gagnerot 'was watching our movements'. No doubt the disinformation and the subsequent observation by Gagnerot was intended to find out whether any action would be taken as well as to ensure that the soldiers could not be surreptitiously warned. Gendarme Rieupeyrout went up to Gagnerot at that time: 'I asked him to tell me where the men were. He led me to the spot and in due course I came upon the British soldiers whom I requested to follow me, which they did immediately. On the way, these men, at my suggestion, got rid of the papers they were carrying.' Laver and Mills were taken back to the barracks of the Police Station at Montlieu where they were well fed and allowed to wash a little.

It was at this point that the escape map (1/25,000 scale) was found on Laver whilst he was being searched and, as it was thought to be a compromising document, it was taken by Georges Rieupeyrout and kept by him so that it did not pass into the hands of the Germans. This map was kept within Rieupeyrout's family papers and surfaced during the research for this book. The maps had been distributed to each team when on HMS *Tuna*. It shows the area that needed to be crossed. Marked on the map was the Demarcation Line, which was under German military control until May 1943. Warrant Officer Rieupeyrout now, reluctantly, informed his section commander Capt. Borie, at the Jonzac office, of the incident by telephone at 2230. Borie then informed the German Feldgendarmarie (Security Police) of the fact that 'two Englishmen were in custody'. Marine William Henri Mills now spent all of his twenty-first birthday imprisoned and being questioned at the Montlieu La Garde Gendarmerie in occupied France.

From an interview in May 2000, we have another report of the day's incident from a twenty-five-year-old man by the name of Jules Bergeon[57], who had heard from his father, via the barber, that two British soldiers that had 'probably escaped from a prison camp' had been arrested by Georges Rieupeyrout. Jules thought to take a look by walking past the front of the police station. With the main door open, Jules saw 'two men standing in the main entrance bare headed with Khaki shirts and trousers' appearing to be slightly older than he was. Jules heard some of the bystanders express a satisfaction, not held by him, to the effect that these Englishmen were in the hands of the police. Between Gendarme Rieupeyrout's telephone call and a detachment of Feldgendarmarie arriving at midnight to pick up the prisoners, Rieupeyrout, through an interpreter, was allegedly fed some fantastic information that seems quite incredible given the circumstances. If we are to believe the following, Laver and Mills must have trusted Rieupeyrout implicitly to relay this, which is also recorded within the gendarme's report post war. 'The men [Laver and Mills] stated that they had been dropped in the area four days before, i.e. on Monday evening, and that they had to find a group of comrades at the said place Chez David.' Georges Rieupeyrout goes on to relate, 'Indeed, the next day I found out that about one hundred metres from the place where these two men had been met by Gagnerot there was an officer and three men equipped with a wireless set and explosives. The party stayed for four or five days in the woods where they were fed by a civilian.'[58]

The only linked evidence to secure this report of other English soldiers is the following report No. 1-594/2 of 20 December 1942 from Division Chief Joliot[59], stating that the commander of the Charente Maritime Division sent a telephone message on 14 December 1942 at 1500 which read, 'The interrogation of two English soldiers arrested at Montlieu in Charente Maritime has revealed that there are other English soldiers in the region. The soldiers arrested were in uniform and armed. Please continue the search for others. This message has also been transmitted to departmental commanders ... The German security police at Bordeaux as well as the Préfecture have been informed.'

Capt. Borie's then secretary, Gendarme Gibaud, also made a statement post-war in which he related how Borie accompanied the Feldgendarmarie from Jonzac to Montlieu (about twenty miles) and that Borie had 'boasted that he himself was glad to have disarmed the two men [Laver and Mills] and to have handed them over to the Germans'. Borie subsequently made a report denouncing Gibaud for his 'anti-German activities'. Gibaud was deported to Germany but on his return accused Borie of collaborating. It seems that once the prisoners had been taken out of Gendarme Rieupeyrout's custody he was unsure where they were taken but thought the destination was La Rochelle. Gendarme Gibaud actually states in his deposition that 'the Feldgendarmarie took the two men to La Rochelle the same night'[60], which is quite some distance from Bordeaux. This is especially surprising, as it can be evidenced that they were interrogated by[61] Lt Harstick at the GIS Station, Bordeaux, by at least 19 December. Here, the situation report reveals that 'a marine states [that the] previous statement that they landed on 14.12.42 was false. They landed on 8.12.42 with the commando which had laid mines in Bordeaux. Harstick also gives away the fact that 'both stated at the interrogation at Saintes that they had buried their charts. This is obviously untrue. It will be ascertained where the charts are.'

It seems very likely that Laver and Mills were not taken to La Rochelle given the distance involved and, perhaps, were taken to Jonzac, to stay at the section office overnight, before the evidenced stay and initial interrogation at Saintes, then brought all the way back to Bordeaux by 19 December.

There can, however, be no confusion of the validity and identity of the two men taken prisoner at Montlieu La Garde, as they also gave their full names with their full postal addresses to Gendarme Rieupeyrout; he also confirms that 'they were dressed in full military uniform, with blouse bearing the words Royal Marine on the shoulder and two crossed rifles'. The uniform worn by each of the force during the escape consisted of rope-soled shoes or felt-soled boots, battle dress trousers, olive green and black camouflage waterproof jacket, with Royal Marine and Combined Operations badges sewn on each shoulder, web belt and holster, Colt .45 auto, fighting knife, Blue Balaclava, identity discs.

There is some additional information that is gleaned from further documents related to the interrogation of Laver and Mills once they were taken to Bordeaux; it has to be remembered that various sections within the Wehrmacht were themselves interested parties to the information they could impart. Laver and Mills were handed over to the *Sicherheitsdienst* (SD) when they arrived in Bordeaux. As soon as the SD had control of the marines, they set about the interrogation, but needed someone who could speak English; this is that officer's brief report.

According to Lt Franz Drey[62], who was the 'head of the port guard post of Bordeaux' (the harbour security office),

[Laver and Mills] were imprisoned in the Army prison[63] at Bordeaux. I remember it so clearly because I received a phone call in my office, I believe the SD, if English speaking officers were present at my office, who should interrogate the two English soldiers who participated in the sabotage act. I answered the question in the affirmative and went with Lt Gauteer to the Army prison. I met two English soldiers there in a room who wore combination uniform on which insignia of rank was shown on their arms. The two prisoners were bound. I refused an interrogation of the two soldiers with the reason not to carry it out as long as the soldiers were not freed from their bounds. I emphasised, furthermore, that in my opinion the security measures in the building hindered the possible escape of the prisoners. My request was granted.[64]

In the course of conversation with the English soldiers, of whom one was a Sergeant[65], as far as I know, I learnt by questioning that they were trained by a special unit, which was stationed in the Scottish Fjords, for this action. On my question, to tell me the place of the training, the soldier answered that I could not request him to do that in any way, as the German Air

Force would probably bomb this place a day after the place had been named. He could bring his own comrades into danger and as I am a soldier like him he believed that I would have an understanding for his refusal. I answered this in the affirmative. On being questioned by one of the English soldiers, if I was of the opinion, that they were to be looked upon as saboteurs and not soldiers I emphasised that I regarded them as soldiers by reason of their special uniform with rank insignia on their arms.

Drey related his findings to his superiors at HQ Atlantic Coast. Drey reports,

I was asked by a member of the SD about the interrogation results after the interrogation. He was especially interested in the place of the training. I gave him the answer of the English soldier together with my opinion. According to my knowledge the English soldiers were interrogated again by Rear Admiral (Korv. Kapt) Dr Krantz and Lt Corssen from the camp Westertimke at Bordeaux a few days later. Some time later … I learned that these soldiers were transferred further, I believe in the direction of Paris, but I do not know which authority. I heard later that these English soldiers had been shot.

In fact, Admiral Dr Krantz and Lt Corssen did not arrive until after Lt MacKinnon and Marine Conway had arrived. Laver and Mills were already in separate cells within the prison at Bordeaux.

Here we begin to understand the journey and the process that the men were taken through. It will also be remembered that the Sonderführer Heinz Corssen had originally been tasked to interrogate Wallace and Ewart but had been recalled then given a post at the HQ of FOIC in Paris. But, before Corssen and his Admiral had arrived, further interrogation was undertaken by Lt Harstick.

Marine Mills was still feeding some disinformation to Lt Harstick, as he reported that, due to the fact that his canoe was 'driven back by the current', it did not reach Bordeaux, so they laid mines on a large ship in Bassens. It seems that Laver also had sport with this interrogator at least. During the Laver and Mills interrogations, a great deal of time was used up relating quite inconsequential details such as his time serving on the battleship *Rodney* as a gunner, including an account of the engagement with the *Bismarck* which was lapped up by the German Naval officers. As Wallace and Ewart had already told the interrogators about the training of the outfit and goal of the mission in the UK, Mills' account yielded nothing new. Probably, in a further attempt to send any searchers in the wrong direction and to ensure the focus was away from Ruffec, for the sake of the Resistance and his colleagues, it is known that Laver told his interrogators that the route intended was to make for Spain where they would make contact with someone in the British Consulate in Bilbao. Eventually, most of Operation *Frankton* was given up along with other 'home' details. Even the name of (Norman) Colley was noted down as the reserve. (Norman had no idea his name had reached the bowels of the Security Services until the author informed him of this fact!)

A/Ty Cpl Corporal Albert Friedrich Laver and Marine William Henri Mills had started their escape at Blaye travelling by night, using a compass, in a north-east direction, crossing two main routes, and made their way as far as Chez Ouvrard only to be informed on by an unkind and sour-hearted individual. They were then taken to Montlieu La Garde, then to Jonzac, then Saintes and, finally, back to Bordeaux, where it is now believed that they ultimately met their end – but at least along with their comrades in arms.

The date of their execution was alleged to have been 23 March in Paris but given the precedent set with Wallace and Ewart together with the information as shown within MacKinnon and Conway's last days, this seems very uncertain and the alternative reasoning is given.

Lt John Withers MacKinnon, Marine James Conway and *Cuttlefish*

Following the third tidal race and with only three cockle canoes remaining in formation, *Catfish*, *Crayfish* and *Cuttlefish* all rafted up prior to making the open passage past Le Verdon jetty. The intent was for each canoe to slip the distance individually with MacKinnon and Conway bringing up the rear in *Cuttlefish*. For some reason, they did not show, even though a good amount of time was spent waiting for them with the mew cry of a gull used. Hasler made the decision to proceed without them, and *Catfish* and *Crayfish* made their way up to the first lying-up point before daybreak on 8 December.

After that loss of contact, there is no real measured route which tells us exactly what happened to the to canoeists in *Cuttlefish*. However, two incidents many years apart have helped to add to the likely scenario of our *Cuttlefish* pilots just before the beginning of the escape. In 2001, Bill Sparks attended commemorations at Blanquefort[66]. It was during this time that a Frenchman approached Sparks and said, 'I am happy to meet you after so many years, in memory of the fright you gave my father and me fifty years ago.' It transpired that this gentleman had definitely seen two commandos at that precise period in 1942 on the river, but given the timing and situation it cannot possibly have been the crew of either *Catfish* or *Crayfish* as, if nothing else, they had not set off until 2330 when the flood stream began to run.

Further investigation brought the second part of the story. The Frenchman's name was Jean Raymond, and during the night of 8 December at about 2200, Jean and his father were illegally fishing near the shore of Fort-Médoc. This night-fishing had been forbidden by the Germans. From their boat, the two were fishing with a net about ten metres long, which was hung straight down in the river. This net fishing is typical of that carried out today from the pier structures that periodically are found along the Gironde. It was Jean who had first heard the unidentified noise disturbing that night's silence. The noise increased in its volume together with the sound of low bass tone of hushed voices talking in a foreign language. Jean's father, thinking it was a German patrol, said to Jean, 'Lie down in the boat and they'll pass without seeing us.' Fearing being caught, they lay motionless as a single canoe paddled past them without noticing that the incumbents were being watched just twenty metres away.

Given the series of events, it can only have been MacKinnon and Conway in *Cuttlefish*, who then must have crossed the channel between the Île Fort-Paté and Île Verte to reach Île Cazeau and unknowingly spent the daylight hours of 9 December on the same island as the other two canoe crews, nearer to Bordeaux. It is not entirely clear what happened to *Cuttlefish*, but a little light can be shed by delving into the German archives and that of the files taken from the war crimes investigation. Some of the information given over by the marines is believed to contain either errors or disinformation, but it is included. It is assumed that information given to the Germans on the whole was correct. Events from 15 December, due to corroborative statements, are believed to be accurate.

MacKinnon and Conway had spent the night on the Isle of Cazeau. We know that *Cuttlefish* was further up the river than the other two canoes. We also know that neither group knew of the other's position. It can be assumed that MacKinnon had decided to launch earlier. He may have awaited the favourable tide and then pressed on. After leaving their hide-up and before being able to proceed to the destination of the targeted area, *Cuttlefish* was at the point where the Garonne and Dordogne join at the Bec d'Ambès. It is believed that it was then that *Cuttlefish* hit an obstacle and holed its thin, flat ⅛-inch plywood bottom. It is further believed that it was through this that MacKinnon sustained a slight injury, possibly in the form of a splinter to the back of the knee, resulting in the boil talked of later. They were eventually beached at about 2100 on the east side of the Island of Cazeau off Bec d'Ambès.

According to other details in the German interrogation documents, MacKinnon had refused to say anything, so it is from Conway that the following information was derived by the interrogators, who reported, 'They were forced to leave the boat as well as the explosives and its entire equipment with the exception of the bag containing money, iron rations and maps [escape box].' MacKinnon managed to swim back but Conway 'had become entangled with the bag attached to the lower leg of his trousers and the canoe as the canoe was sinking in the very strong current. Conway 'had to struggle to free himself because the pocket on the lower leg of his trousers had caught in the canoe.' MacKinnon lost sight of him. Apparently they were reunited at the village of Margaux.

Conway had told his interrogators that they 'swam back to the Isle of Cazeau and were picked up by a fisherman and rowed to the western bank of the Garonne where they had received assistance at Margaux'. It is unsure whether this assistance from the fisherman was during the day or night or if it did happen at all; if the night, it would have been another 'illegal' fishing event. Conway had then told his interrogators that they had walked for three days, sleeping in the open on the first night and in a barn the second night 'before reaching La Reole'. This assistance at Margeaux is doubted, as Conway is reported to have told the interrogator that 'according to the instructions received aboard the submarine [Margeaux] was the one where they would receive help'. Given what is known of the planning, this Margeaux story has to be a ruse and the Germans thought the same, but for a different reason, as the interrogator wrote, 'GIS substation will make investigations in this village' and that someone had 'evidence that the Marine is trying to conceal the actual name of the village to spare the French people'. The interrogator came to the conclusion, 'Since Conway states that they were taken over the Demarcation Line by a Frenchman, the whole story of the route to the Demarcation Line and the village of Margeaux is improbable.' Although not mentioned, the Germans could have thought that the village in question was that of Macau.

From the various documents and depositions, it is possible to begin to understand certain aspects of their escape route. We do know that when they were arrested, according to the German reports, at least Marine Conway 'was wearing very light canvas shoes which showed no signs of hardship'. This description of the footwear matches the same footwear provided in the escape set. Given the distance travelled, the same thought prevails, as it did for the German interrogators when they said, 'Presumably the two Englishmen received civilian clothes and help at an early date and reached the point at which they crossed the demarcation line by train or in a car'. The Germans determined that the point at which the Demarcation Line was crossed 'must lie in the vicinity of Lagnon'. These assumptions were all made without the knowledge that is provided below.

The exact route that was taken is unknown, but it seems as if they somehow managed to either get assistance via road, which took them to the west of Bordeaux, or, given their next appearance, were delivered via the river network. Their first contact is known to have been in the village of Saint-Médard-d'Eyrans. It is possible at this point MacKinnon and Conway had decided to separate but headed in the same direction; this could be because MacKinnon's knee was preventing him from making as effective progress as Conway. Towards the end of the day on 13 December, MacKinnon was 'sitting on a pile of rubble by the roadside' and saw a young girl passing, herding her cows, and decided to speak to her using what little French he knew. The young girl in charge of the animals was Anne-Marie Bernadet[67], who understood that the man needed help. In the full knowledge of the consequences, MacKinnon was warmly welcomed by all those at the farm she lived at. They gave him food and allowed him to sleep in the barn amongst the hay. He was also treated by them for 'blisters and wounds' on his leg and knee. Before he bedded down for the night, MacKinnon had asked about a way he could cross the Gironde at Langoiran and had showed the hosts his escape map that he produced from his bag. He apparently told them that he had a contact on the other side of the river. If this is taken as true, this would indicate that the pair were assisted after they had got to dry land and to such an extent that they had been transported as far as it was possible in the direction of Saint-Médard-d'Eyrans. They were then given details of a contact at Langoiran by whoever had assisted in the arranging of the transportation. This transportation seems likely, given the lack of wear on their footwear when arrested and the fact that MacKinnon was not as advanced in the ailment department as he would have been if he had walked all that distance.

Meanwhile, Conway was noticed wandering in the village early the next day and was linked with MacKinnon due to the fact that he was also wearing an identical shoulder bag and blue naval-pattern pullover. It seems that the two were reunited care of the locals, as it is reported that both escapees left the village of Saint-Médard-d'Eyrans on the morning of 14 December and were en route to Langoiran. It is possible, given that the crossing over the river to Langoiran would have been well guarded, that the pair managed to cross the river by boat, but this is only speculation. Regardless, the next known and evidenced place of arrival is the village of Baigneaux on the evening of 14 December.

Le Pot de Confiture

We can evidence from witness statements taken in 1945 that the route taken by Lt John Withers MacKinnon and Marine James Conway was not that thought or known of by the Germans. It is also important to note that, through the study of these documents, we also learn that the Royal Marines ensured that not only did they keep the identity of the French individuals from the Germans, through every interrogation method, but they also kept their French hosts from knowing who had helped them previously.

The anecdote below was verified by a resident of Baigneaux named Monsieur Delorge-Guilhon and added to with the memories of Claudie Delorge-Guilhon.[68] Whilst it is true to say a few people in the village knew of the incident with the two soldiers, no one spoke about it. It is also true to say that it was many years before anyone knew the connection between the kindness shown to the two Englishmen and the 'Cockleshell Heroes'. This connection only came about by 'unexpected chance'. The first reported contact is from a twenty-nine-year-old Baigneaux resident at the time named Edouard Pariente[69]. Edouard is reported to have been a stonemason, was married to Felicie and had two young children; he had just finished working at the local quarry for the day. Everyone working there was also heading homeward just as darkness was approaching; the busy streets were draining of its populace. Conway was in the short lane that descends to the centre of the village between the school and the church. Edouard was also near the church in the main street when he saw a good-looking, well-dressed man in neat civilian clothing who was looking a little anxious. He thought that he had just got of the recently arrived bus. Pariente was approached by this younger man, who proceeded to speak in a foreign language that was not understood. Fortunately, Edouard did manage to understand one of the words that this young man in front of him began to repeat at the same time as he pointed to himself – 'English'. Post-war, Edouard had revealed[70], "He comes up to me and starts chattering in a language which has no resemblance to French. I finally understand that he's an Englishman and wants to cross the Demarcation Line (a line which separates the zone occupied by the Germans from the zone called 'Free', which passes through Sauveterre).' As Pariente could not understand English, he must have discerned this from someone else.

In this small village, on the road from Bordeaux to Sauveterre-de-Guyenne, it became apparent to Edouard that he was in the presence of an escaped British soldier. Edouard was himself a 'foreigner' who had emigrated with his parents to France in 1926. He, like most of the French people, had the same natural instinct and wanted to help this man. Edouard was a poor man and his humble abode was just that; it was simply too small a place to offer any kind of refuge to this soldier, let alone the other escapee that Edouard did not know about. His words describe his situation better than the author can when he explains, 'My house is very small; we sleep four to the same room, and yet I can't abandon this man who has certainly come here to help rid us of the occupiers. It is night and there is danger everywhere and we can't just leave him to anyone.' Edouard refused to leave Conway in the street to a fate unknown and his thoughts turned to the one person he knew that spoke English; a notary named Guilhon.

On that evening, Edouard knocked on his next-door neighbour's door. It was answered by a young boy, Jacques, who was but nine years old. He looked up at the familiar face of Edouard, who was accompanied by a stranger. Unfortunately, the lawyer Guilhon was not at home. Within the house was a pregnant Madame Guilhon with Philippe, her nine-month-old baby, an eighty-four-year-old Uncle Jules, her eight-year-old daughter Claudie and the aforementioned nine-year-old Jacques.

Given the circumstances, and the thought to preserve her children from the perceived threat of the presence of 'a German spy sent to test our political opinions', Madame Guilhon understandably refused to let the fugitive in. Again, Edouard found himself alone on the street with this stranger and the night was drawing in. Edouard recalled his actual thoughts at that time: 'How about if I asked Pouget to take him in? There are three bedrooms in his house and he's just back from two years as a prisoner in Germany,[71] so he can't love them too much. He doesn't miss a chance to profit from them, black market, and all sorts of trafficking.' So it was that Edouard knocked on the door of his workmate and neighbour.

Robert Pouget lived with his wife Cecile at 'Chez Loulou'. He, without a moment's hesitation, agreed to accommodate this high-risk visitor right away and is reported to have said to Edouard, 'I'll feed him and bed him down – I'll take care of it.' (Given Pouget's known penchant for making a profit, it may well be that money exchanged hands for this 'favour', given the known amounts of money carried and that which remained upon capture. It would seem only fair – Pouget, after all, had risked his life.) It is believed that Edouard returned to his home once he had been sure of securing a place for his Englishman. It was not until many years later that Edouard would know of the events he was party to.

At some stage, Marine Conway collected Lt MacKinnon from the nearby hiding place, for it is known that Monsieur Pouget is recorded as noticing that Lt MacKinnon had problems walking; Pouget noted that he was dragging one leg. Whilst the two commandos had taken turns in establishing contact, no doubt the pain that MacKinnon was suffering from prompted the decision for Conway's action at this village. A man dragging his leg might attract unwanted attention. That night, they were given food and a haven by a Frenchman who was willing to risk all for these unknown warriors. The morning and the afternoon of Wednesday 15 December passed with MacKinnon and Conway secure under the roof of true patriots. Following another workday at the quarry, it had been possible to secure a courier in the form of yet another brave soul and workmate at the quarry. Monsieur Cheyreau volunteered his life to take MacKinnon and Conway to yet more kind French people.

Monsieur Cheyreau[72] was entrusted with the precious cargo, and they were led along a disused railway track that led to a tenanted property just off the line, the small farm of just a few acres in Seguin, near the village of Cessac. Spotting the three from his window as they walked along the line, Shepherd Jaubert came out and greeted them and was told who the men were. Jaubert is recorded to have said post-war, 'From the window of our little house we saw our neighbour approaching along the railway track. He was followed by two unknown men. Monsieur Cheyreau told us they were two Englishmen who came from Bordeaux.' Louis and Louise were true blue patriots, no doubt abetted by the fact that they had a son who had been in the army and who had been evacuated from Dunkirk. Their son had been well treated in England and had written to them of this before he had been taken prisoner when he was repatriated. This was not a family of wealth but one that had great courage and love for what was right. Madame Jaubert was 'in loco parentis' for the two marines and tended well the ailing officer's knee joint, which had become infected with an abscess. It is believed that the skill they held with the ailments of sheep assisted in tending to MacKinnon's joint.

Despite his acute need for the proper medical treatment, MacKinnon decided that he could not put in jeopardy these good people any longer. It is believed that Jaubert, Cheyreau, MacKinnon and Conway went to two cafés in Frontenac in an attempt to make contact with someone from any underground organisation; it does seem that the two marines were less cautious in the security department than was good for them. It also had proved impossible for Monsieur Jaubert to make any type of contact with the Resistance network at La Réole, but it was not going to stop the two soldiers from getting there. 'Mac' asked Jaubert if he could find out the cost of the train fare to Toulouse. They had been well looked after and had fed well on mutton of all recipes during the three-evening stay at the Jauberts' farm; to the marines, this was a five-star hotel. It is believed that MacKinnon and Conway left the Jauberts in the early hours of 18 December with a third unidentified 'friend', who guided them along the circuitous fifteen-mile route and over the Demarcation Line to La Réole. Louis and Louise offered the marines what little money they had but with grateful thanks MacKinnon explained that they had sufficient. It is known that at the Juaberts 'Mac' had 1,000 francs remaining;[73] when he was arrested at La Réole he only had 600 francs. It is believed that money was given to the guide that took them over the Demarcation Line; either just 400 or an additional amount from Conway's cache. 'Mac' had told Jaubert that they were heading for Bilbao. It is evident from the details below that thought had been given to getting some word back home via the Jauberts. This would ensure that this would not be the last time Monsieur Jaubert would be in contact with a MacKinnon[74]. (See the chapter, 'The French Affair')

During the three-day respite and care in the secluded surroundings of the farm, the marines had imparted quite a lot of information concerning the operation and other personal details. In a statement[75] taken from a forty-two-year-old[76] Louis Jaubert, he related that the marines arrived in civilian clothes ('navy blue serge suit and rubber soled shoes'[77]) and gave him their names and full home postal addresses[78]. He learnt from them that they had been assigned the task of 'blowing up some ships in the harbour of Bordeaux and had escaped from that town; that Marine Conway had passed through Targon and Lt MacKinnon through Baigneaux and that they had separated but 'had found each other again at Frontenac' by prior agreement before arriving at Cessac. At enormous risk to himself, the sheep farmer, Louis Jaubert, and his wife Louise, had given shelter and fed MacKinnon and Conway for three days and evenings from 15–17 December. Jaubert wrote in 1945 that 'we would have liked to have helped them [more] but that was not possible as we were in danger. We had Germans in the neighbourhood and the neighbours knew we had two Britishers. There were also a few bad Frenchmen so we were not able to help them. They wanted to rejoin their party at Bilboa in Spain'. The marines had been warmly received with much love and kindness, so much so that MacKinnon and Conway made a promise that they both would write, and one day they would visit them. Louis is quoted as saying, 'with tears in our eyes … we embraced them, they were such nice boys.' Lt MacKinnon thanked them as they parted saying that 'they were going to La Reole'. Monsieur Jaubert reported that he knew 'that they spent the night near Sauveterre where they passed the demarcation line' and that 'afterwards we heard rumours that they were supposed to have been arrested at La Reole'. It should be noted that it is believed the story of passage and mention of Frontenac given by the marines was deliberately falsified in order to protect those French people who had assisted.

According to statements made on the same day of the arrest, 18 December, the Adjutant-Chef[79] Jean Bernard Barbance and Gendarme Pierre Hennequin made the arrests of MacKinnon and Conway. This station office was the Langon section of the Gendarmerie at La Réole. The two marines were apparently 'coming from the occupied zone and proceeding in the direction of La Reole'. Barbance and Hennequin stopped them and requested to see their identity documents as a matter of course, given the circumstances. They were then arrested for their 'lack of identity documents'. The gendarmes 'immediately ascertained that these two persons were two foreigners of British origin'.

This seems to be at odds with another report from Hennequin, who relates in a post-war deposition that a 'Madame Olivier, seeing two apparently suspect persons through the window of her room in the section office in La Reole, immediately warned her husband, the Captain commanding the Gendarmerie in La Reole, whereupon he at once sent a gendarme to check their identity'.

It can be established that the timing of the sighting and subsequent arrest of MacKinnon and Conway was likely before daybreak, which would have been around 0830 at that time of year. It is suggested, given the timings below, that first sighting by Madame Olivier was somewhere between 0630 and 0730. Given the following information, it seems likely that the story to be believed should be that of the reported event with Mme Olivier.

Following the arrest, it was Gendarme Pierre Hennequin who questioned MacKinnon and Conway due to the fact that Hennequin had a good grasp of the English language. It should be noted that the first descriptive word used for the investigation was 'questioned'. This then is the reply by MacKinnon and Conway during the subsequent individual questioning which was completed by 1000 on 18 December 1942. Both the replies from the marines are related in full, as these are the last known quoted words from the pair. (From other testimony, it seems that Hennequin mistranslated the text to favour the marines.)

> My name is John MacKinnon. I am 21 years of age, born 15 July 1921 at Oban, Scotland, the son of James MacKinnon and Helen Withers. I am single. I am a lieutenant in the Navy. I am not in the regular service. I was a member of the British force which landed at Dieppe in September 1942. I was not afloat; I used to serve on shore duties. I was a volunteer for the Dieppe raid and was given a party of 30 men, all volunteers for this raid. We embarked on a boat that had no name. We landed at Dieppe, were in some street fighting, but were cut off from the harbour by the Germans. The ships then left and we were able to [dis]embark. Realising this we set off for the countryside, and since that time, with one of my men, we have been living from farm to farm in the country with the intention of getting to Spain. It is not possible for me to give you the names of the people who sheltered us.
>
> I left my uniform in the outskirts of Dieppe and the occupants of a farm gave me the civilian clothes which I am wearing at the moment. I have never been a prisoner of the Germans, as I was never caught. We had to fulfil a task in accordance with the plan confided to us. It was a question of destroying some factories. It was not possible for us to carry out this task and we duly abandoned the explosives we had been carrying with us. I am not in possession of any passport or any documentation authorising my stay in France.

Hennequin then explains,

> We informed MacKinnon that for contravention of Article 2 of the decree dated 2 May 1938, we were placing him under arrest and that he would be brought before the public prosecutor at La Reole. On being carefully searched he was found to be carrying the following effects and valuables: 1 pocket knife, Army pattern; 1 small metal saw 12 cm long; 1 compass; 1 watch; 1 Michelin map and 600 francs in French notes. He had a knapsack containing one pair of shoes; rectangular box containing some vitaminised iron ration tablets, a box containing some tablets for sterilizing water, a sweater and pair of stockings. He was relieved of these belongings and valuables, which will follow him to his destination.

When Lt MacKinnon was arrested, he was sporting a small moustache and dressed in black trousers, grey overcoat with a blue, naval-pattern pullover under and was wearing a beret, and shoes with yellow socks. It was also noted that MacKinnon had a slight limp of the [left] knee. The rest at the Jauberts seemed to have improved matters somewhat. It seems likely that following the questioning it was decided that medical attention should be sought which resulted in MacKinnon being admitted in the hospital either that night or according to the hospital records the following day of 19 December.

When Marine Conway was arrested, he was wearing grey trousers with a blue sailor's pullover, a grey overcoat, beret and sandal shoes. In his possession, it was found that he was carrying a greater sum of money than that of his lieutenant, namely the princely sum of 1,700 French francs[80]. He also had in his knapsack one electric lamp; a small metal saw, 12 cm long; a pocket knife, Army pattern; a rectangular box with 'iron tablets'; some meat, a piece of bread and *a pot of jam*. He was questioned, it is believed, by Barbance with Hennequin 'acting as interpreter'. Conway too gave the Dieppe story, and it is possible to note that the word 'interrogation' is now used in this statement taken. The report quotes the Marine as saying,

> My name is James Conway. I am twenty years old and was born on 28 August 1922 at Stockport, England, the son of Thomas Conway and Mary Felly. I am single. I am a marine and have no regiment or formation. I was under the orders of Lt MacKinnon at the time of the Dieppe expedition in September 1942. After having landed we were in some fighting. Our task was to destroy some factories. We were not able entirely to fulfil our task and on being cut off in the rear by the Germans we were unable to embark again. We then left the town where we had dumped our explosives and went into the country. We left behind our military clothing and the inhabitants

of the area gave us some civilian wear. We then lived in the country, but I cannot name the people who gave us shelter. It was our intention to go to Spain. I was not taken prisoner by the Germans. I am not in possession of any passport or any document authorising my stay in France.

A full physical description including that of the facial features of both men was also provided. Again, the effects and valuables were taken from him and accompanied him onto his destination, although the non-concentrated food stuffs did not. All documentation was distributed to the Public Prosecutor at La Réole, the Regional Prefect at Toulouse and the Prefect of the Department of Lot and Garonne, with one copy kept for the file.

The text was translated by Hennequin by the evening of 19 December, and it is from another deposition by him during November 1945 in support of Captain Olivier that some interesting facts are revealed that otherwise would have been lost due to the effluxion of time. After liberation, Captain Olivier had been arrested at Nancy during November 1945. Whilst Barbance and Hennequin were still in their occupations, it seems that Capt. Olivier was termed as 'formally in command of the La Reole section'. Hennequin gave his post-war deposition to a Lt Jacques Aubertin of the Direction Générale de Justice in connection with a war crimes investigation and in doing so gave the reason why MacKinnon and Conway became known to the Germans. It seems that, according to Hennequin, it was Captain Olivier who had placed them under arrest. This fact could be to try to put a greater emphasis on the part that Olivier played and assisted him in obviating any scurrilous charges he faced. This is borne out to some degree by Hennequin saying that Olivier had threatened him with punishment following another gendarme informing Olivier of the fact that Hennequin had 'voluntarily mis-translated the text, thus endeavouring to save the situation for these two allied airmen'. Hennequin also bore witness that Capt. Olivier had telephoned his Colonel at Montauban and had received the order to 'fix' the matter for the Englishmen'. It became evident to Hennequin that even the 'Procureur', on being informed, was also party to hushing up the affair.

Lt MacKinnon had been transferred to the hospital in La Réole and began treatment on the posterior left knee. Meanwhile, the wheels started to turn and Marcel Galibert, a forty-one-year-old lawyer (Doctor at Law) at the civil court of La Réole, was 'briefed by the Juge d'Instruction of the town to conduct the defence of two foreigners' who had been

La Réole hospital, from which MacKinnon was taken by force.

found without identity papers. With the relevant information, Marcel Galibert was 'duly provided with a permit to communicate with them'. His testimony, sworn before Capt. R. A. Nightingale of WCIT[81] in November 1945, gives us another important insight. Marcel was obviously in on the conspiracy to obviate any German interference as he relates,

> I immediately went to the prison where I made the acquaintance of an Englishmen who told me his name was Conway. He was dressed in rather worn working clothes. He did not want to tell me how he had arrived in La Reole, and moreover did not speak a word of French. I went to see him on several occasions and took some books and cigarettes. Two days after our first meeting he asked me to write to his family, whose address he gave me, which I did at once.
>
> On leaving the prison I went to the Hospital. There I found another Englishman lying in bed with about ten young people from the college around him. He was in a ward with other sick people, and there was a gendarme about who was there to guard him, but who did not stop his talking to visitors who brought him [MacKinnon] books, cigarettes and fruit. He told me his name was MacKinnon and that he was an officer, but did not want to tell me from what branch of the service, neither how he landed in France nor how he had arrived in La Reole. I gave them to understand that the Juge d'Instruction had put them under close arrest to prevent them being handed over to the Germans and that in due course they would probably be freed. I said I would then endeavour to accompany them to the Spanish frontier.

Unfortunately, Marcel Galibert could only report further that 'a few days afterwards I heard that the Germans had come to arrest them'. (This is slightly odd, as it is assumed that he was present at the time when MacKinnon and Conway were given over to the SD; see below.)

This might seem like a done deal, but the following testimony shows that the Germans met with some resistance! Another Marcel was on the front line, in a battle that he was unable to win, but did give an adequate account of himself and his office. On the morning of 29 December, a gendarme named Marcel Drouillard was in the brigade office and was standing in for Adjutant Espere, who commanded the Brigade. Two NCOs of the German Army arrived at the office stating that they belonged to the German Security Service (SD) in Bordeaux and wanted to interrogate the Englishmen.

The events of the day are best left to Gendarme Drouillard's testimony.[82]

> On my refusing to supply them with any information at all, and pretending not to be aware of the arrest, I replied that only Adjutant Espere was in a position to deal with them. I went to look for [Espere] to whom I at once reported the facts. Adjutant Espere got in touch with the two Germans and explained that the two Englishmen in question had been detained on the order of the Juge d'Instruction for unlawful presence in France. Accordingly it was up to them to apply to [the judge] to obtain all useful information.

Gendarme Marcel Drouillard was instructed by the Adjutant to take the SD to the judge, who listened to their demands. The judge politely refused them and 'seeing that they could obtain no satisfaction they left in a temper stating that they would return the same evening'. The SD had contacted their superiors, who had then telephoned the Ministry of the Interior at Vichy, which had in turn telephoned the judge at 2245 and gave the order to hand MacKinnon and Conway over to the Germans. Gendarme Drouillard records that 'at about 2300 the same evening, a large detachment of Germans, numbering perhaps fifty, again arrived on the scene and armed with numerous automatic weapons, surrounded the hospital and the prison. In the presence of the prosecutor[83] [Galibert?] they took over the two Englishmen.' The gendarme could only identify that there was one German Lieutenant who gave the orders.

A document issued by the hospital dated 1984 confirms that, on 19 December 1942, 'MacKinnon, John. Profession; Lieutenant in the British army' was admitted into care. All that is evident of his release is that of 'treatment not completed' on 29 December by the hospital authority; all that is detailed about his leaving the hospital is that he departed 'non gueri', which simply means, 'Not recovered', i.e., not cured/ healed. Gendarme Marcel Drouillard had known, as everyone else, that they had kept the two marines in the situation precisely to avoid them being handed over to the Germans. Prosecutor Galibert was noted to have said, 'In my opinion it was wrong to let the young students from the college go to the hospital. They talked to their families about it and it was perhaps because of this that the Germans became aware of the Englishman's presence. What makes me think that is that, when they came, it was to arrest only the Englishman in the hospital. They appeared unaware that there was one in the prison.'

It is not known the fate of Capt. Olivier. The testimonies do show that the captain was not thought locally to have been in the pay of the Germans. The only caveat in the events was that too much publicity seems to have been given to the new arrivals and due to MacKinnon's injury, some time was needed before he could depart. Unfortunately, during the enforced stay, word spread and the vital information prejudicial to the safety of the escapees was not retained within a village. And as a result, the two were arrested despite best intentions.

No blame can be levied at any of the individuals. Gendarme Pierre Hennequin's point of view was that 'Capt. Olivier cannot be accused of having betrayed these two English soldiers to the Germans; but through his two sons, who are at college, [they] gave the matter such publicity that the whole town got to know about it and the arrest of the Englishmen was the result'. The mistake was that once the pair were officially presented, the French local authority had to simplify the offences in order to keep their 'books' in order for the Germans and to secure a legitimate release. The judicial process was in order to enable MacKinnon to recover. The injury necessitated the hospitalisation, thus keeping the marines too long in one place with word allowed to spread. The adoration from the students of the collage was an innocent fatal flaw in the plan. MacKinnon and Conway seemingly became celebrities and 'advanced publicity' was broadcast of this event.

There is enough secondary evidencing, especially given the time of the arrest, to suggest that the two marines, once taken by the SD, were overnighted at Lagnon[84]. They were then delivered to GIS Substation in Bordeaux and questioned by a series of interrogators who learnt little of consequence. It should be noted that the date of the interrogation at Bordeaux was given as 29 December. This could not have been the correct date, as they had not left La Réole until 2300 on the 29th at the earliest, and it would not have been possible to have arrived at the city in time to record this day as the day of the interrogation. The date recorded could well have been that of an interrogation which had begun at Lagnon before midnight and was to continue in Bordeaux the following day. Regardless, the SD did record, 'The Marine has made a full confession; the officer however, refuses to give evidence.' But, in the event, all that they learned concerned the training and preparation for the operation, which matched closely with the information already taken. The only seemingly different matter was the fact that it was Plymouth they were billeted not Portsmouth and an odd fact claimed that the Limpet mines in the canoe had exploded prematurely by accident. The SD knew about *Al Rawdah*; Gourock; Hasler; the submarine, pennant number and crew strength; the intent and the subsequent accident with *Cuttlefish* and the intended escape to Spain, but only via La Réole. One thing they never did learn was the names of the French people who had helped them. Given the possible methods of interrogation used, for which there would be little hope of holding out against, especially the time involved, it is believed that MacKinnon and Conway had purposefully ensured that names of the French helpers had not been known by them. This is borne out to some degree in a letter written by Jaubert mentioned later. Whilst the two marines did not deny receiving help from French civilians, they claimed that they could not remember the locations or any details about the people involved.

The SD did notice that MacKinnon wore, 'together with his identification discs, one Spanish coin, dated 1937 on a chain'. They even noted down the value, which was then 20 centavos. But for some reason they saw beyond this and with an uncanny hint of the amateur wrote, after being told by MacKinnon it was a lucky charm, 'that he became involved in contradictions on being asked about its origin. Presumably this coin was used as a recognition sign'.

Whilst the interrogations continued, two letters arrived in Britain. One went to 22 Clarendon Street in Glasgow and the other was delivered to 20 Heaton Mersey View, Larkhill Road, Edgeley; both dated 29 December 1942; possibly the date sent to the UK, not that of Galibert's posting. Monsieur Marcel Galibert, the prosecuting solicitor at the civil court of La Réole, who took books and cigarettes to MacKinnon and Conway and had been entrusted by them to write to their families, had faithfully kept his word to these Royal Marines.

Only a short message was sent, enclosed in a prepaid envelope stamped by the British Red Cross.[85] It read, 'Dear Mrs MacKinnon – I expect that you and the whole family are rather well. Seen last week John who was healthy and well, Sincerely yours.' Another much relieved mother, a Mrs M. A. Conway, had 'rushed down to the Red Cross Bureau' to see if they knew anything more after receiving her letter which read, 'Have seen James last week, he is healthy and conveys New Years greeting to you, don't worry.' At this very time, unknown to the letter writer, the interrogations were continuing. If not for this Frenchman, the last words and contact to their loved ones from these two men would never have happened. Mrs Conway wrote that 'during my time of anxiety I felt greatly relieved to hear he is alive'. Both mothers' hopes were subsequently dashed.

The Christmas period provided no more than a brief respite from the constant interrogations, as certain personnel had taken leave. It has been alleged that these marines were also moved to the Headquarters of the SD in Paris. This is very unlikely and makes no sense. The familiar 'under the pretext of the preservation of life and the assurance of good treatment to obtain information of importance to Operational Control before shooting' was again a feature used, but this time with more menace. For MacKinnon, Laver, Conway and Mills it was a *fait accompli*.

Including Wallace and Ewart, the details of the deaths of all six victims were recorded on the fake burial cards which were captured from the Germans. These documents show that all the men had suffered death 'by drowning in Bordeaux harbour'. The certificates show that Wallace and Ewart's date of death was 8 December with their place of burial, on 12 December, being that of the POW cemetery at Bordeaux. There was no such cemetery. One of the questions that was asked at the time was why, if the bodies (the latter four) were found in Bordeaux harbour, were they then brought the considerable distance to Paris simply to be buried there? We know the report of drowning is fictitious.

Nothing is known of the ultimate treatment of four of the six men except from a report[86] from a Major Reichel wherein it says that 'all those captured were shot in accordance with orders on the 23 March 1943'. One of the comments during the war crimes investigations of October 1945 was that, even given Reichel's reporting of the shooting, it was felt that 'on the whole [this] is unlikely, in view of the precedent set by the case of Sgt Wallace and Marine Ewart'. Also, that 'the particulars of the cause of death in the burial certificates are, of course, completely false'. The date of death on the cards for MacKinnon and Conway is 22 December 1942, which is also evidenced to be fictitious. A point that seemed not to have been highlighted at the time is that Reichel also made a mistake in saying that six men were shot on one date. We know that Wallace and Ewart were shot in early December. One specific piece of information may be a clear indication that indeed they were never taken to Paris. Notably, we find that the personnel of the interrogation section had returned to Paris on 5 January, with Sonderführer Heinz Corssen possibly having had to return to Bordeaux for clarification of any outstanding details.

The war crimes investigation was not able to come to a conclusive decision on what had happened despite much effort to do so. This included an important request[87] from WCIT to the pathologist, Major Morris, at the HQ of British Army Staff at Paris: 'required disinter four bodies in Paris cemetery; Bagneux Paris. Location in one hundred and eleventh division first line number fifty. Identity of bodies not known, reported to be German officer buried 30 Mar 43. cause of death and full description. No rep[ort] of team coming to Paris. Report to T.A.G. on return.'

It is the author's contention that it seems extremely unlikely that the four men were taken to Paris; there would be no reason, as the interrogator(s) had already travelled a good distance to them in Bordeaux. Given the urgency to dispatch Wallace and Ewart, in fear of incurring the displeasure of the German HQ hierarchy for failing to carry out the 'commando order' in good time, it seems logical that the same urgent fate awaited MacKinnon, Conway, Laver and Mills. It is possible that the four had languished in the cells until March but, on the whole, the contention is that, once the interrogations had reached the ultimate point, there was no need to allow them to live any longer, therefore fulfilling the 'Hitler Order' – 'The *Kommandobefehl*' – at the earliest time. The executions may well have been anytime after mid-January when Sonderführer Heinz Corssen had returned to Paris. Given the method of dispatch for Wallace and Ewart, it does also seem likely and indeed probable that MacKinnon, Conway, Laver and Mills were also dispatched in the same way, quite likely in the same place (near Bordeaux), blindfolded and bound with their hands behind their backs. A place previously sought out as secluded enough that it could be used during the early hours of the morning darkness.

A/Ty Cpl George Jellicoe Sheard,
Marine David Gabriel Moffatt and '*Conger*'
The evidenced narrative of where the bodies were found

Following the capsizing of *Conger* in the second tidal race, Sheard and Moffatt now faced the subsequent waterborne tow by the rescuing canoes *Catfish* and *Cuttlefish*. The tow took the pair to between 219 and 437 yards (200–400 metres) of the shore. It was dark and very cold. Sheard and Moffatt had paddled for some 5½ hours with another hour in the ice-cold water, hanging on to the rescuing canoes, kept buoyant with the aid of their Reliant life jackets. They were shivering uncontrollably and at their limits of endurance. Now, with their release and attempted swim for the shore, their clothing waterlogged, hypothermia took hold of the body and mind and they drifted away, slowly, from the shoreline.

As soon as cold water hits a person's face, a diving response is triggered which reduces the blood supply to the skin and most muscles, saving the supply for the heart and brain. For our two marines, resuscitation was not forthcoming within the period required for a complete recovery. They succumbed to the body's shutdown and on into an unconsciousness from which they were never to be awakened. We can determine that the bodies began drifting on the surface on the morning of 8 December.

According to signal Marbef. West nr.27356[88], a body was found near strong point 'Fanny', south-west of Bois en Ré, on 17 December 1942. It is believed that the actual location was on the stretch of sand near Le Bois Plage en Ré, on the Île de Ré. Unfortunately, bodies of the Allied forces were frequently found on the beach on the Île de Ré, mainly due to air raids on La Rochelle. An elderly gentleman who had been a young boy on the island during the war told[89] of the fact that the locals would hide the body to give it a Christian burial at a convenient time due to the fact that the alternative was to allow the German forces to commit the cadaver, unceremoniously, to a mass grave. Given the fact that it is reported that a body was found on 17 December, it is likely it was washed ashore the night before at the earliest. The cadaver would not have lain there too long before it was spotted by the inhabitants. We only know that the body was buried on the 'Ridge of Dunes' due to an extract taken from Official German Totenliste[90] No. 128 after it had been 'washed ashore 17/12/42 Le Bois en Re'. This news came from correspondence known to the Admiralty during early May 1943. The Chief of Staff's office 'considered that the date of death … should be assumed for official purposes to be 17 December 1942, i.e. the date on which his body was washed ashore'. This date of death is unquestionably inaccurate. In the Totenliste document, the body 'buried in the sand dunes' was identified as that of 'Moffatt'.

It should be noted that the current on the coastline is quite fierce and the two bodies had been in the water for up to ten days. It is known that putrefaction of a body is less pronounced in water temperatures persistently below 45 degrees, although this advances with rapidity once removed from water, as would have been the case once washed ashore. Indeed, there would have been some maceration of the skin given the distance travelled; it would not have been a pretty sight; hence the reason why Moffatt's body was only carried a short distance and then buried.

As there is no detailed documentary evidence of how the Germans arrived at their conclusion, it has always been assumed that they knew the body washed up was Moffatt's due to his identity disc. There is no choice but to accept the information provided in the German records that they successfully identified the body, even though it is plain that the Germans were happy to falsify other records, including the fake burial cards for those that they executed. An added indication that this information is true and correct is the fact that the name is correctly spelled,[91] just as it would have been on the identity disc.

Up until this point, no suggestion has been put forward as to what had happened to L/Cpl George Jellicoe Sheard, the No. 1 in *Conger*. There has always only been a presumption of death but how and where has never been alluded to.[92] Within a Naval Intelligence document written by E. G. N. Rushbrooke (ref. NID 24/T.155/45[93]), there is an indication of what may have happened to the body of Sheard. In a signal originated by Field Marshal von Runstedt on 28 December[94] 1942, a warning was issued to the various units and a list of recent incidents given, dating from the capture of Wallace and Ewart on 8 December, Laver and Mills' capture at La Garde on 14 December to the capture of MacKinnon and Conway on 28 December. The two other incidents mentioned are for 14 December, stating that a 'canoe with green-black camouflage [was] washed ashore on Ile de Re', and the other dated 18 December, stating, 'Bodies of two Englishmen washed ashore at Les Sables d'Olonne and Île de Ré, one of these presumed to be a saboteur.'

Interestingly, the report[95] that mentions the canoe find, at around 1600 on 14 December, shows that the canoe was found 'south of the Ile de Re' and that there was 'no sign of occupants'. It was then stated that they believed that there were British sabotage troops 'now at large on the Ile de Re or near La Rochelle'. The HQ replied that 'increased vigilance was required … with the strongest of methods'. This simple report does show that the canoe arrived on the beach before Moffatt's body. It should be noted that the distance from Pointe de Grave to Le Bois Plage en Ré/Le Bois en Ré on the Île de Ré is about 45 miles (70 km) and Les Sables is about 70 miles (90 km).

From another document, we know that, during interrogations of those captured, the Germans established 'that the name of the canoe is painted on the port side in blue paint, and had been painted over in camouflage paint a few days before embarkation in Scotland'. Further investigations carried out on 3 January 1943[96] found out that Sheard and Moffatt's 'boat had drifted ashore some time ago on the Ile de Re and had been secured at La Pallice [in the port of La Rochelle]. After removal of the camouflage paint the name *Conger* was found.'

If we accept the identification of Moffatt as certain, we can then positively place one man and the canoe *Conger* in the region of the Île de Ré. It is uncertain how it was determined that the second body found at Les Sables was that of an Englishman. Given the fact that only Moffatt's body was 'presumed to be a saboteur', either the individuals who dealt with the second body at Les Sables found that it was either stripped of any identification (certain clothing, identity disc) or that the body was found with items of identification but reported to the Germans as if none had been found. It was thus determined by the French, and related by the Gendarmerie to the Germans, that the body was that of an Englishman. The latter is thought far more likely given the garb known to have been worn. Given the state of the body it would have needed to be buried nearby or else picked up by vehicle and taken away. It is probable the Germans would have been content just to know of the fact that a body was reported and buried, accepting any information available. Either way, it is too coincidental that the Les Sables d'Olonne body of an 'Englishman' was not that of George Jellicoe Sheard. It is the considered opinion of knowledgeable individuals that, given the time of year and the currents, a body drifting from Pointe de Grave could have ended washed up on Île de Ré. Without being prompted, the same individuals, when quizzed where a body might next be washed up, if it did not land on the Île de Ré, instantly identified the site to be that of Les Sables d'Olonne.

As an added footnote, a captured report, by a Major Reichel, states that six marines were shot on 23 March 1943 in a propaganda story saying it was 'to counter the Kharkov trials' and that Hasler, Sparks and *Sheard* had escaped. This at least shows that Cpl Sheard did not feature in any direct contact with the Germans. Clearly, he did not make it back to the UK. Until now, Marine Moffatt's official date of death has always been recorded as 17 December; the date his body is recorded as being found washed up on the shore[97]. The canoe, however, capsized in the early hours of 8 December and survival in the cold waters for them would have been in the minutes rather than hours. It is therefore considered that it can be determined that the date of death for both A/Ty Cpl George Jellicoe Sheard and Marine David Gabriel Moffatt is 8 December 1942. Unfortunately, at the time of writing, the Commonwealth War Graves[98] website gives George Sheard's date of death as 7 December, while David Moffatt's is given as 17 December; quite clearly, this is inaccurate. The question of whether it is possible to finally determine the place and or date of death of the others of this Royal Marines Boom Patrol Detachment from Southsea needs to be addressed.

For decades, reliance has been placed with an individual who has an untrustworthy history, the need to impress his superiors and the want of propaganda – Major Reichel. We already have proof that great deceit was used for the cover-up with the fake death certificates. It was shortly after the war, through investigation, that it was deemed 'unlikely' that Reichel's report had validity. What we can be certain of is that there existed a great will to ensure that the 'saboteurs' were shot under Hitler's Commando Order – and swiftly. All concerned were concentrated on this fact. Why then would four of the marines be kept alive for such a lengthy period, only to be taken to Paris to be shot? The evidence shows that the interrogator(s) came *from* Paris and had returned *to* Paris by 5 January with only the possibility that they might return to Bordeaux. All we have to rely on is the word of Reichel, who supplemented his diatribe with a justification of the action and whose testimony can be proved to be inaccurate. Despite an extensive search, none of these men's bodies were found. Without firm evidence to the contrary, it is only truly possible to come to the following conclusions:

Cockle canoeists Corporal Laver and Marine Mills died in a manner and on a date and place not certain, following an extensive interrogation at Bordeaux.

Cockle canoeists Lieutenant MacKinnon and Marine Conway died in a manner and on a date and place not certain, following an extensive interrogation at Bordeaux.

Cockle canoeists Sergeant Wallace and Marine Ewart were executed at a sandpit somewhere outside the area of the city of Bordeaux on 11 December 1942 following a short, inept interrogation.

Cockle canoeists Corporal Sheard and Marine Moffatt undoubtedly died from hypothermia, rather than drowning, in the early hours of 8 December 1942; they had been wearing life jackets. Their bodies are believed to have been found on the beach at Les Sables d'Olonne and the Île de Ré. Sheard's body is likely to have been buried near the beach at Les Sables d'Olonne; just as Moffatt's body, washed up on the stretch of sand near Le Bois Plage en Re[99], was buried in an unmarked grave near to where it was found on the 'Ridge of Dunes'. The identity of Moffatt's body can only have been taken from the identity disc.

Mrs Helen MacKinnon, Jack's mother, contacted the Imperial War Graves commission in May 1947 regarding her son and James Conway. By October 1947, the Admiralty had replied confirming 'that the German entry regarding the burial [at Bagneaux, near Paris] was false'.

In a letter dated 10 December 1947 to Mrs MacKinnon, it was related by the Admiralty at that time, 'The Graves service, Western Europe, report that the records of Bagneux cemetery have been thoroughly scrutinised but there is no record of the grave, nor is there any information regrading 'unknowns' having been brought to that cemetery by the Germans. It is very much regretted that no further action in this case is possible.'

The remains of MacKinnon, Sheard, Laver, Conway and Mills have never yet been found. The author believes, given the research, that the last resting place of MacKinnon, Laver, Conway and Mills is somewhere in a wood, approximately 5–10 km outside and to the north-east of Bordeaux. It is believed that the 'discussion and arrangements for their shooting of these four men most probably took place between 1 January 1943 and 23 March 1943' with the thought that they were executed at some time between 6 January and 30 March 1943 with the burial occurring directly afterwards. It is not believed that any of these six men were ever taken to Paris to be disposed of.

This account, at the very least, gives some closure, enabling a more intimate understanding of exactly what happened to the men during captivity. It should be noted that once a more cohesive attempt was made to interrogate the prisoners by the SD, a great deal of the plan, training sections, and very much more was known. Bill Sparks wrote, 'I can't believe that our lads disclosed so much, and in particular the mention of our training in Scotland, and the development of the two-man sub.' Given Hitler's Commando Order and that the interrogations were to be conducted 'with no methods barred', Sparks could be forgiven for not realising that the body can only tolerate so much.

As regards Wallace and Ewart, they had mistakenly walked into a military installation, but they kept tight-lipped about the actions of the others. It is assumed that Wallace had told Ewart that he would field all the questions asked; he had time to make that clear. Admiral Bachmann's[100] urgency to comply with the 'commando order' saved them from anything other than 'soft interrogation'[101]. MacKinnon, Conway, Laver and Mills, however, had to face the post-attack attention and intense interrogation levied upon them. They cannot be criticised for the information given up. That is the nature of interrogation. Four of the men executed clearly received help from the French people and were interrogated at length. It is quite evident that at no time did these Royal Marines give away even the place names that they had received assistance from. This gives an indication that the interrogation did not reach a point that they could not withhold such information. Normally, it is 'When' will the subject give up the information not 'If'.

CHAPTER 7
The Great Escapade

Springtime in Cornwall

An expected aeroplane slowly approached the south-west coastline of England in the afternoon of an April spring day. The Dakota[1] had avoided the Luftwaffe, operating from Bordeaux and Brest, by vectoring on Cape Finisterre as it journeyed from Gibraltar, having left early that same day. Now safe within the range of fighter cover, one of the few occupants within sat with a grin on his face as wide as a Cheshire cat. He was experiencing that semi-euphoric feeling that one gets when arriving home after having been away in a foreign land for a long time. For this man, his break from Britain had lasted for 123 days. Now he had been sent home as an 'urgent signal' – with the 'utmost priority'. As the coastline became a patchwork and more defined, he could see the familiar places that he had sailed along stretching out below and to his right; this warmed his heart and filled his mind with the possibilities of routes to be sailed in the future. With Start Point in the far distance and the Lizard Peninsula ahead, the beauty of Cornwall and Devon was laid out before the eye; here, springtime arrives earlier than anywhere else in the mainland of the British Isles.

The sun was shining and the lush, green grass of a mild maritime climate was evident. The final descent was made, and apart from a few spring thermals eventing themselves, the plane landed gently and taxied down the fighter station aerodrome at Portreath on 2 April 1943. Sporting a tailored, single-breasted, light-coloured jacket with a white striped shirt, and a tie with a small Polka dot pattern, the near six-foot frame of a blue-eyed, well-dressed man with more than a hint of a bronzed face, felt the Cornish soil beneath his highly polished size eight shoes. The circle was complete. He strode across the grass and was welcomed by the uniformed station commander with a knowing smile. The civilian-clad military man noted that the daffodils were in full bloom.

Unbeknown to Acting Major Herbert George 'Blondie' Hasler, OBE , or indeed anyone else at this time, the only other certain survivor of the *Frankton* Raid was Blondie's No. 2 from the Cockle canoe *Catfish*, Marine William 'Bill' Sparks, and he was yet to board the troopship from Gibraltar to the UK.

The escape part of the operation began on 12 December with disembarkation from the canoes. In truth, the successful repatriation was entirely due to the kindness of the French individuals who risked their lives and that of their families and friends.

As Military Force Commander of Operation *Frankton*, Blondie Hasler's responsibilities were many and varied, and they did not end with the placing of Limpet mines on the Axis shipping. Hasler had methodically begun to place in his memory every detail of the operation during the lying-up hours. This methodology was used during the escape route, continually going over and over the same information gathered in order to write his report when safely out of harm's way.

Hasler made his report to MI9 first, then compiled his report at COHQ by 8 April 1943. Hasler's diary reveals the entry '3rd April – 8th April at COHQ writing report on *Frankton* and celebrating return'. This then is the narrative of that successful escape of the only two survivors from a group of ten men. It is compiled from Blondie Hasler's original initial personal typed notes of 9 April 1943, following his interview with MI9. Together with the margined pencil notations, the report from Hasler remains the only strictly factual document from which to draw. Other than the quoted passages derived from his report, there are no other recorded conversations during this period.

Until this time, much of the information previously reported has been guessed at, and it is only through detailed research that the whole evidenced story is possible. Now, we have the other parts of the story intimately told by those who were there at that time. These are faithfully reproduced and interconnect with Hasler's report.

By the Armistice of June 1940, France was divided by a demarcation line. German troops occupied all the country to the north and west of this line. South of this line was the Free or Unoccupied Zone. The civil jurisdiction of the 'Vichy Government' extended over the whole of metropolitan France with the exception of Alsace-Lorraine[2], which was under the eighty-five-year-old Marshal Henri-Philippe Petain, who hailed from Vichy.

The Long and Winding Road Home

A total of 91 nautical miles, or 105 land miles, had been paddled by Hasler, Sparks, Laver and Mills. Having said their goodbyes to Laver and Mills, the CO and his No. 2 had carried on and paddled a short distance just as the flood tide was returning. As they turned to the shoreline, they saw a bank some six feet in height ahead of them; it proved an 'awkward climb up the mud bank. Forcing a way through the dry reeds made a good deal of noise,' reported Hasler. This bank was

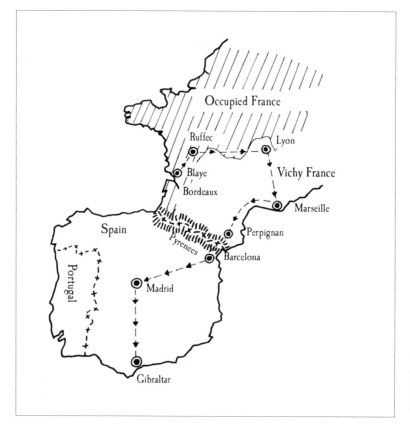

A map of the escape route, also showing Occupied and Vichy France.

typical to the river with its reed-topped crown. They had climbed out of their Cockle for the last time and scuttled her with the slash of the knife. There was no time to be melancholic about the matter; she was a work horse that had come to the end of her useful life and needed to be hidden from view – underwater. They had taken the Nos 4 and 5 bags out and placed them on the top of the mud bank before pushing *Catfish* out into the darkness of the mid-stream flood to sink along with the broken-down paddles inside bow and stern. Once the reeds had been navigated, they found themselves in what appeared to be an open field but soon discovered that they were having to climb over a series of wires of a vineyard on an upward-sloping terrain; once they realised this, they opted for the easier but longer method of transition. The CO again reported that 'the hinterland in this area consists of flat cultivated fields and vineyards, intersected by deep ditches. The vines are supported on wires 3 ft high spaced about 4 ft apart, which makes them difficult to cross except when going in the same direction as the wire.'

They headed in a north-east direction, having landed at Saint-Genès-de-Blaye at around 0500.[3] Still euphoric with a successful outcome to their efforts, they ignored the aches and pains of extended walking, and gradually they warmed in their sodden clothing. Sunrise was due around 0800. They were still in uniform and carried their weapons along with enough fresh water for two days, as well as what was left of the compact rations. Much of the available darkness had been wasted having to zig-zag their way through the vineyard, but they had progressed to the tracks beyond; covering but two miles. With the approaching dawn, our two foxes went to earth as the first birdsong was heard, taking shelter in a conveniently placed wooded area at 0730 somewhere between Saint-Genès-de-Blaye and the village of Fours, about a mile from the railway line. They set about making their beds with the available material having briefly washed in the nearby stream, boiled some of their remaining two litres of fresh water to make tea using the solid fuel carried and had a breakfast from the rations. Later that day, they washed thoroughly, the first time they had done this for many days, and had the regular shave; no more the restrictive movement of the operation. In Hasler's words, they 'spent a peaceful day in the woods [before moving] off as soon as it was dark at about 1900.'

They walked across the countryside during the night until they were 'about a mile south of the large village of Reignac', which they needed to avoid. With morning daylight on 13 December, a decision was made to chance their luck at the various farms for clothing. At daylight around 0800, while all the countryside seemed empty of people, they neared the hamlet of Brignac and decided to make contact with a short, elderly man, presumably a farmer, sporting a black beret and a cigarette in his mouth, who was tending the garden of this isolated farmhouse. They made eye contact, but the old man proved uninterested and continued with his work. It is reported that Hasler made the close approach and explained that they were English soldiers escaping from the Germans and made a request of some old clothes. This request brought a momentary perusal of the two oddities by the old man, who shrugged his shoulders, passing all decisions on to 'her inside', then ignored them by carrying on with his business. The lady of the household was as much a grumpy thing as the alleged head of it. She was described as a middle-aged, stout woman of dynamic soul who was clearly not impressed with the knock at the door, which caused an interruption of the scheduled chores. The request was repeated and 'surprise and indignation' were recorded on her face in equal measure. The reply was made in some language that Hasler did not understand; he only gathered that she felt that they could not possibly be English and that she would not assist them. Despite protestations that they were indeed English, Hasler realised the predicament he had put her in. As she disappeared from their sight, Hasler and Sparks looked at each other wondering what was coming next. To their surprise and delight, she returned brandishing trampish items of headgear and without any particular affirmation said, 'They are very old, but we have no good clothes left. It is the war. Now go away, please, and do not tell anyone you have been here.' With much thanks, Hasler and Sparks retreated with no further indication from the beret-wearing gardener that he was aware of their presence. Off they went into the fields with the old cap and a beret. At the second farm they went to, they met a woman who has been described as a 'real sour puss' and a 'crabby witch'; either way, the response was to the negative, and they left empty-handed in full uniform. Hasler recorded his feelings, saying that 'at both the first and second farms the people seemed suspicious of us'. They now attended yet another farm nearby, hungry and anxious to get into something more comfortable, preferably without military badges affixed!

Like a couple of encyclopedia salesmen going door to door in a recession, they next tried their luck at a kitchen door. Hasler proffered his usual to a more promising candidate, a woman looking not only kind of face but, Hasler thought, like one with fire in her belly. She disappeared after few but positive words. They were not used to waiting and a sense of nervousness grew; there were no telephone lines, so nothing of grave consequence could be happening, thought Hasler. They waited and waited until the woman trundled back with a bundle of clothes. It turned out that, in this instance, Sparks ended up with a rather nifty number in the form of a very old jacket, a poacher's coat, and matching trousers whilst Hasler was furnished with trousers and, latterly, when he asked for one, a sack. This enabled the carrying of the little food and water they had together with the 'gloves, stockings and balaclava helmets' that they had taken with them.

The positive event uplifted the spirits, bolstered by the woman's smiling face and words of good luck. They continued walking in the daylight, which was beginning to be a most pleasant option as opposed to being on the night shift, and it was not too long before they utilised a copse for the purpose of concealing their uniforms and weapons in the canopy floor. Buried were the Colt .45 pistol and fighting knives together with the warm khaki trousers, which were, with some reluctance, exchanged for the thin civilian freebies. Unsurprisingly, their service underwear whilst jolly warm had an odour all of its own and was only tempered by the stale smell of newly donned tramp-like clothing. In rural France, during an occupation, this was an excellent choice of disguise.

Our two fashion gurus emerged from the wooded glade, the older man sporting a coiffured blond 'walrus' handlebar moustache, featuring a beret without jacket, a delightful blue naval sweater, adequate trousering and an exquisite pair of early felt-soled commando boots. The younger man was wearing the same ensemble but with the added advantage of a rural retro, nondescript jacket together with a smile on his face that seemed to highlight the utter delight of the situation. They seemed to be making progress in every department, and it was this that kept Hasler punching on heading north-east across the countryside, solely due to the lack of roads in that direction. With their body clock now adjusting to daylight hours, feeling dapper, they chanced their arm at being somewhat bold by entering their first village during daylight; no more than a hamlet with a few houses either side of a road that skirted first south then north-eastward.

The following details are described as from Hasler's own hand and to a large extent without any influence from the author, as it is felt important to relay what is evidenced. Hasler takes up the story and informs us, 'four miles or so further on, in a small village, we got a jacket for me and another sack'. It is thought that this village was Brignac. He continues, 'We spent the night [of the] 13th/14th December in a wood just south of Donnezac. On 14 December we started about 0630 hrs, about an hour before daylight and walked to Donnezac. There we turned north-east to the main road and north-east up another road which brought us approximately to the 'T' in Montendre.' Hasler refers to sheet 29 of a 1:250,000 map that he carried during the trip. These were in addition to the silk handkerchief map, and up to a point, they were accurate.

Hasler says, 'We then went NW on a side road to a village under the figure 6 on the map. On the main road we walked SE for a short distance, and then turned left to Rouffignac (the light railway shown on the map does not exist).' Hasler notated the word 'rain' in the margin, which gives an indication that the weather was a trifle inclement. 'From Rouffignac we followed a cart track to Villexavier (sheet 24) and thence to Ozillac and St. Germain-de-Vibrac, near which we spent the night of 14/15 in a wood.' That same evening, Laver and Mills were being arrested by the reluctant Gendarme Georges Rieupeyrout. 'The next day (15 Dec) we went on to Saint-Ciers-Champagne, and then east along the main road from which we turned left for Barret. (Here again a light railway marked on the map does not exist). At this point a margin notation records a problem with a compass. From there, we walked along the St Médard road, turning left for Touzac. At a village 1 kilometre south of Touzac we tried to get food at a garage, our own supplies now being exhausted, but without success. About ½

The approach to Saint-Preuil for Hasler and Sparks was from the top right of this picture.

a mile NW of Tousac [Chez Courtin] however, at a group of houses we got some bread and chicken and were told there were Germans in Lignieres-Somerville. We crossed the main road and turned right for St Preuil, where we were given shelter for the night (15/16).'

Le Poulet est Bon!

From this point onwards, there is enough evidence to support the story in a broader sense in addition to that provided by Hasler's clinical account. The next encounter is supported by an interview with one Robert Patient as well as Robert Pasqueraud, the then eleven-year-old son of the now-headlined 'Fiery Woodsman'. The reason for this pseudonym will become clearly apparent.

As a repetition for emphasis, it should be pointed out that for the French people there was a palpable fear of reprisals from the Germans. For these individuals, who had the heart and soul of a lion and who wanted to help, there was no way of knowing if those presented before them were German provocateurs or deserters rather than British escapees. Human nature is a difficult thing to determine, and spiteful or careless talk from a neighbour could result in dire consequences, as we will see.

The distance covered in the rain during 15 December had been nearly twenty miles, and their hunger was getting the better of them. Eventually, that evening they reached a farm called Maine-Laurier, and it was here that Hasler decided to chance his luck. Whilst sympathetic, Madame Malichier was indeed wary and frightened of both the request for shelter and their presence, which, despite Hasler's entreaties, only resulted in the attendance of a tall mid-teenaged youth called Cadillon, the son of a local vineyard worker – all arms and legs and seemingly a sandwich short of a picnic.

Madame Malichier, having given Cadillon some instructions, told Hasler to accompany the youth, who would lead them to shelter. With that, Cadillon duly led the pair about a kilometre down a very muddy cart track towards a hollow surrounded by woods in which stood some very old buildings which funnelled the noise of a barking dog from within. The household they were about to be introduced to was an impoverished one. Cadillon received the wrath of the head of the household, a rotund individual with broad shoulders and a barrel chest, early middle-aged – around forty – dressed in farm worker's clothes that would not have been out of place with those worn by the escapees.

This, then, was the aptly named 'Fiery Woodsman', so called by Hasler due entirely to his most aggressive manner, obvious anger at being presented with strangers, and the fact that he was a woodcutter! Here stood, during a rain-sodden night, two unknown individuals without even a forewarning. Hasler noted the scene behind this anger-filled Frenchman who stood full-square in the door. Within was a slight, thin woman seemingly cowering in the shadows with her children. This 'Fiery Woodsman' demanded to know who the strangers were and who had sent them. Cadillon replied that the wife of the boss had told him that they were escaping Englishmen. Adding that 'the Trouillets didn't want to know them at La Pitardie and she couldn't keep them at Maine-Laurier, so I should take them to Clodomir Pasqueraud[4] at Nâpres'.

With that, the woodcutter aggressively beckoned them all inside the dimly lit, ground-floor room. There was an air of poverty, gilded with the escaping wood smoke from the cooking range that dominated the room. There was very little furniture; a large bedding area was evident at the far end of the room. All other life in the room, including the dog, was wedged in a corner. The smell was a concoction of body odour, wood smoke, and heated food laced with garlic; the latter prevailed in the olfactory senses of our walkabouts. The 'Fiery Woodsman' eyed Hasler's six-foot frame, challenging him to say who he was. The answer was duly given, but this did not satisfy our inclement Frenchman. The woodsman would not believe that they were English. They produced both identity discs from their underclothes and the display of materials from the escape box. During the interrogation, the only thing that started to calm the woodsman was the word 'commando'. A strange turn of events now occurred that seemed to settle the matter.

All the while, both Hasler and Sparks had remained calm, but with Sparks becoming somewhat redundant, his own ear became locked onto a familiar sound from the radio that was bleating some English words. The BBC broadcast was reaching this homely hovel in the depth of France. For Clodomir Pasqueraud, our 'Fiery Woodsman', that noticed attention to the radio sealed the deal, and his persona change somewhat. The interrogation would not finish there, but Clodomir sent Cadillon away and closed the heavy door behind him. From hostility to the epitome of friendliness; they had been accepted.

The next words spoken were definitely the sweetest they had heard for a good while and worth every syllable of the harsh and anger-filled moments they had experienced. 'Are you hungry?'

Sparks did not miss a trick and, even though he could not understand the Frenchman's 'English', reported to Hasler using the words 'horse' and 'eat'. The household swung into action and became much more relaxed; even the dog stopped growling! There was a multitude of questions and a delivery of an act of intent aimed against the Germans with the assistance of the RAF. He was 'Clodomir the Communist', and he was intensely proud of it; that was why Madame Malichier had sent them. Everyone knew his political allegiance and knew of his impetuous nature. Clodomir's only gripe was that he thought he was being regarded as the centre of the local resistance and as a consequence this could result in attention from the Germans, who might arrive in the form of British soldiers.

Clodomir Pasqueraud's wife was called Irene, the children known of were Yves, Marc and Robert (all of whom were attending to the chores of preparation) and a baby girl[5]. Clodomir became his animated self, asking questions and proclaiming his communistic stance; this display of exuberance reached a crescendo as he related, in an act worthy of the stage, that many Nazis would be killed with the pincer movement of the Russians and Pasqueraud! Unfortunately, almost at the very moment of Clodomir's acting display reaching its peak and Irene Pasqueraud placing the closely monitored steaming serving dish of food on the table, there came an ominous knocking at the door. The result was that a mini whirlwind crossed the room in an urgency so great that it stunned all. Clodomir had, en route, secured a pistol in hand, opened the door and with seamless efficiency befitting that of a Commando pressed the muzzle of the pistol under the chin of what was now a very frightened boy. This is the kind of event that would be imprinted on an individual for life, and even years later, Robert Patient could relate the incident with great clarity.

The knock had come whilst Clodomir was in his excitable, self-obsessed other world, and he reacted accordingly. Once Clodomir had realised the identity of the 'intruder', he explained to his guests that this was the baker's errand boy from Segonzac, Robert, who, because he was a friend to Clodomir's son, also named Robert, occasionally and secretly supplied a few bread rolls, which aided the feeding of the family. This secreting of bread rolls was unknown to the baker boy's boss. Robert Patient, once relieved of the bread rolls, was dispatched with the kind of look that would secure his silence for very many years. With the impromptu distraction over, the smell of the food beckoned. The last time Hasler and Sparks had had a decent meal was from Gypsy Joe on the *Tuna* on the morning of 7 December. They now sat at the table with a French family who offered them the lion's share of the hot dinner. Sparks could not wait to consume the truly wholesome vegetable soup, which was then followed by roast chicken with potatoes and onions – with a side order of freshly delivered bread – it was truly Manna[6] from Heaven. This substantial meal was followed by the local wine, which was provided *ad infinitum*.

With the wine flowing and bellies filled, the children paid more attention to their guests, whispering the word 'Anglais' to each other. Clodomir and Irene had five children, two girls and three boys. With Sparks' engaging smile, they warmed to him. Hasler continued his conversation with Clodomir, which involved reference to the outstanding piece of technology sat in the corner – an old wireless set. It transpired that the BBC was a regular tuning in point with messages noted for the people in France. It was at this juncture that Clodomir insisted that when Hasler returned home a coded message was sent by the BBC so that Clodomir would know his two guests had returned safely. Hasler promised to send the message – it was to be 'le poulet est bon'. This promise was kept. It can only be imagined how Clodomir reacted when he heard the coded message … but it was not sent for a long time.

And indeed 'le poulet' was so good that Clodomir, despite his enthusiasm, realised that the guests were now extremely tired due to the large quantity of food and wine that had diverted the blood supply from the head to the stomach. Clodomir intended for them to have the marital bed, which was situated on the first floor, but, mostly due to his height, and the fact that he was sleepy, Hasler truly whacked his forehead on a cross-beam[7] over the staircase. Immensely apologetic, Clodomir then detoured the dazed Hasler to the bed of Yves and Marc, the two elder sons.

Their hosts were not done tending to their guests needs, and Irene Pasqueraud insisted on washing the marines' outer clothes whilst they now slept in their service underwear. Irene and Clodomir might not have had very much but what they did have were huge hearts beneath the rough exterior. The clothing was dried in front of the stove. Clodomir's effervescent nature and excitable ways were not always welcomed by all; expressing his enthusiasm was not an issue for him.

Hasler and Sparks awoke refreshed; they had spent the night without the nervous tension experienced before. They washed, shaved and put on the now pleasant-smelling clothes. They both had a wonderful breakfast before Hasler explained that they needed to depart before too long and reluctantly rejected the fine hospitality offered for yet another night. Irene Pasqueraud ensured they left with some bread and the rest of the cooked chicken. Clodomir told his son, Robert, to replace the tea in their flasks with red wine. Even into the new millennium, Robert remembered this with some amusement.

Hasler told Clodomir that they had to cross the River Charente as well as the road on its northern bank as early in the morning as possible. The next order from Clodomir was aimed at Yves and Marc, who were instructed to take Hasler and Sparks via Saint-Preuil towards Vinade bridge in order to cross the river and then towards Lantin. Clodomir also told the boys to take their bikes. There was a great welling of the heart on the departure of their guests. The oldest son, Marc, seemed to take after his father and had to be asked by Hasler to stop whistling the Marseillaise on the journey. By the time full light came, the boys had left them. As a footnote to this part of the story and to emphasise what could happen, it is know that in 1944 these two sons of Clodomir were deported to Germany and were never to be seen again; there is no indication that this deportation was connected to the night in

1942. Hasler remembered much of that visit for in his scant report, made long afterwards, he pencilled the words 'communist', 'Le Poulet est Bon' and 'weapons' in the margin between the typed lines of words.

Hasler's report tells us only that 'the next day (16 Dec) we went NE to St Meme-les-Carrieres. This was the only place we saw German soldiers. We got the impression there were only a few and were told they had moved in a few days before. That day we continued to Triac, Latin, Fleurac, Vaux-Rouillac and Le Temple and spent the night in a disused hut S of the light rlwy near the latter place.'

This journey was undertaken during another rainy day, and having walked on muddy paths and across fields, they ensured that they maintained the heading, which was not helped by another compass that fell foul of the weather (notated in pencil on the report). There was little shelter to be had in the dilapidated shed. It was cold and all they could do was eat what was left of the provisions given to them by the Pasquerauds. Ruffec was now just some thirty kilometers away, but two days walking.

As Hasler and Sparks began this day, the body of one of their kind was being washed up on the Île de Ré shoreline. Hasler's report begins, 'On the 17 Dec we walked to Montigne, Bonneville, and Mons. We avoided Aigre, turning left at its outskirts on to the road for Oradour, from which we turned right along a cart track to St Fraigne. By this time it was evening and we had run out of food. We continued to Beaunac (not marked on map) just E of St Fraigne. After trying several houses, we found one where we got some food, and were allowed to sleep in an outhouse. As we had to go to several houses the whole village knew of our presence and only about ½ of the villagers were favourably disposed towards us, the rest being suspicious.'

Hasler and Sparks were unaware of a manned German watchtower situated some 200 metres from the hamlet. They were also unaware that they were being observed by André Latouche, and it was he who welcomed them at just before 2000 hrs, gave them bread and pâté and sheltered them in a barn for the night, where the straw made for a comfortable and dry bed. Before they went to sleep, they heard some raised voices in the houses adjacent.

Hasler's report continues but does not and could not contain the subsequent events that occurred in the village. He follows on with events from 'about 2300 hrs [when] our hosts[8] wakened us and told us we would have to leave because some of the villagers had sent for the police. We heard in Ruffec 2 days later that the police had actually been enquiring in the area for two people answering to our description. We got out at once and went by cart tracks to a road SE of Souvigne, where we spent the night.' Here in the margin he writes the word 'haystack' and 'compass'.

It is due to a visit in the summer of 1960 by two Royal Marine probationary second lieutenants on initiative training that some interesting facts can be revealed as a footnote to this part of the story. Whilst following the escape route taken by Hasler and Sparks, they had the good fortune to visit the right house in Beaunac and met a 'very reserved plump woman' who turned out to be the wife of Lucien Gody. Over a beer in an enormous kitchen, Madame Gody related why her husband had been forced to ask Hasler and Sparks to leave the village before the Germans found out. About a week before Hasler and Sparks arrived, a couple of Germans had come into the village disguised as English escaping soldiers. This had the effect of making the whole village rather nervous. As a consequence, when Hasler and Sparks arrived, they had a 'very inhospitable welcome'.

What happened after they had been warned is related and shows what can happen in a divided village where spiteful words or careless talk are prevalent. News had apparently spread around the ten houses that made up the small village, and the neighbours were curious to see the two strangers. André Latouche could not be certain if these two visitors really were British escapees or not. André decided personally to go to the mayor at Ebréon, a Monsieur Bineau, whose domain included Beaunac. Hasler and Sparks had been asleep in the stone barn for a couple of hours when one of André's neighbours, a Lucien Gody, warned the Englishmen that he believed it would be a good idea to depart due to the fact that they had lost their low profile within the village. The two celebrities spent the rest of the night in the hollow of an old, uncovered haystack near the Souvigné woods. Another compass had now given up the ghost.

With the information supplied to him by Latouche, the Mayor of Ebréon told the gendarme to go and investigate. As the Mayor was also expected to advise the local Gendarmerie, he decided to contact the station at Aigre, knowing no one would investigate until the next day, and by that time, the alleged foreigners should have disappeared. As expected, the Gendarmerie did not turn up; however, they did write up a report and forward it to the Préfecture in Angoulême. It is believed to have implicated certain individuals. The report was then passed on to the Feldgendarmerie, who visited Beaunac and arrested Messieurs Latouche, Bineau and Picot on 22 December only to return on Christmas Eve to arrest Maurice Rousseau as well as Messieurs Gody and Souchaud. One of these was the village pharmacist. Obviously not wanting to spoil their Christmas Day, the same authority returned on 26 December to arrest the sixteen-year-old René Rousseau. The two like-named individuals were not related. It was in this atmosphere that three individuals from those arrested were never to be released by the German Feldgendarmarie. As a direct result of being implicated with the escaping commandos, Lucien Gody, Maurice Rosseau and the sixteen-year-old René Rousseau were deported together. Only Lucien Gody is definitely known to have died in Germany. It is extremely likely that Maurice and René Rousseau suffered that same fate, for they were never seen again. Their names will always now be remembered with the Cockleshell Heroes on the new memorial[9] at the Pointe de Grave in France.

The reason why these Frenchmen were 'picked on' and deported lies in the type of thing that happened all over Germany and the occupied countries. In Germany, certainly in the early part of Hitler's rise, ordinary citizens found they could influence the Gestapo by denunciations. This led to the Gestapo spending a considerable amount of time sorting these out. Some Germans were denounced by gossip alone and often with no firm evidence. It might have been as simple as an individual not fitting in or being disliked, and if enough neighbours wrote letters, it often led to the targeted individual being sent to the concentration camp. These were simply hate crimes, no different from those meted out to the Jews. Set in this atmosphere, you had to be brave indeed to assist any Allied soldiers in any way. In the village of Beaunac, human nature was no different, and it would seem that these three individuals were themselves targeted for some reason; perhaps a little 'horse trading' was going on; after all, what crime could the sixteen-year-old René Rousseau have commited? It could have been that either one or both of the unrelated Rousseau villagers had been with Gody when he alerted Hasler and Sparks. After the war, the Marquis themselves dealt out their own kind of justice against collaborators – it was another opportunity to settle old scores.

A Piece of Cake at the Chef's White Hat

Of the journey for the escapees, Hasler's report says simply, 'On 18th Dec we walked via Raix and La Faye to Ruffec. From Ruffec our journey was arranged for us.' Almost at the same time on this day, MacKinnon and Conway were being arrested at La Réole some 170 km to the south.

It is now important to relate some information regarding the town. Ruffec's position during 1942 was on the Route Nationale 10 where it crosses the main Paris–Bordeaux railway line. Situated as it was just 10 kilometres from the Demarcation Line, it was an important town for the Germans with their headquarters within the main square. The routes leading into the Demarcation Line were guarded by the Germans at this time.[10] It should be noted that, about forty days or so before Hasler and Sparks arrived at Ruffec, there had been a disaster for some individuals of the Resistance. Some twelve people were arrested, one returned, the others were never seen again. This terrible event might have served the marines well, as the Germans would have been sated by their find and more 'relaxed'. It is in this recent atmosphere that two strangers rolled into town.

The two vagrants entered the town at Viellemorte. They tentatively crossed the town centre, back and forth, slowing in front of the near-to-empty shop window displays. No one was interested in these 'outcasts', not even the police. Hasler had received no precise information of who to contact, just that a contact could be found at one of the town's restaurants. He tried to gauge every eye movement from those they passed, but there was no indication of a possible contact. Hasler cased one bistro from outside and decided its clientele, prices and *patronne* could be worthy of a foray.

The part of Hasler's report that describes the introduction to Ruffec is again brief, saying, 'On our journey from St G. de Blaye to Ruffec, which is described in my report, S and I used special mounted maps of France, 1:250,000 and escape-aid compasses and boxes. We had been instructed before leaving that Ruffec was a good area for which to make. On arrival at Ruffec just after noon on 18th Dec we walked round for a bit, as we had no specific instructions where to go. We went into a restaurant and ordered drinks and soup (the soup could be got without ration cards). When paying our bill we passed the patronne a note saying that we were English. She sheltered us for 24 hours and got in touch with 2 of Marie-Claire's contacts in Ruffec. They visited us in our room.'

It was hoped that this briefest of reporting could be expanded on, beginning with the testimony of a French restaurant owner named René and his waitress in occupied France, but the restaurant was owned by a woman and the waitress was *not* named Yvette[11]. Fortunately though, a little-known testimony exists that does give a complete picture of events at the Bistro. This informal testimony came from the two Mandinaud sisters in 1960.[12] The restaurant was on the corner of Rue de l'Hopital and as close as 100 metres from the German HQ. It was known as La Toque Blanche.[13] The restaurant had a high reputation – until 'two dirty men' arrived. The two tired and weary travellers in their pitiful clothing entered the establishment at around 1230[14]; it had but few customers. The two rough-looking escapees sat down near the door. Hasler had, unknowingly and by good fortune, found patriots to the cause – even if they did not 'belong' to the Resistance organisation. The friendly-looking woman serving was Alix Mandinaud, who was in her thirties and also did some of the cooking. Yvonne Mandinaud, Alix's sister, was the owner of the Bistro. It is known that Hasler did see another individual, a man, René Mandinaud and had assumed at the time he was married to the waitress; in fact, René was the third sibling and helped in the kitchen.

Hasler, as we know, had what can be described as an odd accent! He ordered 'potage' for two with coffee. The soup did not require coupons; they had none anyway. Two quiet, nondescript,

Early photo of Hôtel des Sports known as 'La Toque Blanche' in 1942.

down-on-their-luck men just passing through sat awaiting their meal. Meanwhile, 'Alix was suspicious of Hasler's French and thought the two marines were German deserters, she went into the kitchen and ordered "two potatoes for the Germans".'[15] The earthenware bowls filled with a substantial soup arrived quickly along with coffee.[16] Sparks had to be told not to eat so fast, but as far as his belly was concerned, there was little need to hesitate when hungry. Try as he might, the hot, thick potato and vegetable soup simply would not stop being swallowed – presently another round of soup and coffee was ordered. Alix is known to have mentioned to her brother something to the effect that they 'had a funny lot in the restaurant'[17]. No doubt, this comment also covered the fact that the two vagrants were rather smelly. With the initial hunger somewhat sated, the soup was now measured in its consumption by Sparks, now knowing the importance of trying to outstay any other customer; but even this failed. It was noticed by Alix that these two 'seemed to be starving'. As time passed, Hasler then decided that there was nothing left to do but take the plunge and wrote a message on some paper which read in French something like, 'WE ARE TWO ESCAPING ENGLISH SOLDIERS. DO YOU KNOW ANYONE WHO CAN HELP US?'

It is reported that this inscribed paper was then folded into a 500 franc note. Hasler caught the waitress's eye and gestured for a bill. Pensive Hasler knew this was all or nothing. Alix Mandinaud came over to the table and told him the charge and in turn Hasler passed her the pencilled note wrapped within the money. Without giving away she had clocked the additional paper, Alix went back to her station and expressionlessly read the message and then told her brother of the content. Alix returned and gave Hasler the change as well a note which read that they were to order more soup and then wait until all the other customers had left and told them to keep quiet. Their third bowl of soup took an age to arrive. This could mean one of three things: the French woman was playing for time, was in the process of informing the Germans, or they had run out of soup. Hasler discounted the latter two and put the odds in his favour; probably the best bet of his life, and it paid off – the soup arrived, much to the delight of the hungry cockney, who had now developed a big smile, having seen the soup on its way to the table.

Knowing that the other customers were just waiting out the last of the lunchtime and not about to order anything further, Alix felt confident in asking them to leave as she busied clearing their table. Two men still eating would not cause any suspicion to those being ushered out even slightly prematurely. In total, the two marines had waited two and a half hours before they could get any help from the ladies. Unfortunately, Sparks, who had downed the soups rather faster than Hasler, promptly fell asleep and remained so for nearly two hours!

The Mandinauds had been busy: they had telephoned around trying to make contact with the local Resistance network. The first call was to a like-minded individual, the local receiver of taxes, Jean Mariaud; in essence a Resistance worker. After the Bistro had closed, the ladies quickly got the marines round to the back and even then they were not convinced that the 'tramps' were English escaping soldiers until Hasler and Sparks produced English sweets and lavatory paper from their escape boxes! Hasler and Sparks had no idea how much danger they were in or quite how much risk these French people were putting themselves in. Due to the fact that there were *two* staircases in the hotel, the Germans who were staying at the hotel never knew they were sharing it with two British saboteurs.[18]

The next stage of the plan was to secrete the pair in one of the rooms upstairs on the second floor. Hasler was worried about soiling the clean beds with their filthy clothes, but they were well attended to. They were furnished with a hip bath, hot water, towel, soap and instructed to leave their clothes by the door. Alix, with kindness in her eyes, would wash the clothes, including the undergarments that had remained in situ for far too long. Service wear or not, they would not have been pleasant. Alix's last words to them as she left them in the room had been, 'Dont worry, we are going to take care of you.' They both washed and shaved, and even though it was only late in the afternoon, Hasler was the first to sleep armed with nothing more than the reassurance of a kind Frenchwoman. It can also be revealed for the first time that Yvonne, the owner of the Bistro,[19] had a very frightening moment when the French Gendarmerie came and actually asked her if the 'two men she had upstairs were

English escaped soldiers'[20] – when she gave them a negative answer, they simply went away. It was revealed by the Mandinaud sisters that the French Gendarmerie were very pro-British and that, had Hasler and Sparks known this, they may have been less anxious whilst walking along the streets in Ruffec. Another probable reason why the Gendarmerie did not pursue the issue could have been that Lt Henri Peyraud, the commandant of the Gendarmerie Nationale in Ruffec, was reputed to have been a member of Mary Lindell's gang[21].

It is further revealed by the Mandinaud sisters that the reason why the French Gendarmerie had visited the Bistro was that a woman from Souvigné had seen the two marines climb out of their last hide in the haystack near this village and had reported this to the Germans.[22]

In an interview in 2007, Jean Mariaud, then a bright-eyed ninety-four-year-old[23], said of Hasler and Sparks, 'They were very fortunate; if they had gone into any other establishment they would have been betrayed and captured.' Jean was very mindful and had great respect for the assistance rendered by the Mandinauds. It is quite amazing to find that, even though eleven people had only just been 'removed' from Ruffec, there were others, not part of the Resistance network, who were willing and kind-hearted enough to take a chance, risking their lives in order to harbour two individuals who could well have been German spies sent to catch them out. It was a fact that, despite their bravery, they were very frightened people. Tax man Mariaud was himself suspicious and feared a German trap. Some months earlier, Jean had been arrested by the Gestapo. Because he had been forewarned, he had had time to burn incriminating papers. When the Germans arrived at his home, the oven was still warm. Despite their suspicions, Jean was released after a day of questioning; it is believe he was one of the twelve who were mentioned earlier. So it was that Jean Mariaud took another risk, and if it was a trap, Yvonne, René, Alix, Jean, and the retired teacher he was about to enlist the help of were the very least that would be arrested and dealt with.

With the considered opinion that they should establish exactly who these two men were, Jean Mariaud contacted a retired teacher friend, Monsieur Paillet. This individual had taught the French language in England before the war and, now living in France, had named his dwelling 'Villa Livingstone'! He was best placed to establish if they were, at least, Englishmen. Hasler and Sparks, now wearing clean underwear, were interviewed in their room above the café. The identity discs, Hasler's poor French with a German accent and Sparks' grasp of the English language, which could not be replicated unless you were of a specific London descent, made the pair the genuine article as far as the teacher of language was concerned. Jean remembered Paillet saying of Sparks, 'He is a Cockney; no German could replicate that accent.' With this confirmation, Bow bells[24] or not, the brave Frenchmen accepted Hasler and Sparks for what they were.

How Hasler and Sparks came to be inducted into an escape organisation is not alluded to within Hasler's report, for all he says is that at 'about 1400 hrs on 19 Dec we were taken in the back of a baker's van to a wood just SE of Benest (sheet 25). At dusk a guide took us about ¾ mile across the Line of Demarcation to a farm owned by another member of Marie-Claire's organisation. We stayed on the farm 18 days while the farmer tried to get in touch with Marie-Claire or her son. Marie-Claire had been injured in a road accident. She was in hospital for about 6 weeks, coming out just before we left the farm.'[25]

Fortunately, the intimacies of exactly what was going on are available from another source. We know that the Mandinauds were amongst a number of like-minded individuals who were well aware that the proprietor of Hôtel de France occasionally had a certain kind of clientele who mysteriously departed without leaving any trace of them having stayed. It was with this knowledge that an attempted to illicit contact with the escape network began at that hotel. A number of Germans were also lodged at Hôtel de France, it being one of the better establishments within Ruffec.

Unfortunately, the owner, Monsieur François Rouillon, kept up the veneer of ignorance to do with any such reception for escaped Allied servicemen. The most that François Rouillon admitted to was an association with the manager of the local Red Cross, who in turn knew an English woman by the name of Marie-Claire; and that was all Rouillon would say even when he was severely pressed on the subject. Marie-Claire was known to be married to a

French aristocrat and had been to the hotel many times. Still, François Rouillon refused to budge. He admitted to knowing Marie-Claire but repeatedly said he knew not where she was or how to contact her. With this flat refusal, Mariaud visited Madame Marthe Rullier; this woman was indeed very well acquainted with Marie-Claire. As far as everyone else was concerned, the Englishwoman's name was Marie-Claire but Marthe Rullier's knowledge extended further than this. She was not about to impart this information freely. They had known each other for many years and had recently become reacquainted, with Marie-Claire having turned up unexpectedly at Marthe's house. This was a lovely homely place set in huge, well-kept gardens with a long drive which, at the time of the visit, was requisitioned for German officers who were billeted there unbeknown to Marie-Claire until she arrived.

Once the cards had been laid on the table, Marthe told the two men that she and Marie-Claire had been nurses together in 1915. She also admitted that, although she had seen her in Ruffec a number of times, Marthe truthfully had no idea where she was. (Marie-Claire was subject to the enforced absence during this time.[26]) The Demarcation Line had been drawn up and this had previously been advertised in the newspapers; it plotted the boundary between Petain's France and the occupied zone. In most cases, it was just a roadblock consisting of a small contingent of German soldiers, huts and a barrier which required all that passed to supply the necessary permit to cross. This German guarded area was closely matched by a French set of officialdom. Whilst Marie-Claire had the ability to obtain a pass, the same was not the case for the escapees; hence the ability to cross the line at a secluded place was needed. A decision was made to transfer the two escapees to someone on the other side of the Demarcation Line in Marvaud. Marthe Rullier knew that Marie-Claire was in contact with a farmer called Armand Dubreuille, and it was this man that the 'parcels' would be sent to in the fashion prescribed via Farm 'A'. But those arranging the 'transfer' did not know anything about Marie-Claire's set-up other than the contact with Armand. The method of transfer was decided upon as well as the driver. It was imperative not only to have a willing volunteer but to know that that individual could be trusted. Jean Mariaud knew such a man by the name of Monsieur René Flaud the future brother-in-law who lived, just a few doors away from the hotel, at 21 Rue Jean Jaurès in Ruffec. It is thought that Flaud until this time was not part of the Marie-Claire escape network.

Yet another Frenchman, the baker René Flaud, was willing to risk his life to be part of this link in the chain for the two Royal Marines. Surviving yet another wash, the freshly laundered clothes awaited Hasler and Sparks as they woke by internal clock early on 19 December 1942. Their heads were clear and thoroughly refreshed; well fed from the evening before, they were chipper. They had been through a lot in the last twelve days; now they knew they would be completely relying on others. Breakfasted, they had known since the day before they were to be moved that very afternoon. Packed and ready to go at just past midday, Hasler and Sparks were led downstairs by Jean Mariaud and out via the dining room and momentarily onto the main road before getting into a black van which had its side and rear windows painted black. 'Another photograph trip,' thought Sparks, remembering the taxi in London. He commented the same to Hasler after boarding. The engine was already running in the gas-powered van as the two 'parcels' boarded. As soon as the door was shut, the van trundled away. René Flaud ignored the whistle-blowing of the French gendarme and carried on, avoiding the main Champagne-Mouton–Confolens route, because of the spot checks, instead taking the back roadways through Condac, then Bioussac and Messeux. En route, Flaud picked up another passenger near Benest; the intended courier Fernand Dumas got in beside René Flaud. Fernand Dumas was himself from Benest, had a darker complexion, and it is believed he was a cobbler, kept goats and was in receipt of a small stipend for his services of crossing the Demarcation Line with Allied airmen; but mainly this assistance was done out of love. The cobbles gave way to the smoother country track and the van pulled up after about thirty minutes. Hasler viewed the open countryside with some relief, and without a pause, 'Smuggler Dumas' was guiding them through the adjacent wood as the van sped away.

With his hat as chauffeur replaced with the hat of baker, René Flaud returned to Ruffec and signalled a successful drop with the aid of the car horn as he passed the workplace of Jean

Mariaud. He arrived back at the Mandinaud restaurant in time for a lunch break complete with a celebratory drink no doubt. René Flaud is quoted to have said, 'It was a piece of cake.' Considering he was a baker,[27] this was quite apt.

After being trained to be independent, Hasler and Sparks now had to rely and depend on someone else, totally – an odd experience for anyone who is used to being in control. They were now in a wooded area between Benest and Saint-Coutant. Fernand Dumas, their personal smuggler for the day, reassured them both that all was well. He told them that the farm was no more than a kilometre away, and provided they were careful, they could cross the Demarcation Line despite the dog patrols. The three waited quite a few hours until the night had set in and then began to walk.

Unknown to our errant Royal Marines from Portsmouth, their destination was that of the Marvaud Farm near Saint-Coutant. The Germans did not frequent this area often. This was termed as Farm 'B' by those operating the route, which was exclusively for Englishmen. According to an interview during 2002 with the owner of the farm, Armand Dubreuille,[28] 'It was the first time we had any Englishmen.'

The original set-up or escape route had been orchestrated by Marie-Claire due to her previous association with Madame Rullier. It is known that an Inspector Riou in the Paris police had become a great worker in the newly set-up Resistance movement, and it was this connection and that of Marthe Rullier which had prompted Marie-Claire to go to Ruffec to see if her friend knew of any other farms that straddled the border of the Demarcation Line[29]. Through this visit, Marthe Rullier became Marie-Claire's new local contact in Ruffec. Marthe's husband, who was an insurance agent, knew most everything that happened in the area, and he was able to tell Marie-Claire what would indeed be ideal for the proposed route. It turned out that this route had already been used by escaping Frenchmen. The first farm was in occupied France and owned by a farmer called Maxim[30] de la Vergne[31] who knew the area intimately. Farm 'B' was owned by Armand Dubreuille, a tall, fit man around twenty-six years of age. The farms were roughly four kilometres apart. This is where the original arrangements were made for the transit between Farm 'A' and Farm 'B'.

As Marie-Claire was not available and due to the fact that no one had expected the two Englishmen, it is thought that this normal transfer between the two farms did not take place, as there is no report other than that it was Fernand Dumas who delivered the men directly to the Marvaud farm, Farm 'B', owned by Armand Dubreuille. At around 1930, a long and low building near the woods was reached; Fernand Dumas knocked on the door and was received by Armand, who recognised him as a bona fide courier. They had been told, via the Marie-Claire network, probably via his cousin Flaud, to expect a visitor. Hasler, as instructed by Jean Mariaud, then told Armand that he was one of two 'parcels' care of Marie-Claire. Before Dumas the courier departed Armand briefly talked to him before Hasler and Sparks were invited into the house. We know from Armand that he knew of Marie-Claire's contacts in Ruffec, and he commented post-war that 'her contacts were sufficient guarantee for us'. Armand also explained that Marie 'told me that ... one day she would be in need of my help. Her escape network was already up and running and I had accepted to become part of it ... she moved around a lot ... it was agreed that she would let me know two or three days before the arrival of 'packages' and they were to stay only a short time at Marvaud – two or three days at most – before being picked up to continue their journey'. Clearly, the first ever transfer had not followed the intended process and would continue to be quite different from the agreed plan of actions and time frame agreed upon. Hasler and Sparks therefore were Armand's first, but not his last, British escapees. Fernand Dumas walked back to his home in Benest that same evening.

The hosts[32] of the Marvaud farm were Amelie[33] aged twenty-three and Armand aged twenty-six, both pleasant and quiet in nature but neither of whom could speak English, which is the probable reason that their guests were immediately shown into a room, also on the ground floor, adjacent to the main living room. Hasler observed it seemed to be reserved for visitors. Clean and tidy, it contained a table with two chairs, a smaller table on which was placed a washing bowl, towels and china jug and a double bed. Armand told them not to leave their room during daylight hours and to keep the two doors locked. He recalled during an interview, 'They could get fresh air in the courtyard at night. If they needed the toilet during the day, they were to use the small privy by the stable, but they had to check first that no stranger was around. My wife and I were obliged to carry on with our normal life, so they would not see us at all during the day. My wife brought them dinner in their room that evening and I said we would talk more the next day.' At 2000, Amelie served them with their first meal at the farm.

During their time at the Marvaud farm, Amelie and Armand tended to their guests with great care. They enjoyed good home-cooked meals, all brought to them by Amelie in their room. Most of the time, these meals were a thick soup with beans, entirely wholesome and satisfying. On occasions, they had lamb or chicken but always with plenty of red wine. There was, of course, coffee with home-made bread, butter and jam. Within the first two days, Armand had sent a message to Marie-Claire and informed Hasler of the fact. Only once did Armand ask Hasler about the reason they were in France and asked no more when Hasler replied, 'We did our job.'

Hasler became as bored as Sparks, even with the newspaper supplied each day, but busied himself and, with the aid of knives supplied by their host, began to do some wood carving. Sparks tried his hand as well and, even by Sparks' own admission, Blondie 'had a real talent for it'. Over the days, Blondie had produced a little goblin smoking a pipe and a human figure. Sparks carved a rudimentary elephant and gave it to the nearly one-year-old boy named Michel[34]. They were given as Christmas presents to the family and treasured for years.

In a most recent interview, Amelie[35] told the author these gifts were lost when she moved house. Amelie still has a necklace that Hasler made. It was many years later (1969) that it was realised that Bill Sparks' life jacket had been used by Michel for waterskiing. Most of the other things were given away to various individuals over the passing years.

Every evening was a BBC evening, when all listened to the news on the radio. When Christmas Day arrived, Amelie came to the room with Armand in tow declaring it was Christmas Day and proffering a plate of pancakes. New Year's Day duly arrived, and a familiar object appeared in a different guise. It was roast duck which was served with a strong sauce. The yard that had to be crossed to get to the privy had one less aquatic waddling Anatidae to get underfoot! Also in the yard, there was a dustbin-lid warning signal alarm which fortunately never went off.

The Elusive Marie-Claire and the Parcels of Food

About the same time as HMS *Tuna* was making its way down the west coast of the British Isles, Marie-Claire suffered what can only be described as an intentional attempt to kill her by two principal collaborators in the area as she and an associate were bicycling near the village of Blois at the Demarcation Line. Marie-Claire had returned to Ruffec and had gone directly to Marthe Rullier's, where she stayed overnight before cycling to Maxim's farm, Farm 'A'. Her associate was also badly injured.

Marie-Claire never did get to Maxim's farm that day. Her injuries were so severe that one attendant individual thought the body only required a death certificate. She then had been carried across fields for at least five kilometres. Marie-Claire had then narrowly avoided the Gestapo as she was sheltered in a Loches hospital bed. The elusive Marie-Claire was still extremely ill, having fought for her life over a couple of days. She was told that she would not be able to move for forty days due to her age and injuries. The Gestapo could not find Marie-Claire, and true to form, they then arrested her estranged husband as well as the doctor of the hospital; both were eventually released due to lack of evidence of complicity. Marie-Claire had previously rejected the original candidate for the job of radio operator, and with London having not supplied her with the promised replacement,[36] this meant that she had no way of being advised of the imminent arrival of any Royal Marines from Bordeaux.

It was on Christmas Eve that Marie-Claire's son visited her in hospital and enjoyed a dinner of turkey and seasonal pudding. He also had to inform her that the new route over the mountains was proving more difficult to fix than had been anticipated. Our heroine's son was called Maurice. He was of military age and had enrolled at the Law Students' University in Lyon in order to escape military service or deportation to Germany. But in order to have time for his Resistance work, he secured a fellow pupil to present the arranged double papers, just attending the odd lecture.[37] When Maurice returned home, he found a letter from Armand Dubreuille, who wrote that he had 'two important parcels of food for him'. Sensing an urgency about the matter, Maurice returned to the hospital to see his mother, who decided on a course of immediate action. Her words as recorded were, 'I'm not supposed to be out for another three or four weeks, but obviously I can't stay here; go to Armand and advise him that you will pick the men up on 6 January. In the meantime go back to Lyons and arrange for their reception at once. The day after tomorrow [26 December] I shall leave here and go back to Lyon to see that everything is all right at your end.' She had also instructed her son that, on arrival at Armand's farm, Maurice should take the escapees to Roumazières on bicycles and pick up the night train from there to Lyons, where the stationmaster, who was also in on the deal, would be able to assist.

Still waiting to hear news, the Dubreuille family and friends settled in for the Christmas period. Sparks thought about the nightlife in Pompey and Hasler dreamed of sailing along the Devon and Dorset coastline. It had been a full year: from nothing to a fully functioning detachment of specialists, two of whom were now trying to avoid capture in the corner of a foreign field.

Once Armand had been contacted by Maurice, he was a much happier man, although, even sixty years later, Armand still remembered his annoyance at having to wait so long. The longer the escapees stayed, the greater the risk for him and his family. He told Hasler and Sparks that Marie-Claire's son would be calling for them on the morning of 6 January. Meantime, 1943 blew in through the doorway. On the appointed day, Maurice was introduced to his 'parcels', and in perfect English, this handsome eighteen-year-old apologised for the delay, explaining about his mother and the altercation with a car. He also outlined the plan of action as dictated by her. Whilst pleased with the impending continuation of their journey, this very young man noted the concern on Hasler's face about using the railway. He reassured them that his 'chief' would be awaiting their arrival in Lyons.

Maurice told them that they were not to talk on the train, saying that should anyone speak to them the best avoidance measure was to use a guttural voice and say 'Breton', explaining that there were many people in Brittany who did not speak ordinary French. Before the off, Armand asked them if they carried anything that could identify them as English. The result was that their identity discs were left with him along with Sparks' Reliant life jacket. To this day, Hasler's original identity discs still remain in France.[38] Armand then asked a favour. He asked if Hasler would send a message via the BBC especially for them to indicate the two had safely arrived back home; it was agreed that the message should be 'the two chickens have arrived'. Both Hasler and Sparks looked at each other and laughed; the deal was made. Armand had hidden the two Royal Marines for eighteen days,[39] which was far more than he had ever envisaged. Once Armand had realised the reasons behind the delay, he accepted the sojourn as unavoidable. The longer any escapee stayed, the greater the risk for the hosts and their twelve-month-old firstborn son. Amelie must have had great faith and love in her husband to risk her child.

The two extra bicycles Armand had acquired were mounted, and they set off, accomplishing the eleven-mile country route to Roumazières within a couple of hours. The 'parcels' waited outside the station as Maurice bought tickets and spoke to the accommodating stationmaster. Maurice then walked along the platform and signalled to them to a position where easy access to the station could be had. Hasler and Sparks joined a group of people and awaited the next signal from Maurice. When the train arrived an hour later, Maurice selected one of the third-class carriages, and they joined a sleepy bunch of French travellers and endured the seemingly interminable halting at every station to Limoges. They then caught the night train to Lyons as arranged. The train rolled into Lyon in the early hours; none of the three had slept due to the hustle and bustle.

Marie-Claire had discharged herself from hospital, much to the chagrin of those who had cared for her, but this Marie-Claire was an extremely determined woman. She had expected to find a car awaiting her arrival at 0730, but this did not happen and she was forced to walk the entire distance into the city centre. She eventually found the lodgings that her son had arranged for the escapees but was not at all pleased when she realised a cardinal rule had been broken – the family Maurice had placed the 'parcels' with had children. And so it was that the memorable meeting came to pass after a few days; Hasler and Sparks met the indomitable and formidable Marie-Claire at her flat in Lyon. From that moment on, both men had great admiration and affection for this woman for the rest of their lives. Before them stood an upper-class woman wearing a Red Cross uniform with English and French ribbons and medals on the breast. She also sported the results of the car attack; her leg was still in plaster and her arm had become at risk of gangrene. Hasler sported the very magnificent and too typically English moustache that caught her eye immediately. At some stage, this moustache was limited in its overall volume to a great degree at the behest of this diminutive and punctilious woman, who produced a pair of scissors for the action to be undertaken post-haste. Hasler did not offer any argument, much to the amusement of Sparks. After the shave, bath and breakfast, Marie-Claire's real name became known to Hasler and Sparks. Now they knew her simply as Mary.

Before Marie-Claire took them via tram to get their photographs taken for the identity cards, she had a long and interesting discussion with Hasler. He described the raid and explained the journey undertaken in order to pick up the escape line at Ruffec. During the conversations, Marie-Claire informed them both that there was only one rule they insisted on and that was the 'No Girls' rule. The journey was fraught, but after they had received their identity cards with the requisite fictitious French names, a further afternoon of conversation continued. Marie-Claire told Hasler he might like to take the opportunity of using her visit to Switzerland for treatment in order to send a message back home. With this offer, Hasler then compiled a message* ready to be coded with the No. 3 code they had learnt. Unfortunately, once the code had been applied and produced the meaningless gobbledygook, Hasler realised that he, and Sparks, had forgotten quite how to convert these letters into the plain, innocent language needed. Regardless of this failing, the message was given to Marie-Claire, and Hasler hoped that an astute cipher clerk in London would realise what had gone wrong.

In the evening, Maurice led the 'parcels' through the darkened avenues and on to a house which was the home of one of Lyons' town councillors. It was an imposing but quite beautiful dwelling occupied in one wing by the owner's German mother-in-law who hardly ever went anywhere else in the house. The woman's husband had, conveniently, taken a tumble when getting off a tram and was incarcerated in hospital for the duration; this was an added bonus, as he was a Vichy supporter! Hasler and Sparks were moved many times during their month in Lyon and both the men's lack of activity and the fact that they were not allowed to go out made them feel claustrophobic. For active and fit men, they simply had to endure this strange waiting game; there was no alternative. Sparks does record that during the long time waiting to be advanced both he and Hasler were 'going slightly insane'; he also recognised that, due to the fact that they were unable to get any kind of exercise, they 'were growing fat and soft'.

Marie-Claire had received treatment and seemingly managed to make contact with the Swiss Intelligence Service, who made arrangements for Marie-Claire to return secretly to Lyon. Again, despite her injuries, she crossed the frontier at Annemasse. On Marie-Claire's return, she told Hasler of her problems with her route over the mountains. With this lack of fitness, they knew the impending trek over the Pyrenees would not be an easy task. Still feeling desperately ill, Marie-Claire knew that she must return to Switzerland for further treatment and that she would have to hand the marines over to another organisation. This would ensure both speed and safety. Maurice made the contact, and it was during one evening that a 'little French Communist' named Martineau came and collected the Marines. He told Marie-Claire that the pair would have to 'go over in our name'. Marie-Claire agreed but added, coldly, 'I'm not doing this on commission.' Hasler and Sparks said their goodbyes. Fortunately, despite Marie-Claire's dice with death in Ravensbrück concentration camp, she, Hasler and Sparks met a number of times after the war and each time it was with great rejoicing. She remains one of the most 'extraordinary personalities in the chronicle of escape'.

Hasler does not report on many of the events as described above, saying only,

> Eventually, on 6 Jan 43, Maurice, the son of Marie-Claire, came to the farm. We left with him that day on bicycles for Roumazieres, where we got the night train for Lyons. We had not been supplied with identity cards, although they had the blank forms at the farm, as they had no means of taking our photographs. We arrived at Lyons on the morning of 7 Jan, and were taken to a flat, where we met Marie Claire. Through her son we were lodged that night in a large house on the northern suburbs of Lyons. We were there [Lyons] for 12 or 14 days, during which MC was trying to re-open her line through the Pyrenees. As she was unsuccessful, she got in touch with Mr Carter, a member of Pat's organisation[40]. We were transferred to Carter's care. I was sent to live with M. and Mmme. Bonnamour. Mme. Bonnamour is the daughter of Mr Barr, manager of Barclay's bank in Baker St.[41]
>
> I stayed with the Bonnamours for 6 days with the exception of one night, when I was sent to a flat belonging to Paul Reynauld. Carter then obtained the use of a large villa on the northern outskirts of Lyons, belonging to Mr Barr. There Sparks rejoined me, and we were looked after by a young Frenchwoman who assists Carter. We remained in this villa for another 6 days, till one of Pat's men (Fabien) arrived to conduct us to Marseilles (Early February).
>
> In Marseilles we lived in a flat overlooking the observatory gardens. The flat is rented by a member of Pat's organisation (Albert or Robert), and run by a French family called Martin. We were there until the early hours of 1 March, when we left with F/O de Merode and F/Sgt Dawson. From this point until my arrival at Barcelona my journey was as described as de Merode's report. From Barcelona I was sent to Madrid by car and was there 6 days before being sent to Gib, which I reached on 1 Apr.

Meanwhile, back in England, the only information available came from the Germans, who had reported that 'a small British force, planning to carry out acts of sabotage, was spotted in the Gironde estuary and, following a brief fight, was wiped out'. In the RMBPD War Dairies Capt. Stewart posted all of the men as missing on 31 December 1942. It was following a communication to Capt. Stewart, as commander of the RMBPD, that on 25 January 1943, he officially declared the ten men as 'missing in action'.

The following extract is taken from the report of Flying Officer Prince Werner PMG de Merode, of 350 Squadron, Fighter Command, which ties in with Hasler's report.

> We spent a few days in Toulouse with a members of the orgn [organisation] and then went on to Marseilles, where we stayed about a fortnight with Mme Martin, 12 Boulevarde Cassini. Pat visited us on 28 Feb. I left Marseilles on 1 Mar. in a party that included Maj. Hasler, Mne. Sparkes, and [Flight] Sgt. Dawson. We went by lorry to Ceret, whence we crossed the Pyrenees with a guide we crossed via Las Illas and Massanet-de-Cabrenys. After 4 days walking we were about 9 km N. of Banolas, where we spent 3 or 4 days in a hotel, seeing people who were in touch with the Consulate at Barcelona. Through them arrangements were made for our journey to Barcelona by lorry.

Espadrilles and the Pyrenees

The one thing that ate away at Hasler and Sparks' souls was the inactivity and boredom of just waiting for things to happen. It did occur to Hasler that they could have returned to the UK quicker if a small sailing yacht had been issued to him.[42] The events of the efforts to retrieve the two Marines are brief, but certain highlights are related directly from Hasler's annotations.

Following the move to the Marseilles flat, they spent an interminable amount of time in the company of as many as twelve other RAF men. There was a brisk turnover of individuals during their time at the flat, great food but no activity other than board games. Our two 'saboteurs' were eventually joined by four other individuals who were due to undertake the journey with them. On 1 March 1943, each of the pilgrims was issued with two pairs of Espadrilles and a canvas rucksack. Now the group numbered five and consisted of a young French guide, Hasler, Sparks, F/O de Merode[43], F/Sgt Dawson. The guide took them on a train journey, arriving at Perpignan in the afternoon. As they hopped on an old gas-powered lorry that contained crates, they were now joined by a tall, well-read Frenchman who notably carried a pile of books tied up with string. They were driven the twenty kilometres to Boulou and then on westward. The road passed through Céret and Amélie-les-Bains running parallel with the border crossing it at the 1,600-metre-high Col d'Arras. The air became distinctly colder as the lorry climbed. They had already been told that the crossing place was so rugged and difficult that it proved ineffective for either the Spanish or Germans to maintain border guards.

At a secluded point, the van stopped and two dark-skinned men, wearing warm clothes and black berets, stood menacingly ahead of them. The five pilgrims now became the charge of the two Catalan guides, who led them away from the road as the van continued on to the Prats de Mollo border crossing. The path was scarcely visible, but an hour later, they reached a pile of dry stones with a roof of mossy slate and home for the night. The next morning, before the sun had risen, the party departed, climbing steadily upwards into the increasingly thinner and colder atmosphere of the snow-covered mountains that towered above them – the Pyrenees. Another night was spent in a cave before they set off again. The lack of fitness was something that Hasler and Sparks found difficult to tolerate, and it embarrassed them as Royal Marines. Incredibly, these two Marines, who had been at the height of physical fitness, were the ones struggling to keep up.

Whilst the guides were used to the altitude, the rest were not, particularly the Marines. By midday, they found themselves in a rough, desolate landscape with no other signs of life. Visibility was proving difficult due to the low cloud, and despite some arguing from the guides as to the direction, the trip concluded for that day with a night spent at a farmstead. The following day comprised yet more miles on foot before they eventually reached a small hotel 9 km north of the town of Banolas where Hasler records them staying from 4–7 March.

It should be highlighted at this point that in a letter written to Marie-Claire in February 1961 Hasler referred to his inability to trace the two guides but went on to relate some other interesting information. He recalled that 'they were most inexpert and kept getting lost and the initiative was really taken by the young Frenchman who was with us and who … was subsequently suspected by the British Consulate in Barcelona as having been a stool pigeon, and implicated in the blitz on that particular escape organisation that occurred soon after we crossed'. It is known that this gaunt Frenchman had disappeared on arrival in Barcelona.

Barcelona and the British consulate was another sixty miles away and the transport now provided by the Catalan guides on the afternoon of 7 March was another covered lorry, which contained ceramic toilets surrounded by great quantities of straw, in which they duly concealed themselves for the forthcoming police check point. At the Consulate, when all matters had been clarified, three of the four escapees that were now left from the party were obliged to remain confined within; Sparks was eventually joined by two RAF officers, who taught him the 'rudiments of Bridge'. The Consulate arranged for Hasler to be kitted out with new clothing and to have his photograph taken for the identity card. Armed with the identity card, he was able to convince the police that he was a commercial traveler, and appearing above the military age, he obtained a police pass. Thus he was 'old enough'[44] to be given the freedom of the city and it was possible for Blondie to sample the delights of Barcelona from the Hotel Victoria in the Plaza de Cataluña during the fifteen-day stay until 22 March. This 'utmost priority' individual was eventually found a car to take him and his cardboard suitcase on to Madrid. Sparks meanwhile remained to be forwarded at a later date.

Taken in Barcelona for the identity card, 1943. (Source: Hasler)

Blondie's mother, Annie, had been told in the January of 1943 that her son was missing in action. Then, in late February, she had been informed that her son was alive and well. It was via the diplomatic pouch that his mother received another letter at Glyn Corrig, Catherington, in Hampshire sometime in late March. It had been penned on the notepaper from the Hotel Victoria on 12 March and signed 'Love George'. Within, Blondie had been able to tell her, by means only she would know, of his present location[45]. He told her, with his usual understatement, that he was 'still flourishing and happy' – quite all a mother would want to know – besides the fact that he was 'enjoying it all very much'. He told her that 'he was supposed to be on his way home' having had a 'most interesting time since I last saw you'. As a good son would, he also told her 'not to worry about' him and finished with hope 'to be with you again soon'.

Within Hasler's personalised pencilled footnotes, we learn that he spent from 23–30 March in the flat and care of the naval attaché, who took him on a tour of parties and galleries including that of the Prado, of which he retained a catalogue as a keepsake. Hasler, whilst only writing single words to remind himself of events, shows us that he even enjoyed suckling pig!

From Madrid, an embassy car ferried Hasler, minus Sparks, to Gibraltar but made a stop-off in Seville for one night on 31 March, where the Flamenco dancers proved a distraction to the attendant German officials at the adjacent table. The next luncheon appointment was taken at Jerez, where he notes that he partook of a glass or two of the local Tio Pepe. Hasler finally arrived in Gibraltar during the afternoon of 1 April 1943.

So it was that on the morning of the next day, in brilliant warm sunshine, Hasler viewed the Rock of Gibraltar and its strategic importance from aloft. No doubt, he could not help wondering how easy it might be to penetrate the harbour using the same technique he was to improve on. During the flight homeward, he thought about the events of the last four months. The submarine trip, the journey up the Gironde, that special night with the 'sticky' Limpets and then the most difficult part, the escape. He remembered those who had helped to save him and each place name. From Saint-Genès-de-Blaye to Gibraltar via Brignac, Donnezac, Rouffignac, Villexavier, Saint-Germain-de-Vibrac, Saint-Ciers-Champagne, Toussac, Saint-Preuil, Nâpres, Saint-Même-les-Carrières, Triac, Latin, Fleurac, Vaux-Rouillac, Le Temple, Montigné, Bonneville, Mons, Beaunac, Ruffec, Saint-Coutant, Roumazières, Lyon, Marseilles across the Pyrenees and now, flying high, he, or at least the pilot, was avoiding the Luftwaffe.

Capt. Dickie Raikes was to write later that, at the promised arranged meeting in a London restaurant, he noticed Blondie had aged 'ten years'. As soon as Dickie knew Blondie was back in the UK, he booked a table not at the Savoy as had been previously recorded but at Kettners in Soho 'where we thought the food was better'. Hasler records only, 'Monday 12th April 0819 train to London … 1100 met Raikes at COHQ. 1140-1215, giving verbal report on '*Frankton*' to Plans Committee. Lunch with the Raikes. 1430 conference.' At this overdue luncheon date Dickie introduced his wife to Blondie for the first time.

It can be certain that what little colour remained in what little hair he possessed before the event had turned grey by the time he had arrived at Barcelona. Poor old Bill Sparks was obliged to wait in Madrid for a month before being taken by train to a border station before the short walk into Gibraltar. Sparks then faced the ignominy during his journey home by sea of being secured in his cabin in order to avoid contact with other passengers; seemingly, his only contact was during meal delivery. On his arrival at Liverpool, he was put under escort for the night trip to Euston station by train. With a continuing deflated spirit, Sparks manage to get away from his escort due to their inattentiveness in the locked door department. With his training, and the desire to visit his father to ensure him he was very much alive, he arrived at the Finsbury Park home and stayed there for two days before presenting himself to an army sergeant major at the approved and original destination of Euston Hotel. Sparks eventually rejoined the RMBPD at Southsea.

Whilst Bill Sparks could be thought of as being hard done by; spare a thought for Hasler's fellow officers at Dolphin Court HQ who had just received the news of Hasler's imminent return to the camp at Portsmouth. They had to swiftly rally round to get enough money and replace the more-than-substantial amount of alcohol that they had 'legally' pilfered[46] from Blondie's private stock after he had been posted missing just before the new year of 1943.[47] They might have had a good New Year's drink on him at the time but the meagre wages they received meant that they were all 'boracic'[48] for a good few weeks.

The Message from Switzerland

The message, compiled by Hasler in Lyon, was taken by Marie-Claire to Switzerland. She entered the neutral country in a fishing boat on Lake Geneva. It was received by Intelligence Staff at the War Office on 23 February 1943. It was finally broken by a very clever Wren, Second Officer Marie Hamilton, purely by her imagination and skill. The message read,

> COHQ. *Tuna* launched five cockles seven Dec. Cachalot torn in hatch. Pad hatches[49]. In bad tide-race SW Pte de Grave Coalfish lost formation fate unknown. Conger capsized crew may have swum ashore. Cuttlefish lost formation nr Le Verdon fate unknown. Catfish Crayfish lay up in bushes Pte aux Oiseaux. Found by French but not betrayed. Ninth in hedges five miles north of Blaye. Tenth in field south end Cazeau. Eleventh in reeds thirty yds south of pontoons opp Bassens South. Attack eleventh. Catfish Bordeaux west three on cargo ship two on engines of Sperrbrecher two on stern of cargo ship one on stern of small tanker. Crayfish Bassens south five on large cargo ship three on smaller liner. Back together same night. Separate and scuttle cockles one mile north of Blaye. Sparks with me. Fate of Crayfish crew unknown. Hasler.

*The message was then passed to COHQ, which resulted in much rejoicing and relief in London and Portsmouth. Quite how the message was broken is related by a man who was to become one of Hasler's best friends, Major Ronnie G. Sillars, RM, who had been at the War Office on the afternoon of Wednesday 18 November 1942, when Hasler and MacKinnon received instruction in the No. 3 Code. He later wrote to Hasler explaining the situation:

> It was an evening I shall always remember. Those of us who knew of the operation were tensely awaiting news of the raiders. Much sooner than were expected, your coded report arrived. Only night duty staff were on, and there was no-one in the decoding section who could make head or tail of it. That was understandable in view of the manner in which the letters were strung together. By great luck, our extremely competent Wren 2nd Officer Hamilton was doing her homework in the office and I suggested to her that she might have a go at your message on the assumption that you had superimposed No. 3 code on a kind of bogus cipher, or the other way round. Marie Hamilton had both imagination and amazing skill as far as codes were concerned and it wasn't long before there was a cloud of cigarette ash as she leapt to her feet coughing, 'it's coming out – it's coming out!' When she got the hang of your method (which was excellent for that particular message, and made the code virtually unbreakable by any outsider, however expert), she quickly had the report decoded. She was just 'fey' that night. Shortly afterwards the decoded version was on its way to Combine Ops by special D.R.

CHAPTER 8
A Repeat of Operation *Frankton*

Four to One Against

One of the questions that may be asked is whether Operation *Frankton* brought about a significant enough impact to prevent the movements of the blockade runners and, given the losses sustained, was it all worth it. Any determination in the explanation must be done with understanding of the climate in which war was fought and the situation in which Great Britain found itself at that time.

Statistics can often be a cold method of quantifying success, especially when it is done with people's lives. But in truth, if you are quantifying sabotage raids, these have to be represented in the context of the overall war effort. When one compares the loss of a submarine, then costing £350,000, or a bomber at around £70,000 with a large bomb costing £100[1] and then compare it with the outline plan to attack Bordeaux with two divisions, it is easy to see that, for a total cost of less than £1,000 in materials for canoes and explosives, the RMBPD action represented a lesser monetary risk. It is an unfortunate accounting statistic that the training of a canoeist was considerably less costly than training their counterparts as aircraft crew. The unquantifiable calculation is the measurement in morale that successful raids like this produced, and in warfare, this is another important factor, along with the great psychological principle of offensive actions. This offensive does confer the initiative and with it liberty of action and the denial of it to the enemy. For the French people, in this instance, the *Frankton* Raid showed the Germans not to be the 'master race', but those who could be shown to be vulnerable and lesser individuals than the propaganda broadcast by them suggested.

German propaganda reactions were significant evidence that the impact of the raid provided deep psychological damage upon the German morale and served as a reminder to the French people that all efforts were being made to disrupt the German war machine. This one operation moved a German naval officer[2] to describe the *Frankton* Raid as 'the outstanding commando raid of the war'. In real terms, this was only a pinprick in the overall offensive actions undertaken, but the intent was that there were to be many pinpricks. The overriding factor is that the *Frankton* Raid did achieve a tactical surprise. Had it not been for the 'Hitler Order', the only casualties suffered would have been those sustained by ordinary peril. For true success in war, there is a need for the maintenance of the objective as well as offensive action, for the objective must be ruthlessly pursued with the maximum concentration of force. This was something Corporal Hitler, best General on the Allied side, neglected to a staggering degree in major matters. It can be honestly said that the Allied side were not always right but made far fewer transgressions. *Frankton* was the pursuance of one of the principles of warfare. One thing that the *Frankton* Raid was undoubtedly successful in was not providing the excuse for the Germans to undertake reprisals against the local inhabitants.

Within the Admiralty docket (The *Frankton* File) on the attack on French ports of October 1942, stress was laid on the vital importance of the blockade runners to the German economic strategy, which dated back to before July 1942. It highlighted shipping targets, dredgers and floating dock servicing the port of Bordeaux. These identified targets were also subjects of discussion for the Chief Planners of the Plans Division of the Admiralty during mid-1943. The problem of the blockade runners post-*Frankton* still existed. It was for this same problem that offensive action was still required. More importantly, the area of interest centred on shipping ready to sail at that time as well as others that would be ready to sail shortly afterwards. These ships were especially interesting, as they were reported to be carrying spare U-boat parts for the Far East, and it was considered important to prevent them sailing. Again, an attack by airborne forces was mooted during August 1943 and examined at the same time were methods of attack by seaborne forces.

The first of these methods was the original 1942 idea of the Mobile Flotation Unit (MFU), and at first sight, it was believed that the MFU was the ideal means of carrying out the operation, but due to the fact that any submarine carrier would require considerable structural alterations, it was not thought a viable option. (The MFU was then being developed for carriage in surface craft, but because of the urgency, this method of attack was out of the question.)

The Plans Division also seriously considered a 'repeat of Operation *Frankton*', which was discussed with Blondie Hasler, and the following conclusions prevailed. The previous operation (*Frankton*) was carried out in a condition of flat calm which was most exceptional, and the odds were against that occurring again. It was pointed out that, in spite of the calm weather, two canoes were lost in the tide race, and Hasler was of the opinion that, under any other sea conditions, it was unlikely that *any* of the canoes would have got through the race. The possibility of using more seaworthy canoes was examined, but the view was that it was not practicable without sacrificing other features essential to the success of the operation. (Even by August 1943, canoe development had only just begun in earnest.) Hasler believed that, in view of the experience gained, it was likely that once the mouth of the river had been passed, the passage up the river could be carried out as easily, or even more so, than on Operation *Frankton*. Hasler's view was that the most difficult part of the operation would be the actual attack on the ships. The NID were able to inform the planners that, for four months after *Frankton*, the Germans took all possible precautions to prevent further attack, but it was also reported that those measures had been discontinued by mid-1943, and the state of alert was even less vigilant than it was before *Frankton*. Given the intended period of attack, November 1943 – January 1944, it was thought difficult to believe that the occupying forces would not reinforce their precautions during that same period, especially given the presence of the valuable ships, which were the subject of the proposed attack. It was also pointed out that, from the *Frankton* night intruders' viewpoint, the weather conditions were bad: flat calm and bright, starlit night. It was considered that the probability of getting the same unfavourable weather during the proposed months was low.

An interesting point at that time was that it had already been decided that Hasler was not to go on the operation should this type of attempt be made again. That being the case, it was probable no other officer would be available that had the skill in the same type of work. Although a decision had yet to be made, it was pointed out that, if a repeat of the *Frankton* Raid were mounted, it would take at least one month to train the force and assemble the stores required. Such an attack could have been mounted at the end of September or the beginning of October 1943 during the dark period, but a decision would have to be made immediately, i.e., August 1943. The Flag Officer Submarines (FOS) had already proved willing to provide a submarine during the desired dates. It was considered that the chances of bringing off another operation on the same lines as *Frankton* were about *four to one against*.

Other methodologies of attack by seaborne forces were considered: 'Intermediate Carriers' – this was being developed by Hasler at that time (mid-1943) and was thought to be a possible way of getting the attacking canoes through the tide race and into the mouth of the river; 'Suit Cases' – involving dropping boats by parachute (akin to air/sea rescue then being deployed), but this suffered due to the lack of an advanced stage of development; Swimmers and 'Sleeping Beauties' – thought to be a more efficient system than the canoe option, but it too had not reached a sufficient state of development for immediate use; Wellman and Well-freighters – this suffered from the same lack of development. An interesting point was raised with regards to the use of Limpets. In the case of normal harbours where vessels lay alongside quays in a depth of water that had only been dredged out sufficiently to take them, it was pointed out that Limpet attacks were unlikely to make a vessel a total loss, as it would result in the vessels resting on the bottom, and at low tide, salvage could be affected. It was know that, if the engine was targeted and had been flooded, this would result in said vessels being out of action for at least three months in the case of steam-driven and considerably longer in the case of a diesel-engined vessel.

It was also for consideration whether a device on the same lines as a Limpet could have been evolved which did not take action until the ship was at sea. It should be noted that some work had already been done on these very lines.

It was considered that the same problems remained with regard to bombing, yet this was the only viable method of attack in the immediate time frame. Evidently, due to the lack of advanced designing, the only hope was to produce something more satisfactory for the job than the Limpet. The most obvious action would have been to produce this device and have it attached so that the vessel or preferably vessels would explode simultaneously when in deep channel in such a place that would make any salvage very difficult and would then prevent further traffic of blockade runners using the port.

Until the RMBPD came about, there was neither the personnel nor the method of deployment; even then it was all rather rushed, but the best of efforts were undertaken, which resulted in the *Frankton* Raid.

The Results of 'the Outstanding Commando Raid of the War'

As Hasler, Sparks, Laver and Mills had made good their escape over land, the Limpets were busy fizzing away underwater fixed to the hulls of the ships. The daily journal of the Commander of the Port (Kühnemann) had recorded the fact that a telephone message had been received on 11 December stating that two suspected saboteurs had been captured at the mouth of the Gironde and that the cargo ships had been instructed to be of increased vigilance. The report of the events beginning on the early morning of 12 December are extracted from the information taken from accounts in German documents.

The ships damaged by explosions at Bassens and Bordeaux on the morning of 12 December were the ex-French ship SS *Alabama* (5,641 tons), SS *Tannenfels* (7,840), SS *Portland* (7,132) and SS *Dresden* (5,567). Two of the ships were lying alongside the quay at Bassens facing up stream and two alongside the quay on the west side of Bordeaux harbour.

All of the explosions occurred on the seaward side of the vessels and the first of five explosions on SS *Alabama* occurred at 0700. During the panic that followed, no casualties or deaths occurred. The following is the definitive account of the damage to the ships.

Ship	Time	Where Damaged	Actual Damage Reported
Alabama	1. 0700	Near hatch 5	Hole about 1.4 x 0.8 m
	2. 0703	Near hatch 1	Near hatch 1. Splinter from this
	3. 0800	Near hatch 4	this explosion made hole in
	4. 1005	Aft	starboard side above waterline
	5. 1305	Forward	line. Second explosion
		All 1.5 m below	caused bulge below 1st hole.
		water-line on	Hole about 1.25 x 0.7 m.
		port side	near hatch 5 and a bulge
			similar to that near hatch 1.

Aerial view showing Quai Carnon at Bacalan and the ships damaged by Hasler and Sparks' Limpet mines. This image was taken within days of the explosions. Note the floating crane, tenders and the degree of list of the ships.

Tannenfels	1.0830	Between hatches 2 and 3	2 holes 1 x 0.6 m.
	2.+ 30 secs	2.5 m below waterline	
Dresden	1. 0845	Near hatch 4	2 holes 1.25 x 0.8 m
	2. 0855	Near hatch 5	Also hole in shaft tunnel.
Portland	1. 0955	Near hatch 1 Starboard side, 1.5 m below water-line	Hole 1.8 x 0.85 m

It was reported that an explosive charge was discovered on the pier side of SS *Portland*, which would account for the lack of a second reported damaged area on this ship. A further explosion occurred about 1030 on the seaward side of a *Sperrbrecher* (believed no. 5, ex-*Schwanheim*[3]), but it was reported that no damage was caused, as it was presumed that the Limpets (L4 and L5) had dropped off the ship's side and exploded on the riverbed.

The damage to ships was reported as follows: *Alabama*, water penetrated through hatches 4 and 5; *Tannenfels*, water penetrated through hatches 2 and 3 into hold, ship had list of about 18 degrees, which increased rapidly to 24 degrees, but countermeasures were successfully undertaken to prevent the ship from capsizing; *Dresden*, holds 4, 5, 6 and 7 filled with water, stern of the ship sank to bottom, leaks were sealed by 2130 but work was necessary until the evening of 12/13 December, and by the morning of the 14th, the holds were emptied; *Portland*, little water penetrated and the hole was soon sealed provisionally. (By February 1943, SS *Portland* was ready to sail and was loaded with machine tools and spare parts and left once but returned to Verdon.)

All the ships were empty at the time of the explosions. All damage was reported as being slight. The work undertaken by the divers made it possible to seal both *Dresden* and *Tannenfels* (moored alongside the Quai Carnon at Bacalan). These were re-floated at the next high tide and remained afloat.

In these reports, there was no mention of the single and last Limpet (L8 on the diagram on p.88) placed under the poop of a petrol tanker later identified in some reports to have been *Cap Hadid*[4], 4,000 tons[5]. The full ramifications of the Limpet attack on this ship were not realised until this research. In fact, at the time of the *Frankton* Raid, the Limpet mine identified as L8 said to have been placed on the petrol tanker reported to have been the *Cap Hadid* was in fact placed on a conventional-looking merchant ship with engines amidships named *Python*.[6]

At the time of the raid, this *Python* was attacked with at least one Limpet. Interestingly, it seems that, during the time prior to 1942, the *Python* moored at Bordeaux was possibly a *Tarnschiff* (camouflage ship) – a decoy – if the commissioning date is to be believed. During the *Frankton* Raid, the (previously a decoy ship) *Python* was being employed as a *Versorgen* – a supply ship refueling U-boats at sea. *Python* was not a bulk tanker in the conventional sense but was equipped to transfer diesel fuel and other stores such as fresh food as well as mail to U-boats at sea; there was a U-boat pen at Bordeaux. This fits in well with the fact that even the SOE agent at the time said that he had 'not seen a tanker in Bordeaux – all the oil arriving in barrels'.

Hasler never knew the true use of this ship. Through this research, it can be claimed that *Python* turned out to be quite an important target.[7] Given the report saying that the explosion resulted with the ship settling and fire breaking out, it would seem that the damage caused was substantial enough to prevent *Python* being used in her role as a *Versorgen* and converted into an expendable Sperrbrecher 122 in February 1943, in some quarters reported as a mine barrier breaker. This is the only ship that was damaged enough for it to be relegated to a more dangerous and expendable role. Ships like *Python* were converted with their hulls being reinforced and fitted with a large number of anti-aircraft guns. They led convoys through any dangerous waters. Vessels such as these were much larger than purpose-built minesweepers.

Of the *Sperrbrecher*, named *Schwanheim*, mentioned in the report, which was moored at Quai des Chartrons, it seems that these Limpets had fallen off, and as they detonated, a tall geyser of water and mud plumed skywards. Each ship was evacuated during the ensuing explosive event and guards were posted all along the quay and simply watched in fear and awe as each of the explosions occurred.

At the time, the harbour master requested the intervention of the French Fire Brigade and the Coastal Mine Defence Service (CMDS); indeed, the Italian Admiral Polacchini, who was busy improving his submarine base security, gave up three of his deep-sea divers to help the CMDS technicians and began to examine the damage but had to be recalled due to the continued explosions until it was deemed safe for them to continue. Both the CMDS and the 'on loan' Italian divers did succeed in preventing any of the damaged ships from capsizing. By using baulks of timber and bags of special cement, they managed to block up the holes in the hulls, enabling the vessels to be pumped out. Both the Italian divers and the French firemen were singled out for praise in the way they conducted themselves.

An amusing anecdote can be related about the French Fire Brigade based at Bacalan in this regard. Whilst Commander Kühnemann reported that 'the fire teams arrived immediately and carried out their work with the pumps efficiently and with remarkable enthusiasm', he did so without the knowledge that some of the firemen were members of the Resistance movement. Chief Engineer Raymond Brard[8] was responsible for equipment and security in the port, whilst the Chief of the Fire Service, Captain Paduch, had rapidly deployed in the areas concerned the port's pumping tender, the 'Stockling', along with six motorised pumps. Whilst the enthusiasm was noticed by the Germans, they had not noticed that instead of pumping water *out* of the ships, some pumps were, in fact, pumping water from the Gironde *into* some of the ships' holds!

It became apparent that the repairs to the ships were abetted by the fact that two ships sank on an even keel in very shallow water and were repaired quickly. A third heeled over on her side, but the Germans managed, presumably by flooding her tanks, to right her so she then fell over on the other side, leaving the damage exposed with temporary repairs made.

Right: Fire tender and crew.

Below: Bordeaux Port fire brigade on the quay.

Even then it took a long time before one ship came out of dry dock. Immediately after the raid, no one in the locale knew what had happened, and the common gossip was that the Italians had sunk the ships in revenge because the Germans did not intend to allow them to use the U-boat shelters nearby. At the time, 'everybody said "it is just the sort of thing the Italians would do, sinking merchant ships in the night"'. Once it had been realised what had actually transpired, 'vigilance was very greatly increased'. It should be noted that when the submarine shelters were finished in March 1943, all the German submarines in the port were housed in the shelters and the Italian submarines were left outside, 'much to the indignation of the Italians'. The SOE agent at the time (Scientist) did feel that 'the best way of getting at the German crews of the submarines was through the Italians, since very bad feeling exists between the two'.

Apart from the fact that the whole town had been instantly placed under the strictest of military control, certain countermeasures were proposed by Commander Kühnemann, which included a strengthening of patrols and pickets guarding shore installations and an increase in harbour patrols; a night boat patrol for the entire harbour including that of Bassens; an increase of the crew of the guard vessel at the harbour entrance with instructions that the searchlight was to be used to sweep the shore at regular intervals; ships in harbour were to be illuminated from shore with immediate effect; the domestic quay lighting was to be restored to full working order; the sea area had to be swept repeatedly by searchlights at high tide, provided the air situation permitted; any shore installations not included in the rounds were to be protected with barbed-wire entanglements and the Pauillac floating dock, the gate of the Gironde wharf and the large stone bridge at Bordeaux were to be protected by river booms. Two other orders were made: if an explosion occurred on the side of a ship, the sides of that ship and of all ships in the vicinity had to be searched by means of poles for further charges; merchant ships in harbour had to have two sentries posted, one on the gangway and one on the seaward side of the ship. The Gironde Estuary itself was now to be guarded by two patrol vessels between Pointe de Grave and Royan and by three searchlight batteries at Fort Royan, St Georges and Le Verdon, all to search at regular intervals. In addition, land patrols were to be conducted on either side of the river. At the time, it was unclear how long these measures actually lasted before apathy set in once more.

At first, the Germans were under the impression that the attack on the ships had been carried out by drifting underwater weaponry, but as soon as the men from the unit began being captured, together with the discovery of equipment, it was soon revealed how this operation had been conducted. One of the first secret messages received by Naval Intelligence (NID), dated 21 December 1942, reports, 'The merchant ships *Dresden* and *Alabama* and three others were damaged by mysterious explosions on December 12th. Two ships were at Bassens and three at Bacalan. The damage can be repaired.' From an extract from a captured Italian document, it can be shown how these *mysterious explosions* came about: 'In Atlantic Port 4 German merchant ships have been damaged by explosive devices applied to the hull, probably the work of Commandos disembarked unobserved.'

Following the raid, it became dangerous for any individual to go on the river or the banks, as anyone could be shot on sight without warning. The morale of the French people was low before the raid but became very high afterwards and remained so for some time.

Definitive accounts were required in order to assess the impact that Operation *Frankton* had on the blockade-runners traffic. An interview between an officer in Naval Intelligence (NID) and a well-informed French officer who had been in Bordeaux until mid-March 1943 gives some indication. It was said that cargoes were cleared quickly, and he mentioned that unless bombing could be done within a day or two of arrival, it was thought it would be a pointless exercise. He was able to say that the blockade runners were in excellent condition and the morale of the crews was first class as was that of the naval crews. The naval crews and the Italian U-boat crews both had the belief that they were winning the war.

In recent years, much has been made of an intended SOE attack on the blockade runners in Bordeaux, yet this seems to be based on very little. Whilst it is a fact that many SOE documents were consumed by fire, there seems to be no firm evidence that the SOE action was at an advanced stage except anecdotal information from the SOE official historian, Professor M. R. D. Foot, who is related as saying, 'The SOE were actually on the quay making their final recce before they attacked the following night, when they heard some quiet pops below the water and their targets started to settle into the water under their noses. They were furious.' It is believed that this overstates the actual events, as the requisite PRO file informs us only that 'Scientist was well on the way to organise an attack on his shipping targets by the introduction of a reasonably large quantity of explosives through dockers and the paint sealers working on the vessels. At the critical moment the commando attack took place.'

The statement that 'they heard some quiet pops below the water' does not ring true, and it can be evidenced that great plumes of water were sent heavenward following the Limpet explosions – hardly 'quiet pops'!

Claude de Baissac, alias Scientist, was miffed by the RMBPD attack, but again, apart from alleged intent, nothing firm has been found to unquestionably prove that an SOE action was as imminent as Foot describes; it is therefore suggested that Foot's comment is not based on fact[9]. In London, an SOE debriefer wrote of Baissac, 'Scientist, rather indignantly, asks why he was not informed of this attack upon one of his targets.' Baissac was indeed *allocated* targets within Bordeaux including the blockade runners and their cargoes, but that does not mean that his 'show' was the next day or days. If one looks at the intent from Baissac's file, it can be shown that inroads had been made to smuggle in explosive via tins of food, but that is all.

In truth, it is unknown what kind of attack the SOE had in mind. If the SOE recce on the quay was indeed as related, then the reprisals against the French population would have been swift and deadly. In order to negate these reprisals, an attack would have had to be planned in order for sizeable explosives to have detonated en route either in the Gironde or at sea not at harbour.

With the RMBPD effort, no French nationals were executed or imprisoned; the Germans were sated when they knew it was a Commando action. With this in mind and the fact that the blockade runners were active post-*Frankton*, the SOE agents could still have carried out an action with the ships en route with the knowledge that the Germans would have suspected another Limpet mine action by Commandos rather than a Resistance effort. Such an action would have been especially easy given the fact that a state of reduced vigilance was evident during the summer months. Since no actions were documented or reported in this regard by the SOE, the validity of the claim regarding just how far the SOE action had progressed is brought into question. If the SOE action had been so far advanced, requiring the strategic planting of a considerable amount of explosives in the interior of the ships, i.e., the engine room, it is likely that these explosives would have been found during the subsequent checks on the damaged ships. No reports of this kind were filed by the Germans. There would have been no time to recover these explosives, and it is suggested that none were planted. Most interestingly, what can be proved is that certain operatives had only been placed in Bordeaux by November 1942. These two agents were given rubber and other cargoes entering the port as main targets in the following order: the ships, cargo in the ships, cargo on the wharf or warehouse, cargo on rail. It is also known that at that time repeated efforts had been made to get stores to this group 'but only one has been successful, on 20th November 1942'. This was a mixed consignment of arms and explosives; the explosives consisted of 60 lb of Plastic explosive and 15 clams.

With this information, it does seem likely that the intent to attack might have been that aimed at cargo rather than the ships themselves at that time. Given the known quantity of explosives, the local knowledge that the ships would only sink to one metre and that they could be salvaged quickly, as was the case post the *Frankton* Raid, it is doubted that this (from the SOE perspective) would have proved a viable way forward. Despite the fact that there was an urgent and crucial requirement to prevent or at least curtail the blockade runners operating from the Port of Bordeaux, it was deemed unacceptable to bomb the port. Even though it was in range from the airfields of the west of England, this bombing action would have only alienated the local populace.

Agents of the SOE in Bordeaux and elsewhere were of the view that too much sabotage at certain points would result in reprisals and that tended to deplete the French population. An SOE report recorded that 'when innocent folk suffer the populace gets very bitter'. On one occasion, when a container of ammunition was blown up, two men were arrested, and the following morning, the entire village was taken to jail including the children. The villagers were released after fifteen days but became hostages and faced being shot should another subversive act be perpetrated within that district.

The SOE agents would therefore have ensured any sabotage action was not seen to be emanating from the workers at the port. It is, of course, possible that the SOE agent concerned (Baissac) was just lining his own nest in this regard and made more of the facts than the reality. Either way, the records[10] do not reveal anything other than an intent that was not at an advanced stage. It is believed that much has been made by modern-day sensationalists searching for a 'new' twist on the *Frankton* Raid story. These 'researchers' provide alleged infringements on SOE agents' targeted areas in the Port of Bordeaux, but these are un-evidenced. Baissac was only parachuted into France on 30 July 1942, was injured on landing, then found it difficult to initially recruit personnel, and his profile was recorded as being 'extremely French and volatile' and with 'excessive self confidence'. This serves only to show that whilst he had been given targets and some planning had been done, that was the extent of his efforts. As his instructions were to certain cargoes of rubber either aboard ships or stored elsewhere, it is uncertain where the alleged intended smuggled tins of explosives were destined for. No doubt Baissac was miffed that his 'turf' had been infringed upon, and given his volatile nature, it is likely that he gave an enhanced report of his efforts in attacking the shipping. It does seem odd that Baissac should himself point out the error in making attacks resulting in the deaths of French civilians, which could be avoided by other methods, only to commit to an attack that certainly would have resulted in heavy reprisals. What can be certain is that the intelligence Baissac provided regarding the blockade runners operating from Bordeaux was graded as 'very high' by MEW and the Admiralty.

Conflicting opinions about the impact Operation *Frankton* had on the war effort prevail. The loss of life for the sake solely of morale boosting seems offensive; regardless, there is absolutely no doubting the bravery, courage and endeavour of all the participants. It has to be remembered that, without the '*Kommandobefehl*' being in existence, the only real peril would have been a domestic one. It was an unfortunate twist in warfare that led to the execution of the captured men.

One other rather interesting facet remains seemingly unresolved. It was known by MEW that cargo being shipped to Japan was believed to consist of prototypes of various weaponry such as radar as well as other equipment used in manufacture that the Japanese did not possess. We also have firm evidence of intelligence regarding ships sailings and the cargo carried. We therefore can rightfully assume that, in rough terms, it would have been possible to identify when and which ships would be carrying the most important radar equipment. Baissac himself had been instructed which cargo to target and given specific areas in which to operate, but none mentions any cargo to do with radar or prototype weaponry.

It was thought that the *Frankton* Raid was unlikely to succeed or would result in 100 per cent casualties probably after the event if not before, but given the need for action, it was authorised. But why was it authorised? Was there something of such great importance over and above that of mere organic materials? Maybe the truth can be gleaned from a post-war comment emanating from Mountbatten himself via HRH The Duke of Edinburgh when he said, 'The raid was specifically planned in order to destroy four German ships which were about to sail for Japan with radar equipment.'

Presuming the intended targets of *Frankton* were the new technologies, it is possible there would have to be specific intelligence to show that this cargo was on board at the time within specified ships. This information does not and may well not have ever existed. It is likely that, if the developing technologies were the target, the *Frankton* Raid was speculative in this regard and that, with all or most of the five teams placing each of their eight Limpets apiece on shipping, the odds of getting these 'important' technologies would be high. Either way, with up to forty Limpet mines exploding in almost uniform pattern, this would have been most spectacular and extremely disconcerting for the Germans. It is also likely that had more Limpets been placed the forces would not have been able to cope and more damage would have occurred, with certain ships turning on their side and blocking more of the shipping channel.

Alas, only a maximum of sixteen Limpets were available for the task on the night. Regardless, given the fact that the ships were easily repaired in situ due to the shallow draft afforded in the harbour to these ships, it would seem that this one flaw, i.e., the lack of this knowledge, existed in the intelligence of the *Frankton* Docket. The SOE ground troops knew of this caveat to the attacks to shipping at the quay, and knowing this, they would not have mined the ships at the quay. This reasoning gives more validity to the argument that the SOE were not on the quay as Foot suggests and had no impending desire or intent to do mischief to the ships whilst tied up on the quays.

It is a known fact that other targets were identified by SOE agents within Bordeaux and included the floating cranes and the dredgers of the harbour.[11] The latter were imperative to the access of shipping to the port and were in almost continual operation. It is known that the SOE agents were aware of this importance and considered these as viable entities; it is believed access to these was the only problem. If the dredgers were so crucial to prevent the silting up of the harbour, the question has to be asked why these were not dealt with by the SOE. There are many questions that could be posed.

The facts are that it proved viable and possible to undertake an operation that was thought to be so implausible that it was a mission too far – pointless, impossible. But that is the point. If we were to take that view of an impossible mission, even today, we would never have specialists in our nation who show us that the impossible is achievable. There can be no half measures in warfare – 'Moderation in war is imbecility.'[12]

CHAPTER 9
The 'Not Forgotten'

'Ar dheis De go raibh a n-anamacha'[1]

'There are two kinds of people in my world, valley people and mountain people. Valley people seek the calm and comfortable ground of shelter, safety and security. Mountain people have decided that valley life is not for them, and seek to test ambition on the toughest climbs. They take the risk of winning because, to them, there's no such thing as a risk of losing.'[2]

It is difficult for anyone to fully describe any individual unless they have spent a near lifetime knowing them. Of those souls that ventured out for their undertaking on the *Frankton* Raid, only two can be written about to any great degree. Of the others, very little is available, as most had not yet experienced enough of life. It seems inequable, but the author, with every endeavour[3], has tried to ensure that the memory and character of the individuals who had their lives dishonestly taken from them are finally and fully recorded even after the many years that have past. This compilation of information has, without doubt, been enormously assisted by those relatives who it has been possible to contact, even after all these many years. They have not forgotten them.

All these individuals who were part of the Royal Marines Boom Patrol Detachment (RMBPD) were men who made choices that determined their part in the history books; for most of the raiding party, this cost them their lives. Some of the information is surprising, some is amusing and some of it is saddening. It is, however, a reflection of the essence of human nature. This is the unbiased reporting, taken from oral histories and documents, of the known details of each of the men who were chosen for this most difficult of hazardous service. From some of the men are reported correspondences; the other men no doubt sent similar letters to loved ones. If these men had survived, they would, no doubt, think their little escapade was of no special significance, and the role they played was just one of many of that era that was acted out during a conflict that would remain etched into the history of mankind.

They were just ordinary men, the few from what was available, Volunteers for Hazardous Service, that made the grade, who were then moulded into something very special. Few things are stronger than the heart of a volunteer. Some of those volunteers lived and gathered a lifetime of precious memories; it is the nature of warfare that most on this famous intruder raid did not. Of the thirteen men mentioned, ten that launched their canoes on the night of 7 December were posted as 'missing in action' on 31 December 1942.[4] These are the few who left a legacy that has and will continue to inspire very many others from many walks of life. These men were not anxious to die – just anxious to matter.

The Doors We Choose to Open Define the Path in Our Lives

'Do you realise that your expectation of a long life is very remote?'

This quoted sentence is one of the vivid memories from 1942 recalled by Marine Norman Colley, who was volunteering for a place in the new formation that became known as the Royal Marines Boom Patrol Detachment. Solely due to a game of rugby, this man's destiny was changed forever.

Each man who answered the call for 'Volunteers for Hazardous Service' was asked this rather rhetorical question by Major Herbert George 'Blondie' Hasler before he finished each and every interview. Each man now picked, and in Blondie's care, had different reasons for applying.

It is probably best to recall Blondie Hasler's own words when he said of the men that they were 'just a good cross section of average young fellows and we had to do the best with what was offered to us'; this should be remembered as each vignette of the thirteen men's lives is read. The *Frankton* Raid became the prominent feature in the deaths of those that did not return and in the life of Bill Sparks. This, however, was not the case with Herbert George 'Blondie' Hasler, who felt the actual expression of 'the Cockleshell Heroes' was inaccurately embarrassing, and that the incident, whilst of great valour, itself was of little significance in the war effort as a whole. For Blondie, it was certainly not a feature prominent in his well-documented life.

In truth, he sought not to profit from or revel in the limelight given in the subsequent media coverage. As the man who was responsible for the action, he knew well the likely outcome, as did Mountbatten. A realist, Hasler was always mindful of those who did not return.

This photograph was the last picture taken of most of those picked to go on the *Frankton* Raid. Taken off Southsea Esplanade on 10 September 1942 (note distance of drop from wall to stone beach), it shows testing of Goatley's collapsible assault boat as pictured in the Father Cockle chapter. Top photo, front row, left to right: MacKinnon at the helm, Sheard, Moffatt, Ewart, Laver. Bottom photo, front row: Sgt Wallace, Conway, Fisher, Mills.

Herbert George 'Blondie' Hasler, DSO, OBE
'An Indefatigable Experimenter and Tinkerer'

Blondie Hasler

No truer words have been written of Blondie Hasler than those of HRH The Duke of Edinburgh: 'His lifelong passion was small boats which his Commission in the Royal Marines did nothing to abate. What became famous as the "Cockleshell Heroes" raid on German shipping in Bordeaux could only have been conceived and led by someone with a deep understanding of – and faith in – small boats.'

Even as a small boy, Blondie had a symbiotic relationship with the wet stuff that was to last for very many years; it can be said that the sea was always to be his mistress. He was originally responsible for bringing about the single-handed transatlantic yacht race after a conversation with David Astor in 1957; it is believed that he was also involved with a half-crown[5] wager with Sir Francis Chichester about the event!

A great deal has already been written about this man; here, a brief synopsis of his character is offered. What can be made plain is that, without any doubt, the men of the RMBPD admired him immensely, even though the regime for them was extremely tough.

It is true to say that Blondie Hasler was a decent sort, a few faults but no more than average for anyone who is so single-minded. Very few definitions of character are found. He had 'a capacity to see the hidden depths in a volunteer'. Those that greatly admired him found him 'somewhat unpredictable'[6]. Another individual reports that 'he had a way of commanding respect from all who knew him for his bearing and ready smile, quiet humour and the practical way he approached any task they gave him, leadership qualities so rarely found in others. I've seen officers and senior NCOs stop what they were doing just to watch him walk from A to B then get on with their job with renewed vigour; it was as if they had received a tonic.'[7] One senior officer[8] wrote of him,

> Thinks clearly and expresses himself well, particularly on technical subjects, and has a lively imagination with a leaning towards development or invention. Despises cant, but is apt to classify in this category too readily. He is intolerant of opinion which he does not share, often despite lack of knowledge or experience to back his own opinion. He has not yet fully realised the need for the petty day to day methods of maintaining good discipline and for this reason appears to lack firmness in dealing with his subordinates. He often fails to hold a balanced point of view on general subjects. He is in the centre of work which borders on a hobby for him and works exceptionally hard and long.

The same officer also believed Hasler was 'too good to be true for the job he was employed'. Another officer[9] was to write that 'Blondie's contribution to Allied victory in the Far East has never been adequately recognised'.

Of accolades, sometimes it is better to quote from individuals who are known to carry humour and the sense of the ridiculous in their heart and mind and therefore give a better understanding and a more balanced viewpoint. One such man was the captain of the submarine who ensured the safe launching of the five Cockles and ten men that were finally and successfully disembarked for the *Frankton* Raid. Even though Capt. Dickie Raikes had only days of Blondie's company in HMS *Tuna*, he made an important observation many years later when he said of him that 'he was a chap that never showed any emotion, for him it was just the next job'. The captain can also be quoted as saying, 'I think Blondie was without doubt one of the very finest men I ever met in my whole life'... and that Blondie was ... a 'born leader, no bullshit about him at all. He was quiet; he was a character'[10]. Dickie Raikes

Hasler at different stages in his career.

'remained in touch with him all his life' and was proud to state that on record. Another observation by Raikes reveals he believed that 'there can be several fulcrums in anyone's life but without doubt the *Frankton* Raid was definitely one of them for Blondie Hasler'.

In 1953, Blondie gave a surprising little insight into his view of how the war years were for clandestine operations, and in a 'parting thought', entitled just that, he wrote, 'In peace time, the oceans of the world are becoming increasingly littered with eager Britons making long passages in boats as small as 18 feet in overall length. Often they report having made vain attempts to attract the attention of steamers passing within one mile in daylight. In war, the national genius for making ourselves at home, but invisible, in the Ocean does not seem to have been exploited at all.'

In truth, there is very little that can be written that has not already been said and to do so would be inappropriate given the fact that the others from his team were not so fortunate. Here then is a whirlwind tour within just a few words. It has been said that he was 'a prolific author; portrait painter; cartoonist; musician[11]; gifted amateur hydrographer; a diligent searcher for the Loch Ness monster; inventor and an Ocean racer'. Interestingly, even though they were only together a short time, it was through the production of the film *Cockleshell Heroes* another friendship was made, between Blondie and the lead actor José Ferrer. Ferrer wrote of Blondie, 'I could write a short book on him, for he was an example of what each of us can be if he wants to, and if he sets his standards and ideals high.'

However, there are windows that have never been opened. A hint into his dry humour can be evidenced by referring to copy from a *Daily Express* article that briefly reported on the reunion of the two surviving 'Cockleshell Heroes' and their French helpers at the presentation of a commemorative brass plague at Ruffec in France. The story was relegated to page nine, where their visit shared the page with a story of a 'Model (19) mauled by [a Siberian] Tiger' on John Aspinal's Estate; she attempted to try to tickle the 'tame' tiger under the chin! Hasler's humour was evident when he mentioned that had the headline been 'Tiger (19) mauled by model then they [the Ruffec story] would never have made it' at all. He also noted that the paper had even omitted to mention the fact that they were Royal Marines!

Hasler had earned the nickname of 'Blondie' during his early years in the Corps, but by 1942, the then acting major, at the age of twenty-eight, had already lost most of his pale reddish-golden hair but had retained the 'flowing mane of a moustache' of the same colour, which he sported with some distinction. He had a well-formed, strong frame and at 5 feet 11 inches tall not only did he look like an individualist, his actions told you he was. He had what can only be described as an eye for detail, and to some this can be an irritant, not only because it requires a like-minded individual to understand, but because it can show others as lesser people. He was most certainly one of a few, not one of the many. He did, however, have a naivety of commercial matters that in civilian life proved to be his Achilles' heel, and he was taken advantage of on more than one occasion.

He was reported to be 'less of an expert in men than in things', saying himself, 'I can never bring myself to punish anyone if it can possibly be avoided.' He had the ability to talk to the common man in their language, could assert his authority and seemed to mean it, but was not apt to carry out matters too far. He wanted his men to put every effort into training and provided an objective which had to be met; he thought to penalise was a negative thing; he was not a bully and would not tolerate any of his men being bullied from whatever quarter, and was keen to allow his men to stand on their own feet and make their own decisions.

Blondie would reserve drinking sessions with his marines for special occasions and even then only when he was invited. He did prefer to associate with small groups: the company of those he knew and liked. Some thought he lived in a world of his own, and unlike others, he was free to pursue the world of the things he enjoyed. He really disliked reunions, preferring to look forward than backwards, but out of duty attended with gusto.

Blondie was both choleric and phlegmatic. It was said that he 'took a completely unconventional approach to everything he attempted and often had a profound influence on things as a result'. He had 'an inquisitive mind' and possessed a great energy.

He married late in life at the age of fifty-one in the October of 1965 and soon found that a 'small daughter who effectively sabotages all other projects'[12] was replacing one passion for another. It was once remarked that, as we have two ears and one mouth, a good leader listens twice as much as he talks; it is evident that Blondie was a good leader of men. 'A courteous man who was quietly spoken'[13] is how the now-ninety-one-year-old Norman Colley remembers Blondie, 'He would never ask you to do anything he couldn't do.'

A Service of Thanksgiving was held on 19 June 1987[14] at Portsmouth Cathedral for the life of Lt-Col. Herbert George 'Blondie' Hasler, DSO, OBE, and most of the assembled knew that he had been a distinguished Royal Marines officer in the Second World War who was responsible for many of the concepts that led to the post-war incarnation of the Special Boat Service.

He had served as fleet landing officer in Scapa Flow in 1940 and was then sent to Narvik in support of the French Foreign Legion in the Norwegian campaign, for which duties he was appointed OBE, Mentioned in Dispatches, and awarded the Croix de Guerre. At the age of twenty-eight, he planned and led Operation *Frankton*, for which he was subsequently awarded the DSO. In 1944, he became OC of the Special Operations Group (SOG) in Ceylon. Following being invalided out of military service at the age of thirty-four, Blondie spent four years living on an 18-ton yacht on the Hamble River in the winter at the Moody's Yard at Swanwick and summer cruising with a small crew sometimes around the coast of Britain but more often the coast of Spain. During this time, he also produced a book on the harbours and anchorages of the north coast of Brittany amongst his many other writings. He devoted two years in the mid-fifties to the development of a new rig for sailing boats in conjunction with Vospers Ltd. Blondie retired in later years to a home in Scotland, where he pursued organic farming well before it was all the rage and the reinvention of certain agricultural methods.

He was born in Dublin on 27 February 1914 and died in Argyll on 5 May 1987, and whatever else has and could be written, it has to be said that Blondie Hasler did have a hunger that propelled him and his men unknowingly into the history books.

To get an unbiased viewpoint seems impossible, and that is perhaps the best of accolades anyone can give. The last words are given over to Sparks, who is recorded saying that Blondie was 'never one to be selfish' and 'as well as [his] dry humour, he possessed an incredible amount of patience'. Speaking of how Blondie handled him during the escape route, Sparks said, 'I often reached a point of such frustration that I would loose off with a long succession of complaints. He never admonished me for it, he just waited for the storm to abate and calmly said, "Have you finished?".'

He was the Commanding Officer of the *Frankton* Raid, which was solely his brainchild, and was also 'A' Division Commander and No. 1 in Cockle canoe *Catfish*. He was described by Mountbatten during this role as showing 'courage, skill, discretion and perseverance in the highest degree'.

Like the indomitable pair Sherlock Holmes and Watson, it was inevitable that Blondie Hasler would be always inextricably linked to his No. 2 in Cockle canoe *Catfish* or perhaps this slightly built, curly haired, wiry cockney with an infectious laugh was forever to be linked with Hasler. Either way, this shoe repairer, until the outbreak of the war, was always known as Bill Sparks or, as he is recorded as saying, 'Ned, to my friends'.

William Edward Sparks, DSM
'The thing I enjoyed the most was unarmed combat.'

Bill Sparks

Bill Sparks, DSM, a Royal Marine corporal and wartime Special Forces commando, was born on 5 September 1922 in Holborn, London, and died in Alfriston, East Sussex, on 30 November 2002 aged eighty. Blondie had predeceased him by fifteen years.

Of the things that Blondie Hasler is reported to have said of Bill Sparks, he can be quoted for this accolade: 'He was a brave, fit, enthusiastic young man.' Even by his own admission, Bill tended to 'sound off' when he became anxious. He could not cope with being idle; he was one of the true outdoor lads. He hated the dentist's chair so much that it is not known if he ever visited as an adult; he suffered with teeth problems as a result. He was a young, wild boy, rough around the edges, keen to bend rules in order to spend time at home, tending to arrive late from leave, a reasonable swimmer and a heavy smoker of roll-ups. He had an infectious laugh, but when things became difficult, he would overcompensate by cracking jokes. In tight corners, he had plenty of fighting spirit, indeed he was bred for it. He liked a good drink and a fight, but when the fight was over, he would be best of friends with that very person. He too often had cause to be depressed about a given situation. In truth, he had a heart of gold.

Bill started life off as a marine and progressed to the rank of corporal by the end of the war. He was the son of a serving seaman and worked as a shoe repairer until the outbreak of war. William Edward Sparks was twice married, having all his children (three sons, one daughter) from his first marriage. One of his sons also joined the Royal Marines and rose to the rank of lieutenant, and then captain as a reserve in the Royal Green Jackets, something that Bill was extremely proud of.

Bill Sparks was brought up in Shoreditch, in the East End of London, and left school at fourteen to become a repairer of footwear or as Bill would have said ... cobbler's. At the outbreak of war, Bill volunteered for the Royal Navy, intending to follow in his father's footsteps as a stoker, but this was dashed by a clever recruiting sergeant who diverted him to the Royal Marines, and on the face of it, this was to become a better deal.

Bill was drafted to HMS *Renown* in August 1940 after completing his training at Deal in Kent. For the next eighteen months, he was part of a 4.5-inch dual gun crew on convoy duties to Malta and searching the mid-Atlantic for the *Bismarck*. It was during a refit and

Above: Hasler and Sparks post-*Frankton* during PR for the film in London.

Below left: Sparks as a bus inspector, London Transport

Below right: Young Sparks taken at an Islington studio before he joined the RMPBPD.

In training. Note the life jacket, believed to have been taken just after Sparks joined the RMBPD.

Sparks in Palestine, 1944, posing in a disused aircraft.

The elderly Sparks during an event at Southsea in the 1990s sporting his well-known broad smile.

subsequent leave in London he received news that his brother Benny[15] had been killed while serving on HMS *Naiad*. This temporarily unhinged Bill, who then proceeded to drown his sorrows for the rest of his leave. It took all his father's efforts to persuade Bill to return to Plymouth.

Bill was confined to barracks for seven days as a punishment for being two days late back. This became fortuitous, as he spotted a notice calling for volunteers for 'hazardous service'. This gave Bill the idea that this could be the chance to avenge his brother's death, and following an interview with Blondie Hasler, he was accepted. The standard question posed by Blondie of 'Do you realise that your expectation of a long life is very remote?' only made him smile; and what a smile.

Eastney Barracks beckoned, and he reported himself in July 1942 along with other volunteers. The men were put through their paces, training in the use of the canoe, navigation, explosives, diving, and escape and evasion. Many volunteers fell out, but Sparks remained focused and uninjured, which resulted in him becoming one of a team of thirteen that formed No. 1 section of Royal Marine Boom Patrol Detachment headed by Blondie Hasler. This led to the legacy that was the 'Cockleshell Heroes', and for his actions on the *Frankton* Raid, Bill was awarded the Distinguished Service Medal.

When he returned to duty, the military service continued with the Royal Marines, serving in the Aegean with the 'Earthworm' Detachment. In 1946, Bill returned to civilian life as a bus driver, then joined the newly federated Malaysian Police Force as a lieutenant for a short while before returning to London only to find work was a difficult commodity to come by. Bill first took employment as a labourer on a building site during a harsh mid-winter, then as a casual worker at the Post Office sorting office, then in desperation as a shoe repairer again. The next job was as a milkman, but he then contracted severe winter bronchitis, which took him from the fresh air and into a plastics factory. In 1948, he was requested to attend a war crimes trial in Hamburg to bring to justice those who had been part of the killing of his comrades on the *Frankton* Raid. Following his return to work at the plastics factory, he was given leave to be one of the technical advisers for the film *Cockleshell Heroes*, which was filmed in Portugal. Following the premiere in London, further promotional tours occurred in America and Canada, and then on to France, where Bill met up with Armand Dubreuille at another premiere. After the bout of stardom, Bill tried the insurance business, then worked as an ice-cream vendor, and eventually he returned to bus driving and then became a bus inspector.

We now arrive at a point in time when both Bill and Blondie attended the 1969 commemorative reunion in France at the English Church in Bordeaux where a plaque was unveiled. It was during this time that Hasler had learnt that Bill was 'hop[ing] to get a job as a range marker at Lympstone'. Probably unbeknown to Bill, Blondie had swiftly written a letter to the Administrative Officer, Lt-Col. Bayly Jones, at the Royal Marine Lympstone barracks in support of Bill's application. Blondie wrote 'that [Bill] was devoted to the Corps' and that he 'really did want to stop working as a bus inspector … if he could get the right sort of job in a Royal Marines Establishment'. It is believed that Bill's health became an issue, which is why he took a job as a garage inspector with the company and stayed there until 1986 when he began to have further respiratory health problems and retired from London Transport. It was two years later that Sparks' invalidity pension was cut by £1,000 a year, and despite media coverage and family disagreement, he decided that he had to auction his medals. He was quoted as saying about this episode, 'I have tried not to feel bitter about this, but when I went to the DHSS and explained my case, I was told absolutely nothing could be done. How can I feel anything else but bitter and disappointed?'

Regardless, it has to be said that he had a right to decide whether to sell or not. It is reported that some pressure was levied on Bill to sell his medals to the RM Museum. Sparks' rejection of the pre-auction offer of £11,000 was probably down to Sotheby's estimate that the medals would reach in excess of £12,000, and it failed to endear him with the establishment. When Lot 208 sold for £31,000, the anonymous phone bidder also made it known that he or she would allow Bill to wear the medals for veterans' parades. The under bidder was the RM Museum.

It is true to say that Bill loved the Isle of Wight and would have moved there if things had been different. This attraction to the island was in no small way down to the regular boom patrol paddles he had to undertake from Southsea to the island. After his first wife Violet died in 1982, he eventually remarried in 1994. Bill was instrumental in the erection of and participated in the dedication of a memorial to the fallen Cockleshell Heroes. He did get a surprise to see his name carved in the Purbeck stone memorial when it was unveiled at the SBS HQ in Poole on 11 December 1983. The memorial was very quickly funded by public subscription through a newspaper appeal.

In 1983, at the age of sixty-one, Bill paddled part of the river Gironde to Bordeaux and raised considerable money for cancer research. In June 2002, Bill also enjoyed a sixtieth anniversary visit to places on the escape route he and Blondie took. This route is now called the '*Frankton* Trail' and is a historical hiking tourist attraction. He died just months later, but had been fortunate enough to understand what others thought of the heroic effort by ten Royal Marines even after very many years had passed.

On Thursday 5 December 2002 at 2.30 p.m., a Service of Thanksgiving was held for the life of Corporal W. E. Sparks, DSM, at St Andrew's church in Alfriston. Bill was one of five children. The Loughton War Memorial is one of a handful that records his name.

He became the last living survivor of an intrepid band known as the 'Cockleshell Heroes' that undertook the raid on Bordeaux.

John 'Jack' Withers MacKinnon[16]
'Jacky' – 'A Real Gem'

On 25 June 1942, Major Hasler visited the Royal Marines Small Arms School (RMSA) at Browndown and interviewed ten second lieutenants. Only two were selected[17] for his new unit, Temporary Second Lt 'Jack' Withers MacKinnon was one of those two.

Jack was born on 15 July 1921 in Oban, North Argyllshire. A little-known piece of information is that he was actually baptised as 'John' with this entered on his birth certificate; in family circles and even in his last homeward-bound letters of 1942, he always signed off as 'Jacky'. Temporary Lt J. W. MacKinnon was the son of James and Helen Ogilvie (née Withers) MacKinnon. Helen was known as 'Nellie'. She had previously been a chambermaid in a hotel in Oban. Jacky's parents married in Oban on 30 September 1919. After moving from Paisley with the family, Jacky then spent most of his formative years living at 22 Clarendon Street, Maryhill, in Glasgow, a typical but moderately ornate sandstone tenement building with narrow sash windows. This may sound quite ordinary, until you realise that family life, for the then five individuals, was within a second-floor flat with one sitting room, one bedroom, one kitchen/dining room and one toilet – but no bathroom. The family bathed in a tin bath within the kitchen/dining room. There were double bed recesses in both the kitchen/dining room and the sitting room. James and Nellie slept in the kitchen/dining room, Margaret and Isabella slept in the sitting room, and Jacky slept in the bedroom; heating was afforded by an open fire and cooking range in the kitchen.

His father, James, was formally a Piper in the Argyll & Sutherland Highlanders. He had served in the First World War, after which he returned to Oban, where he worked as a bowling-green keeper. Jacky joined the Maryhill Road Boy Scouts troop just around the corner from the flat. He showed leadership skills and became a leader in the cubs group. He also had been a Scout master and fond of life in the open air, playing all games with great ardour. He was an exceptional young man with a real love of life. He is known to have cycled some fair distances and took regular trips from Glasgow to his aunt's house on the Isle of Cumbrae. With his friends, he used to enjoy camping in the surrounding countryside. Even as a boy, he was athletic, a good swimmer, enjoying hiking and playing football with his friends. He enjoyed supporting Partick Thistle, known as the 'Jags', his local team.

Nellie MacKinnon had another baby boy called James, who sadly died of whooping cough, aged about three months. When Jacky was about fourteen years old, his mother gave birth to another boy named Douglas. All the children attended the primary school at Napier's Hall and Woodside Senior Secondary School.

As a young girl, Isabella, one of his two sisters, went to the Albert Ballroom in Bath Street with her own friends and used to see Jacky dancing with the girls there; he was handsome and popular with the girls! Being a good ballroom dancer, he spent many an evening there. Isabella was three years younger than Jacky, and his other sister, Margaret, was seventeen months younger.

Sometime during his twentieth year, he had volunteered for Hostilities Only, and on 7 April 1941, the Combined Recruitment centre at St Mary's Halls in Moffat Street, Glasgow, sent him a letter requiring him to report to Moffat Street. Duly found fit, he was sent to Port Division at Exton the very same day. Po/x 105495 John 'Jack' Withers MacKinnon became a Royal Marine.

Jacky had previously been employed as clerk at a coal merchant's. Meanwhile, Jack's sister, Margaret, joined the WRNS. Isabella wanted to join the Land Army, but her parents did not consent. Instead, she worked in Barr & Stroud as an engraver of gun sights for the duration of the war.

By the January of 1942, it became apparent that his natural abilities had been noted, and he had advanced to the rank of corporal. Jack had joined HMS *Atherstone* on Tuesday 26 January 1942 and, apart from an early bout of slight seasickness, had settled down and was

Above left: Lt Jack MacKinnon in dress uniform.

Above right: Right to left, Jack, father Jimmy, mother Nellie, sister Isabella and brother Douglas in front. Taken at home in the back yard of the tenement block at 22 Clarendon Street, Glasgow, during leave, March 1942.

Above left: A fifteen-year-old Jack.

Above right: Jack (right) camping with friends at Helensburgh.

enjoying the quantity and quality of the 'first-rate' food and the company of his three fellow Scotsmen from another nearby mess. These four lads had 'been everywhere aboard asking silly questions and [had] been as awkward as a herd of elephants'. The ship was helping to protect a convoy and his first action was within days of joining.

This 'exciting and enjoyable voyage' for Jack culminated in the shooting down of a Junkers 88. It had dive-bombed the convoy, but Jack and the other Marines had shot it down astern before it could get away. Four nights after this event, they also had gone over 'to the French coast and shot up a German convoy – sinking two ships'. In one of his early letters, he wrote to his mother and is quoted as saying that he 'was enjoying every minute'.

Jack related, 'We had the best time of our lives. The captain of the ship sent a message to the Brigadier telling him of the fine work we had put in on the ship's Lewis guns. The Brigadier sent for me personally and congratulated me on downing "first blood" for the 103rd RM Brigade, was I pleased or was I.' By 10 February 1942, Jack had returned to shore and was at the Dalditch Royal Marines establishment near Budleigh Salterton in Devon. His only gripe was the fact that he could not get any Palmolive shaving cream in southern England and was hopeful his mother would post some to him. It wasn't until mid-March that he managed to get ten days' leave, which he duly took in Glasgow at the family home with the hope of seeing snow for the first time that year.

It is probable it was the events with the convoy that got him noticed with his superiors, who recognised his ability and sent him to officer school. By 15 May 1942, he had completed his officer training at the RM Military School on the South Devon coastline at Thurlstone and had been commissioned, graduating top of his class.

The very essence of this man's character that made him universally liked, loved and appreciated by all with whom he came in contact is first indicated by Lt K. C. Harris in a letter to Jack's mother where he says, 'I congratulate you on your son's success in getting a commission. He did extremely well in this course and expect great things of him. I had the great honour of being his Platoon Commander and I thoroughly enjoyed every moment of it. I hope he will write occasionally and let me know how he gets on – I will always be very interested. Give him a good leave, he thoroughly deserves it.'

At Browndown, he met up with Pritchard-Gordon with whom he became inseparable. Both were accepted by Hasler into the RMBPD. Known as Jack, but to those in the RMBPD as 'Mac', his intuitive and dynamic approach coupled with great intelligence made him the perfect instructor.

On 16 July 1942, Jack wrote what can only be described as a letter written from the heart. He had just been inducted into the RMBPD.

Dear Mum, Yesterday was the great day, I was 21. I am now supposed to be a man, but I dont pretend myself that I am, because the one man I am aiming to be like is my father, and until I am as fine a person as he is I shant be strutting about with a big head. I wonder if children thank there parents for all they have done for them. I dont know if they do, but I want to thank mine. Thanks for everything you have ever done for me, for all the sacrifices you have made, and for the many, many, times you have given me things which you really couldn't spare. Thanks to you mother especially, for the way you have looked after me and brought me up and the way you have stood up to the strain of day after day of working in the house, cooking washing and above all bringing up a family. I think your swell. Thanks to you dad for all those little things you brought me when I was a boy, which you may have forgotten about but which I never will. Remember my cricket bat and how you shortened it down for me and the pair of football boots which I bought with the money you loaned me and never paid back, and then there are dozens of others too. I dont think they are making any more like you dad. I am not finished thanking people yet, would you thank Margaret, Isabella and Aunt Maggie for me for sending these lovely cards and presents. (I am writing to Aunt Maggie to thank her myself. Tell the girls the next time I come home on leave they will have the finest night of their lives to repay them. Do you remember when I used to knock them about well tell them I am sorry. I am still keeping very well and feeling like a young hog so dont worry about me I have a better job now than I had in 'civvy street'. Well

Right: Early days of a fine career at Exton. Po/x 105495 at Exton on 18 May 1941. Jack wrote, 'These two lads are my chums. The big one is McIntosh and the other is McFaden. Dated 18 May 1941 RMRD Exton.

Below: Third from right, 16 May 1941, RMRD Exton.

On leave, Cpl Jack and his brother Douglas at home.

L–R: Nellie, Margaret, Isabella, Douglas and Jack.

Cadet officers MacKinnon and Pritchard-Gordon, second row from back, eighth and tenth from left.

RM Division Platoon Weapons Course 25 May – 27 June 1942. End of row, second and third from back Messrs Pritchard-Gordon and MacKinnon.

dearest, I think I have said my say so dont think this is a sad letter for a mother to read, you should be glad and proud of yourself to think you have born and bred the greatest animal in the world today:- A Man. So dont be sad be glad. Will you give Douglas a big hug and kiss for me please. Cheerio just now and lots of love to all. Your loving Son, Jacky xxxxxxxxxx. I am sending you this flower from my cake as a souvenir. Love Jacky.

Two things happened during early September 1942 – he received his Commission Sheet and the unit had bought a twelve-week-old female Cocker Spaniel, which was also billeted at Spencer Road; Jack had named it 'Tich'. Meanwhile, Jack was working hard, but by the time October arrived, his workload had increased and he was doing an eighteen-hour day, 'conducting tests and experiments up and down the country'. He was looking forward to 'moving around'.

Throughout his military career, Jack tried to maintain contact with his mother, writing as much as possible (she called them 'short notes'), but even this diminished due to his workload. He explained that was due to the fact that he 'was only good for bed when [he came] home'. His mother and others wrote often and sent presents, some of which came in very handy during the cold days at sea before December. He was particularly grateful for the sea boat stockings (socks) that she sent in October. He was always reassuring her that he was safe and happy in his 'secret work' and she 'was not to worry about' him.

The very day they all had been told of the intended mission, Jack wrote his last letter to his mother from aboard HMS *Tuna* in the late evening of 30 November 1942 following the testing of the hoisting gear at Scalpsie Bay. He had visited his home in Clarendon Street, Glasgow, just three days before. In his letter, not one hint of anxiety is evident, and this shows that he did not want to alarm her. It reads,

Dear Mum, This is just one of my well known short notes, which everyone thinks are just a waste of time. However it is just to let you know that I am still in the best of health and enjoying life to the full. I got down and aboard again in tons of time on Saturday [28 November] so everything was alright. Well, I want to confirm the fact that you will not hear from me for a number of weeks, so dont on any account worry over the fact you get no letters. Would you please tell Margaret this as I have not had time to do so myself. Remember dear, look after yourself and Dad, and the children, and I will 'carry on watching crossing the road'. Well cheerio just now, and above all dont worry about me. With lots of love and kisses to you all, Your loving Son, Jacky. xxxxxxxx xxxxxxxx.

On 21 April 1943, within nineteen days of Hasler returning to England after his escape, he wrote to Mrs MacKinnon. In this hand-written letter from Dolphin Court Headquarters in Southsea, his view and appreciation of Jack is evident:

Dear Mrs. MacKinnon,

I am writing to you in respect of your son, who is a very valued member of my unit besides being a close personal friend of mine.

I well realise the anxiety which you must be experiencing in the absence of any further definite news of him, and you may rest assured that I will let you know as soon as I hear anything further.

He is the sort of chap you can rely on to look after himself and make the best of any opportunities he gets, so I hope we shall have further news soon.

Yours Sincerely

(H.G. HASLER)

Major R.M.

Without a doubt, Jack was the favourite with those marines of No. 1 section and indeed well liked and highly thought of by many others. Norman Colley really rated him and thought he was 'a wonderful man, very approachable'. Even Capt. Dickie Raikes knew that Blondie Hasler 'had a lot of time for him'[18], also saying he was 'a terribly nice boy, a real gem'. Lt MacKinnon was also extremely well thought of by Sam Wallace, who held him in high esteem.

Jack drank very little, was a non-smoker and had a passion for enjoyment. He was good company, sociable, pleasant, helpful, responsible, very kind and thoughtful, and always enjoyed a party!

He played the jazz drums with some relish at the unit's parties. His character was that of a jolly, debonair individual and 'bonny fighter', an eager-spirited individual. He was an excellent swimmer, but never became a proficient seaman. He was noted for his party trick: launching himself high from the concrete wall of the Esplanade at Southsea and jumping bare-footed onto the shingle beach; at the time, this was a considerable distance from the top of the wall. A definitive description was once given[19] of Mac: 5 feet 7 inches (1 m 70 cm), with light brown hair and eyebrows, a straight forehead and nose with a normal size mouth, blue eyes, an oval face with a fresh complexion and he sported a small moustache. He took to wearing a lucky charm on a chain around his neck along with his identity disc – a Spanish coin dated 1937. How Jack MacKinnon died has been known since just after the war, but when and where he died is *now* subject to renewed speculation. Contrary to what is thought, the author submits that he was murdered outside Bordeaux and buried nearby – as were the other five men.

Helen MacKinnon wrote to Louis Jaubert on 30 March 1945 thanking the Jauberts (who were the sheep farmers near the village of Cessac) for their letter of 13 March (see 'The French Affair' chapter) and what they had done to help her son. In Jaubert's reply on 22 April he said, 'I felt it was my duty as a good Frenchman to do my best towards your son.' Even then, no one knew what had happened to the men.

In June 1945, Pritchard-Gordon, now a major, had written to Mac's mother enclosing some documents. Mrs MacKinnon thanked him for his kind letter, saying, 'I appreciate it very much,' adding that she would be pleased to take up his 'kind offer to help me in tracing Jack'. Helen MacKinnon had done much to try and trace the whereabouts of her son but related that 'the Red Cross say they have no news at all' and that she had written to the Admiralty. She was putting all hope in a letter from a Frenchman who only knew that Mac was a prisoner of the Germans. Mrs MacKinnon told Pritchard-Gordon that she was 'most anxious although I am doing all in my power to get news this end'. Even in her grief over many years Helen MacKinnon had great determination and despite the Admiralty letter confirming her son's death in September 1945 she made great efforts to contact those who had known him. With news of her son's death, she wrote to Madame and Monsieur Louise and Louis Jaubert. They had tended and assisted MacKinnon's problem knee as well as feeding and sheltered both Marines for three evenings. Louis had written a letter to Mrs MacKinnon within days of the two marines leaving their farm. Louis Jaubert, until Mrs MacKinnon's letter, had thought Mac and James Conway were still in prison. Jaubert replied saying, he 'was very sorry to learn that your son was dead. My wife and I both share in your sorrow. He [Mac] did not deserve what has happened.'

On 22 October 1945, Helen MacKinnon wrote to Pritchard-Gordon, who was then at HMS *Stuart* at Teignmouth in Devon, and asked if he knew where her son's personal effects might be. He replied the very same day giving his commiserations saying that she had 'waited a long time for such news'. Due to his service abroad, Pritchard-Gordon only knew that 'these [effects] were put away in early 1943 for safe keeping' but assured her that he would 'turn the place upside down to find these'. He also wrote, 'I want you to know just how much we all thought of Mac: He was the finest friend and soldier; Col. Hasler has always spoken of him in the highest terms of praise. Mac's last words to me was that he was honoured to be selected for it [the mission] and I know he did his share.'

Unfortunately, it took until 16 January 1946 before matters had been resolved and the personal effects forwarded. Helen MacKinnon at last had something to remember her son by. Jack MacKinnon had put aside all the normal day-to-day items ready for his return to 9 Spencer Road in Southsea: his wrist watch and strap; pocket diary; Bank of Scotland cheque book and account book; registration card; identity card; assorted photographs; RM reserve depot pamphlet and his leather wallet. Helen

MacKinnon's grief did not leave her, and perhaps in an effort to reach out and make any further contact with anyone she could, she traced Bill Sparks, who by 1952 was a police officer in Malaya. Sparks tried to offer some comfort and duly wrote as much as he could about Mac, also saying,

> Your son, Mac. was my section officer, and a finer man would be impossible to meet, he was loved by all who served under and above him, and I say with all sincerity, a man that everyone was proud of.
>
> When I last spoke to him, on the night of our tragic parting, he was his usual cheery self, and an inspiration to everyone around him, not the slightest sign of fear, but a symbol of courage and manhood.

Pritchard-Gordon was the other officer selected by Hasler on 25 June when he visited the RMSA at Browndown. One of Jack MacKinnon's last conversations with this friend who had been there from the beginning was reported as, 'Well, goodbye, Bill, I shan't see you again.' Pritchard-Gordon said he was talking 'nonsense'. 'No, I don't think I shall, Bill.' Jack did not see in his twenty-second birthday. He was just one year older than his co-pilot in *Cuttlefish*. Lt Jack MacKinnon was commander of 'B' Division and No. 1 in Cockle canoe *Cuttlefish*. Mac's No. 2 was …

James Conway
'Proudest lad in the land'

One can only hope that Ply. X. 105763 Marine James Conway had Mac beside him when he too was murdered by the decree of Hitler. He met his death in France in early 1943. That is certain. As with the three others who were captured during their escape through the French countryside, Jim Conway's actual place of death and burial remains uncertain. He did not celebrate his twenty-first birthday.

Jim Conway was a Stockport lad born on 22 August 1922[20] and, at the time of joining, lived at 20 Heaton Mersey View, Larkhill, Edgeley, with his mother, who on 29 January 1943 received a telegram notifying her that he was reported as missing. He was the son of Thomas and Mary Ann (née Felly). He can be quoted as writing back home that being part of the RMBPD made him feel the 'proudest lad in the land', where he was well thought of, and he himself was happy to be in this special band of brothers. James had an elder brother in the Royal Marines, which gave him the boyhood ambition to join the Corps.

He was described as a 'handsome young man with an open and honest face' by one French person who remembered him.

From differing sources, it can be said that James Conway was quiet, yet quick-witted, good-natured and liked by all. He enjoyed cycling as well as swimming and his horse. This solitary subject became one of a constant stream of stories: his time with his horse and cart when he was a milkman for the Co-op wholesale society before war broke out. He told all in his section that he would talk to his horse about all matters under the sun, often spending hours in its company; it was the only thing he truly missed.

Upon his capture, this definitive description was taken: 1 m 68 cm (5 feet 6 inches), with light-brown hair and a straight nose which was broad at its base. He had blue eyes and a large mouth with thick lips, a small chin and a low forehead. He was clean-shaven at the time of arrest.

Samuel Wallace
'Old Stripey'

This sergeant of 'Hasler's Party' was the author and director of the special and famous 'Southsea Stroll' for which the Royal Marine Boom Patrol Detachment were known.

Samuel Wallace was baptised into the Church of Ireland. His shipwright father also bore the same name. His mother's name was Ellen, and he had two sisters, Christine and Margaret, as well as a half-brother and sister. He went to school in Lower Rutland Street in the north of Dublin. He was a member of the Boys' Brigade (for whom he played football) at St Barnabas' church, East Wall, near the mouth of the River Liffey and had worked in a builders' merchant's next to The Custom House on the Liffey called 'Brooks Thomas'.

Applying for and getting into the Royal Navy or the Royal Marines was not an easy task for Sam. He had originally sent a letter on 9 November 1930 to apply to enlist in the Royal

Marines. He received a response from the recruiting Major Evans at Liverpool saying that only in special cases were applications considered for enlistment from the Irish Free State. Sam would have to obtain two references 'from persons of high standing, one of which should be from an Officer on the Active or Retired Lists of the British Services'; this would include someone in the Royal Irish Constabulary.

It seems that Sam did indeed fulfil this requirement, for on Monday 24 November 1930, this six-foot, dark-haired, tough, Dublin-born Irishman was requested to attend his *provisional* medical examination with Dr Scott at Clarinda Park East Surgery in Kingstown, Dublin, at 4 p.m. by the Recruiting Staff Major Evans. He subsequently joined the Royal Marines in 1931. He then qualified as a gun-layer working on 'X' and 'Y' turrets on HMS *Queen Elizabeth* and HMS *Rodney*, and during this time, he was awarded his colours for boxing.

Regular Ply. X. 665 Sergeant Samuel Wallace had his home at Summerhill in Dublin where he attended Rutland Street School before he, at the age of seventeen, joined up. In his twelve years of service, he came to develop an engaging sense of humour, becoming the No. 1 section senior NCO, possessing so much cheerful determination that it inspired the men to keep going. This exuberance was sometimes so enthusiastic that when the Admiralty wanted to find out how long a man could keep afloat in full gear, he volunteered immediately. It took five minutes before he sank with the tin helmet resting on the water's surface like something out of a Buster Keaton movie; the good thing was he could laugh at himself – the rest of the men did! Sometimes this ball of energy led him to be somewhat impulsive, and this eagerness sometimes made him act without thinking.

'Stripey' Wallace became a tower of strength to Lt MacKinnon, and he became quite devoted to this younger officer. He told Lt MacKinnon's sister, Isabella, 'I would follow Major Hasler and Mr 'Mac' anywhere in the world' … and he did, even to his death. Thus it was for the men who had great respect and affection for 'Old Stripey'. He remaining a tad distant; his expectations required them to drill well, and they did – Southsea style. Tall, dark and good looking, with a fine physique, he was the embodiment of a professional soldier with the ability and efficiency in the instruction of drill, weapon training and military life to prove it. His cheerful willingness got the men into the right spirit of things. He could easily rally the troops.

Old 'Stripey' Wallace gave his next of kin as his elder sister Mrs Christine Clabby, who lived at St Margerets Road, Marsh Mills, in Plympton near Plymouth. Ply. X. 665 Sgt Samuel Wallace was born in Lower Buckingham Street, Dublin, on 24 September 1913, and at the age of twenty-nine, the No. 1 of Cockle canoe *Coalfish* met his death in a sandpit in front of a firing squad somewhere in a wood just outside Bordeaux, France, on 11 December 1942. The place of his burial is not known. Sergeant Wallace no doubt died whilst still doing his duty as a Senior NCO, giving verbal moral support to his No. 2 in the Cockle, the young man …

Robert Ewart
'My Bobby'

In France, on 11 December 1942 at 0300, life ceased for Marine Robert Ewart. Both he and his sergeant had been executed in the same location and manner and pronounced dead by a naval surgeon brought along for that purpose. Robert Ewart had only just celebrated his twenty-first birthday on board HMS *Tuna* as they steamed towards the coast of France with his RMBPD buddies. Only a few days later, he was listening to his sergeant encouraging him to be strong, moments before they were both then murdered and buried in an unmarked, unrecorded grave.

He left behind him a young girl who he loved and who loved him. Fortunately, 'Bobby' Ewart had written a letter to her. It shows his fears, as by this time he had been told of the mission. It had been written on submarine *Tuna*. It had been entrusted to 'the care of Norman', his best friend. Robert Ewart did not know where he was, so he penned a question mark as to his whereabouts along with his name and Ply. X. number at the top of the letter, written from the heart, to a girl he loved … it read …

Dear Heather, I trust it won't be necessary to have this sent to you but since I don't know the outcome of this little adventure I thought I'd leave this note behind in the care of Norman who will forward it to you should anything unpredictable happen. During my stay at Southsea as you well know made me realise what the good things in life are and I'm glad I have this opportunity to help bring the pleasant times which I'm sure you always had and you were made for.

I couldn't help but love you Heather although you were so young, I will always love you.

as I know you do me, that alone should let me through this but one never knows the turns of fate, one thing I ask of you Heather is not to take it too hard you have yet your life to live, think of me as a good friend and keep your chin up, some lucky fellow will find you who has more sense than I had and who can get you what you deserve. You are young yet for this sort of thing but I had to do it, so please don't worry and upset yourself about me, with your picture in front of me I feel confident that I shall pull through and get back to you some day. I won't have you read more Heather but I will thank you for all you have done, I pray that God will spare me and save you from this misery so hoping for a speedy reunion I'll say cheerio and God be with you. Thanking you and your mother from the bottom of my heart, at present in your care.

God bless and keep you all.
Yours for Ever.
Bob.
Chin Up Sweetheart.

Heather called him 'Bobby'. The love they shared was chaste; she was, in truth, totally besotted with this young, six-foot Scottish boy from Glasgow with the piercing blue eyes. The mutual attraction was apparently evident straight away. Maybe 'Bobby' was Heather's first love – but he was to be her last.

After Robert Ewart wrote his letter, it was collected by Hasler, who then gave all the letters to Norman Colley. Norman discharged his duty and ensured it made its way to its intended address in Southsea via the commandant of the Plymouth Division of the Royal Marines.

Ply. X. 108880 Marine Robert Ewart found ordinary soldiering boring, with life too pedestrian in his posting pre-RMBPD in the Orkney Islands. This was a simple, honest-natured young man who had a great respect and affection for his parents, James and Annie, who had produced four boys, James, George, Tom (who died at a young age from asthma) and, of course, as he was always referred to by the family, Bert. Even at an early age, brother George remembered Bert as a dare devil: 'I remember him using the holes in a big pigeon house to climb to the top – he was always up to something. He really enjoyed swimming.' He enjoyed being with his family and preferred the company of his father and brothers at the local public house playing the green baize game; he also enjoyed the simple art of an evening conversation with his mother.

The family had originally lived on the east coast of Scotland in Scone near Perth with his father working as a farm labourer; then they had moved slightly southward to Alloa, near Stirling, before moving westward to Glasgow. It was here that Robert Ewart was born on 4 December 1921. He joined the ranks of the Boys' Brigade, where his keenness for running won him many an award. One of his first real jobs found him entering the textile industry: a local factory in the city. His refusal to take employment in the local munitions factory, and a want to serve his country, brought him voluntarily into the Corps family.

'Jock' Ewart was a skin and bone lad, but he was a tough cookie, and his running abilities allowed him an almost effortless skim over the pebbled Southsea beach during the near-daily runs, his keen determination and most enthusiastic efforts seeing him through everything thrown at him. Norman and Robert used to spend most of their off-duty time playing snooker and billiards.

'Bert' put pen to paper and wrote to his family. As the named next of kin, his mother would have received the 'missing in action' telegram first and then this letter sometime afterwards. It was written on submarine *Tuna* during early December 1942, just days after it is believed he had taken the opportunity to visit them at the family home in Cowlairs Road, Springburn, Glasgow. Bert wrote,

Dear Mum Dad and Brothers,
    I'm taking this opportunity to write you these few lines, although I hope they won't be necessary. As you know I volunteered for a certain job, which I trust you will learn about at a later period. I've enjoyed every minute of it and hope that what we have done helps to end the mess we are in and make a decent and better world. You will see by recovery note whether I am prisoner or otherwise, which at present isn't worrying me in the least. I have a feeling I'll be like a bad penny, so please don't upset yourself over my safety. My heart will be with you always, you are the best parents one could wish to have. Anyway Mum you can always say you had a son in the most senior service, and, though I say it myself, 'one of twelve heroes'.

Little could he have known that is exactly what *ten* of them would be known as forever more.

Along with Bobby's brief glimpse of life, the story of Heather is mentioned here for the simple reason it is fitting to do so. Heather Powell was the only child of Mrs Leonora Powell and her serving Royal Marine husband. She had great admiration for her father's clan and treated the billeted lads the same way. She had a maturity beyond her tender fifteen years. From the beginning, a special attachment grew between Heather and Bobby. Heather had no realisation that the day they were picked up to go on to Scotland was any other than a normal day; the Blues uniforms were still hanging up awaiting their return. No doubt Bobby's eyes looked into Heather's the same way they had each time of his departure. It is said that Heather had some kind of premonition at this particular departure time. Bobby's last words to her, as he and the others left in the usual high-spirited fashion, were to 'look after our things, we will be back soon'. As the lorry drove away, Heather broke down in tears saying, 'Oh mother, they'll never come back. I know they'll never come back.' This emotion was followed by diary entries that mentioned 'letter from Bob' and 'wrote to Bob'. Heather had been advised by an NCO to keep a twenty-first birthday present she had bought for him until he returned.

The reported German radio announcement of 'commandos slaughtered' relayed in the local Pompey papers had been seen by Heather, and even though she had no reason to make any connection with her Bobby, somehow she linked the two and this caused her to become ill. It was the end of January 1943 that Mrs Ewart had sent a letter from her home in Glasgow telling of the 'Missing in Action' telegram to Mrs Powell at the White Heather. This caused a further plummet into despair for Heather and culminated in her being admitted to hospital for observation. The three men who had returned on the submarine had been kept separate from even their fellow Boom Patrollers of No. 2 section for a short while; then they had returned to White Heather. Following Heather being admitted to hospital, Norman Colley remembered how Leonora Powell had asked him and Eric Fisher to vacate the dwelling. On returning to the UK, Bill Sparks called at White Heather one evening, and the door was answered by Leonora Powell, who, whilst pleased that he had returned, was also anxious to hear about the others. Bill divulged nothing but his face spoke volumes, despite his words that the 'others would be back later'. Leonora told Bill about her daughter, and he then visited Heather in hospital. Bill remarked that 'she was weak, unwilling to fight her illness'. His inability to tell her anything comforting only served to worry her further. Heather was released from hospital and returned home only to find all the men's belongings had been taken from the wardrobes. She knew that others had returned[21], but this was no comfort and she broke down again. Despite reassurances from any quarter, her mind was set, and this fuelled a further decline with Tuberculosis being diagnosed. She was finally admitted to hospital, where she died. Records show that she died in the second quarter of 1944. She was nearly seventeen, and her father had returned from sea on leave. Her forlorn state no doubt attributed to her demise.

Robert Ewart's mother had accused her son of 'kidnapping' when he told her of his feelings for this young girl. Following the early months of the New Year and having received news of her son 'Missing in Action', Mrs Ewart visited Heather and her mother and realised why he had been so attracted to this young girl. When they died, Bobby and Heather were apart; in words, they are now together.

This state of mind, not in direct relation to Heather, is referred to by Blondie Hasler in a letter he wrote from his abode at that time at Moody's at the Swanwick Shore boatyard. Following on from someone highlighting the premonition of death relating to MacKinnon, Blondie states quite rightly, 'I have been worried about the story of his premonition of death – more than once I have run into this, and I often feel that when it is fulfilled it is not so much a case of amazing intuition, but of fatalistic resignation and losing the essential hope of survival. In other words, a man who has had a premonition of death does not fight for his life.'

In October 1947, a letter from the establishment was written regarding the presumed death of the *Frankton* personnel seeking approval to clarify matters for the parents of these men. It refers to letters sent to the parents of Wallace and Ewart (in the case of Wallace, the letter was to his sister) dated 30 July 1945, which gave the information available at the time. It was thought that, in view of the knowledge that had since been forthcoming, the information did 'not represent accurately to the next of kin the circumstances attending the death of their relatives, and that although some distress [might] be caused to them in that a period has elapsed, a further letter should be sent, if only to prevent them going on a wild goose chase to see the supposed grave'. It was also at this time that the date of death for two was amended from 8 December to 11 December 1942.

George Jellicoe Sheard
'The Married Janner'

Ply. X. 1369 Temporary Corporal George Jellicoe Sheard had volunteered for hazardous duties and had been interviewed on 1 July at the Plymouth Division of the Royal Marines by Blondie Hasler. Preliminary training commenced on 24 July 1942 in the Portsmouth and Isle of Wight area.

Being 'free of strong family ties or dependents' was one of the prerequisites required. It is presumed that George would have mentioned his newly married status to Blondie Hasler, and it was the fact that George was a regular not a 'Hostilities Only' entry that allowed Hasler to accept him. The archive records at Plymouth Reference Library show that George Jellicoe married Mabelle Irene Bates in Devonport in the second quarter of the year (April–June). George and 'Renée' started their married life living at 3 East Cornwall Street in Devonport along with George's mother; as George was away much of the time, this was the obvious arrangement.

George Jellicoe's father, George William, served in HMS *Vivid*[22] in the Royal Navy; his mother was Beatrice Maud (née Bullen). George J. Sheard was the youngest of twelve children; two siblings died in infancy. His oldest sisters were already teenagers when he was born and must have spent much time caring for him. In childhood, he had very poor health and was sent to an 'outdoor' school (presumably for asthmatics). For the family, it must have been a bit of a shock when he came home and announced that he was signing up for the Royal Marines as a regular.

By 29 January 1943, the chaplain of the barracks at Devonport visited the family home at 3 East Cornwall Street in Devonport to say that George was missing; the requisite letter confirming this was sent out on 30 January. Irene was now Mrs M. I. Sheard and the next of kin. At that time, it is believed that Irene had either moved back to her family home at

Above left: A young Sheard.

Above right: Taken on the wedding day in the backyard of the flats in Cornwall Street, Devonport, with 'Renée'.

At home in Plymouth.

21a Sussex Road in Ford, Devonport, or had been visiting, for on 13 June 1943, she was killed there, aged twenty-six, during a bombing raid.

Following this event, a sanction was duly obtained from the General Officer Commanding, Royal Marines, to regard George Jellicoe's mother as temporary next of kin. Once this had been accepted, she was notified by letter on 28 July 1945 that her son was missing, presumed killed.

It was believed by Bill Sparks[23] that George Jellicoe's wife, Irene, was 'expecting their first baby'. For Bill Sparks to have known this, he would have had to have been told by the proud father-to-be. This being the case, it is likely that the last thoughts of George Jellicoe were of his wife and child. When Irene died in June 1943, she had only been informed that her husband was missing in action. Unfortunately, the fate of any child is not known, it is possible that the pregnancy had not run its full term or the child had not yet been born. No children or babies were reported as being killed in that house in Sussex Road.

Norman Colley remembered that Sheard's nickname was 'Jan'. This was probably a derivation from the word 'Janner', which is a British regional word used to describe people from Plymouth. George Jellicoe, who had a strong regional accent, was born in the Devonport area of Plymouth on 2 May 1915. Described as short and tough, sporting plenty of initiative and the power to command, this witty man was not averse to making fun of himself. Norman also related that he was contacted via letter by one of George's sisters, Lilly, who lived in London. In an effort to find out any information, she asked Norman to travel up to the capital and treated him to a good dinner at a brasserie. This occurred sometime well after May 1943, and he told her what little he knew. Any information would have been second-hand from Sparks. It should be remembered that it was forbidden for any of the men to talk about the matter.

George Jellicoe's name is remembered by the local populace at the North Corner Quay in Devonport on a granite coping stone, which was dismantled in around 2000, from number nine dock of the historic Devonport Royal Dockyard. The rectangular-shaped stone has a polished black granite plaque inserted flush, commemorating the North Corner Heroes of the Second World War and was unveiled in 2002. The medal group awarded to Cpl G. J. Sheard comprises 1939–1945 Star, Africa Star, Defence Medal, War Medal 1939–45. These are held by the Royal Marines Museum in Southsea.

In the absence of a definitive legal definition, the cause of death for George Jellicoe is very likely to be that of hypothermia rather than drowning, given the circumstances surrounding his last contact with colleagues; he was wearing a life jacket. The time of death is also very likely to be near to 0400 on 8 December 1942. He died in France. Although George Jellicoe's body has

Taken on 10 September 1942 during workouts with Goatley's assault craft at Southsea just months before the *Frankton* Raid. Sheard is on the left, Sgt Wallace on the right.

never been found, it is more than a possibility that it was his that was reported as being found at Les Sables d'Olonne, mentioned in the same report as that of Moffatt and canoe *Conger*. George Jellicoe Sheard was the No. 1 of Cockle canoe *Conger* and his No. 2 was …

David Gabriel Moffatt
'The Mimic'

Ply. X. 108881 Marine David Gabriel Moffatt's body lies buried somewhere in the Ridge Of Dunes on Le Bois en Ré in France. It is believed that the body was identified by the Military ID Disc and recorded in the official German Totenliste No. 128 as being 'washed ashore on 17/12/42'. This can be considered a certainty, as the 108881 number was confirmed. Further information to the exact location is given within signal from Marbef. West nr.27356[24] a body was found near strong point 'Fanny', south-west of Bois en Ré, on 17 December 1942. It is believed that the actual location was on the stretch of sand near Le Bois Plage en Ré on the Île de Ré.

Originally, the Chief of Staff's office 'considered that the date of death … should be assumed for official purposes to be 17 December 1942. This is simply inaccurate, as it can be safely assumed that, as with George Jellicoe Sheard, the cause of death has to be that of hypothermia, which occurred on 8 December 1942 at around 0400 hrs.

During David's stay in Portsmouth, he, as with all the other RMBPD members, wrote home to his loved ones. He was able to keep in contact with Francis Quinn, who had joined the RAF, and Bert Jolly, who had kept David informed of the dances held in the hall at the local St Joseph's school. Fortunately, one letter written by David on 11 October 1942 does exist. It was written from the White Heather in Southsea, and the address includes 'c/o Mrs Powell'. Within this letter, we get a first-hand account of the life for David and all the others. He writes to Elsie Ambler[25] at her family home in Halifax.

He begins by apologising for the long delay in writing and also in posting the letter but explained the delay was down to the fact that they were away over the weekend and he could not get to a post box. He asks, 'How's things at '28' still the happy home I suppose, does Geoff still polish his boots? Tell him I'll be having a look at them next time I'm around that way.' He also explained that it had been his intention to write the previous week at the same time as he was writing to his mother Elizabeth, 'but I forgot … I hope you let me off this time'. David then relates that 'we're still hard at it', also mentioning that 'it's a bit cool in the water these days' – meaning the water at Southsea beach. He then explains why he was on seven days light duties at that very time. He reported,

We were rope climbing the other day up a 30ft wall, at the bottom of which were a few rocks and then about four feet of water. Well we secured our rope and climbed down, with every thing in order, then I began to climb up. I got half way up and my pal, instead of letting me get to the top, started to climb too. Well this was too much for the stake to which the rope was fast and out it came. I was higher up than him and that enabled me to push myself out and land in the water and so I came off lucky with a slight sprain on my ankle. The other chap landed on the rocks and got a pretty bad sprain on his ankle. We then both got into hot water for securing our rope to a weak point. Were both pretty lucky not to have broken something.

He ends by telling Elsie that 'my ankle is quite better now', giving his best wishes to Elsie's Mum and Dad, Eveline and Geoff, saying to keep smiling 'till next time', and signs off with 'God Bless', David.

Within this solitary letter to survive the decades we can glimpse not only the level of the constant training in the RMBPD but that all-important link with family and friends.

Before the outbreak of the war, Elsie lived at at her parents' home at Chester Road in Halifax. She had been a Girl Guide and upon reaching the age of eighteen in 1938 became a Ranger. All the groups, Cubs, Brownies, Scouts, Girl Guides, Rangers and Rovers, were combined and operated from St Bernard's church rooms. All the St Bernard's group got to know one another, and friendships were formed that would continue into adulthood. Before the outbreak of the war, the group would jointly all go to camp and put on a pantomime each year. As with others, David Gabriel Moffatt started off in the Boy Scouts, and on his eighteenth birthday, he too became part of the senior group known as Rovers. One of the earliest photographs of David was taken during a Scout outing of around 1938 showing the young David in a rowing boat on the river at Knaresborough, Yorkshire. Others who were part of the Rovers group were Basil, Bert Jolly, Francis Quinn and David's best friend Owen Murphy.

As a consequence of the friendships, they all walked home together and the route took them past Elsie's parents' house. David and Owen spent much time at the Ambler household. Elsie Ambler had two siblings: Eveline, the younger sister by two years, and Geoff, the youngest of all. David Moffatt became very fond of Eveline; he was known to be sweet on her, but they were just good friends. David Gabriel was a popular member of the Scout group. When war broke out, all but Owen went off to war. Owen, being in a reserved occupation as an engineer, was rejected when he applied to join up but became a member of the Home Guard. Elsie joined the ATS and, due to her mother's ill health, obtained a local posting very near Halifax on compassionate grounds. Elsie married David's best friend in 1944 and became Mrs Murphy. David always visited the Chester Road address when he was on leave; it is believed that the last time he came home to Halifax was in September 1942 when the entire No. 1 section of the RMBPD were given seven days' leave.

David Gabriel Moffatt was born at 97 Butler Street in Belfast on 20 November 1920,[26] to John and Elizabeth (née Mallon), from an Irish family, but was a large, strong Yorkshire lad who had his family home in Halifax. It is believed that David had two brothers and a sister. The youngest of the three Moffatt boys was Shamus and the eldest was John. Sadly, David's sister, Catherine, died at an early age. It is believed that David's mother, Elizebeth, returned to Belfast purposely to give birth to each of her children and that she also ensured the baptism of each of her children took place at the Roman Catholic Church of the Holy Cross in Ardoyne in Belfast. Certainly David Moffatt was baptised according to the Rites of the Catholic Church on 26 November 1920[27], and this was sponsored by Thomas and Mary Ann Mallon. When he became an RMBPD member, David Moffatt was nicknamed 'the preacher' either because he could give a sermon when explaining something, because of his second Christian name, or because he could and would impersonate the clergy with all due solemnity. No doubt, this ability was the result of the links with St Joseph's church, which he frequented as a boy. He also had a wry sense of devilment. Otherwise, he was shy, reserved, very considerate and had 'a lovely nature' and, to quote one person who knew him,[28] was really good looking. After joining the RMBPD, he became friends with Eric Fisher, rarely drank any alcohol, had a very good sense of humour, and was surprisingly careful with his choice of words – he didn't swear!

Taken at the 1939 Scout and Guide camp at Knarsborough. Of the two young men standing together David Moffatt is the one on the right smoking a pipe which he was trying out. He soon gave it up. Seated third on the left is Owen Murphy.

The twenty-two-year-old David had given his next of kin contact details as his mother Mrs Elizabeth Moffatt, who had presumed that he was safe in Portsmouth. The telegram that stated her son was 'missing in action', presumed dead, had arrived at 62 Wheatley Lane, Lee Mount, on the afternoon of 29 January 1943. All those who knew David from the early days in the Scouts 'were very sad to hear of his untimely death, but we were proud of his achievements'[29].

Albert Friedrich Laver
'Never to be the Best Man'

The only NCO to have reached the desired targets at Bordeaux, he was awarded the oak leaves of Mention in Dispatches, being ineligible to receive the recommended DSM as it could not be awarded posthumously.

Ply. X. 3091 Temporary Corporal Albert Friedrich Laver was born on 29 September 1920 at 5 Hind Street, Birkenhead, in Liverpool. He died in France during the first three months of 1943. It is likely that he, along with his three 'Blues brothers', was taken to a remote place outside Bordeaux and executed by firing squad. There is no marked grave. All that any relative had known of him at the time was from the letter stating that the individual concerned was reported as 'missing in action', which had been sent out in the January of 1943. Even Blondie Hasler's mother had received a letter bearing the same news about her son.

Albert Friedrich Laver was known as 'Bert' by his siblings. He was one of five children from the union of John 'George' Laver (a shipwright in the Royal Navy as of 1916) and Marion (née Williams). The eldest of the Laver children was John Jack (b. 1918), then 'Bert' or Albert Friedrich (b. 1920), May (b. 1926), Gwendoline (b. 1929) and Marion (b. 1934). It was said that 'Bert' was a bit of a daredevil when he was a schoolboy; he and his brother Jack went to school in Westham. Bert would fight all his elder brother's battles due to Jack's weak heart from an early childhood bout of rheumatic fever.

Bert's protective pugilistic intent was proven when, as he grew up, he went on to win many boxing trophies. Fourteen years after Bert was born, the family moved from Birkenhead to Friern Barnet, near the football ground. His sister Marion was born at the new home, and she recalls that there was much fuss over the fact that, when the war began, Bert wanted to join up as a regular in the Marines. It is thought that Bert either was successful in forging his father's signature or, more likely, that his mother signed the papers for him, as his father objected, believing his son was too young. The reason for believing the latter is that his mother appears as next of kin. It is believed Bert bought her some chocolates for signing the papers. Bert, prior to joining up, did have a part-time job as a butcher's assistant, and it is amusing to learn that, during a Christmas period, Bert's mother couldn't understand why he was taking so long in dispatching one of the home-bred chickens until she found him in the shed with the still live bird – he could not kill it! Mother Marion had to do the job herself. Sister Marion remembers that, whenever Bert came home on leave, he always refused to go into the Anderson shelter in the garden and would rather stay in his bed when the bombs were dropping. It is also known that Bert injured his foot during training and came home to rest it; this is likely to have coincided with his leave on 16 September 1942.

Fortunately, it has been possible to put together a little of his service history, his thoughts, wants and aspirations during his time after enlisting. These snippets are derived from the letters that he wrote to certain individuals. Bert wrote a good deal of letters to his mother and father as well as many others. Here is the first account available. It was written to Phyllis Janet Page, who had been Bert's elder brother's (John Jack) girlfriend before the Christmas of 1940.

Phyllis, her sisters Doris and May, and the rest of Bert's family had sent him Christmas cards; Phyllis' card had some welcome news for Bert. In his reply, Christmas Eve 1940, from 71 Mess aboard HMS *Rodney*, he thanked them for the cards and took the opportunity to tell Phyllis that he had a definite date for leave and would be home either on 28 or 29 December of 1940.

Laver at different stages in his career.

A much more relaxed young Laver at home in the back garden during leave.

He was looking forward to having the unexpected bonus of the New Year at home. He hoped that Phyllis was going to a dance on New Year's Eve and, if so, that she would ensure that his 'big brother' got him a ticket, as he would not be writing to John before his leave date.

Even though he was aboard ship, Bert had heard that High Barnet had 'been having a rough time lately', meaning the bombing, and hoped they would fair better over Christmas. The welcome news that Phyllis had previously written about was that 'John has managed to pop the question at last'. He continued, 'Well, I'm very pleased to hear that and you have my blessing (I have always had a hidden ambition of being a 'Best Man' anyway). Seriously though, I wish you both all the best and I hope that brother of mine realises how lucky he is.' He ended this letter with a p.s. saying, 'Save me a dance please.'

Another letter, written from 71 Mess on HMS *Rodney*, is dated 1 March 1941. He begins, 'Well, I am afraid that nothing has been happening here lately except we have been having some awful weather the last few weeks but it isn't so bad now thank goodness.' Within three months, in the early morning of 27 May, HMS *Rodney* engaged the *Bismarck* with Bert Laver as an ammunition handler for secondary armament in the forward turret, port side. Bert continued, 'I['m] afraid I haven't got a girl in every port nowadays Phyl, I used to know quite a few girls in different places, but I don't see or write to any now (except you of course), when we are able to get ashore I usually go with a couple of chaps and we have a very quiet "run" ashore, probably have a few drinks (of lemonade) go to the pictures and then "turn in" like good little lads, so you are quite mistaken about me.' It seems that Bert's father had previously written and told him that he had become a firewatcher,[30] and Bert had 'pulled his leg about it'. Now Phyllis had told Bert that she had also become a firewatcher. This prompted Bert to write, 'I hope you look after yourself during the raids, because I don't want to lose my sister in law before I get one – do I Phyl?' He closes with 'give my love to the family, Love Bert'.

Just before dinnertime on Sunday 19 April 1942, now L/Cpl, Bert had again taken pen to paper and written to Miss P. Page at Carnarvon Road in High Barnet, Hertfordshire. This time, he had upgraded to heavyweight linen paper and envelope and was writing from the Junior NCOs Club at the Royal Marines Military School at Thurlstone near Kingsbridge in Devon; the parade ground was on part of the golf course! He had time to compose a touching letter addressed to 'Phyl and All'. He had been away for the wedding of Phyllis'[31] sister Doris, and inquired whether Phyllis and May had been bridesmaids. This led him to comment about his own life in the future, saying, 'Perhaps I'll get married myself soon (after the war, about five years time, if I last that long). Now all I'm waiting for is to see that brother of mine get married, so I can have a lovely sister-in-law and have children call me "Uncle Bert", won't I be proud!!!' The reason Bert was now in this idyllic part of the world with its beautiful coastline and sandy beaches just yards away was that he was trying to advance in the ranks. He says, 'Well this NCOs course is very nearly finished and in less than a fortnight I'll know whether the Royal Marines want A. F. Laver to be a 'Corporal' or stay as a Marine. I hope myself that it will be the successful one, because I've always wanted to "boss" people about and now I'll have my chance.' His letter finishes by saying, 'I'm thinking of going for a swim this afternoon, as we've had some warm weather and the sea looks very tempting.' He ends with 'Love Bert' and adds in a p.s., 'As I'm allowed to put Xs in letters, I'm making the most of it' … he then pens some eighty small xs in an inch square. Such was his affection and humour. Bert managed to make the Thurlstone post box for the last collection at 1930 hrs.

The most interesting letter from this archive collection reflects Bert's time after being accepted into the RMBPD. Even though it is undated, it is possible to attribute the letter to a precise moment in time, namely, after they had returned from Exercise *Blanket*. It was written on Tuesday 17 November 1942, the second day of being back in Southsea, at White Heather just before they travelled via London to the Loch in Scotland to undertake additional training immediately prior to the covert Operation *Frankton*. It is worthwhile relating most of this letter because of its importance.

Interestingly, he begins,

Dear Jack, I'm sorry I haven't answered that letter of yours earlier, but we've been so busy the last few weeks, getting ready to go on that trip, and while we were on it we didn't have an hour to call our own, so I kept putting of[f] writing to you until now. Well Jack we've been back at South-sea here only two damned days and now we've got to go on another blue-pencil so and so trip again, for about the same time as the last one. I don't mind so much the trip but the damned rub is if you're getting married next Sat your little brother Bert will probably be at the other end of England, and I can't stand for you as Best-man Jack, talk about cursed luck. I don't doubt for a minute that you'll manage OK without me but ever since you've been engaged to Phyl I've been looking forward to being at the wedding very nearly as much as you have, but there it is. If only you hadn't changed the date and had got married at Xmas I'm pretty sure I could have made it, because we're sure to get leave after this trip, but it's no good moaning that won't change it, so you'll have to get me a sub – and if its possible next Sat for me to get a shore leave I'll have a couple of big drinks to celebrate your wedding. I hope that you and Mum have patched up that row you had, because I'd like to think that if I can't be there at least all the family will be to wish you luck, so don't let me down Jack see what you can do will you? Well here's wishing you and Phyl "All the Best" and may your married life be as successful as Mum's and Dad's, perhaps I'd better shut up before I get sentimental, but you know what I mean don't you Jack, so cheerio for now, hope to see you soon, give my love to Phyl, Yours Bert.

P.s. If you want to write to me use this address I'll get it OK. B.

pps DON'T forget a piece of the wedding-cake. B.

Jack and Phyllis married on 21 November 1942 at Barnet church without Bert. Jack and Bert had always got on very well. Bert had left home at a young age, as he 'could not get settled', and had joined up. Understandably, Jack was very upset at not having his brother stand as his Best Man. Even if Jack and Phyllis had kept the original December wedding date, they still would not have seen Bert attend. During the entire month of December, he had either been on a submarine, the mission, evading capture or prisoner of the Wehrmacht.

We see from these precious accounts that Albert Friedrich Laver was a kind and considerate young man, 'of quiet demeanour, fair-haired, stocky, round-faced' boy who kept 'himself apart from the evening drink and singalongs'. When Bert was on HMS *Rodney*, not only his family wrote but the entire Page family, even Phyllis' mother. When Bert became part of the RMBPD, they knew not where he was except that he was in Southsea … sometimes. They had no clue as to his whereabouts at any time, as Bert never divulged any details; 'he never said a word about the training' – this had been instilled in them all by Hasler on the very first day. He was 'a lovely young chap, though, not a rowdy soul'. He was 'quietly spoken and loved to go to the dances'. He had better navigational skills than others, was a keen swimmer and could run well. One of his first opportunities to 'boss someone' came on 14 August at Southsea when the L/Cpls were given the opportunity to take charge for PE swimming and signals in order to give them experience.

It was mid-September of 1944 that Albert's father, a carpenter by trade, had decided to write a letter from his home at 119 Sherrads Way to the commandant of the Royal Marines division in Plymouth to illicit, not unreasonably, news of his missing son. This letter had been forwarded to the Admiralty in London.

On 18 October 1944, the Admiralty replied to him saying that they wished to inform him, 'in confidence, that your son was a member of a small force of Royal Marines who carried out a successful seaborne operation of a hazardous nature against enemy-held territory in France during early December 1942. A few of those engaged returned home safely; the fate of the remainder, including your son, is as yet unknown. There is evidence that certain members of the raiding force may be held prisoner of war in enemy hands but confirmation has not yet been obtainable through the international Red Cross society.' The commandant went on to say that he 'and all within the service fully understood the anxiety caused by the absence of news and desired to alleviate this uncertainty, but in order to safeguard any captured personnel against reprisals which are sometimes taken against those engaged on unorthodox offensive warfare', they regretted they were unable to divulge any further details. Mr Laver was also told that, as Albert's mother was the officially recorded next of kin, she would be the one who would receive any further information as soon as it became available via the commandant at Plymouth. It must have been of little comfort, but it was all that could be offered.

His sister Marion was able to write that she was only eight when Bert was captured in 1942, and she remembered vividly the anguish of her parents but particularly her father. It took many years before they knew Bert had died. She believes that as a result of the trauma and worries her father suddenly collapsed and fell from a scaffold which he was on from the low height of only 12 feet. It is thought that the trauma of losing Bert, the uncertainty during the years that followed, together with the death of her husband was too much to bear and Bert's mother Marion drowned her sorrows and succumbed to the excesses of drink.

Bert Laver was noted in the RMBPD for an extraordinary night paddle covering 34 miles with Capt. 'Jock' Stewart. On another 'jolly', before compasses had been provided, on Patrol Margate to the IOW on 17 August 42, the pair used a bright moonlit night to venture out into the Solent. They found themselves lost in a dense fog of a smoke screen that the army had introduced due to an air raid over the area of Portsmouth. Unbeknown to them, the exercise had been called off at 2300. They had no option but to remain where they were in the middle of the waterway for a number of hours until they eventually made for a dummy barge anchored in the Solent and, soaking wet, took refuge and slept on it.

After the *Frankton* Raid, in May 1943, Blondie Hasler wrote in support of Marine Laver's efforts during the operation and said he had 'handled his boat skilfully and displayed initiative and coolness in making his independent attack'. It didn't matter what was said by anyone else, for as far as an eight-year-old girl was concerned, 'He was my hero'. The little girl was Marion, his sister.

Ply. X. 3091 Temporary Corporal Albert Friedrich Laver was the No. 1 in Cockle canoe *Crayfish*, which, being the only other 'insignificant vessel' to have successfully reached the intended targets, placed Limpet mines and began the escape. Laver was ably assisted by his No. 2 …

William Henri Mills[32]
'Full of Life'

When William Henri volunteered for hazardous duties, he might have thought that his celebrations for his twenty-first birthday would have meant a night of fun and the high spirits he was known for 'on the town' at Portsmouth – instead he was spending a night in the cells before any celebrations had taken place; he had been arrested by a French policeman the day before. William Henri had now drawn the shortest straw and landed the worst of a bad deal.

Ply. X. 108159 Marine William Henri Mills was close friends with Bill Sparks; whilst Sparks called him 'Bill', William Henri called Sparks 'Ned'. Had they both been in Pompey that night, they would have had a real good time celebrating. To quote the words of a close family friend,[33] 'Bill was a boy of an extremely lovable character, full of life and always ready to do someone a good turn.' He enjoyed playing the clown and kept all the section amused with the practice. He had attended the local parish school before being employed at Kettering's sports and rubber stores. His education was of a higher standard than most of the others and had served in the civil defence force before joining up. He was of course a very fit lad, well liked, being an accomplished swimmer and footballer and had a girlfriend who he had intended to marry.

William Henri Mills was born in Kettering, Northampton, on 15 December 1921 to William Henry and Mary Ellen. This stocky, high-spirited 'boy' with brown, wavy hair was

Taken just minutes before he journeyed back following home leave; note the rucksack on the window sill behind to the left.

gunned down by Hitler's direct order in occupied France in early 1943. It is likely that he was murdered near Bordeaux, as with the five others who had been captured. William Henri or 'Bill' was one of three children. His elder brother was called Les and his younger brother was named Brian.

It is known that Mrs Laver had been in touch with the Mills family either by telephone or letter[34] and this is borne out by the fact that at the very same time that Mr Laver had written to the commandant at Plymouth, the mother of William Henri, Mrs Mary Ellen Mills, had written a letter from her home at 11 Lime Road in Kettering, to Lt-Col. John Profumo[35] – her MP. John Profumo in turn passed on her letter to the Admiralty, who replied to Mrs Mills with the same content that was relayed to Mr Laver.

On one occasion during the training period near Hayling Island, William Herni and his No. 1, Laver, had become so trapped in the metal barriers of the boom, due to a fierce tidal race, that they both had to be rescued. Neither suffered any injury. This stood them in good stead during the tidal races that they were to encounter at the mouth of the Gironde and that claimed the life of two of their number.

On 13 May 1943, the accolade for Marine Mills' Mention in Dispatches from Hasler reads that he 'carried out his work in a cool and efficient manner and showed considerable eagerness to engage the enemy'. Marine William Henri Mills was also recommended for a DSM. Due to rulings, he was only awarded the oak leaves of Mentioned in Dispatches for his part in what even the Germans described as 'the outstanding raid of the war'. The MID is held by the Royal Marines Museum.

William Henri spent his twenty-first birthday in Montlieu La Garde Gendarmerie in occupied France. William Henri 'loved life', and like many young lads of that period, he just didn't get the opportunity to fully enjoy it.

William A. Ellery

Originally from Soho in London, he was by all accounts an excellent swimmer, being the best in the unit, yet he suffered claustrophobia with the underwater gear used. He was a good medic having a natural ability in this regard and 'knew his stuff'. Ply. X. 108875 Marine W. A. Ellery was a broad-shouldered, 'husky' fellow with a black head of hair who was noted as being a 'fine footballer' and was believed to have had trials for Chelsea Football Club. His original motivation for joining the team was that he wanted to 'have a go at the Germans' and was 'defiant in his attitude' toward them.

Sparks is recorded to have believed that Ellery 'knew how to con his way through life' and told of one incident that displays his ways of getting what he wanted. Sparks relates,

> Inside the barracks we were forbidden to use the NAAFI because we were billeted in civilian lodgings ... one day he disappeared into the NAAFI, leaving us outside and wondering how he expected to purchase anything that was out of bounds to us. A short while later he came back out carrying half a dozen chocolate bars. Ellery is reported to have said to them as he handed out the chocolate, 'I've got a rule in life, Everything you can't have, I will have'.

Ellery became Sparks' closest friends before the raid.

The author writes 'before the raid', as it is known that it was not until at least late April 1943 that Sparks returned to Southsea, and with the following information given by Norman Colley, the reader will understand why the two are likely not to have met again.

When Ellery, Fisher and Colley had disembarked from HMS *Tuna* and returned to Southsea, it is believed that it was Ellery[36], as 'the other rank' who was taken to COHQ in London by Capt. Stewart on 15 December 1943 to see Lt-Cdr L'Estrange; there are no documents found which provide a definitive account for the trip from Portsmouth. During the next few weeks, the three returning marines were 'segregated' from the others. Norman relates that, about six weeks after their return, say mid-February, Ellery 'just disappeared without any warning'. It was about mid-April 1943 that Norman and some others from No. 2 section went to watch football at Portsmouth Football Club ground at Fratton Park. It was then that Ellery surfaced, wearing full uniform and stood with the four other marines watching the game. Norman reported that not a lot was said, and he didn't recall any explanation from Ellery of where he had been or what he was doing, only that after the game Ellery again disappeared. Norman has his own view of events from the night of 7 December onwards, but without any positive evidence, this can only be given as a viewpoint from one who was privy to events at that time.

One thing is certain, Ellery did not feature in the famous 'blues' photograph of No. 2 section that Colley, Fisher and Sparks had now joined. This No. 2 section was ultimately sent out to the Aegean and became known as the 'Earthworm' Detachment, and Ellery did not feature within that group or within any other RMBPD section. Given the circumstances, it can only be assumed that Ellery had become wayward, he simply could not continue[37]. Perhaps in the end he just was not up to the task he had volunteered for. Whatever the reason, the consequence is that no more is heard or known of Ellery; even though he is reported to be an all-round good man to rely on by Sparks. Ellery was chosen to be No. 1 in the canoe team for canoe *Cachalot* with Eric Fisher. It is reported that when the damaged occurred to the canoe Ellery looked 'glum'.

Eric Fisher
'Swam like a Frogman'

It's cool in the trees – Palestine, 1944.

Ply. X. 108151 Marine Eric Fisher is known to have physically broken down and sobbed when he realised his chance to go with the others on the mission had been scuppered by the damage caused to canoe *Cachalot* on the hatch clamp.

Eric Fisher was a very likeable chap who was slightly older than the others in the section and had more in common with Moffatt than anyone else; both came from Irish stock and neither really drank very much or smoke, and as a consequence, they became good friends.

It was Lt MacKinnon who taught Eric to swim from sinking in less than six months, but even then he only just managed! But below the surface Eric was to become a very competent underwater frogman. This is hardly surprising, as you don't need to 'swim' underwater! Described as a stout-built, round-faced young man with a reddish cheek complexion, he was a keen lad with plenty of determination. Eric was from West Bromwich, near Birmingham, and had been a painter's machine minder in the printing trade. Eric had originally been paired up with Bill Sparks, who thought that 'if there was anything that could go wrong, Eric did it'. It appeared that the two did not get on. Regardless of the clash of personalities, he was, along with the two others that remained in the RMBPD, drafted into No. 2 section, which became the 'Earthworm' Detachment, the HQ based at Azzib, Palestine. Many of the operations were speculative due to the fact that many harbours did not contain sufficient enemy shipping to merit a canoe attack.

In one particular canoe operation with this detachment, Eric was part of Operation *Sunbeam A* during 16–18 June 1944 on Axis shipping on the island of Leros in the Aegean using three canoes (Mk 2**) named *Shark*[38], *Salmon*[39] and *Shrimp*. The latter was crewed by Corporal E. W. 'Johnny' Horner[40] and his No. 2 was none other than Marine Eric Fisher. The result of that Leros raid was that two Italian 'Guardian' Destroyers, crewed by the Germans,

Above left: From the famous 'blues' photograph, Earthworm Detachment, before the section went to the Aegean.

Above right: Colley, rear, Fisher, left, and Duncan, right, in Palestine.

were severely damaged and subsequently sunk by RAF when being towed to a repair base, with three further escort vessels sunk. Eric was also part of the reinforcement crew for Operation *Stripling*, which was a month before the *Sunbeam* Raid. Norman Colley said of him that he was 'not the toughest but one of the best you could meet'. Of Eric Fisher's accomplishments, his most outstanding claim is that he managed to survive the war even though he put himself voluntarily in harm's way.

Norman Colley
Mr Hurts and Wounds!

In truth, this man owes his life to a game of rugby and a M183 Certificate. Ply. X. 108877 Marine Norman Colley was originally paired up with Lt Jack W. MacKinnon as his No. 2 in an Mk 1 canoe[41] during early training upon joining the ranks of the RMBPD. But fate was to spare Norman's life twice given what transpired during the *Frankton* Raid. Even after the many years that have passed and with the knowledge of his certain death had he gone on the *Frankton* Raid, he still experiences some guilt that Marine Conway did not return.

Postman James Richard Colley received his first-born son into this world on 22 November 1920. Norman was to become the eldest of four brothers. Most of his childhood was centred around Pontefract, attending Love Lane School, which was close to an army barracks. His secondary modern education was also taken care of in Pontefract, but after leaving school, he started work in a grocer's shop in Featherstone by delivering groceries on a three-wheeled bike. In 1941, Norman was called up for his National Service, signing on at Leeds recruiting centre. As with Sparks, it was a sergeant at the centre who agreed with Norman that the Royal Marines would be a good place for anyone who did not want to join the army. Norman was on holiday from work when his mother, Ellen, shouted upstairs with the news that his

Our 'Mr Hurts and Wounds' Colley in full dress, left, and right, a photo taken in Palestine.

papers had arrived saying, 'you're to join the Marines in Plymouth'. A few days later, on 16 April, the blue-eyed, 5-foot 6¼-inch tall, twenty-year-old grocer's assistant with his fresh complexion had boarded a train at Leeds. He changed at Bristol Temple Meads and was receiving a cup of hot tea and biscuits from the WI at Plymouth railway station just as the sirens sounded the all clear from one of the many bombings in the area. The next port of call was the barracks, where his initiative and aptitude were put to use and he was given the job pointing the new recruits in the right direction. The Royal Marines accepted Norman into their ranks and he was then subjected to the physical testing during the three months of recruit training. The posting in the Orkneys beckoned with Norman being a part of the Labour Corps (813), which entailed the building of accommodation blocks for the employees of an oil exploration company. His highlight of the time was being part of a Guard of Honour during a royal visit to the Isle of Hoy for King George VI. Norman can be quoted saying, 'I would have volunteered for the Girl Guides if it meant I could have got away from Scapa,' such was the want to be doing something of meaning. He wanted a 'bit of excitement'. This want grew and his need to get away ensured that he would keep an eye on the Daily Orders. His attentiveness was rewarded when the 'volunteers for hazardous duty' ploy was posted on the notice board. He applied. Norman soon found himself in front of Blondie Hasler in Plymouth and accepted into the newest established unit of the war – the RMBPD.

A number of the other ranks were selected, some were RTUd, and the remaining thirty-three, including Norman, proceeded with the tough training regime, which included the new art of canoeing.

Norman had been partnered up with Lt MacKinnon for canoeing training. This allegiance was on course to send Norman into the history books as one of the 'Cockleshell Heroes' but for an incident during one of the many organised games for the men of the RMBPD. Norman found himself in a hospital bed sporting an injury of the metatarsal variety. It was Friday 31 July 1942, and as with all the others in the section, he had been playing rugby in bare feet on the grass near Eastney Barracks.

The Hurts and Wounds Certificate (M183) was verified by Lt MacKinnon and reads, 'Fracture base of metatarsal, right foot, no displacement.' It was Lt MacKinnon who came to visit Norman in hospital to ensure that the injured soul did not take sick leave, as this would have meant that Norman would have been Returned to Unit (RTUd). Norman assured Lt MacKinnon that he had no intention of taking sick leave, and this then ensured that Norman was kept on the team in No. 1 section.

Norman volunteered and was picked to be the reserve man; had he been needed, he would have been happy to go on the raid. Norman acknowledges that the injury sustained 'saved my life'. Unquestionably, Marine Colley would have been MacKinnon's No. 2 on the *Frankton* Raid if it had not been for his untimely recreational injury. History now records the fate of Marine Conway, who had taken Norman's place.

Norman, Eric Fisher, and Bill Sparks when he returned, were all eventually drafted into No. 2 section where, known as the 'Earthworm' Detachment, some were part of a number of actions, such as Operations *Brother*, *Sister* (subsequently changed to *Stripling*), and *Sunbeam*. The latter saw both DSCs and DSMs awarded.

Norman excelled at football, cricket and swimming; he also enjoyed cycling. A Plymouth Albion scout had spotted him playing football in 1945 and asked if he was interested, but at that stage, all Norman wanted to do was go home and marry his sweetheart. Promotion did not interest him for the same reason; as with most men, he just wanted to get on with his life.

At the age of sixteen, Norman had got a job at a company that supplied groceries. Alma worked in the office for the same firm and became the only girl for Norman – the love of his life. The men were not allowed to marry until hostilities had ceased in Europe, all having to ask permission to do so. He proposed to his sweetheart by telephone from Teignmouth on VE day: Tuesday. The following Saturday, the hallowed day for playing football, saw Norman take the bus to Torquay town centre. He gave up the afternoon of playing football to buy a 9ct engagement ring. They had to scour all of Leeds to find the elusive 22ct wedding ring for their wedding day on 23 June 1945 during embarkation leave; two other men of the RMBPD also got hitched that same day. At that time, RMBPD were scheduled to go to the Far East, but their deployment was cancelled after VJ Day.

Norman's best friend had been Marine Robert (Bob) Ewart. After joining No. 2 section and the 'Earthworm' follies, Marine Duncan became a good friend, and they kept in touch by letter for several years thereafter. It was on 23 March 1946 that Norman left the Royal Marines; he would have stayed in if he had not married – but he had met the right woman. The last time he saw Stonehouse barracks was on his demob day. He never wanted to live at his parents' home but was content to live with the in-laws until Norman and Alma found their own home. Norman went into engineering for seven years before becoming a self-taught baker and confectioner in South Elmsall, Pontefract, an occupation that lasted for twenty-three years. Converting the shop next door to the baker's, he became a sub-postmaster until 1985 when, upon retiring, he and his wife travelled the world visiting every continent, ocean and temperature; Norman's love, Alma, died in 2003.

Norman saw the 1953 *Cockleshell Heroes* film three times. The first time was in London at the premiere, then in Leeds, where he met up again with Bill Sparks, and in Bradford. As with Hasler, he wasn't impressed with its accuracy and said that there was 'too much romance and Hollywood'.

Only recently has it been possible to trace Norman, and it was through an enabling nephew that in 2007 Norman's wish to see the *Frankton* Memorial at the SBS HQ at Poole was fulfilled, care of an invitation to a *Frankton* Dinner. Norman was made an honorary member of the SBSA. The author is privileged to have met and been able to have many a conversation with this man, who retains a wealth of memory that has enabled the finer details to be presented within the body of this work.

Norman only stopped swimming at the age of eighty-seven due to ill health. Whilst his mind is as bright as a button, his body is quite tired out, but with the care of those who attend, he still 'carry[s] on'. Of Norman's soldiering, his medals consist of the 1939–45 Battle of Britain Star, the Italy Star, the Defence Medal and the 1939–45 War Medal. Being 'young and daft' is Norman's only excuse for his escapades during the war. Young he was, daft he ain't, of character he is.

Human Will and Determination

In 1984, a memorial was unveiled to all the men who undertook the *Frankton* Raid, including Bill Sparks and Blondie Hasler, who were present at the ceremony at Hamworthy SBS HQ in Poole. Although he did not attend, HRH Prince Philip, Captain General of the Royal Marines, wrote of the efforts of the operation: 'The sheer size of an operation has never been a criterion of its importance or a measure of the popular response to its outcome. The men who took part in Operation *Frankton* have written one of the most glorious pages in the long history of the Royal Marines. The memorial to those who died is as much a tribute to their personal courage as it is a record for posterity of what can be achieved by human will and determination in the face of adversity.'

These were the men who used their skill with an 'Insignificant Vessel' to caress their quarry with the ingenious stickiness of the Limpet Mine and *paddled* their way into the history books – forever.

CHAPTER 10
The RMBPD's 'Southsea Stroll'

In order to better understand the reasons for the establishment of miscellaneous small units, we first have to understand the environment in which these were fostered. After the fall of France in 1940 and with it the termination of continental warfare in the West, there became a requirement for small-scale reconnaissance and 'nuisance' raids upon the enemy-held coasts. The craft first used by the few that undertook certain actions was that of the privately held requisitioned canoes or those that belonged to the officers or men of the units so employed. These 'borrowed' canoes consisted of various types, some of which were quickly proved to be unsuitable for even training purposes. The evolution of small craft for special purposes even until 1943 was a result of the requirements and enthusiasms of individual units. One man and one unit were ahead of the subsequent co-ordinated and planned result of operational experience, which then provided the required craft. This man was Blondie Hasler, and the RMBPD was the first unit to have its own type of specialist canoe for its own purposes. Through his leadership, his detachment was afforded something lacking elsewhere – self-reliance and clarity of purpose. This is the brief story of the unit and its raison d'être.

'We were young in those days. You did not think it was going to hit you. It might be somebody else.'

Capt. Dickie Raikes

'Free from close family ties'

As a unit, they were self-sufficient. They did not adorn themselves with any special distinguishing markings. They had great independence and greater responsibility. They became supremely fit.

This was 'Hasler's Party'. He is recorded as saying to them, 'I don't mind what you do with yourselves off duty, within reason, so long as you appear on Parade next morning – fit.' The whole ethos was one of seeking challenges rather than avoiding them, and that takes a special kind of individual. These were the boys with a truly mixed background, thrown together in a secretive situation, moulded by Blondie Hasler and based, initially, in Portsmouth at Southsea: a seaside resort with a fine promenade and pier, sporting the 'canoe lake' nearby and overlooking the Solent Water with the Isle of Wight on the horizon. Whilst the beach surface content was far from perfect, lacking in the fine and unbelievably sticky sand found at Hayling, the long stretch of pebbled higher beach proved to be of great use.

The combination of Limpets and the canoe was not a new idea, having been part of operations by the Special Boat Section in 1941. The Royal Marine Boom Patrol Detachment (RMBPD) came about, in rough terms, due to Hasler's idea of combining canoes with underwater swimmers. These could be launched offshore from above or below the water in order to attack enemy shipping whilst in harbour. Hasler had produced a paper largely ignored by the Admiralty on this subject using covert approaches. Hasler also knew about the ingenuity of the Italian's Explosive Motor Boats (EMB) and the 'Chariots' used in the prosecution of their craft of being sneaky. The EMB was a high-speed planing craft that carried about 500 lb of warhead located in the bows. The Italian technique was to enter a defended harbour at night either by stealth or through a breach in the obstructions made by other means. The driver would aim the boat at a stationary ship, accelerate at full speed, pull the cocking lever and bail out over the stern with a small balsa raft when the boat was still 200 yards from target. The charge was set to explode either on impact or hydrostatically when the bow component of the boat had sunk to a predetermined depth alongside the target. This effort only afforded the driver the opportunity to be captured. By April 1942, only two attacks by EMB were known of: one on 26 March 1941 by six EMB on HMS *York* at Suda Bay in Crete and another on 25/26 July 1941 at Malta. Hasler's views eventually filtered to Mountbatten, and in Hasler's words[1], it was a sheer stroke of luck that the Italians demonstrated that ship attacks by clandestine small craft could be successful and that somebody had remembered turning down similar proposals made by an unknown captain serving in a non-combatant unit – meaning himself!

On 26 January 1942, now Acting Major, Hasler joined the Combined Operations Development Centre (CODC); its head at that time was Lt-Col. Langley. Within only hours of arriving at his post, Hasler and Tom Hussey (at that time co-ordinator at CODC, very soon becoming commandant) met with Commander Peter Du Cane, OBE, from Vosper Shipbuilders and inspected an EMB that had been brought back from Malta, where it had been found beached outside the Grand Harbour following an abortive attack. It appeared to be, and was referred to as, an Italian Prototype, which, in mid-April, was in the process of being reassembled by HMS *Hornet* in order for trials to be run by 25 April. For ships with anti-torpedo bilges, the EMB was known not to be effective, other than to cause skin damage. The method of delivery to the scene of operation was always by surface craft, which lowered the EMB into the water by crane or derrick.

It was following the verbal briefing on this subject that Mountbatten required Blondie to concentrate on 'the development of a British version of the [Italian] explosive motor boat paying particular attention to methods of attacking ships in harbour'. This Boom Patrol Boat (BPB) was developed in accordance with the Staff requirements of TSD 276/42 as a close copy of the EMB.

There followed a paper proposal to investigate and develop the means of transporting the BPB by air, which would greatly increase its scope, as well as to develop methods of using the boat to destroy boom defences, beach obstacles and dock installations. It had been proposed (the 'Tadpole' idea from Hasler) to develop a craft so that it could be dropped by parachute from an aircraft for raids on enemy ships in European harbours. This 'toy' was an integral part of a power boat section headed by Lt David Cox, RM, later Captain, who was awarded a military MBE for being the first man to be parachuted from an aircraft in a boat (BPB) into the sea, off the Harwich coast.

From 26 January to 28 June 1942, Hasler was allowed to concentrate almost exclusively on the development of all types of small boat attack on enemy coasts and harbours; but at this stage, this centred on the BPB. By arrangement with C-in-C Portsmouth, the Experimental Party night exercises were combined with operational patrol of the Eastern Boom (Patrol Margate) using canoes equipped for counter-attacking Human torpedoes and other enemy small craft. This technique had been provisionally adopted by the Director of Local Defence as a standard method of defence. This type of affair continued during the first six months. During the experimental and trials stage, the BPBs were handled by Commander Du Cane, Hasler and the CODC's Experimental Party of one corporal and one private from the No. 3 Commando of the Special Service Brigade. The maintenance was carried out by Vospers Ltd, who also made arrangements for the initial trials. The only suitable British-made engine was the Lagonda V12. The engines were not in production at that time, but there were ten engines available at the works, four of them incomplete. The ten Boom Patrol Boats provisionally ordered were to be designed to be powered by the Lagonda engine, but the engine bearers were to be designed to accommodate a V8 Mercury as an alternative, giving a maximum speed of 29 knots.

The projected personnel required for the operation of the initial ten BPBs was suggested by the new commandant of the CODC, Capt. Hussey, on 20 April. This totalled twenty-four for the establishment, consisting of one Lt-Cdr RN (or equivalent rank), two officers and twelve other ranks as drivers, with one officer and three other ranks for maintenance. There was no suitable craft available in which to train the CODC's Experimental Party for their role as drivers in the experimental stages. At this time, there was a need to requisition three training boats from civilian sources 'without delay'. These were named and determined as 'a robust craft' of Chris-Craft type of 25 knots, 'a moderate type' of 35 knots, and a 'racing motor of "Ventnor" type of 50 knots', with the intent that the drivers would graduate from the robust to the racing type.

The EMB had a 16-foot multichine hull capable of a speed of 30 mph with an explosive charge fixed in the hull. It was powered by an Alfa Romeo 2.6-litre six-cylinder water-cooled petrol engine driving through a friction clutch to an inboard/outboard 'leg'. The driver was located near the transom, and when the craft was put on course for its target, he would then clamp off the steering wheel and bail out[2] over the stern onto a balsa-wood float, as previously mentioned, which formed part of the after cockpit. Through a bumper bar arrangement to the explosive charge, the craft would explode on impact.

Following on from suggestions, a temporary base for the engineering division was sited in a civilian yard taken over by Combined Operations' landing craft operational and training base of HMS *Tormentor* located in the Hamble River near Warsash, on Southampton Water. The site was used as a repair base for landing craft.

The training craft, as suggested, were a 16-foot Chris-Craft 'Spider Boy' runabout, a 12-foot Whippet-class 1½-litre Hydrographic plane 'Elinore', and a 4-litre 'Ventnor'-type Hydrographic plane-powered Uhet.

The engineering division of the RMBPD was moved to HMS *Northney* on Hayling Island near the Maypole Public House, Fishery Lane. The Italian boat was inspected by the DNC staff with all necessary drawings taken in order to replicate. With this, an order was placed with Vosper's at the then Porchester Yard for seventeen craft. Initially, only ten were shown as being laid down. These were subcontracted out to the firm Percy M. See of Fareham, who had experience in building small reverse-clinker inboard and outboard racing craft; they were also responsible for building the special IRSB-designed cutter for launching two Mk 2 canoes as well as the two-man MFU Kayak. It should be pointed out that the BPBs were never used operationally.

The order for contra-rotating propeller inboard/outboard drive was placed with Lagonda at Staines. These were found unsuitable, and American Gray Marine 'Fireball' 6/140 side-valve engines were used in the operational airborne craft and Vosper Marine Ford V8 conversions used in the training craft. The captured Italian boat was then used for training in Chichester Harbour. This study of bringing about the Boom Patrol Boat (BPB) also led to Hasler's remit of the use of canoes 'in co-operation' with the BPB.

Hasler turned his attention to the improvement of the EMB, which included the ability to get it past any harbour defences with the added benefit of rescue to the pilot; this he did with the help of the SOE. The writing of papers for the BPB began on 15 April. So it was that the search to provide a canoe to fit in with operations was begun, and it was duly found in the already designed, flat-bottomed craft from Fred Goatley on the Isle of Wight. Whilst the study and intent of redesigning the BPB was being applied, Hasler's ideas would change. The method of the insertion of small raiding craft, covertly, into enemy-held territory was still to be advanced.

It was during a hot-water wallow in a pristine and modern bathroom at Dolphin Court[3] in Southsea during late April 1942 that Hasler came up with an idea for a more active service role for himself, and a couple of days later, discussions had taken place about an operational arm of the CODC which would be required for trails and operations once the targets had become available.

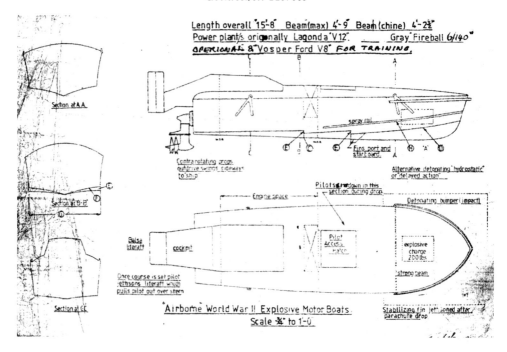

Boom Patrol Boat, also known as Airborne WWII Explosive Motorboat.

With that in mind, the commandant of the CODC had written to the CCO with proposals for a formation of the RM Harbour Patrol Detachment on 12 May 1942 saying,

> Tactically, the main disadvantages possessed by this type of boat [BPB] appears to be the difficulty in negotiating the boom defences. After careful investigation, it seems more than doubtful if the present boat will be able to pass over any form of surface obstruction in darkness without assistance. To overcome this difficulty it is proposed to develop the use of Cockles in conjunction with BPB. The outline of the concept that each BPB should approach its objective in company with a Cockle. The function of the Cockle would be (a) to clear a passage through the surface obstructions using explosive cutters or (preferably) some more silent method (b) to take station by the gap and exhibit some form of screened leading light until the BPB had passed through. (c) to follow up the BPB for the remainder of its approach with the object of attempting to pick up the driver after he had baled out and escaping with him. Smoke floats could be used at this stage to give concealment. In order to achieve the close liaison necessary it is evident that the crews of Cockles and BPBs must be raised and trained as a single unit, preferably interchangeable.

The commandant had recommended Hasler as CO due to his abilities and knowledge in the required field of small boat attack.

It was at this time that Hasler, armed with a proposal of an all-Royal Marine unit, attended a conference chaired by Mountbatten's RM Chief of Staff, one Colonel G. E. Wildman-Lushington. The idea of the Harbour Patrol Party had been mooted but was then changed from the Royal Marine Harbour Patrol Detachment to the Royal Marine Boom Patrol Detachment during the same conference at COHQ on 26 June. With encouragement from Mountbatten, Blondie was granted authority in accordance with the CCO's Q.481/3/928 of 27 June 1942 and the verbal instructions given to him to form the RMBPD. The proposed establishment was for a total of forty-six individuals including the administration and maintenance staff, with each of the two sections comprising one lieutenant and one sergeant, two corporals, and ten marines.

Third row from front, MacKinnon second from left, Pritchard-Gordon second from right.

Hasler had already visited the RMSA School at Browndown on 25 June and selected two volunteers for hazardous service in the form of two second lieutenants, namely W. Pritchard-Gordon and Jack MacKinnon. On 30 June, he had reported to the commandant of the Portsmouth Division of Royal Marines to explain the detailed proposals for raising and training this unit. The proposed form of the circular to units from which the personnel were to be drawn informed that a small Royal Marine unit was about to be formed under the CCO. It explained that the work consisted of offensive operations of a commando type and called for exceptional individual qualities and listed, in order of importance, that 'all volunteers *must* be: eager to engage the enemy; indifferent to personal safety; intelligent; nimble; and free from close family ties or dependants; able to swim; of good physique and eyesight. Previous knowledge of the sea and small boats [was] desirable but not essential.' The categories targeted were cadets, corporals and marines. Most interestingly, the circular ended with the statement 'the name of this unit, when published, should not be taken to indicate its true function'.

Hasler's frustration was evident, realising that whilst there were plenty of men serving who had small-boat knowledge, it was a fact of life that they were the very ones that would not be allowed to volunteer. He was quoted as saying, 'There must be thousands of keen young yachtsmen wasting their time in the Army and the RAF, but of course we can't tap them.' As it turned out, not one of the volunteers had experience of small boats, which shows that, with the support of Hasler, the determination of those who had volunteered shone through. No wonder they had great admiration for him and pride in what Hasler had turned them into.

With the daily bulletins having been previously posted, on 1 July, this brought in twenty-eight marines (twenty were drawn from the RM Auxiliary Battalion), three corporals and two sergeants, from whom Blondie selected one sergeant, one corporal and four marines as candidates suitable for training as instructors. By the end of the interview each man had also been asked the timely rhetorical question by Hasler, 'Do you realise that your expectation of a long life is very remote?'

It should be noted that none of RMBPD had done the Commando course at Achnacarry before the *Frankton* Raid and as such none of the men were actual Commandos but were trained to undertake clandestine raids. It is believed the general request for 'volunteers for hazardous service' has been corrupted since the war to imply that the RMBPD men were all Commandos. This is similar to '*Force Viper*' in Burma in 1942, who held a similar status to that of the RMBPD but were not Commandos. The *Frankton* Raid was a commando raid with a small 'c' not a Commando raid undertaken by Commandos.

Hasler had now picked his principal officer, Ty Lt J. D. Stewart, who was discharged from MNBDO II at Hayling Island and then reported at Portsmouth in the evening of 3 July to take up his duties as second in command whilst Hasler was dutifully mowing the lawn and 'putting more cotton on strawberry beds at his mother's house at Catherington.

Stewart was a Scot with whom Hasler had fought in Norway and whom he admired for his administrative and technical abilities. Stewart took over the operation at Southsea, carrying on with developments when Hasler was away on Operation *Frankton*. He was a reservist; since 1939, he envisaged no other goal but the eventual victory of his country. The men's admiration for his efficiency and respect for him was high. His nickname was the 'Old Man'; he was the same age as Hasler. 'Jock' Stewart was the only other officer who was informed of the purpose of the mission that Hasler was to undertake.

With the nucleus of the other ranks arriving from Plymouth on 6 July, a medical inspection took place at 2100 followed by a 'short talk on rugger ground'. All the RM officers, the administrative section and the instructors were now assembled at Eastney. The two sections then commenced training on the morning of 7 July 1942. All ranks were given 'a short talk on security' by Hasler. The nucleus now received instruction directly from Hasler in seamanship, small arms, explosives, swimming and PT. The system of instruction was that Hasler would demonstrate the correct method, then the class carried out the lesson, and he then critiqued. At a later period, he dictated notes to class on various lessons he had taught them. These notes were subsequently used for instructors' hand books due to the majority of subjects taught not being catered for in normal naval or military text books. Each week during this time, it is recorded that 'all ranks [were] given personal reports, pointing out their faults and good points'.

Meanwhile, the whole of the remainder of the volunteers still at Plymouth (less the rejected NCOs) were formed into a squad and put through a course of parade training, swimming and P & RT. During this period, some men were taken out of class, and others added, at the discretion of the Adjutant, Plymouth Division.

Before the main body arrived from Plymouth, the nucleus received a final talk from Hasler on 23 July 1942. A squad of twenty-three Marines finally joined Portsmouth Division on the afternoon of 24 July 1942 and was addressed by Ty Lt J. D. Stewart on security. This brought the total strength of operational ranks to twenty-nine NCOs and men. As this was three in excess of the establishment, it was proposed to 'weed out' the surplus on the conclusion of the preliminary stages of training[4]. Thus the nominal list of the unit with their rank at that stage in the July of 1942 was

CO Major H. G. Hasler, OBE, RM.
2nd i/c Ty Lt J. D. Stewart, RM.

No. 1 Section	**No. 2 Section**
2nd Lt J. W. MacKinnon	2nd Lt William Pritchard-Gordon
Ply. X. 6655 Sgt Samuel Wallace	Ply. X. 1457 Cpl J. M. King
Ply. X. 3091 L/Cpl W. S. Laver	Ply. X. 1412 L/Cpl Robert Johnston
Ply. X. 1369 L/Cpl G. J. Sheard	Ply. X. 2559 L/Cpl E. S. T. Bick

Main Body No. 1 section comprised	Main Body No. 2 section comprised
X.108881 Mne David G. Moffatt	Ply. X. 105040 Mne J. Saunders
Ply. X. 108159 Mne W. N. Mills	Ply. X. 108660 Mne R. N. Ruff
Ply. X. 108877 Mne Norman Colley#	Ply. X. 108876 Mne Alexander Duncan
Ply. X. 108875 Mne W. A. Ellery[5]	Ply. X. 108871 Mne P. G. Turfrey

Ply. X. 108878 Mne Dennis Blaymire*
Ply. X. 3664 Mne W. E. Sparks#
Ply. X. 108151 Mne Eric Fisher#
Ply. X. 105763 Mne James Conway
Ply. X. 108879 Mne Clement Carroll*
Ply. X. 108880 Mne Robert Ewart
Ply. X. 108144 Mne L. T. David*
Ply. X. 1816— Mne W. G. Hughes*

Ply. X. 105862 Mne W. S. Stevens
Ply. X. 106070 Mne Gordon Lambert
Ply. X. 4114 Mne R. W. S. Martin
Ply. X. 108873 Mne G. F. Cattrell
Ply. X. 108883 Mne Alexander Watson
Ply. X. 108884 Mne John McCarroll
Ply. X. 1026 Mne Lawrence Ashton

* known to be RTUd[6] along with others.
# Following *Frankton*, these men were absorbed into No. 2 section.

On 28 July, it seems that certain alterations to this first nominal list were made, with Marine Hughes RTUd from No. 1 section and another added to No. 2 section, namely Ply. X. 108872 Mne E. W. O'Dell.

Administrative
X 18979 Clr Sgt W. S. Edwards
Ply. X. 18609 Mne W. J. H. Drew (Storeman)
Ply. X. 20545 Mne Robert Brown (Orderly)
Ply. X. 103924 Mne F. J. Phelps (MT Driver)

The RMBPD was not issued with a unit badge of any kind; just the commando dagger and combined ops flashes were worn. In outward appearance, in uniform, a member of the unit would look like any other Royal Marine. The unit developed into a spirited one with pride in their physical fitness, but this did come at a price. Some marines were RTUd, normally through injury. Hasler forbade all to use the steps leading to the beach from the esplanade, and it was the high jump from the concreted barrier onto the far lower beach with large pebbles that each had to negotiate. On more than one occasion, this, and the rough play, resulted in injury. One chap landed on the shingle so badly he damaged both his heels and was RTUd. Others, like Norman Colley's room mate Blaymire, were RTUd simply because they were not up to the requirement – not a slur on that marine, just a fact of life. It is believed that four from the initial intake for No. 1 section succumbed. Even Colley himself had an early incident, which as discussed actually saved his life in the end. Hasler expected a great deal from the men that became the RMBPD.

The functions of the RMBPD were to operate Boom Patrol Boats with or without attendant canoes; to be capable of undertaking at short notice any other form of specialised small boat operation; to provide expert personnel for carrying out small boat trials, experiments and development under DXSR. The 'job description' for the health and safety nuts of today would have required the intent, which was that the detachment should concentrate chiefly upon small boat seamanship, navigation, underwater work and transport by air, with the object of evolving new methods of attacking ships in harbour. It was not intended to specialise in small-scale raids on coastal positions, demolitions ashore, reconnaissance of beaches, routine patrols in submarines or the landing and re-embarkation of agents, since those functions were already covered by SSRC and the SBS. The role was viewed as more of a naval one and less of a military one. The proposal was that the unit would be under the direct operational command of CCO, administered by RALB, with Hasler as CO still a part-time member of the CODC, where he would deal with the development of equipment and techniques. The Headquarters were at Dolphin Court in Southsea, Portsmouth. Even today, it is a pleasant block of apartments of a near Art Deco style, overlooking a small body of fresh water used for recreational purposes (which used to be known as the 'canoe lake'). It is set back from the higher main road that runs adjacent and parallel to the beach.

At 0815 on 24 July 1942, Hasler inspected and addressed the new troops for three quarters of an hour on the functions of the unit and security. Then the training of the main body commenced by the nucleus, and the first test of their seamanship, or lack of it, began. Hasler's diary says it all: 'new troops almost drowned themselves', with the second entry telling us that the afternoon was spent in 'salvaging boats and continued training'. Fortunately, due to Hasler's foresight and the unbroken rule that life jackets should be always worn during this training, there were never any drownings, despite the high spirits of the men who thought this to be 'jolly' worth the effort. The war diaries simply mention 'three capsizes occurring in the first day of training. No casualties. All boats salvaged'. Hasler, as a young boy, had himself learnt the art of canoeing on exactly the same part of the beach.

The game of covert patrols began with each section, on a rota basis, patrolling the 'Boom' off Southsea to the Isle of Wight. It would prove adequate to test the techniques needed of the men destined for this new formation. This boom was a miscellany of surface and underwater nasties that stretched out from the beach opposite Lumps Fort at Southsea for six miles in dogleg fashion across to Seaview, near Ryde on the Isle of Wight, the remnants of which are still visible at low water today.

When they reached the island, they had a cuppa and a bite to eat from a canteen nearby. So it was that the training continued, consisting of small boat operations by day and night in canoes, assault boats and fast motor boats, together with the use of weapons from these craft, as well as boarding tactics.

They had to learn coastal navigation as adapted to these smaller craft, signalling, physical training, close-quarter fighting, Limpet attacks on shipping, explosives and shallow-water diving.

The training base was at Lumps Fort; the canoes and equipment were stored in one of the two Nissen huts, one of which was used for stores, the other for training, lessons and assembling machine guns, etc. They had the whole sea front to themselves from just shy of the pier all along the beach area including the promenade. The unit patrolled the boom on night and day exercises, often probing the defences at Portsmouth. On 27 July, the very first Margate patrol exercise was carried out with officers and NCOs, in a 'full moon and calm water'. It was here that the very first Mk 2 uniquely designed flat-bottomed canoes were to be tested during the regular Margate Boom Patrol across to the Isle of Wight. In the canoe,

Canoe testing showing adjacent Boom in background.

the forward man was armed with a Tommy gun and the aft man with six 5-lb charges and six No. 36 hand grenades with three-second delay fuses (not thrown from the canoes). The island was also the home of the elderly designer of the canoe that Hasler would put so much trust in. Ultimately, only twenty-six of the eventual 876 Cockle Mk 2 canoes were produced here. Perhaps the greatest importance of canoe history is attributed to the RMBPD because of its associations and involvement with certain operations. This was the unit that had not only had first use of the Cockle Mk 2 canoe, but had used it for the first time on an operation – the *Frankton* Raid, which Hasler commanded. Without the input from Hasler, and the formation of the RMBPD at that time, canoe development and that of other hardware might not have moved ahead as quickly as it did.

On 8 July, Hasler had inspected the first two BPB, which were framed up at Fareham by Percy M. See. For Hasler, there was one episode that nearly scuppered the entire process. Sub-Lt (E) R. W. Ladbrooke had joined the RMPBD on 20 July. Shortly after the men of the unit started training in Portsmouth, Hasler and Ladbrooke, the engineer, were at Hayling. Whilst all things marine were Hasler's forte, the speedboat was not his preferred choice of craft. Hasler's first encounter with the EMB was at full speed minus the balsa-wood raft platform, which he had removed. At 25 knots, Hasler had belted along Mengham Ryde and then shut the throttle down in order to measure its stopping distance. The absence of the balsa-wood raft platform that should have protected the craft from the wake that swept across the now-open stern rendered the craft sunk on a shallow mud bank. The platform was subsequently refitted.

At that time, the BPB was still a reality, with the projected delivery of the first craft in October and the men ready for operating the same just a fortnight after that date. Hasler also envisaged that his men would be prepared for simple canoe operations by the end of August. The number of men working together would depend on the operational task, and no more than one section would be employed on any given operation. The unit would also be available for a secondary role in larger operations.

During the development, it soon became apparent to Hasler that the canoe option would be better employed in 'methods of attacking ships in harbour' rather than the BPB. With this in mind, Hasler believed that small parties of men used in destroying the economic targets of the enemy would be the way forward, with both canoes and divers.

Billeting

With the formation of the RMBPD, there was a need to have independent accommodation; furthermore, the RMBPD personnel would not be available for administrative duties, as cooks, guards or fatigues. Billeting was proposed and granted with a special (commando) rate of subsistence due to 'their work consisting largely of night operations, thus necessitating unconventional hours for sleeping and feeding, as training progresses it will be necessary for them to change localities frequently'. Colour Sergeant W. J. Edwards, 'the spotless, shiny marine from the top of his head to the tips of his toes', had been recalled from the reserves and was an active pensioner acting as the RMBPD sgt major. The lads called him 'Bungy' Edwards. Whilst friendly, he kept the lads at arm's length. He had found lodgings for all the boys, who were then transported in the 3-ton Bedford OY from the Esplanade to the first stop of White Heather in Worthing Road. The landlady was a Mrs Powell who had a sixteen-year-old 'very attractive' daughter named Heather. This was the accommodation for the entire No. 1 section, including Messrs Ellery, Ewart, Fisher, Moffatt and Sparks. Apart from Wallace, Laver and Sheard, all the rest of the men were initially accommodated at White Heather, each paying their commando subsistence of 6s 8d per day[7]. Mrs Powell's husband was also in the Royal Marines serving with HMS *Aurora* at the time. Bill Sparks said that he slept like a log that first night at the White Heather.

With No. 2 section billeted at 35 St Ronans Road with a Mrs Montague, the officers had been accommodated at Eastney Barracks before moving into the furnished rented property of 9 Spencer Road on 7 September. The gardener attended to the bulk of the work in the garden, but they did try their hand in the cultivation department as, no sooner had they moved in they, as Lt MacKinnon mentioned, they 'had planted winter cabbage'. It was also at this time in September that a female was recruited by the unit. Lt Jack MacKinnon reports, 'Our unit has bought a small 12 week old Cocker Spaniel and I have adopted it. It is funny to see the tiny pup and our big St Bernard playing together'. He called her 'Tich', 'as this is the only word she understands'. It seems then that the unit had an existing 'mascot' as well as this new recruit who was billeted with the officers. 'Tich' was to become a feature in the lives of all who remained.

Blondie had been living at his mother's house, twelve miles from Portsmouth, in Catherington, until they had organised their own mess. The officers had three Marine Officer's Attendants or MOAs named Todd, Oxley and Hoy, the latter responsible for messing and the other MOAs. It was here that others got to know that Blondie had a pint of beer – with breakfast. Blondie instigated a French-speaking-only night three evenings each week.

The relationship between the officers and men was one of quiet informality, and given the nature of the training and exercises, it would have been too unreasonable to expect otherwise. Strict yet friendly. Hasler expressed this when he said, 'They have built up a tremendous spirit and I think if I were to interfere it would damage their morale. Of course, it would be disastrous with poor officers, but my officers seem to be able to fraternize like this without losing respect or lessening their authority. Still. It is a little worrying.'[8] Given the time and what was to transpire, it would seem that this informality allowed the men to put their entire trust in their leader for what was to be an 'ask too far'. The get-togethers were held in various establishments and of those most favoured were the hostelries of The Eastney, Granada and Clarendon, all of which were actually mentioned by name during the *Frankton* Raid itself.

When one section was patrolling the boom, the other section (and later, sections) carried out night exercises paddling to Langstone or Chichester Harbour, often having to find their own way without the aid of a compass – in the dark and trying to avoid all others including the Solent Patrol. Royal Marine Boom Patrol Detachment became more noticeable with the 'Southsea Stroll', a decisive, smart and rapid march devised by Sergeant Wallace. They became known as 'Hasler's Party'. In other ways, they intended to become less noticeable. The stealth technique was honed to perfection at night and in the daylight. Sometimes, the sneaking up on people was self-motivated. On more than one occasion, it is recorded that craft on the Solent were sent out to clear the scene ready for anti-aircraft gunnery practice, and these were often manned by Wrens. These Wrens, during periods of inactivity in the hot summer months, used to sunbathe far from prying eyes, often with very little hiding their modesty. Hasler's Party soon learnt that they could get very close to these bathing belles. The indicator was the shriek of alarm when the young marines had eventually been spotted – all too late. Another stealth approach was during an evening exercise involving a group using canoes. Whilst one crew member stayed with the canoes, the others scaled the ironwork to the pier in Southsea. The plan was that they would 'capture the assembled dancers in the ballroom'; in truth, it was a raid on the assembled dancers' beer, which was purloined without anyone knowing, the intruders clambering down and away in canoes with the booty. It must have seemed to those in charge of the event that the beer really had just disappeared. Self-sufficiency at its best. The first holiday leave granted was for No. 1 section and began on 16 September 1942 for seven days! They had been worked hard during the previous weeks, but the work load was to intensify. By October, they were working eighteen hours a day.

Weapons of War

The RMBPD was the first unit to design, or have designed for them, its own canoe type: the Mk 2 and Mk 2**. The unit specialised in attacks on shipping in European estuaries. The nature of these canoes made them unsuitable to other users.

Hasler taught his men seamanship and how to navigate. He had a different way of moulding an individual. This in turn made them different, a target. It was on more than one occasion that Hasler had to have words with the 'ordinary' officers who sought to persecute his men. With the general training, they got to grips with all manner of craft and equipment. They trained in BPB, inflatable boats, army assault craft of various descriptions, Surf Boats, Boston Whalers, Swimmers Floats as well as the all-important and famous flat-bottomed canoes ... and the incredible and very clever piece of kit that could be paddled and sailed – another canoe that was as happy underwater as it was above the water: the 'Sleeping Beauty', alias MSC (Motor Submersible Canoe). The RMBPD grew, and like that for the BPB, it had its own section given over for the MSC. They also had many different pieces of kit, from the commonplace to the exotic, which included the Matarrassino – an oversized lilo.

Then there was the surface swimsuit and the lightweight thigh waders and rope soles. These were the type used on the *Frankton* Raid and were open-crotched and -legged with wrap-around laces from the rope-soled shoes. Another piece of kit was the Reliant life jacket, which was not only used on the training of the men but the *Frankton* Raid itself.

The RMBPD Nissen huts were 'jealously guarded' by Marines 'Dicky' Drew and 'Jock' Brown. This is where all the 'goodies' were kept and repairs undertaken with the exception of the BPB and MSC. It is also where some lessons were given. The men of the RMBPD were trained to use a multitude of craft and were obliged to test an awful lot of them as well. From the early months onwards, both boats and canoes were paraded at Southsea and Hayling Island. As time progressed, more sophisticated craft were developed. More to their liking in the early development were the Mk 2 and Mk 2** canoes and Motor Submersible Canoe (MSC)[9].

The specialist instructors were brought to Southsea for diving training. The parachute training took place after Operation *Frankton* at the Central Landing School and later at

Part of the workload of the RMBPD was testing craft such as this Dory on their own section of Soutsea beach. Note an Mk 2 canoe in the background.

Above, testing a dinghy, a young Bill Sparks front right.

Dory testing at Southsea.

No. 1 Parachute School Ringway (now known as Manchester airport). No reserve chutes were used, and Norman Colley said that the instructors would advise 'if it doesn't work, take it back!' The first jump was from a balloon and another was into water using the technique of releasing the harness buckles during the descent. After that, from old Whitley bombers. 'After the last jump they were tasked with rejoining their base at Portsmouth, 260 miles away, on their own initiative, dressed as civilians and even in German POW uniforms. The police and armed forces were given orders to stop them, but by train, bus, hitching on lorries, even on stolen bicycles, they all made it back.'[10] There was one night descent but no equipment jumps were done on the basic course.

By July 1942, the unit had completed training, and Norman was moved to remark that 'it had all seemed rather rushed'. Sections not on boom patrol carried out night exercises along the coast in such places as Chichester and Langstone harbours. These included specialist mud exercises, day and night. Apart from the canoes in general, which include the Mk 2 and later the Mk 2**, which were especially used by the unit, a number of other small craft for special purposes were used as 'the weapons of war'. Here is given a short list of the craft that were used or trialled by RMBPD with a brief description as an introduction:

The smaller of these was the collapsible assault boat by Mr Goatley, which was constructed in a similar way to his Cockle canoe Mk 2 and Mk 2**. It was known as the Goatley boat; 12-man assault boat; naval assault boat; and (mistakenly) the cockle Mk 4 (see *The Cockleshell Canoes*, Chapter 7, 'The Pseudo Canoe'). This boat carried ten to twelve fully equipped men and could be fitted with a stern bracket for propulsion by a 10- or 20-hp outboard motor. It was 17 feet x 5 feet 3½ inches x 2 feet 1½ inches and weighed 350 lb. It was used operationally in SEAC and in Europe and was trialled by the men of the RMBPD No. 1 section, and most of them were photographed in them before the departure on the *Frankton* Raid.

The 32-foot version was developed as a store-carrying boat with a maximum load capacity of ten tons. Its normal load was 8 tons with a draught of 18 inches and a beam of 11 feet.

Dories were made in five types and again these were trialled and used by the RMBPD. The Surf boats were similarly trialled and used in training by the RMBPD along with the Cow Boat, an inflatable; the Intruder Boat, a smaller inflatable; Dinghies Q and Y type. The Intermediate Carrier was also used for training.

The Limpeteer's Companion

The 'Limpet' by definition is a mine with the ability to be attached to a target with the aid of its magnets. With a weight of approximately 5 kg, it was designed with hollow compartments in order to give the mine a slight negative buoyancy, which made it easier for the operator, swimmer, diver or canoeist to handle it underneath the water surface. The Limpet was fitted with a secondary 'sympathetic' fuse which was set off by any underwater concussion. This was necessary, because when more than one Limpet was placed on the hull of a ship, it was imperative that the first Limpet detonation did not dislodge any others fitted. The 'sympathetic' fuse was at that stage unreliable, and due to this, the fuse was held in the safe position by a soluble washer which would only begin to dissolve when the Limpet was immersed in the water. This prevented any premature detonation by an accidental knock. At the required time, the Limpets would be taken in pairs and one AC delay cap was removed; the threads were luted, the required ampoule was inserted with the point down and the cap was replaced, ensuring it was tight. A cross was indicated on the original scratch mark on the fuse, and the securing string of the safety pin was untied. Repeat for the other AC delay then turn over, remove rubber cap, small split pin and collar from sympathetic fuse and place the soluble washer or plug in place and replace collar and split pin clear of the sleeve. Open the split pin points, remove the 2 feet of sailmaker and replace cap, then remove sailmaker from safety pin. The next stage was to test the placing rod on each Limpet to ensure it went in freely.

Once the ampoule was broken, the liquid inside would slowly dissolve the washer holding back the striker pin. In the metal tin box containing the various coloured ampoules, a chart showed roughly how long the period of delay would be and how much it would increase given a lower temperature environment at the time. Each Limpet had eight integral powerful horseshoe magnets, which meant that until the Limpets were needed they were stowed aft, in pairs, with the keeper plate separating them. This also reduced the magnetic field which was a problem when compasses were used; when fully loaded, the canoes needed to be 'swung' for compass deviation.

At a predetermined hour before Limpets are required to explode, the safety pins are removed from the AC delays and the spindles are then screwed down fully, then the rubber cap and the safety pin are removed from the sympathetic fuse. With the fuses set, the one canoeist would be able to place the Limpet, whilst the other crew member would ensure a static position of the canoe by clamping the magnetic holdfast onto the hull of the ship. The Limpets were attached at strategic places by means of the placing rod. The placing rod was collapsible (folded up 15½ inches or 395 mm) but fully extended became 58¾ inches or 1,465 mm. The canoeist would lean over the side of the canoe and with great skill and dexterity carefully lower the Limpet mine down on the placing rod, ensuring it was kept away from the hull until it reached the required depth. It was then gently moved towards the hull of the ship, where an audible clumping noise was heard, meaning that it was attached. The placing rod was then unhooked by pushing it downwards. The Limpet would ordinarily cause a hole of damage about three feet in diameter. If three holes were breached in different compartments of the ship, the pumps of the ship would not be able to cope with the volume of water taken aboard. Often the engine room compartment was targeted to ensure considerable damage to electrical installations and engine machinery.

An interesting footnote to this activity is that it seemed that the preferred name given to indigenous dogs taken on as pets was 'Limpet'. This name was given to these detachment pets in Ceylon and the Aegean by, respectively, the 385 and Earthworm, as has been evidenced by portrait photographs taken at the time of these mutts.

The other main project that the RMBPD was involved with was the MSC, which was powered by lead acid batteries. To properly try and cover this important subject would distract unduly from the detachment itself; however, a brief idea of just what the SOE inventive genius had produced is relayed. Affectionately known as the 'Sleeping Beauty', the name was changed to the Motor Submersible Canoe. The original name would have confused all, yet they decided to indicate exactly what this 'Most Secret' piece of kit was capable of! It was a single-seat, electrically driven, submersible canoe with auxiliary paddle and sail propulsion. It had a length of 12 feet 9 inches, a beam of 28½ inches and weighed 570 lb. In easy-to-understand terms, it was an extremely impressive piece of kit. The pilot sat inside with his head and shoulders 'outside' and wore special breathing gear. The interior could be flooded, and when in neutral trim, the craft was controlled by hydroplanes. It was designed to carry small charges for attack against unarmoured ships, during which operation the pilot secured the craft to the bilge keel and could place the charges by hand at the desired location on the hull either in a seated position or when venturing from the craft. For those interested in being assured of the MSC's correct history and development, this is provided for the first time in its entirety within the author's previous book, *The Cockleshell Canoes*.

For the MSC, the RMBPD also had an operational training base with the depot ship HMS *Quentin Roosevelt* in Loch Corrie just off Loch Linnhe in Scotland with another temporary operational base in Lerwick. The administration of the RMBPD was transferred from CCO to DDOD(I), who were already controlling the MFU Flotilla; this was to enable the co-ordinatation of administration and training of Special Forces personnel and the development of special craft. A captain was appointed to co-ordinate the training of the Special Service personnel under DDOD(I) with approval given to the commissioning on 28 August 1944 of an establishment at Teignmouth where the MFU had been base for a number of weeks.

During 1944, the unit itself was under the command of Major J. D. Stewart and had moved to this shore base of HMS *Mount Stewart* in Teignmouth, Devon. This base was commanded by Capt. T. B. Brunton, RN, DSC. Shortly after the move, 'Jock' Stewart was invalided from the service and Major W. Pritchard-Gordon took over the post.

Operation *Frankton*'s Predecessor

It was in springtime of 1942 that a special project had been started under an Admiralty requirement for an attack on the harbour of Bordeaux against the blockade runners, which had been set for November 1942. The first recorded date of a prototype or production date was that of the summer of 1942. The DDOD(I), Deputy Director of Operations Division (Irregulars), was an Admiralty department and the parent organisation of the Bengal Auxiliary Flotilla. The HQ was in Princes Street in London and was headed by Captain Slocum, OBE, RN. It was this department that controlled the Mobile Flotation Unit. According to the officers and men at the time, the MFU was also known by another name!

The MFU concept itself was a steel motorboat with its engine room and cargo space in the form of pressure-tight chambers. It carried two canoes on deck and stores of explosive Limpets in the cargo space. A special sinking and surfacing device was a feature of the design. The crew was six in number, that is to say, four for the canoes plus two others. The method of operation was that, having approached the target by night and anchored, a clock was set to the time the craft required to surface. The craft was then buoyed and flooded to sink to the bottom and the crew proceeded ashore in the canoes. If the clock failed, a diver in DSEA apparatus could dive and turn the clock, bringing the craft to the surface. The project was begun in early 1942 and the original design was to Admiralty requirement (Admiral Renouf) for an attack on Bordeaux in the November of that year. Due to technical difficulties, the production was delayed, and it was never to be used operationally but was used for training under DDOD(I).

Whilst still at Hayling Island, a twin-screw, diesel, steel coastal barge owned by the Rochester Trading Company was converted to carry Boom Patrol Boats (BPB) as well as MSCs manned by personnel from RMBPD. It was commanded by Lt Dingwall, RNVR. This craft also saw service in Teignmouth and Loch Corrie, which provided good training for the RMBPD operational BPB and MSC crews, as the craft was able to move from each base under her own power, albeit slowly. The RMBPD was also the first British service unit to experiment with fins with Cdr Shelford of Siebe Gorman at Isleworth developing the improved shallow-water diving sets of the time, beginning with the Davis Submarine Escape Apparatus (DSEA). It should be noted that these fins were obtained from America and were the only ones in the UK. As things improved, a representative from Dunlop's was almost continually stationed with this section. It was from this liaison that the rubber Cockle suit was developed as well as a two-cylinder Recycling Breathing set. This equipment was used with the MSC.

A noteworthy piece of history that gained an MBE for Lt David Cox, RM, later Captain, was on 10 June 1944, when he and the BPB he was aboard were fitted to the bomb rack of a Lancaster aircraft, and at around 5,000 feet, the ensemble was released and successfully dropped into the sea at Harwich with the aid of specially constructed parachutes. Previous dummy drops had been tried before and two BPB had been lost; one had completely smashed to pieces on contact. It was then decided a live drop was necessary!

Part of the engineering division of the RMBPD, which was responsible for the BPB operation, maintenance and repair, as well as the MSC Section (Detachment Celtic[11]), under the now Capt. Cox, moved to 617 Squadron at Woodhall in Lincolnshire. The first operational task allotted to the section was for a drop in Bergen, Norway. Several abortive attempts were made and subsequently cancelled due to bad weather over the target area. On 22 October 1944, with Detachment Celtic (No. 3 section), six BPBs were loaded into 617 Squadron's Lancasters at Woodhall Spa and flown down to Exeter for Exercise *Skylark*. Those taking part are believed to have been Sgt T. Cooling, Cpl R. Bratten, R. Monstall and D. Page; it is also understood that parachutes with a 96-foot diameter were used in the operation. The following day, all six of the BPBs were successfully dropped off 'The Ness' at Shaldon, a predominantly waterside village adjacent to Teignmouth.

This was the first and only such airborne operation to be carried out by any armed service anywhere in the world. There was, however, little co-ordination of the spectacular event, with a major security alert being narrowly avoided. For historical background information, this craft, the BPB, was based on the Italian Explosive Motor Boat and was some 18 feet in length, 5 feet in beam and 4 feet 6 inches in depth. These were procured by the Admiralty for CCO and DDOD(I) use and a total of seventeen were built by a subcontractor to Vospers.

In early 1945, Blondie Hasler himself moved into a role of development, which took him to Ceylon along with another newly established and even more 'extraordinarily secret' detachment, 385, which does not come under the overall storyline. The RMBPD itself had become much larger as time progressed, with four sections in total being created.

With No. 1 section no longer in existence, the remainder of those men were absorbed into No. 2 section. Although only three sections existed post-*Frankton*, they were referred to as Nos 2, 3 and 4. The function was to carry out offensive demolition against shipping or harbour installations, and they became equipped with special craft, which were carried to the vicinity of the target either by sea or air.

Section No. 2 then became known as 'Earthworm' Detachment, which was moved to Athlit for operational training and then moved to a base camp at Azzib and ultimately onto Teignmouth in Devon with the others by October 1944. No. 3 section meanwhile had become Detachment Celtic, which dealt with all matters 'Sleeping Beauty' (MSC) and BPB.

By the end of 1945, the Teignmouth base was closed with all the craft and equipment for RMBPD and other Teignmouth-based DDOD(I) units being moved to the P. K. Harris Shipyard at Appledore (HMS *Appledore*). This saw a march through Teignmouth, all being assembled on the seafront. In September 1947, the RMBPD moved to Portsmouth and was subsequently amalgamated as an integral part of the Amphibious School RM, eventually becoming the Special Boat Section RM.

It is known that Hasler produced a paper outlining his vision of the future, defining the modern amphibious Special Forces. This was not about, and never had been about, sending men on suicide missions. He knew that inadequately trained men would face certain death and badly planned operations only spelt disaster.

At Courtenay House, Teignmouth. Cpl Bill Sparks, centre, first row.

Courtenay House, Teignmouth. From left: Marines, DUNCAN, -?-, -?-, 'Tich', -?-, Cpl Horner, -?-. Norman Colley in background.

Earthworm Detachment. Back row: J. Duncan, P. Turfrey, H. Oxley, G. Lambert, D. Ruff, T. Stephens, R. Henshall, Norman Colley, Eric Fisher, F. Phelps, -?-, Harding. Middle row, seated: Cpl Horner, Capt. W. Pritchard-Gordon, Lt Richards, Cpl W. Sparks. Kneeling: Sgt J. King, Sgt R. Johnson. Front: Cpl Ashton.

The freedom of the town. 1945 March through Teignmouth, South Devon. They had used the Teign Estuary and the area around the Ness at Shaldon and up to Dawlish Warren as their testing ground.

Action in the Aegean by Detachment Earthworm

One of the notable actions undertaken by No. 2 section of the RMBPD was the raid on axis shipping in Operation *Sunbeam A* on Leros Island in the Aegean Sea during 16, 17 and 18 June 1944. Of the reported operational uses, the Mk 2** canoe is positively identified as the type of canoe used on this raid. It has to be noted that the naming of canoes, which seems to have been started by Hasler in the *Frankton* Raid, was continued throughout the war. An example of this can be seen in Operation *Sunbeam A*, where three Mk 2** canoes were used. They were named *Shark*, *Salmon* and *Shrimp*. Although the Mk 2** could be crewed by three, on this operation, only two men occupied each canoe. *Shark* was commanded by Lt J. F. Richards, RM (DSC), with Marine W. S. Stevens, (Ply. X. 105862) RM, as his number 2. An amusing detail found in the source material was that for some reason it was mentioned that Marine Stevens was 'urinated on'. At first it was wondered if this was some ritual used to 'blood' the individual. Following further research, it was found that both the crew members of *Shark* were unlucky enough to be urinated on by a German sentry; they had not seen or heard him during the very moment of attaching the Limpets underneath the bow of the Italian Turbine-class Destroyer.

Salmon was commanded by Sgt J. M. King, (Ply. X. 1457) RM (DSM), with Mne R. N. Ruff, (Ply. X. 108660) RM (DSM), as the number 2. *Shrimp* was commanded by Corporal E. W. 'Johnny' Horner, (Ply. X. 2968) RM, and his number 2 was Mne E. Fisher, (Ply. X. 108151) RM.

The canoe was beached in a very small inlet and camouflaged, the *Shark* crew having found their hide-out. From 0445 hrs, explosions were heard, and this continued throughout the day until 1700 hrs. This gives a clear indication that depth charges were being used by the garrison, thinking that a submarine was in the harbour, the use of the canoe again fooling the enemy. It should be noted that *Salmon* had been holed, and by the time King had placed six Limpets, the canoe was half full of water; the crew abandoned their attack and proceeded out of the harbour bailing out at the boom.

More interesting information that should not go unaccounted is that Corporal 'Johnny' Horner was mentioned in dispatches, the awards to Richards, King and Ruff being given for that raid. The result of that Leros raid was that two Italian 'Guardian' Destroyers,

Portalago Bay, Leros, Recon photo.

Recreation football in Palestine, 1944. Front left, clockwise: Colley, Turfrey, Fisher, King, Stevens, Oxley, -?-.

Above: The Earthworm Blues in less formal attire.

Left: 'Tich' on the bench at Teignmouth sea front.

crewed by the Germans, were severely damaged and subsequently sunk by RAF when being towed to a repair base, with three further escort vessels sunk. The human cost in casualties to the Germans is not known. The result of this successful raid was that the main raiding assault forces of Brigadier Turnball were able to attack and retake Simi Island with the ability to advance up to mainland Greece.

On Operation *Brother*, again with canoes, and Operation *Sister* (subsequently changed to *Stripling*), both a month before the *Sunbeam* Raid, it is interesting to note those taking part.

For Operation *Brother*, these were Captain W. Pritchard-Gordon, Cpl L. Ashton, Mne C. Lambert, Mne A. Duncan. The spare man was most notably Cpl William E. Sparks, DSM, one of the two survivors from the *Frankton* Raid. Many operations in this area were speculative, since at the time of planning, the harbours did not contain sufficient enemy shipping to merit a canoe attack. For *Sister* or *Stripling*, the same team was to be used: Richards, King, Stevens, Ruff, with Horner and Fisher as the reinforcement crew.

When No. 2 section left for the Aegean, the mascot, 'Tich', the black Cocker Spaniel bitch, was looked after by the other chaps of the RMBPD. 'Tich' had been cared for post-*Frankton* by Marine Duncan, who trained the dog to jump into his arms at the click of his fingers. Even after the long absence of Duncan and co. in the Aegean, on his return the dog still remembered him. The dog was even paraded on the Teignmouth lawns on the promenade with the men. Norman Colley once took the dog home on leave after VE Day when he was arranging his wedding bands. Due to the war ending, certain personnel were demobbed as they were 'hostilities only'; it was at this time that 'Tich' was raffled off – the lucky new owner became Bill Sparks, who as a regular remained with the unit as it moved and changed post-war.

You can praise of all men that ever lived and died
The army and the navy and the RAF beside
But now in my opinion I have found the greatest yet
Their speech and manner may not be good as some I've met
But these things are quite small compared with other gifts of god
The handshake and helping hand, the smile and friendly nod
They do not boast how brave they are or just how skilful too
But most men would be scared if need to do the job they do
They say I will miss them when they've gone, and heaven knows they're right
What shall I do with no-one here to argue with and fight
For though we dont see eye to eye in many little ways
The times I've spent with them have been the happiest of days
And though as long as I shall live to me they'll be the tops
No doubt they will forget the girl who wouldn't sell them slops
So on departing from our base I'd like to if I can
Say thanks for everything and bon-voyage to every man
My heart may not be large but still forever there will be
A little corner marked reserved for the RMBPD

A poem written by N. E. S. Lawnton,
Wren attached to the RMBPD at Southsea
on the date of the RMBPD leaving the area.

2

TIMELY LIVES

Naturally, the focus of attention has been centred on the *Frankton* Raid and the continuity of narrative itself, but there still remain other stories to tell which serve to enhance what has come before. Within these following chapters are individual stories that could not be placed within the main body, as to do so would unduly interupted the flow of the main focus. This section delves into the lives of those who lent themselves for the event in question: the contributions that made all the difference. Most of these individuals have never had their part in this compelling tale broadcast. Some might think that these are just 'supporting roles' to the 'main players' or just 'incidentals', but each and every one contributed in a way significant enough to warrant the term 'patriot'. Of those in France, they risked not only their own lives but those of others. Without them there would be no 'Cockleshell Heroes' or an enduring story. This was faithful service, a great treasure rendered freely, and it is fitting to include this celebration.

None of these individuals are the 'little people'; they are just the ones who didn't have a publicity agent – until now!

CHAPTER 11

Father 'Cockle'

The Unsung Hero from the Isle of Wight; Designer of the 'Insignificant Vessel' – Fred Goatley

It is unquestionably painful to read that in the very few books[1] that even mention Fred Goatley, various 'facts' are incorrectly stated. Some very basic errors in researching have been made at Goatley's expense and need to be addressed.

Given the author's research, it can be stated that, without Fred Goatley designing the Cockle Mk 2 canoe, it would have been very likely that the December 1942 *Frankton* Raid would have been unsuccessful. Simply put, and contrary to what has been written in some books[2], the Cockle Mk 2 was not 'conceived from the Mk 1**'[3] or indeed the Mk 1*. The Mk 2 was entirely different in its concept (as was the three-man version, the Mk 2**). It is important to accurately relay the correct information, which can be found within the 'Insignificant Vessel' chapter.

In brief terms, one needs to look at the Mk 2 construction versus that of the only other canoe then available, which was the latterly named Mk 1*, with nothing else on the drawing board at the time. The Mk 1* had been conceived from the original 'Folboat' or 'Foldbot'; it was barely an improvement, used by the early Special Forces under Courtney that Hasler had received a taster in. The term 'Folboat', or 'Foldbot', is derived from the names given to recreational canoes at that time and are not military terms or names given to military canoes but are simple descriptions used even today by some.

The Mk 1 canoe was not of the correct length or width, could not be assembled very quickly, especially during the night, and was prone to skin damage if run onto any hard projections. The frame would fracture if run onto anything solid, flooded by breakers on a beach, or picked up at the ends with a load in the middle. It also had a large silhouette and took an age to assemble on the deck on a boat. It was available, and if Hasler had thought it suitable, he would have used it. It should be borne in mind that Hasler did not even know about the *Frankton* docket when he began his quest for a suitable canoe to use for the RMBPD. In short, the Mk 1* was not a canoe that would have served the *Frankton* Raid well.

The entire story of canoe development has been comprehensively covered in *The Cockleshell Canoes*, which provides the ultimate understanding of the military canoe in the early years and beyond. For repetition, the Mk 2 was produced in its design nearly a year before Hasler came on the scene at COSD. As far as the nomenclature is concerned, for the very first time, it can be revealed how Fred Goatley may have come up with the name 'cockle' used on his design drawings of the Mk 2 canoe provided to the military. It seems very likely that Fred gleaned the name for the canoes from a time in 1920 when the firm of boatbuilders he was working for, Saunders Roe, was asked to refurbish two 21-foot BMBC-class racers named *Angela II* and *III*, as well as Mr T. Desnos's *Cockleshell II* for the Spring Monte Carlo races in which *Cockleshell II* came second.

Further, as the name 'cockle' seems to have originated from Fred, then was adopted as the code name for military canoes (the first of which thus named was the Mk 2), it can positively be stated that without Fred Goatley, we would not have this evocative memory of

Fred Goatley, designer of the canoe used on the *Frankton* Raid.

the 'Cockleshell Heroes'. Given Hasler's disdain for the term 'cockle', we may have been left with 'The Tadpole Heroes'! Therefore, it is clear that, without Fred Goatley, 'the cockleshell heroes' reference would have not come about. If Hasler had used the Mk 1* canoe, it is almost a certainty that the operation would have failed due to the equipment used. Hasler should not have felt so bad about the 'cockle' name when it was derived from such an illustrious racing company.

The focus of attention of a good deal of the early work on canoes has to be centred around Fred Goatley: he alone was truly responsible for the great strides made with certain types of canoe that bled into the 'new' types that took the canoe into another sphere of development. This information deals with the immediate known facts during the period of interest.

Fred Goatley was a boat designer and builder, a very talented man, who had learned his skill from his father, who had a boatbuilding business near Oxford. When a Mr S. E. Saunders moved his business from Oxford to West Cowes to open 'Saunders Boat Building Syndicate', Fred Goatley went with him.

The idea of collapsible boats occurred to Mr Goatley in 1920, when he was in the employ of Messrs S. E. Saunders in East Cowes on the Isle of Wight, the firm that then became Saunders-Roe. The extreme simplicity of Goatley's craft was the collapsing device, consisting of a few bolts and buckles enabling all his craft to be raised or collapsed. In the case of canoes, this took less than a minute. Goatley also designed a folding boat, which Sir Ernest Shackleton took with him on his ill-fated voyage. The craft was named the *Quest* after the voyage; it could be used as a canoe, rowing boat and even a sleigh.

In 1937, the Managing Director of Saunders-Roe, Maj. Darwin, mentioned to Mr Goatley, then a manager in the firm, that the War Office required an assault boat. This craft needed to have the attribute of requiring very little storage space, which in itself would save considerable transport. Fred Goatley proceeded to design a boat 12 feet 4 inches in length, which was duly constructed at the Saunders-Roe factory. Goatley's design was one of many others that had been offered up to the War Office competition to find a craft to fit the need required. The tests were exhaustive, but Goatley's design won the day.

The 'Goatley Assault Boat' was accepted by the War Office and Saunders-Roe received an order for 1,000 boats. It was during the latter stages of the production process that Fred

Goatley became very seriously ill. Six months passed, and while still convalescing, Goatley was approached by his firm with regard to his retirement and selling his interest in the patent for the assault boat. Goatley felt that it would be a long time before he fully recovered his health and accepted the 'package' offered, which was £1,000 for his interest in the patent with £3-a-week pension for his forty-three years of service. After two years of the enforced retirement, he wished to add his talent to the war effort and started to design at home in his converted garage at 'Tonalba', 157 York Avenue, East Cowes, on the Isle of Wight. In his own words, 'I had plenty of time at my disposal and wanted to do something to aid the war effort, so I decided to concentrate on various types of collapsible craft.'

Goatley's first job was to improve and strengthen the existing assault boat, and he was duly granted a patent. He then produced the 17-foot Mk 4 Collapsible Assault Boat, building the prototype at home. When the prototype had been tested, the firm, now Saro Laminated Wood Products Ltd, received an order for 1,000 boats. It is believed the total production of this craft was some 30,000 from different manufacturers. Saro's then approached Goatley to act as consultant, and a contract was signed for one year, with a salary of £350 per annum in order to put the boats into production. He was subsequently kept on with renewed contracts for another two six-monthly periods.

From 1940 to 1945, Goatley designed and submitted a total of eleven types of boats and pontoons to various departments of the Armed Forces, as well as making experimental models at great expense to himself, with copious quantities of correspondence to the departments concerned. During this time, Goatley became involved with Major Blondie Hasler, who led the *Frankton* Raid into occupied France with six revolutionary Goatley-designed canoes.

This was the 15-foot Collapsible Cockle Mk 2 – quite the most 'famous' of all the types of canoe ever produced. One of the factories was at the Folly Works at Whippingham, East

In this photograph, taken near the Boom at Southsea, the true collapsible nature and portability of the Mk 2** is demonstrated by Capt. Pritchard-Gordon.

A Mk 2** showing the centre cockpit sealed, compass hole, backrest configuration, spray deck clips and paddle stowage arrangement. Note the sponsons were not featured on this early example.

Goatley's assault boat in its folded position.

Goatley assault craft in its built-up form and, below, ready kitted out for testing by RMBPD men at Southsea beach. Note the ballast sand bags in the background (See Wallace and Sheard in the 'Not Forgotten' chapter).

Sailors testing the craft in the confines of an outdoor testing tank.

Middle and bottom: The Goatley load carrier in tests off Hayling Island using an Ack-Ack gun.

The Goatley load carrier in tests off Hayling Island using a 3-ton Bedford truck – the load carrier used the same collapsible method used in the assault craft.

Cowes, IOW. Mr B. F. Miskin took responsibility for ensuring the canoe contracts were dealt with. This is where the six famed Mk 2 canoes for the *Frankton* Raid were manufactured. Whilst the major did have an input, this was Goatley's design, not Hasler's. Even before Hasler was on the scene, Goatley had already produced much of the desired canoe quite unknowingly.

Goatley also produced the Mk 2**, a 17-foot 4-inch two- to three-man collapsible canoe. This canoe was subsequently manufactured by Harris Lebus with Goatley giving the final approval. He also designed a 32-foot collapsible load carrier boat, with the prototype also built by Saro Ltd, under Goatley's supervision. In September 1940, he also submitted to the DSR (patent application No. 9256/40) a design for an unsinkable lifeboat with self-sealing from bullet holes. The Mk 4 Collapsible Assault Boat, the 15-foot and 17-foot 4-inch canoes as well as the 32-foot boat were all produced without any benefit of remuneration.

During March 1946, Goatley, who was by this time nearly seventy years of age and, by his own admission and entreaty, 'a poor man', applied for payment for his work to the Secretary of the Ministry of Supply. The matter still had not been finalised by May of 1948. The design and experiments for the home-built prototype of the 17-foot Mk 4 Collapsible Assault Boat were not included in an original contract in addition to the work on the Mk 2 canoe and required a lot of minor experiments. Other work was the design drawings supplied to Levy for the Mk 2**.

For all of this, together with the design drawings of a 32-foot collapsible load carrier and the design for an unsinkable lifeboat, Goatley is believed to have eventually received £435. When the war ended, Goatley gave up his designing work, and as he said at the time, 'It was an arduous job and gave me many knotty problems to solve, but I was very pleased with the results.'

The military gained much by Goatley's efforts, yet when he was put up for an MBE, even though it would have been richly deserved, for some reason it was not successful. It is a great shame that someone has still not realised the great value of this unsung hero. One can only hope that some form of equal recognition will be awarded posthumously given his unquestionable talents and accomplishments; then it can be said he was never forgotten. Even in his declining years, Goatley certainly was the right man at the right time.

Mr Fred Goatley was registered at his death as being a boat designer and was buried[4] with his wife Beatrice Ethel Goatley at East Cowes on the Isle of Wight on 8 October 1949 at the age of seventy-one.

CHAPTER 12

Submarine *Tuna* and the Trugs

As the Commander of submarine HMS Tuna *remarked, 'It is never given to mortals to relive an episode in their lives,' but it is through this episode in history that certain individuals were able to do just that in the viewing of the film based on the* Frankton *Raid. Much has been written about the principal characters of* Operation *Frankton, but little is known of the other participants, largely due to the lack of research previously undertaken. From the available information, these cameo narratives or vignettes are finally related in order to show how these other individuals played their part to become entwined and inextricably linked with, the 'Cockleshell Heroes'.*

The Submariner, A Fishing Fleet, A Minefield and Black-Faced Villains Lieutenant Richard Prendergast Raikes, DSO, RN

This is only a short account of the life of a fine gentleman, but it is believed the first outing for public consumption; a tale of wartime submarine operations that puts a cold shiver down your spine and makes the hairs on the back of your neck stand on end. Whilst he was only one of many, this short narrative will no doubt illuminate the process needed to become an officer in the British Navy at the time. In parts, it is rather light-hearted, but by all accounts, he would have approved.

Lieutenant Richard Prendergast Raikes, DSO, RN, (1912–2005[1]) had more than his fair share of humour as well as having developed, at an early age, the 'sense of the ridiculous'. Both these attributes as well as full-belly laughter carried him through the fears, tragedies, disappointments and failures that make up life's rich waterway. These qualities of character also endeared him to those who served under him.

At the world premiere of *Cockleshell Heroes*, he found his role as captain of HMS *Tuna* in the film being played by Christopher Lee, a foot taller than Dickie, a slender, rather hard-faced actor of Dracula status. José Ferrer, who directed and acted in the film, gave Dickie a script in which are the words 'Dick, many thanks for your help, sorry we had to pick a good looking guy for your part'. The 'comedic situation' or 'sense of the ridiculous' was not lost on Dickie Raikes, well suited to the confining height of a T-class submarine.

A fitting place in which to use Lt Raikes' thoughts of the ten commandos who disappeared into the darkness on that cold December night in 1942 was found by the author and given

Lt R. P. Raikes. A fine study of a submariner.

pride of place as a title of a chapter within *The Cockleshell Canoes* publication. He was solely responsible for dispatching this 'Magnificent Bunch of Black-Faced Villains' in the 'offspring' with all due diligence.

How Lt Raikes' name, if not his life's story, became known to the world and became a part forever in a nation's history is related. It shows how his experiences during the early years moulded him into the right kind of individual to enable him to be chosen to serve at the right time and place.

Whilst not a historical giant, his kind heart and strong unwavering leadership coupled with a cool, calm personality and commanding presence enabled him to direct without issuing orders; he also had the ability to use quiet deliberation and discussion in any event that went askew. He had the need for perfection, and as a commanding officer with the safety and success of every operation vested in him, this was a mixture that made him truly loved by all those who served under him. He also had a sense of humour.

The Second Man in History to Walk on Water

Dickie Raikes was born on 21 January 1912 to an Indian Army Major. One of five children, he and his brother were boarded at school in London whilst his other younger brother and sisters remained with his parents in India during 1919–22 solely due to the First World War; they were not reunited until Dickie was ten.

The two brothers spent the Christmas holiday with a married aunt in London and the Easter and summer holidays with his doting grandparents and two unmarried aunts in the inherited family pile in Brecon, South Wales. In this large, comfortable Edwardian household, Dickie was carried almost effortlessly through the traumas of childhood, such as the long separation from his father, but he enjoyed the strong family bonds. Dickie's father was one of ten children, and due to the hero worship of the seven brothers for having earned eight DSOs and four MCs during the First World War (two of them had died, one became a general, another an admiral), Dickie became and remained a bit of a family rebel. His own father became a brigadier, but died just before taking up an appointment. The miscellany of family success made Dickie aware of his privileged background and also the very definite duties and responsibilities to those less fortunate.

Following a written exam (a terrifying interview conducted by a bishop, a public school headmaster, a senior civil servant and two Admirals), Dickie, at the tender age of thirteen, managed to scrape into the Royal Naval College at Dartmouth in 1925. For the first time, he really enjoyed schooling and enthusiastically tackled everything. He was made a Cadet Captain at fifteen and a half and in his last year was one of the two chief Cadet Captains who won the coveted King's Dirk, which was suitably inscribed and presented by King George V. During his time at Dartmouth, one of his instructors was Chief Yeoman Arthur Welsman Quick; this should be noted as Dickie Raikes would encounter this name again on HMS *Tuna*.

At seventeen, he joined the battleship HMS *Warspite* in Malta as a snottie[2]. He discovered that life in the navy was tremendous fun as well as being a serious and responsible career and learned to see the funny side of any situation during his three years in his lowly midshipman's position. It was the funny incidents that stood out rather than the long hours, rough weather, irregular meals and lack of sleep. But all of this was to the mettle of the man and each of these played a part in the following years. This life was crammed full of new experiences. At Cowes in 1931, he crewed for T. B. Davis in the magnificent J-class yacht *Westward*[3] against King George V.

From 1932–35, he wore a single stripe of gold lace on his arm as an acting sub-lieutenant, joining the naval college at Greenwich for eight months education to university level. In January 1933, he and the fifty or so subs that had been through Dartmouth together joined the infamous gunnery school at HMS *Excellent* on Whale Island where, in his own words, 'discipline was rigid to a ridiculous degree'. The 'most disagreeable bullshit' that turned his mind towards small ships was the constant courses at gunnery schools, stripping a torpedo, and the drill and marching; he became determined to 'stick to small ships without guns and preferably submarines where bullshit was at its minimum'.

The Gunnery Course was followed by a Torpedo Course and then a Navigation Course. In September 1933, Raikes applied for the next submarine course and soon joined HMS *Dolphin* (Blockhouse) in Gosport for the ten-week training event. They spent about three days each week at sea learning to handle a submarine and deal with all emergencies. These lucky lads lived on an old banana boat called, unsurprisingly, *The Dolphin*, which was not only riddled with cockroaches but had a deck that leaked directly into the bunks!

In the November, young Raikes passed out as a submariner and joined L.22 as '4th hand' (responsible for navigation, the torpedo department, the 4-inch gun and watch-keeping). He did the one-week medical course at Haslar Hospital; because submarines carried no doctor. It is worthwhile noting his memory of the final summing up by the Surgeon Commander: 'Well, young gentlemen, you are now fully qualified medical officers – I hope you have learned the single most important lesson, which is that out of every 100 cases of illness 98 will cure themselves if left strictly alone – of the other 2 per cent, you may be able to help one, and the other will die anyway.' There were some close shaves encountered during his term in L.22, including one with a liner that missed them in thick fog by a matter of single digit feet.

After eight weeks he was appointed to the newly built river-class *Clyde* submarine of 2,700 tons with a crew of fifty-six and, as a crew member of *Clyde*, took part in the 1935 Jubilee Fleet review off Spithead. Dickie Raikes then was fed to the Med and enjoyed the blissful carefree life of a junior officer in the peacetime navy base in Malta, and whilst they all worked fairly hard when at sea during three days of the week, there was much socialising in the form of sailing, swimming, cricket, tennis, picnics, dancing and horse racing. Indeed, a truly wonderful life of fun and that's what life should be about. Unfortunately, all good things come to an end, and this they did. The fortieth prime minister[4] of Italy invading Abyssinia and everything took a more serious footing.

Raikes spent several weeks fighting fires, evacuating a maternity home next to a burning timber yard and building an armoured train during the Arab general strike in Palestine during 1935. By the end of 1936, youngish Raikes had two months of foreign service leave before joining H.32 as first lieutenant under Gordon Duff[5] but was glad to leave for a similar job on *Otway*. By the end of 1937, he was appointed second in command of HMS *Severn* and arrived back in Malta in the first week of January 1938. It was during this stint that Dickie met his wife-to-be – a physiotherapist in the employ of a Lady – but her only interest in Dickie at the time was his ability to facilitate her interest in seeing the interior of a submarine, which he duly arranged. Surprisingly, despite being refused at the first attempt on the battlements of the city of Medina, Joan accepted his second proposal a week later adjacent a large herd of smelly Maltese goats[6], and they became engaged in April 1938. They had only managed to see each other about ten times in the intervening period. A week later, HMS *Severn* sailed for Gibraltar, surviving a frightening underwater collision with a destroyer on the way.

Dickie Raikes married his bride at St Peter's Square in London in September 1938, where Raikes had attended twenty years earlier, and honeymooned at the Montague Arms in Beaulieu in the New Forest, Hampshire.

During 1939, with another short stint in Gibraltar, he was back in Malta in July, and it was around this time that someone had the bright idea that it might be possible to enable a submarine to penetrate an enemy harbour submerged at night providing some way could be found of conning the dived submarine from the surface[7]. After some thought, a tiny wooden platform was fitted at the top of the periscope on which an officer could stand up to his waist or neck in the water wearing only a bathing costume whilst holding onto the periscope and 'conning' the invisible submarine under water through a telephone. The pitfalls to this venture were many, not least the difficulty of retaining a sense of direction and the fact that almost certain death would follow any loss of depth by the submarine. The idea was actually perfected by daylight in the warm waters of a Maltese summer, but not before an alarming incident for some fishermen.

On their last practice, they set out to attack an imaginary harbour in St Paul's Bay through some previously laid buoys. Whilst wearing only a bathing costume, Dickie, as second in command, had enough experience to con in the conditions. They were just approaching the critical entrance when he was slightly alarmed to see the Maltese fishing fleet putting out to sea. There was no real danger, but once the sub began to surface slightly, all the fishermen could see was a naked body walking on water in the same place where Paul of Tarsus[8] was shipwrecked in around AD 30. The result was that the men jumped overboard, most crossing themselves beforehand, and swam for the shore, leaving the fishing boats virtually unmanned. The sub surfaced and picked them up and returned them to their fishing boats. Any further trials were conducted out of site of land. Only the second 'perfect' man to have walked on water!

The Second World War was gathering its inevitable pace, and just before Christmas 1939, Dickie Raikes was appointed to *Talisman* as Number One; his CO was Philip Francis, who no doubt gave Dickie a lesson in the art of command, for he was an 'admirably quiet [man] of great personality and efficiency'. Their first patrol put them off the Gironde river in order to land two agents, one French, one English, on the French coast by canoe[9] with their radio transmitter. It is probable that this was the first or certainly one of the first types of operations using the sub/canoe combination. The sub was so close inshore that they actually ran aground but not before, in the pitch-dark night, one of the agents fell overboard whilst trying to get himself into the canoe. Dickie did likewise, trying to retrieve the situation. Further anxiety was had when, after all the protracted 'goodbyes' were said, the canoe set off in exactly the opposite direction to the shore and the two agents had to be ignominiously hauled back and redirected. The canoe was recovered in order to leave no evidence of the arrival. Even for a new boat on its first operational patrol with a new crew, it still had taken far too long.

All of the lessons in these different situations and waters were to prepare Dickie Raikes for the *Frankton* Raid, and it shows how his coincidental path was to ensure the right man was put in the right place at the right hour. The encouragement from others was another vital ingredient in his education, and he learnt that quiet leadership was much more effective than any shouting.

It was during 1940 that Dickie passed his 'Perisher'[10] command course with the Battle of Britain in 'full swing' and London was in flames. This course was the final part of Dickie's testing and required targeting a live, solid ship. All his training needed to be brought to bear for this task; the urgent translation of theory into the three-dimensional, solid reality. He was judged on how he carried out his tactics in practice, used the periscope, how quickly decisions were made and turned into precise orders, use of the instruments, how he would cope with an emergency and most importantly if he was liable to run the submarine into dangerous situations[11]. It could well be that his course involved targeting HMS *White Bear* or HMS *Cutty Sark*, which were both used as submarine targets and escort vessels.

Dickie's first command was the non-operational L.26, which was used as target for destroyers working up their anti-submarine skill at Scapa. He describes 'a loathsome two months during which I put L.26 aground in a howling gale (8) on my first day in command but got off without damage and without serious recrimination'. This interlude can be swiftly reported thus: Dickie was sent for by the Admiral, 'Well, tell me what happened.' 'Entirely my fault,' said Dickie. 'Any damage?' 'No, sir!' The Admiral replied, 'Well for God's sake let's forget it, because I'm not going through a court martial. Don't do it again.' All these things, as with Hasler's Exercise *Blanket* failure, served only to ensure that subsequent events would run well.

In the September of 1941, Dickie took over HMS *Seawolf*, an operational boat. In a six-month Arctic winter, they patrolled the area round the north of Norway, where they were fairly successful in attacking enemy shipping. With temperatures falling to -52 °C, the boat was heavily encrusted with ice. There was one near-disaster on a crash dive, when due to the depth gauge freezing up, unnoticed, until the boat began to creak and groan, they slowed to a stop at 350 feet – the official deep diving depth was only 250 feet! The recovery from this depth 'took the longest ten minutes of [his] life'. He remained in this area for a year, during which time, he learnt that he had been awarded a DSO. When they had finished the long convoy stint in Russia, whilst en route back to Lerwick, the sub had an encounter with a whale that presumably had mistaken the sub for his mate and kept bumping the sub at an alarming rate. *Seawolf* was given over to a new commander, and Dickie had some well-earned leave in the south.

HMS *Tuna* and her Fish[12]
'The happiest ship that I ever served in'[13]

This is the beginning of the immediate story of the submarine leading up to Operation *Frankton* and covers the detail that is too involved to be included within the main narrative of the Cockleshell Heroes. This addendum gives a few light-hearted and scary moments that do much to add the flavour of what life meant for this crew of HMS *Tuna* (from the 3rd Submarine Flotilla) and who deserve recognition for the part they played in history. Dickie Raikes said that he looked back at his time on *Tuna* with 'enormous affection' and 'of all ships she was my absolute pinnacle'.

After nearly three weeks' leave, Dickie Raikes was appointed to command[14] HMS *Tuna*; she had just finished a refit at Swan Hunters yard at Blythe in Northumberland. Dickie found *Tuna* much larger and more comfortable than *Seawolf*, with ten torpedo tubes and sixteen torpedoes, a 4-inch gun and an Oerlikon anti-aircraft gun, she packed a bigger punch too. She also had more endurance and could stay at sea if necessary for six weeks. Dickie rejoiced in finding his new cabin was 6 feet by 6 feet! He also had a whole new set of officers and a mostly new crew of fifty-six. Of his officers, he had a very experienced and efficient No. 1 named 'Johnnie' Bull, an engineering officer named Abbott and two very young and completely raw sub-lieutenants; one was twenty and already divorced, the other was a newly qualified solicitor named Jump. 'He managed to get *Tuna* into more tight corners than the enemy … he nearly turned my hair grey,' said Raikes post war.

With one day at sea before sailing to Holy Loch, Dickie Raikes impressed on the new sub-lieutenants the absolute necessity of calling him whenever they should be in any doubt about anything and the unforgivable sin of not doing so. Dickie Raikes kept the first watch with Jump for an hour then went below after Jump assured him he was entirely confident. After an hour, instinct took Dickie Raikes back to the bridge, where he found *Tuna* in the middle of an east coast convoy and under fire from the escort, a destroyer. After Raikes had established *Tuna*'s identity to the satisfaction of the convoy's escort, he relegated Jump 'below'. Jump 'thought he could cope', and despite Raikes wanting rid of him, Ionides[15] pressed him to give Jump another chance; a decision which could have been terminal.

On the very first day at HMS *Forth* (mother or depot ship), whilst working up in Arran Water, Jump was on the bridge, and he was instructed to dive 'in five minutes' by Raikes, who, fortunately, remained in the control room. Jump dived the *Tuna* without remembering to shut the hatch behind him as he left the bridge. Raikes, seeing what was happening, slammed shut the bottom hatch leaving Jump excluded, stopped *Tuna* at 30 feet and surfaced at maximum air pressure. With the conning tower full of water, Raikes emerged through the gun tower to see Jump swimming gaily after *Tuna* about 200 metres astern. Without a word, Jump was picked up and, after pumping out the conning tower, *Tuna* returned to harbour and Jump departed for general service.

Dickie Raikes always maintained that HMS *Tuna* was the happiest ship that he ever served in. Of the complement, normally fifty-nine, which first ventured out together were Lt Raymond Henry 'Johnnie' Bull (First Lieutenant or No. 1); Lt (E) Henry Meadows,[16] who was 'pure gold' and 'the best engineer I [Raikes] ever had' (the replacement for Adrian Frederick Alexius Abbot, who went sick); the two sub-lieutenants, Gordon James Rowe, RNVR (Navigator), and (Third Hand) Neil 'Johnny' Rutherford, who was in charge of 'trim'. All the key positions were more than adequately filled. Little is known of the other characters bar the ship's chef, 'Joe' Lawrence[17], a gypsy, excellent cook, and Raikes' steward – shared with the wardroom and Wilfred Griffiths, who doubled up as the wardroom flunky – he had been a valet at the Berkeley Hotel. Of the other crew that can be mentioned and who were often vilified in copies of *Book of the Prophet*[18] were Coxswain Willie Stabb, who Dickie Raikes had served with twice before and was very pleased to have aboard; PO Raymond Arthur Welsman Quick, DSM[19], the telegraphist and 'news editor'[20] (his father had instructed Dickie Raikes at Dartmouth) – Ray became great friends with Dickie Raikes; Second Coxswain PO Harry 'Shakem' Fright.[21]

They went through the usual working-up routine, including a few days at Arrochar at the head of Loch Long discharging torpedoes with daily exercises off Arran. It was at this point Dickie Raikes took the opportunity of giving his wife, Joan, a 'totally illegal' trip by picking her up by canvas boat just round the corner from Holy Loch at the crack of dawn and disembarking her at Arrochar to then stay in a local hotel. Thus Joan's interest in the interior of a second submarine had been met along with a 'fabulous' breakfast in *Tuna*'s wardroom en route.

The first special patrol began on 25 October 1942 out of Lerwick following a quick shake down that made them into an efficient unit. During Operation *Torch*, there were not enough ships to escort the convoy to Russia, so the ships sailed unescorted, singly, at about 100 miles apart. *Tuna* was fitted out as a rescue ship with bunks instead of spare torpedoes as well as carrying a real doctor. They suffered dreadful weather, one roll was measured 50 degrees to port for 30 seconds before righting, all this whilst on the surface. They suffered trouble with a main port engine bearing which necessitated them diving for five hours in order to fix, then came trouble with the lubricating pump, then the fuel pump; they eventually proceeded on one engine. All was made good and they proceeded to move to the convoy route, listening out for distress signals. Some were picked up but these were outside the designated area. Much went on during that patrol, including nearly getting stuck in a land-locked lagoon following up another distress signal. They arrived back in Lerwick after dark on 16 November with all the crew extremely tired.

After six days' leave Dickie Raikes was ordered to report to Admiral Submarines at Swiss Cottage.[22] He did so on 22 November 1942. This was to be briefed about the next 'special patrol' for HMS *Tuna*. It was an operation surrounded in the utmost secrecy and the operation had to be undetected. It was Dickie Raikes who had the final word, and it was he who was authorised to abort the operation if he had any reason to believe that they had been detected. It was to land a small force of Royal Marines close enough to the mouth of the Gironde Estuary to enable them to paddle their canoes into the river proper … at night. The leader of this commando operation was Blondie Hasler; both Raikes and Hasler held the same values and responsibilities for safety and success. Dickie Raikes viewed him as 'a remarkable leader'.[23] They remained in contact with each other for many years after the war. Indeed, it can be said they were both members of the mutual admiration society within a lifelong friendship.

After Operation *Frankton*, they kept a very low profile for the following 48 hours in order to ensure no link with their offspring. They then patrolled a new area until 11 December. During the return journey to Plymouth, in the words of the captain, 'we were badly popped by a heavy and very cold sea' rounding Ushant[24]. *Tuna* and her crew encountered some 'pretty filthy weather', preventing any fixes and almost forced her ashore at the Lizard Peninsula in Cornwall.

When they arrived in Plymouth, *Tuna* was fitted with an early, but primitive, radar system, which took about three weeks. This was the dual-wavelength type 267W[25] with the added ability to show a 3-cm picture of the coastlines on the PPI, as if it were a map.

In January 1943, *Tuna* was then tasked to take the Crown Film Unit to sea for about five days for the making of a film entitled *We Dive at Dawn*;[26] probably around the same time as the midget submarine exercises, she was also used for experiments in carrying 'chariots' mounted on chocks on her saddle tanks, tied down with steel bands located round her hull. Next came two days in Loch Striven in conditions of great secrecy carrying out trials with midget submarines[27] to see if it were practicable to be towed by larger submarines, both being underwater, and with a little practice, it proved to be the case. This was how the midgets reached the entrance to Alten Fjord when they carried out their famous attack on the *Tirpitz*.

In the February of 1943, they returned to Holy Loch and then promptly left for the familiar area of Trondheim. The trip was uneventful, punctuated only with the occasional brief encounters with patrol vessels; but nothing like the number being reported by the new radar toy. Whilst it was a great help in establishing distance off the coast, they apparently were surrounded all night every night by targets until they gave up trusting it at all. On the return journey, when dived, *Tuna* and crew were courted for about three hours by an amorous whale, which occasionally bumped them quite hard before coming alongside the periscope and 'blowing' – with his usual wit, Raikes remarked, 'I was a bit worried about our screws.'

On returning to Holy Loch and after much heart searching, Dickie Raikes decided it was time he had a rest. To be almost omnipresent, knowing and seeing all, to be at readiness for all eventualities required exceptional abilities from any submarines commander, but this mental strain could only be endured for so long. He had a 'most understanding' talk with Ionides and Admiral Submarines and went on leave due to the state of his health, turning *Tuna* over to Lt D. S. R. Martin.

After consultation with the doctor, it was Admiral Claude Barry (Adm S/Ms) who insisted that Dickie went off on two months' leave. Dickie's sleeping improved, and he gradually recovered his mental balance. After the leave period, Dickie was offered a choice of many appointments, and with Barry's recommendation, Dickie was appointed a divisional officer at the officers' training establishment of King Alfred at Hove. But after only three days, Barry's Chief of Staff telephoned to notify of a transfer to the RAF coastal command as the anti-U-boat advisor to the C-in-C. There was a great need for an experienced officer to fill this post.

During the period 1943–45, Dickie Raikes attended the Trend Committee, which oversaw the U-boat war. Raikes then commanded the captured U-3514 and a group of similar U-boats during Operation *Daylight*, the scuttling of surrendered German boats by the Royal Navy. By July 1946, Dickie's health was broken, and he was invalided from the service – without a disability pension! Dickie was offered a job as an operational director in a friend's hotel, thus learning the hotel trade from the bottom up. Dickie became unemployed for the first time in his life in the summer of 1947 due to the financial squeeze and the last in first out nature of employment. Being unable to borrow the capital to buy his own hotel, another move followed. He became membership secretary of the Royal British Legion in Edinburgh, where his talent for writing was spotted by a guest on whom Dickie had once waited when in the hotel business. He was subsequently recruited to the publicity department of Marconi, where he became content and stayed until 1972.

In his career in the Royal Navy, Dickie Raikes served in H, L, O, River, S and T-class boats as well as the German type XXIs and became the sixth captain to command HMS *Tuna*, between 24 August 1942 and 17 March 1943. Dickie Raikes was predeceased by his wife, Joan Margaret (née Edgington) and one of his three daughters. He died peacefully on 5 May 2005 at the good age of ninety-three, still a very good egg, with love in his heart. He wrote after the war, 'I was fortunate indeed to have served under so many fine people and had such splendid and loyal officers and men serve under me.'

Dickie Raikes described the then Lt Bull as a 'splendid chap'. During post-war correspondence, John Raymond Henry Bull, MBE, DSC, RN, described his captain on *Tuna* as 'a small man of great efficiency with whom I struck up a close rapport very quickly'.

The last accolade, fittingly, is best left to Blondie Hasler as CO and subsequently a lifetime family friend. Hasler observed the handling and day-to-day living of submarine *Tuna* and reflected on this object lesson in talent saying, 'Dick Raikes remains for me the very best type of British naval officer.' Of Blondie's recommendations following *Frankton*, he says of Dickie Raikes that he 'cheerfully accepted serious risks in order to fix his position accurately and subsequently to launch the attacking force in a favourable position'. Dickie Raikes name will now be recorded on the new memorial at the Pointe de Grave in France.[28]

Chief Petty Officer Telegraphist Raymond Arthur Welsman Quick, DSM, RN

Much can be lost over time. Fortunately, the research undertaken has allowed another window into history to be secured through the testimony of this gentleman. He became friends with Dickie Raikes and was the link to the outside world from the inside of HMS *Tuna*. He holds a significant place in history as the man who sent the completion message of Operation *Frankton*; apart from all the other messages he was responsible for. He was another important cog that ensured the safety and happiness of HMS *Tuna*.

Is that Speedy? No, it's just 'Quick'

In a letter from the Admiralty dated 5 July 1943, notification was given that the King had awarded the DSM 'for outstanding coolness, cheerfulness and skill whilst serving on *Tuna* in five arduous patrols and a brilliant and successful attack on a German U-boat on 7 April 1943, to Petty Officer Telegraphist Raymond Arthur Welsman Quick'.

In full service dress, he attended the Presentation of Medals Investiture at 11 a.m. on Tuesday 24 July 1945 with his wife, who was the only permitted guest. As they arrived at the gates of Buckingham Palace at the appointed time of 1030, both stood with the other recipients before they were parted. Raymond was ushered into a separate room whilst Mrs Quick took her place to witness this momentous occasion.

CPO Raymond Quick

The King, with a few kind words of appreciation, pinned on the medal, thanked him and shook Raymond's hand. Raymond smiled, said 'thank you, sir', before taking a step back and turning to exit.

Raymond's father, Arthur, had himself left school when he was fifteen to join the navy serving twenty-two years and during the First World War on convoy work to reach the rank of CPO before retiring to civilian life. After the First World War ended, Arthur Quick moved the family to his home port of Plymouth in 1920; the family moved many, many times within Plymouth. By 1925, Arthur received his Draft Chit advising him to report to Britannia Royal Naval College at Dartmouth.

Arthur Welsman Quick was busy at work at Dartmouth Royal Naval College as Chief Yeoman, an instructor in Signals, as his son was being decorated. That evening, he impatiently awaited his elder son's return to celebrate the fine and deserving award at his home at Winner Hill Road in Paignton, Devon. Raymond's younger brother also worked at the naval college and lived at home. With Raymond and his wife living nearby in Redburn Road, Paignton, it was an easy arrangement to get the family together.

Raymond was born at Sidford near Sidmouth on 29 April 1916, joined the navy after he left school at Dartmouth and had been in the navy for about twelve years by 1945.

On 12 February 1930, Raymond entered the Royal Hospital School at Greenwich;[29] his father had recently retired from service but had retained his 'old' job at Dartmouth due to new rules from the Admiralty; the family home in Dartmouth had been sold and they moved to Paignton also in Devon, only a short bus ride from Dartmouth.

Raymond was accepted into the RN proper and duly enrolled at HMS *Vincent* in Gosport, Hampshire. From Boy Second Class with a wage of five shillings[30] plus a bar of soap a week, he became a Boy First Class with a wage of seven shillings and sixpence, also with a bar of soap. During this time, Raymond was to meet and serve under the first of two captains by the name of Raikes; both from the same family. Raymond Quick became Boy Telegraphist

OND/Jx.136656 (Dev) and 'qualified educationally for Accelerated Advancement to Man's Rating' on 9 March 1934 at the age of seventeen and a half. Raymond's first posting was Battleship HMS *Malaya* attached to Devonport.

He entered the dockyard, as many have done, through Albert Road Gate and stood next to the enormous structure that was to be home for the next eighteen months. Raymond soon found that he had welcome connections in the form of the Divisional Officer by the name of Lt-Cdr Mellor, who had been at Dartmouth with Raymond's father; he had asked Mellor to look after Raymond. Another surprise was that the Leading Telegraphist on *Malaya* was Raymond's father's going ashore 'oppo' on HMS *Seawolf*. During all Raymond's years in the service, his father's name would often crop up in conversations with officers due to them being instructed by Arthur at Dartmouth. Raymond managed to see a lot of the world during his time on HMS *Malaya*, even as far as the West Indies. He then served his first foreign commission in the Mediterranean at Malta with HMS *Delhi*. He then volunteered for a position aboard HMS *Basilisk*, then to a First World War destroyer, HMS *Tenedos*. Following a Draft Chit, he found advancement as Leading Telegraphist at HMS *Pembroke* at Chatham Naval Barracks and then onto his last surface ship, HMS *Brazen*. Raymond then joined his 'new navy' with entry into Fort Blockhouse (HMS *Dolphin*) and a submariner's world from 1938 until 1946, again as a volunteer. He married his nineteen-year-old bride (he was nearly twenty-two) at Totnes, Devon, on 7 September 1938[31], then spent the honeymoon evening at the ABC cinema at Castle Circus in Torquay, followed by fish and chips on the way home to Paignton before he joined HMT *Dunera* in October 1938 for a slow six-week voyage to Hong Kong. He joined HM Submarine *Rover*, then *Regulus* in the Second World War. His next draft was to HMS *Tempest*. At the age of thirty-two, Raymond joined HMS *Tuna* as Petty Officer Telegraphist and met the nephew of the first Raikes family member he had met in Gosport – *Tuna*'s Captain – R. P. Raikes.

Raymond would also become friends with the engineering officer Henry Meadows,[32] who would often spend hours during the night chatting in Raymond's office and consuming the rum-soaked raisins that hid there. This 'office' was just a tiny area with equipment, but he did have his own electric fire in this 'room'.

It was on board *Tuna* that Raymond began to produce the 'funnies' for which he became well known and added much to the morale of all aboard *Tuna*. At this point, it is probably best quoting Dickie Raikes when being asked about his crew on the *Tuna*. He said that they 'all had a good sense of humour. One was a remarkable chap. Whatever the weather or conditions he would get the news somehow and he would type it out and circulate it – it was very popular. He was allowed by me to cartoon all of us including me. He started making up the news and did it very cleverly so eventually we were not sure whether we were getting the real news from the BBC or Ray Quick!'

'The funnies' was a daily 'magazine' entitled *Book of the Prophet*, which Raymond not only produced but featured in under the pseudonym of 'Kwikus'. The story of *Tuna* and Operation *Frankton* has been told but Raymond Quick's part in this operation should be noted, as it was he that sent and received all the signals during this operation and indeed the famous signal to the Admiralty – 'Operation *Frankton* completed 2100/7'.

Following on from Operation *Frankton*, 'Kwikus' disembarked *Tuna* in Plymouth and was sent to Portsmouth Barracks to learn about the new installation of an early radar. This new radar would require a further two radar operators. Raymond took his place amongst the other dozen PO Telegraphists – but he was the only one from a submarine. (This system was made from a printed circuit board and sported a simple screen. A line of grass across the centre on which echoes would appear as blips, either to port or starboard indicated in yards on either side from the centre of the screen.)

Towards the end of the war, Raymond became Chief Petty Officer Raymond Quick. He was demobbed on 29 April 1946 and headed to 11 Redburn Road, Paignton, Devon, as a civilian. He joined the National Fire Service then, after a stint abroad in Rhodesia, Raymond, care of Dickie Raikes, ended up working at Marconi's. Following this, he had custodial employment at Kirkham House in Paignton and latterly at Dartmouth Castle.

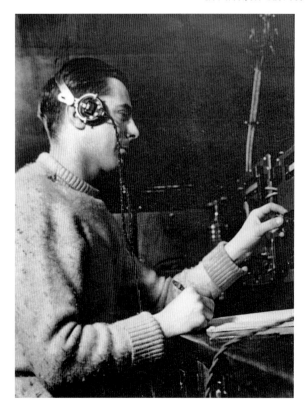

Ray Quick at work – an official photo
necessitating a nice clean sweater.

On 12 May 2003, Raymond Quick received a Commemorative Medal from the Consul of
the Russian Federation in the United Kingdom for the '50th Anniversary of the Victory in
the Great Patriotic War 1941–1945'. Raymond also received the Russian Medal (60th Arctic)
in May 2005; he also holds the 40th medal. It is believed he also served on P552 and HMS
Vitality.

'Kwikus', another good egg, had survived the war largely due to luck and his friend and
captain, Dickie Raikes. In ending and as a tribute to all those who wore the White Woolly
Jumper, a quote from the *Book of the Prophet* … 'Not just anyone can be a submariner.'

The T-Class Wartime Submarine

In order to bring a perspective to the role of this submarine during the war, a brief description
of what life was like on *Tuna* is related together with the specifications, capabilities and some
history. This will assist in showing how, in the already cramped conditions, the 'Cockleshell
Commandos' integrated into this life below the waves during their short trip. Space was at a
premium, but the camaraderie and food was exceptional.

HMS *Tuna*[33], pennant number N94, 94N, 94T was first laid down by Scott's Shipbuilding
& Engineering Company Ltd, Greenock, on 13 June 1938 and launched on 10 May 1940.
Commissioning took place on 1 August 1940. The crest was a badge – a tunny fesswise
proper. She had a displacement of 1,325 tons on the surface and 1,573 tons submerged. Her
normal crew total was fifty-nine. *Tuna*'s was 275 feet in length with a beam of 26 feet 6
inches, a mean draught of 14 feet 9 inches and was propelled by two sets of MAN Diesel
engines, which gave 2,500 bhp with two sets of electric motors that produced 1,450 hp on
twin screws giving a surface speed of 14 knots. The flat-out speed underwater was 8 knots
for an hour and a half or 2 knots for twenty hours. The armament consisted of eight 21-inch
Bow torpedoes tubes (two external), two 21-inch external tubes mounted amidships firing

The crest – a badge – a tunny fesswise proper, blue waves inside a gold rope and crown.

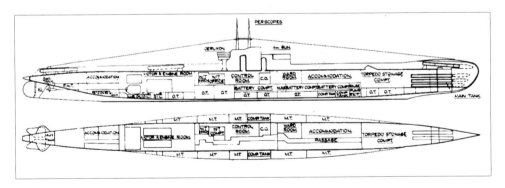

Internal compartments of a T-class submarine.

Tuna ready to berth.

forward (she carried sixteen torpedoes), one 4-inch Mk 12 gun, three .303-inch Lewis or Vickers MG. During the refit in 1942, a single external stern torpedo tube was fitted and to improve the anti-aircraft capability, a 20-mm Oerlikon Gun was mounted on a platform aft of the bridge structure.

HMS *Tuna* was adopted by Aldershot under the Warship Adoption Scheme of 1941–42. Following Operation *Frankton*, *Tuna* returned to Plymouth on 11 December to be fitted with an early radar system. *Tuna* then carried out trials of the development model of the dual-wavelength type 267W. Immediately prior to the *Frankton* Operation, HMS *Tuna* went through a series of degaussing; in fact, it was thought by most of the crew that she was the most heavily degaussed boat in the British Navy[34]. The reason for this level of precaution was that the RAF had sown a vast quantity of magnetic mines in the relatively shallow area that *Tuna* would be operating in.

Degaussing is a process in which a system of electrical cables are installed around the circumference of a ship's hull, running from bow to stern on both sides. A measured electrical current is passed through these cables to cancel out the ship's magnetic field. Degaussing equipment was installed in the hull of navy ships and could be turned on whenever the ship was in waters that might contain magnetic mines; usually shallow waters in combat areas. Done correctly, it provides an 'inviability' to the sensors of the magnetic mines. In Britain, ten wiping stations were active during the war, which degaussed in total about 10,000 ships. In England, these were located in Straits of Dover, Portsmouth, Portland, Plymouth and Falmouth. In Scotland, Firth of Forth, Loch Long, Oban Bay, Rosyth and Cumbrae.

The term was first used by Cdr Charles F. Goodeve[35], RCNVR, during the Second World War while trying to counter the German magnetic mines that were plaguing the British Fleet. The mines detected the increase in magnetic field when the steel in a ship concentrated the Earth's magnetic field over it. Cdr Goodeve developed a number of systems to induce a small 'N – pole up' field into the ship to offset this effect, meaning that the net field was the same as background. Since the Germans used the 'gauss' as the unit of the strength of the magnetic field in their mines, Goodeve termed the various processes to counter the mines as 'degaussing', which was then adopted. With the success of these countermeasures to the magnetic mine, he began to gain a reputation for cutting through red tape and pushing his projects against all opposition. Many of the developments originated from the junior officers in the department or outside. Every single development was examined by Charles and generally improved by his inventor and critic. The two most important inventions of that period were plastic armour and the Hedgehog ahead-thrown anti-submarine weapon, which was masterminded by Cdr Goodeve. He also undertook to ensure the Oerlikon AA gun went into production.

The core of any submarine was the pressure hull; it was cylindrical in section with a constant diameter throughout most of its length but tapered towards the bow and stern; it typically narrowed at the bows but maintained its height to allow room for the torpedo tubes. The saddle tanks were huge blisters along either side of the pressure hull. The hull was fitted with hydroplanes fore and aft to control depth, which could be turned up when the boat was coming alongside in the harbour and were operated by a system of hydraulic telemotors to power both rudder and hydroplanes. The pressure hull in a T (Triton) Class was 16 feet in diameter; the deck featured six openings. From forward to aft: the forward escape hatch; the torpedo loading hatch; gun tower; conning tower; engine room hatch; after escape hatch. The 'soft patch' in the pressure hull was situated over the engine room, which could be detached for installation or removal of the large pieces of machinery. Access to any submarine was usually through the top-loading hatch leading down into the top stowage compartment and through to the second watertight bulkhead, where the accommodation areas were for the crew except the Stokers and the Commanding Officer. The pressure hull[36] was also divided into six roughly equal compartments along its length, each being separated by a watertight bulkhead. Forward in the narrow part of the bow were the six internal torpedo tubes followed by the torpedo storage compartment, with six reload torpedoes on racks on either side with the torpedo-loading hatch above. The space could also be used for crew bunks in hammock form if required.

The messes led off a passageway running down the starboard side; at the end of the passageway was the third bulkhead leading on to the control room and the CO's 'spacious' 6-foot-square cabin. Dominating the control room were the two periscopes in the centre, and along the port side were the positions for the hydroplane operators and the Engine Room Artificer, who controlled the ballast tanks, with the helmsman's positions facing the forward of the two periscopes. Of the two periscopes, one was high power with magnification of 1.5 to 6 and the other was a small or attack periscope, which was less detectable by enemy. When not in use, these were retracted within fixed tubes, which protruded above the conning tower. The control room provided a home for the chart table, ASDIC[37] listening position, attack instrumentation, gyrocompass and the 'Blowing Panel'. The after end of the control room, on the starboard side, sported the all-important galley, centrally situated to aid with the food distribution, with the W/T office (small cabin) on the port side. From the control room, a ladder led up through the conning tower to the bridge, which could maintain communications via voice pipes. Projecting above the bridge were two standards with fitted positions for the lookouts. The gun position was below and in front of the bridge and access to this position was via the gun tower, which led down into the control room. Further aft and through the fourth watertight bulkhead were the engine and motor rooms containing a diesel and electric motor on each side. Through the fifth and last watertight bulkhead, where the pressure hull began to narrow, was the cramped stokers' mess deck and the steering machinery area. The after escape hatch was situated there.

Most of the crew lived between the torpedo stowage compartment and the control room; seventeen of the men lived in an open mess deck. The majority of the bunks were in the mess around the tables where the top bunks were lowered to form the backs of the seats which also served as bunks. This was a good arrangement when nobody wanted to sleep, but in a three-watch routine on a normal patrol, there was always a conflict between the sleepers and those who wanted to read, play cards or uckers.[38] ('Hot bunking' is the process of one man moving into a bunk still warm from the previous occupant.) Bunks were also fitted down the outboard side of the boat off which lay other mess decks. Walking aft down the passageway took you past the separate messes for eight CPOs and POs as well as the five heads before finding the wardroom just forward of the watertight bulkhead leading through into the control room. Most of the batteries for the electric motors were under this compartment and the control room aft. The four officers lived in the wardroom, and although it was furnished more comfortably than the other messes, it was no less cramped. The CO's cabin was no more than a plated-off corner of the control room on the port forward side, but it afforded an opportunity for him to be on his own – yet always aware what was going on outside.

All the spaces in the bottom of the boat were for the lubrication and fuel oil together with the fresh and salt water tanks; the salt water tanks were used as internal auxiliary for trimming and compensating.

The T-class design offered an enhanced standard of accommodation to that previously experienced in other submarines. Without doubt, the conditions were cramped, but this was suffered throughout the ship's company and this situation bred a camaraderie not found in any other branch of the service, which compensated for the discomfort and must have given an uplifting experience to any outsiders who became temporary travellers ... such as the 'Cockleshell Commandos', who found the lack of rationing on submarines a boon. In comparison with the civilian population, submariners lived like kings.

The Royal Navy's T class of diesel-electric submarines were designed in the 1930s to replace the O, P and R classes. Fifty-three members of the class were built just before and during the Second World War. Fifteen pre-war submarines of the Group One boats were ordered under the Programmes of 1935 (*Triton*), 1936 (next four), 1937 (next seven) and 1938 (last three). The boats originally had a bulbous bow covering the two forward external torpedo tubes, which quickly produced complaints that they reduced surface speed in rough weather. These external tubes were removed from HMS *Triumph* during repairs after she was damaged by a mine and HMS *Thetis* during the extensive repairs following her sinking and subsequent salvage. Only six craft survived the war. On 30 September 1945, HMS *Tuna* was allocated to reserve group D, which were those being destored ready for berthing on the mud at Falmouth; by 10 October, *Tuna* was in tow of HMRT *Envoy* to Falmouth and by 31 October had become reserve group F. HMS *Tuna* was sold to be broken up for scrap on 19 December 1945 and scrapped at Briton Ferry, Wales, in June 1946. The Royal Navy disposed of its last operational T class boat in 1969; it retained one permanently moored as a static training submarine until 1974. They played a major role in the Royal Navy's submarine operations. In the decade following the war, the oldest surviving boats were scrapped with the remainder converted to anti-submarine vessels to counter the perceived growing Soviet submarine threat. The last surviving boat served in the Israel Defence Forces and was scrapped in 1977.

Of the full complement that served[39] on HMS *Tuna* at the time of Operation *Frankton*, the names below have been identified. The titles, ranks and awards were not necessarily held at the time of serving on HMS *Tuna*. For the first time after all the years that have passed, the author is pleased to introduce them to you to ensure they are not forgotten.

Lt 'Johnnie' Bull, RN, became HMS *Tuna*'s No. 1 or First Lieutenant on 14 August 1942; he later became Commander John Raymond Henry Bull, MBE, DSC, and Bar, American Bronze Star. 'Johnnie' Bull said post-war, 'The knowledge I acquired and particularly what I learned from Dick Raikes were to prove very useful later on when I was appointed as Captain of HMS *Severn* and later HMS *Clyde* to do Special Operations in the Far East both with Force 136 of SOE and with the American OSS parties.'

Lt (E) Sir Henry Meadows, RNR, appointed to HMS *Tuna* as engineering officer on 15 October 1942, reported to have died in August 1996 aged eighty-two.

Sub-Lt Neil Rutherford, RN, was appointed as third hand on HMS *Tuna* on 20 May 1942. Sub-Lt Micheal Edward Pearson Jump, RNVR, was appointed to HMS *Tuna* as navigator on 21 August 1942 but following the incident as reported above he was swiftly replaced on 26 September 1942 by Sub-Lt Gordon James Rowe, RNVR.

CPO Ernest Tonking, Electrician (looked after all low power, gyro compass, 25v)

Second Coxswain Petty Officer Harry 'Shakem' Fright.

Petty Officer William Stabb, DSM, MiD, O/N J113899 (Devonport). He was drafted to Submarine depot ship HMS *Forth* of 3rd Submarine Flotilla at the Holy Loch for submarine HMS *Tuna*. He was part of the complement aboard *Tuna* during Operation *Frankton* in December 1942 and the U-boat U-644 business off Narvik on 7 April 1943. He was awarded the DSM for his part in the attack.[40] He was promoted to acting Chief Petty Officer then drafted to the submarine depot ship HMS *Adamant* of the 4th Flotilla at Trincomalee, Ceylon, for Submarine HMS *Templar*. Latterly awarded a Mention in Dispatches 'for Far East War Patrols'.[41]

Stoker PO Joe Oakes**. Engine room.

Stoker Petty Officer Charles Spencer Watkins, MiD, O/N P/KX 84385 (Po).

Leading Stoker Thomas Alexander Abraham, DSM, MiD, O/N D/KX 82152 (Dev)

Petty Officer Robert Drydale, DSM, MiD, O/N C/JX 140917 (Ch)

Petty Officer Cook Joseph Albert Lawrence, DSM, O/N

Stoker First Class T. 'Irwin' Uscroft, O/N

Stoker First Class John Murphy, MiD, O/N P/KX 130140 (Po)

Stoker First Class Phillip Robson, MiD, O/N C/KX 117447 (Ch)

Telegraphist Francis Leonard James Toogood, DSM, O/N J113983 (Po)

Leading Seaman (LTO) Ernest George May, MiD, O/N C/SSX 19393 (ch).

Leading Seaman (Asdic) Lee, O/N

LS John Francis Wilband, MiD, O/N D/JX 996550 (Dev)

LS Dominic King, MiD, O/N D/JX 135013 (Dev)

Engine Room Artificer Third Class Percival Ronald Clarke, DSM, O/N P/MX 47365 (Po)

Engine Room Artificer 4th Class Richard McDonald Hodgson, DSM*, O/N D/MX 75596 (Dev)

Engine Room Artificer 4th Class Wilfred Jarvis, MiD, O/N D/MX 74878 (Dev)

AS James Dickson, MiD, O/N D/JX 238092 (Dev)

AS Albert John Snelling, DSM, O/N P/JX 276517 (Po)

Tuna in Holy Loch following a refit. From front: Captain Raikes, second row centre; Ray Quick, standing off centre left of the *Tuna* crest.

Signalman 'Ivory Dome' Smart (name found in log of 5 December 1942 through reported injury). Smart's Christian name has eluded Ray Quick's memory, but he related the story behind Smart's inclusion into the sick list: Signalman Smart was Dickie Raikes right-hand man on watch. Only one signalman was carried aboard *Tuna* and this was Smart. On 5 December, Dickie Raikes and Smart were on the bridge, and during the descent into *Tuna* from the bridge, Raikes attempted to pass Smart an Aldis lamp, or signal lantern, but dropped it on Smart's head causing a gash. This resulted in a day on the sick list and the nickname of 'Ivory Dome' from that day onwards.

** Likely to have been decorated.

CHAPTER 13

The '*Bébé Anglaise*' from Room 900
– Agent 45660

Comtesse de Milleville, a.k.a. Marie-Claire

It is very likely that most readers will never have heard of this lady; it is gratifying to be able to convey just a little of the history she helped to create.

Decorated for gallantry under fire; awarded the Russian Order of St Anne and the French Croix de Guerre with Star; constantly hunted by the Gestapo, captured, interrogated and kept in solitary confinement for nine months, she then escaped; deliberately run down by a car and badly injured by French collaborators; again captured, then shot by the Gestapo. Having had her head and neck rebuilt, she was then deported to Ravensbrück concentration camp and included on a death list. She suffered having one of her sons disappear forever after he was sent to a concentration camp. One of the few Englishwomen to have been awarded a second Croix de Guerre; saving countless Allied servicemen; so very proud to be British.

For all her efforts, and the way she represented Great Britain to the Nazis in France, her only recognition after the end of the war by the British Government was a Mention in Dispatches. This sad state of affairs did eventually change, and she was belatedly awarded an OBE in the late 1960s. She was extremely proud to receive the honour and to be British, even though she continued to live in France. There is so much about this incredible woman that it is not possible to relate all. This is just a flavour of her being and the essence of her character – her life.

To begin, it is fitting to convey a measure of how those who met her felt. Dickie Raikes met Mary in Paris in 1965 and described her as 'a wonderful woman' whom it was 'a privilege to meet'; Mary was seventy years of age. In a letter penned by Hasler in September 1969, Mary, at the age of seventy-four, was still being described as 'indefatigable'. An Englishwoman inspired by Kipling and the example of Nurse Edith Cavell, she was a true patriot, for which not even the Germans faulted her. How she defied the Germans and their regime by sheer pertinacity, daring and guile remains without precedent.

Airey Neave of MI9 described her as 'one of the most colourful agents who combined a passion for adventure with extremely blank speech'. Lt Airey Neave first heard of her on 27 July 1942 when a telegram arrived at the War Office with news of her escape to England. Neave was part of only a few staff of the top-secret section of MI9 at Room 900 in the War Office known as IS9(d). Surprisingly, 'Room 900' only had two rooms in London to conduct their clandestine operations in North West Europe.

By the Armistice of June 1940, France was divided by a demarcation line. German troops occupied all the country north and west of this line; south of this line was the Free or Unoccupied Zone. The civil jurisdiction of the 'Vichy Government' extended over the whole of metropolitan France with the exception of Alsace-Lorraine[1], which was under the eighty-five-year-old Marshal Henri-Philippe Petain, who hailed from Vichy. The situation of trapped soldiers and downed airmen necessitated the breaking of fresh ground in the field of military intelligence and began this entirely novel form of secret service in order to maintain regular lines of escape. This service had been set up in 1941 with Neave joining in May

So very proud to be British, Agent 45660, the indefatigable
Mary Lindell, a.k.a. Marie-Claire.

1942 and was totally devoted to this purpose. The return of the various airmen and others represented a significant renewal of skilled manpower[2]. A newly returned 'evader' was of far more operational value than one who had been cooped up in a prison camp for months. The ultimate price for this was that over 500 civilians from Holland, Belgium and France were arrested, shot or died in concentration camps; very many more died post-war as a result of their injuries – all assisted in the goal of repatriation.

In the Unoccupied Zone, the security forces mainly consisted of the gendarmes of the French civilian police who frequently co-operated with the escape workers. A group of thugs called the 'Milice' were recruited by the Vichy Government and often betrayed, arrested and brutalised their own countrymen. This sadistic group, drawn from the scum of the French jails, were a constant danger to the Resistance Movement[3].

Escape group lines were infiltrated by the traitors. The Gestapo, German security police and security services carried out their business with great brutality against the ordinary peoples who were either caught with or had been known to harbour Allied airmen. The practice was to dispose of those whom they considered unimportant to their inquiries whilst the real organisers were kept alive and submitted to torture; many were eventually sent to concentration camps.

Within the operating field of Room 900 was the knowledge of the balance of sacrifice made by individuals who, through their devotion, had a profound influence on the outcome of the war.

This vignette sets the scene and brings into view just one element within the escape network in France and shows how this one network under one woman agent trained by Room 900 helped save two commandos who are still remembered to this day.

Mary Lindell, OBE, was ninety-two years of age when she died. Her life should have ended many times before that, but she cheated death on each occasion. Countless Allied servicemen were returned to their homeland during the war years; all owe their safety to her charmed life, determination and enormous contempt and disdain for the Nazis.

Proclamation of her nationality, even in the face of Gestapo interrogation, was always evident. When Hasler first came into contact with Mary during his escape after the *Frankton* Raid, he found her to be a 'handsome woman of medium height with greying hair along with clear blue eyes.'[4] He thought she looked like a typical fox-hunting woman. A tad unfeminine with a touch of arrogance – strong characteristics of a particularly English class. He said of her that her 'eccentricity and her commanding aristocratic manner enabled her to get away with a great deal'. He also noted at this first meeting that she wore her two English decorations in front of her French ones. Unashamedly pro-British, flaunting the same to any German in her sight.

The bloodline of Herbert George Hasler and William Edward Sparks would have ended had it not been for the organisation that was controlled and operated by this extremely resourceful, courageous and strong-minded woman in German-occupied France during the Second World War. They both knew this, were ever thankful and kept in touch for many years before her death in 1987. A service of thanksgiving was held in France on 13 February and was attended by Sparks, who commented, 'Wild horses would not have kept me away'. Hasler was not in attendance to honour and pay thanks to her; Mary's old friend Blondie died on 5 May 1987. Sparks was the last to depart on 30 November 2002. Sparks wrote of her with great affection and had 'memories of the most courageous lady I have ever had the privilege of knowing'.

The French farmers, who were a part of most escape routes, including Mary's, suffered great deprivations to assist escapers and evaders. These civilians and their families would have been summarily shot or sent to concentration camps if they had been discovered aiding or harbouring Allied servicemen. Most of the servicemen risked only capture and life in a POW camp, but as with most things, there are always exceptions. Hasler and Sparks were one of these exceptions; if caught, torture and death would have followed, just as it did for the other 'Cockleshell Heroes'; but they, or at least Sparks, did not know this.

Mary Ghita Lindell was born in Sutton, Surrey, England, in 1895, impeccably English in both upbringing and manner and well used to getting her own way, a trait that certainly saved her own life and that of the many Allied personnel. This concise account is her story, which has been taken from the known documents or publications as well as the oral accounts from those who knew her. For some readers, it is repetition for emphasis, for others it is another incredible story that allows a true appreciation of a life given over to duty.

Mary became Comtesse de Milleville through marriage; aliases she used during the Nazi occupation were Comtesse de Moncy and the elusive Marie-Claire which was also the code name for the escape route she orchestrated.

Mary Lindell first served as a nurse in the Voluntary Aid Detachment (VAD) during the First World War. Following an altercation with a diminutive matron with an unkindly disposition towards volunteer nurses, Mary returned home and offered her services to the Secours aux Blessés Militaires, an aristocratic division of the French Red Cross with whom she served during the entire First World War. It might have been only six or so trips along the mud-swamped lanes amongst the bullets, gas and bombs, but she affectionately became known as the 'Bébé Anglaise' by the French soldiers she tended on the battlefield in her white uniform.

Her first transgression or taste of disobedience toward her betters came when she volunteered to stay on at the hospital and had to go over the head of the Chief of Medicine to do so. In the apparent sanctuary of the field hospital, she and only two orderlies tended the wounded who otherwise would have been abandoned as the Germans advanced over the position. At Red Cross Headquarters, she was reported as 'missing, presumed dead', and before any official communication had been published, the news vendors were selling copies of the *Daily Mail* with the headline 'British Nurse Killed on French Front'. Unfortunately, Mary's mother had learnt this news as she was shopping in Kensington and had to be escorted home in shock. Through contacts, the rumour of the early demise of our heroine was dispelled by a noted family friend.

This and other acts of righteousness, love and kindness, even to the enemy of the day, resulted in the 'Bébé Anglaise' being awarded the Military Cross. Amidst one hot and dusty afternoon with thundering guns belching out their foul temper just a few kilometres distant, she stood amongst the bloodied and battle-stained men. A French General carefully pinned on the decoration and remarked at the twenty-three-year-old, 'Very pretty, very pretty,' then kissed her on both cheeks. This became Mary's most emotional moment in her life. (She was awarded the Russian Order of St Anne by the last Tsar of All the Russias in 1917 at the age of twenty-three for her devotion to the Russian wounded and also awarded the French Croix de Guerre with Star in June of the same year.)

In 1939, at forty-five years of age, she was married with two grown-up sons, Maurice (seventeen) and Oky (sixteen) and her young daughter Barbe (twelve). She had married a French nobleman, Count de Milleville, and had a place in the new Parisian Society. Her husband was building up his business and was away in South America when hostilities broke out. With the announcement from Chamberlain and the imminent commencement of another world war, her son, Oky, piped up and said, 'Mama, now you'll be able to go back to war.' In that one fleeting moment, Mary knew this to be true and took out her old uniform, dressed and headed to the French Red Cross Society's Headquarters to arrange a transfer onto the active list. After being denied by a high official due to her being English, she returned to her Parisian flat with a determination to play her part in the war.

Months passed during the phoney war, and after her move to a smaller flat in Auteuil, Mary's introduction into the war was via the request during late evening in March 1940 from the President of her boys' school. The President had been waiting for Mary, and as she attended the hastily convened meeting in the principal's study in her Red Cross Uniform, she was ushered to his side. An operation was needed to accommodate 500 Belgian refugees within the school, and Mary was designated as having full authority to orchestrate the event due to her experience. It was this episode that fuelled unsolicited visitors asking how they could serve the cause of defeated France.

It was not long before she had been tasked to get an English woman out of a rapidly deteriorating Paris. This was the beginning of what seems to be her destiny; armed only with her previously mentioned attitude and persona together with the decorations and Red Cross Uniform, she began her journey, embarking on the most important and dangerous self-imposed mission: her amateur occupation of assisting Englishmen to escape over the Spanish border via the foothills of the Pyrenees.

A decision was made to operate more 'professionally', and she had adopted the code name 'Marie'. Soon, she had connections and a stipend at the American Embassy in Paris and was dealing exclusively with officers. With the sudden influx of Englishmen, her efforts turned towards Ruffec, and she drove down to speak with a Madame Roullier in order to try and find out if she knew of any other farms that straddled the 'border' of Free France. This then became the exclusive escape route for the British. This is where arrangements were made for the transit between Farm 'A' and Farm 'B'. She also managed to begin a trade in obtaining German hand arms.

The first Englishmen to pass through this route were Hasler and Sparks of Cockleshell Heroes fame. On average, the group helped two or three men per week, with each one involving hours of negotiation and planning.

Eventually, she was arrested and interrogated by the Gestapo but not brutalised. She went through a three-hour court martial, was found guilty and given a sentence of two and a half years of hard labour but through her continued argument was eventually sentenced to only nine months of solitary confinement and was imprisoned in Fresnes prison. Whilst she was imprisoned, the members of her group were rounded up and her eldest son, Maurice, also ended up in Fresnes with a sentence of eleven months. She was told that the Gestapo were ready to rearrest her following her release in November 1941. Mary managed to evade them, but during the process, she caught a cold. Due to her being gassed in the First World War and the attack of Spanish flu in 1918, she contracted pneumonia. With Maurice still in prison and her near to death, again the Gestapo arrived at her home to take her back to prison, but due to the protestations of her doctor, all they did for the meantime was put a sentry at the entrance to the flats; eventually Mary slipped away from her guards.

Mary's Route from France

Mary had to provide the money for the journey of each Englishman herself, which was taken from funds she received from the British Government whilst the Frenchmen's primary route of Sauveterre-de-Béarn was paid for by the escaping Frenchmen themselves who could afford to pay their own expenses.

Her disappearance from Paris was the only option, and she made plans that would take her to Madame Roullier's at Ruffec. It took three weeks to gain her strength before undertaking the second part of the journey. Once a message had been sent by her family, Mary made her way to the metro and met her second son Oky on the deserted platform ready to escort her to the Gare d'Austerlitz. They were met by her daughter Barbe, who handed over both money and ticket. As Mary sat with her back to the engine, she looked down at her two loyal children with great affection and tried to put aside the thought of whether she would ever see them again. Her son's face was white with anxiety as he looked up at her. As the train jerked forward, his face turned to intense sadness and he started running to keep pace with it, unable to contain the pain of separation, and as the train advanced, so did the speed of his running until he came to a sliding halt at the end of the platform. He waved frantically until the train was out of sight and Mary permitted a tear to slowly trickle down her cheek. She had no idea that this would be the last time she was to see Oky, as shortly afterwards the Nazis took him for transportation and the last known of him was that he fell into Russian hands and was lost in the depths of the Soviet Union, his death never confirmed.

Her husband the Count was also on the train but did not make contact until Ruffec, but both met as arranged and headed to Mme Roullier's, where a room had been prepared. The Count stayed at the Hôtel de France and said his farewell the next morning before Mary's taxi ride to Farm 'A' and her agent, Maxim.

Her passage was to take her from Farm 'A' to Farm 'B', and from Maxim's point of view, this was highly dangerous mostly due to Mary's hacking cough. Mary countered this by swallowing a large mouthful of Dr Collis Brown's 'Chlorodyne' and after saying goodbye to his large family then set off during twilight with Maxim out through the farmyard. He took her by the arm and using his skills as a stalker led her into the fields, taking every advantage of cover using his countryman's caution at every move. As they reached the most difficult part of the journey, Maxim decided he would go on alone a hundred metres ahead along the valley, and when he signalled, she advanced, walking briskly with her head bent low. Leaving her again, he entered a wood and the process repeated itself, and with a carpet of pungent-smelling leaf mould underfoot, they arrived at a gate in the peaceful solitude of the buildings and barns of Farm 'B'. Maxim walked to the side door, knocked and pushed it open with his foot and at the same time indicated for Mary to follow.

Mary's first view was of an old woman, Louise Dubreuile[5], the mother of Armand, who was sat spinning wool by the side of the fire. Maxim spoke to the elderly Charente woman with the soft words, 'Who do you think I have brought this time?' Only a grunt was received in reply but Maxim proudly continued, 'This is our Marie', which met with a flicker of interest from the old woman's eyes, and she pointed to a chair, which Mary duly sat down on.

Maxim sat next to the table and poured a glass of wine from the bottle that the old lady had brought and offered it to Mary. As Mary declined the offer, he downed the wine, wiped his lips on his sleeve and took Mary's hand and kissed her on both cheeks and said softly, 'You can always rely on me, Marie. Don't forget to send them all to us.' Mary was ill but managed to thank him; with that, he slipped out the door and into the darkness, just as a coughing fit took hold that moved Louise into action. She left the room, but was back within minutes with a huge bowl of milk which she had quickly warmed. Mary's ribs ached badly, and she felt terribly nauseous. 'Take this, child, I've put some honey in it and it will ease your coughing.' Without question, Mary drank and felt a little relieved but knew her temperature was rising. Mary said that she must get the bus to Roumazières to which Louise nodded knowingly but suggested that Mary take her shoes off first, remarking that Mary looked cold and tired. Louise then removed Mary's stockings and began to rub Mary's feet.

Louise told Mary that she could not possible carry on telling her she was very ill. 'If you want to make this journey, you must rest first.' With that, Mary looked at her watch and agreed to rest so long as Louise promised to wake her in time for the bus; she simply nodded and left Mary alone and went to wrap up some hot bricks and put them in a bed. She then opened Mary's attaché case, took out a nightdress and proceeded to help Mary to change.

Louise Dubreuile then led Mary into a tiny bedroom that contained a large, warm bed that was so comfortable that no sooner had Mary's head touched the pillow than she fell into a deep sleep. Louise ensured Mary's clothes were dried and ready on Mary's waking that night. As she woke, Armand walked into the room carrying a lamp; he gazed down from his lofty height and said as he shook his head, 'We cannot let you go, Marie, It would not be right. You are too ill.'

In characteristic manner, even in her very weak state, Mary replied, 'That doesn't matter. I must be on my way. There is too much danger should I remain.'

Armand's retort was overwhelming, 'This is my house and I am master here, no guest of mine is going out on a cold night like this when she is ill. Nobody knows you are her, so you might as well stay.' Despite her feeble protestations, she knew that she was no match for this kindly man. During the following days and nights, Mary's health improved with the careful tending from her hosts. But as she grew stronger, she began to feel quite alone being restricted to the bedroom during the worst of her illness.

During a visit to her room, Mary asked Armand if it would be possible for her to join the family during evening mealtimes, knowing that to do so during the day would be risky due to the many people who called at the farm. Armand was stunned by this and said, 'You could never do that. You are a Countess and we are just peasants, it would not be right for you to eat at our table.' Her face lit up and she gave a little laugh and said, 'My dear Armand, we are comrades in arms. I have never heard of such nonsense, you are risking your lives for me and I should like to feel I was one of the family.'

Armand dropped to his knees beside her bed. With tears forming in his eyes, he kissed her hands and said, 'Very well … you shall eat at our table and in the future there will always be a place called "Marie's place". It will be yours now and forever.'

When Mary was strong enough to travel, Armand took her to Roumazières in his pony and trap. He told Mary about a boy from his village (in actual fact, he was twenty-four years old) who worked as a porter at Limoges and could be trusted and suggested that she contact him.

It should be highlighted that at this occasion he refused to take any money from Mary; she said a fond farewell to him. Armand Dubreuille did not take any payment for men who passed through his hands during the future work he carried out for her, but Mary being Mary was determined that he should receive money for the sustenance he provided for each of her evaders.

Mary caught the train to Limoges, where she made contact with this porter and had a long talk with him. His ultimate end was that of many, and he mysteriously disappeared just before the end of the war having been taken by the Gestapo and shot; but not before he was able to do a most tremendous job of work for 'Marie-Claire'. Her journey continued on to Lyons and a contact was made with the American vice-consul, who in turn had been in contact with British Intelligence.

It was an arrangement made by the British Government with Vichy that enabled elderly ladies to be repatriated back to England. This presented an opportunity for Mary to be smuggled out as a governess on a previously owned British passport in her maiden name of Mary Lindell. Six weeks later, after a celebration in Monte Carlo with her son Maurice, she left on her forged exit visa from her network of helpers.

She reached Spain and the British Consulate, and it was there that the crucial matter was put to her by the Consul-General, 'Mary, I must ask you a most important question. Would you be prepared to go back to France?' Without hesitation, she replied, 'Yes, if I get the help I need. My son is awaiting my return and I want to get back as soon as possible.'

During her passage to England under the cover of a governess, Mary was condemned to death *in absentia* by the Germans, who were actively looking for the Comtesse de Milleville! Mary was urgently transported via a VIP flying boat from Lisbon and eventually landed at Poole in Dorset.

'The evil men do'

By 29 July 1942, Mary had arrived in London and presented herself with the letter she had been given by the Consul-General at 10 Downing Street. After being interviewed by an official and put on standby, she was then told to report to No. 6 St James Street and she met Lt Airey Neave of Colditz fame. As he opened the front door, his first glimpse was Mary standing in the sunshine, her Red Cross uniform well cut to suit her slight, feminine figure. He noted her fine, well-proportioned face with dark-brown eyes[6] and chestnut hair and that she looked considerably younger than her supposed age of forty-five. Her expression was one of intensity and a stubbornness that did not fit her smart appearance, and as soon as Mary spoke to him, he knew why; very defiantly used to getting her own way, she had a commanding mode of speaking with a tone both peremptory and English in every inflection; gruff but beautiful.

After this interview and the initial misgivings, Airey Neave was put in charge of her training, and Mary was then formally introduced to the MI9 organisation formed to promote escape in all ways but especially of airmen shot down over enemy-held countries of France, Belgium and Holland.

With each British bomber pilot costing £10,000 to train and a fighter pilot £15,000 and two years to train, MI9 made good economic sense. With Airey Neave as her field captain, she learnt the art of coding, which she did with great aplomb and application. With this came Mary's indicator phrase of 'the evil men do' and a compromise was found in her user name of 'Marie-Claire'. Then came the training in all aspects of night flying in Lysanders including the laying out of flare paths and parachuting in emergencies; unfortunately, Mary was a bad pupil in this regard. Following this, Mary spent ten days' leave in Cornwall, but this was curtailed, and she found herself rushing to Exeter by car, and then by night train managed to keep her 11 a.m. appointment the next day. Mary then had a coding examination and after about three hours she was declared 'passed'.

Mary was the first woman to be specially trained by Room 900 and was returned to France. Her little platinum ring was engraved with her agent's number 45660, and she was ready to go. Her final briefing was on 20 October 1942 by Lt Airey Neave, St James Street, and just before dusk, they climbed into a waiting car and drove down to RAF Tangmere in Sussex. Here, on the moonlit nights, 138 squadron operated their Lysanders to France. They were met by a squadron leader, who took them into the briefing room, and it was at this time that Neave remembered that Mary had not signed her will! They all had a meal and awaited updates on the weather. Mary was travelling in her blue uniform of the French Red Cross and was misty eyed and looking forward to her mission. Before take-off, she was introduced to the slim little Canadian sergeant pilot, he was a Battle of Britain hero and was wearing gallantry ribbons on his battle dress. He took both her hands in his and not knowing the best way to express himself said, 'I just wanted to say thank you for … for going over there,' his voice trailing. 'I can't tell you what we feel about it but all the boys have tremendous admiration for what you are doing.'

Taken aback, her throat constricted slightly, and in characteristic fashion, she managed to say, 'How astounding … don't say a thing like that. You make me feel quite ill. I feel ashamed to stand before you. After all you are one of the Battle of Britain heroes.' The young Canadian pilot smiled sadly at Mary and said, 'Yes, but tonight I shall be back and sleeping in a warm bed without any fear. But where will you be? And the terrible thing is that you're going out there for us. My God, to think that you're going out there to help us back should …' With that, Mary interjected with 'well, I hope I don't have to help you'.

He grinned and said, 'Well, I've been lucky so far, anyway, I just wanted to say thank you from all of us.' He smiled, turned around and walked rapidly away.

This anecdote gives expression to the whole purpose of the work Mary and all of her kind undertook.

Minutes after Mary was being equipped with her parachute harness, Mae West and inflatable dinghy, she was driven towards the silhouette of an all-black Lysander. A few hours later, the report of her safe arrival in France was received back in Britain.

The SOE had agreed that Mary should fly to one of their reception committees; a field about sixty miles south of Limoges and fifteen miles from the small town of Ussel. She had a considerable amount of money with which to finance the escape route along with her nurse's French identity card from the First World War in the name Ghita Mary Lindell and a French Red Cross card forged by MI9 in the name of Ghita de Milleville; either could be used according to circumstances.

Mary met Maurice in Monte Carlo and the next morning they both took the train to Lyon. From there, Mary left to make contact with all her friends at Ruffec.

Mary's idea had been to set up alternative escape routes across the Pyrenees. With this in mind, she had previously decided to set up an alternative bolthole in Ruffec after she had turned 'professional'. The first HQ of the Marie-Claire line was Hôtel de France. Mary had decided on this hotel because it had the advantage that five or six rooms were usually available, enabling passing airmen to be assured of a night's sleep before they moved on; the building itself was old and in parts built on a low elevation; it straddled across a large area, which made it difficult to surround and provided any number of hiding places and means of exit; and most importantly, she knew that its owner, François Rouillon, 'could be trusted absolutely'.

Mary then returned to Lyon on 1 December 1942 to see how Maurice was getting on with the task of setting up alternative escape routes across France. Her money was running out. Mary had not been supplied with a radio operator and therefore could not be advised of the arrival of the *Frankton* Raid commandos, who at this very time were on their way aboard HMS *Tuna* just out of Scalpsie Bay in Scotland having practised hoisting out canoes for the last ten hours. The commandos however had, unusually and possibly for the first time ever, been told the location to head for to meet up with the escape organisation.

Once Mary had finished her business and satisfied herself with regard to the work undertaken by Maurice for an alternative escape route, she returned to Ruffec, but this time by a different route. She decided to cross the Demarcation Line at Blois, on the River Loire, between Tours and Orléans. Unfortunately, at the time and place that they could cross, there were two German soldiers on duty seemingly awaiting something; both Mary and her guide had to wait for them to be withdrawn. During a second reconnaissance, she and her guide, François, pedalled towards the river where they were to cross. They had only travelled a short distance, and on a clear road the advancing car became menacingly focused in their direction and at speed. It purposely hit them from behind. Both were severely injured and Mary was unconscious. Several of the villagers nearly lynched the occupants of the car (they were collaborators and intended to snatch Mary and her two agents in order to whisk them over the border). Meanwhile, unnoticed, two of the villagers picked up François on a gate, while an associate helper scooped up Mary in his arms and carried them to a remote farmhouse. It took them two hours to travel the five kilometres, but with frequent rests, the three helpers eventually arrived at the farmhouse with the blood-soaked bodies. Mary was placed on the farmer's bed and presumed dead but was just deeply unconscious. The farmer's wife attended to François as best she could; a doctor was sent for but was away on his rounds, so they telephone a friendly chemist, but he lived some distance away; the farmer started to dig a grave in his garden for Mary but told Mary's uninjured helper that he could not bury her until a death certificate had been obtained. Mary was now moved under the greatest of secrecy to a hospital in Loches some fifty kilometres away. Mary had suffered a serious head wound, five compound-fractured ribs and injuries to her leg and arm. Her lungs, liver and intestines should all have been pierced, especially after being carried for over five kilometres across fields.

Such was her situation, Maurice was called to her bedside and arrived three days later only to be dispatched by his mother, who told him to go back to keep an eye on the operations in Lyon. Mary was told that it would take more than a month of convalescing in order for her bones to heal due to her age.

Ten days after Mary's arrival at the hospital, the Gestapo turned up hearing that there was an English agent who had been seriously injured. They searched the hospital but found nothing; Mary had been secreted behind a pile of wood in the cellar by the nurses. The Gestapo were still suspicious and the doctor who attended Mary was arrested but kept denying any involvement and was eventually released after three months. Mary was taken back to her room, but she could feel her collarbone had again been dislocated and was feeling extremely ill. On Christmas Eve, Maurice visited his mother at the hospital and explained that he was still trying to fix the new route but it was proving difficult; he stayed for a Christmas dinner of turkey and Christmas pudding. When Maurice returned to Lyon, a letter from Armand Dubreuille was awaiting him explaining that he had 'two important parcels of food for him'. Considering that the message was an urgent one, he returned to the hospital, and once Mary had been apprised she formulated a plan of action which, even though she was not supposed to leave for another three to four weeks, involved her travelling to Lyon within the following two days.

The plan was that Maurice should go back to Lyon to arrange for the reception of the men in question and then to inform Armand that the men would be picked up on 6 January by Maurice. This then is how Mary Lindell and her French agents became part of the Cockleshell Heroes' story and a lifelong friend of the only two survivors – Hasler and Sparks.

By May 1943, Mary had been introduced to a lieutenant in the Swiss Intelligence who was a friend of Britain and could be trusted; she had officially arrived in Switzerland. Mary's pay was fixed on a sliding scale and came in batches from London usually via a military attaché. She was drawing a mere £45 per month whilst in Switzerland but considerably more when in France. She continued to take instructions from Neave in London on keeping the line open. Whilst in Switzerland, she collected letters via friends who received her letters from France. One letter from Monte Carlo read, 'Maurice is very ill and has been transferred to the clinic', which when decoded meant that Maurice had been arrested and sent to prison and was at the mercy of the Gestapo; as it transpired, it was the notorious Mont Luc prison. Mary contacted London and asked how much she could use to try and obtain Maurice's freedom. London replied, 'Secure release without delay. Finance as required.'

Mary returned to the Gestapo-infested Lyon, where her sixteen-year-old daughter Barbe was. Mary's husband, the Count, had already told Barbe to find out about the situation, and it turned out that the German officer in command was fond of the ladies, and as Barbe looked older than her years, this officer had already invited her to tea. Mary instructed Barbe to find out the price of Maurice's freedom at this meeting with the officer in command, *Hauptmann* Barbier. Armed with sixty thousand Francs, Barbe managed to secure Maurice's release by 11 a.m. the following day. It was not until 2.45 p.m. that day Maurice staggered out of the prison and was shadowed back to the flat owned by the Belvaise family (who had also accommodated Hasler and Sparks). Back at the flat, the full extent of his injuries was discovered – he had been beaten across the face with a thin brass chain. Maurice received the best in health care, Barbe returned to Paris and Mary made for Switzerland. Mary's husband was eventually arrested and sent to prison for two years because Mary had outwitted the Gestapo yet again. It was during 1943 that the Gestapo accumulated much information and evidence against Marie-Claire. She was known in at least five regions. She was under sentence of death in Paris.

Mary again ventured into France to reinforce her workers in the field with money for the cause, via Paris to Ruffec on 9 May 1943. During this period, an important piece of paid information via a pilot[7] in Bordeaux was received concerning the blockade runners' return to Japan. With the dates and times, it was passed on to London, and due to this important piece of intelligence, Mary received a Mention in Dispatches for her part in the operation that sent the entire convoy of blockade runners down to the sea bed as they came out of the estuary.

Maurice had returned to Lyon and restarted operations and on several occasions Mary had only just managed to evade the ever-closing net for Marie-Claire. Due to the ever-increasing number of evaders being handled, people were caught, giving the Gestapo the upper hand. As the operations became more dangerous, Mary assumed more direct command and interrogated more evaders and travelled up and down the line constantly. She disbursed the money herself, found new agents and paid off old ones.

With the help of the Swiss Intelligence on her last visit to Switzerland, she changed her name from the Milleville name the Gestapo knew well to the Comtesse de Moncy, which matched her embroidered underclothes with the little crown and the 'de M'. At this same time, she had begun a system of guides for airmen crossing the frontier at Andorra.

On 24 November 1943, Mary was arrested at Pau railway station by the SD following a betrayal by a worker in her escape line; a bitter and twisted woman who had nothing but hatred and selfishness in her heart.[8]

Despite a huge sum of money paid for her ransom without the sanction from the War Office in London, Mary was eventually removed from the SD headquarters in Biarritz and escorted by train to Paris. During the journey, Mary dived from the train in an attempt to escape but was shot by the guard in the back of the head and another bullet pierced her cheek. Upon waking, she found the bullet in her mouth. She was taken to a hospital in Tours, where she was operated on by a skilled German surgeon who saved her life. Mary recovered but was taken to the notorious Dijon prison in February 1944, where she remained for eight months, suffering savage treatment from the SD.

Even in prison, the Gestapo had tricks to ensnare more quarry into their net. When the prisoners arrived, they were given five pre-stamped postcards with the explanation printed on them that food was in short supply; the idea was that the names supplied would net associates in league with the prisoner. It did not work in Mary's case. There she stayed in cell number 108 under the name of Doctor Marie de Moncy until she was transferred to the black hole of Ravensbrück concentration camp in September 1944. Even in this evil place, she did not stop helping others, saving several women including one from the SOE from the gas chamber as she carried out her duties in the camp hospital. Mary herself was included on a death list, but she was warned and managed to avoid being in the chosen group.

Mary was never particularly religious, but she lost the little faith she had after witnessing the horrors of Ravensbrück concentration camp. A little of this is related in order for the reader to fully understand how difficult it was to survive in the sea of animosity and hatred that was Ravensbrück. It was the only major Nazi concentration camp for women. It was surrounded by a high wall with electrified barbed wire on the top. Prisoners were treated as human Guinea pigs; this was just one of the many killing centres of the Nazis. The SS prided themselves on their lack of pity. In private, they talked about the policy of genocide, never in public. All concentration camps were riddled with corruption; it was easy for individuals to profit from the vast hoard of valuables that streamed into these pits of despair. When a senior officer was tasked to investigate, solely because the Reich was being cheated, he deemed those caught as 'degenerate and brutal parasites'!

The first prisoners arrived in May 1939 with the number of prisoners increasing dramatically: gypsy women from Austria and then the first women from Poland. By the end of 1939, the population of the camp was 2,290.

After the war began, the prisoners came from twenty European countries. The conditions of life in Ravensbrück were as shameful as in all the other concentration camps with death by starvation, beating, torture, hanging, and shooting happening daily. The women who were too weak to work were transferred to be gassed at the Uckermark 'Youth Camp' located nearby to Auschwitz. Others were killed by lethal injections or used for medical experiments by the SS doctors. Various SS-owned companies operated on the camp where the prisoners had to work day and night until they died by weakness and illness.

Due to the constant growth of the population, the camp had to be enlarged four times during the war. Ravensbrück had a crematorium, and by November 1944, the SS built a gas chamber. More than 132,000 women and children were incarcerated in this death camp. It is estimated that 92,000 of them died in the camp by starvation, executions, or weakness. The cruelty and the sadism of the Nazis against the children had no limits. In the early months of Ravensbrück, children were immediately killed. Newborn babies were separated from their mother and drowned or thrown into a sealed room until they died; most of the time this was done in front of the mother. Many testimonies exist telling of children thrown alive into the crematorium ovens or buried alive, poisoned, strangled or drowned. Children were also used for sadistic medical experiments. Hundreds of little girls, some as young as eight years old, were sterilised by direct exposure of the genitals to X-rays. The SS doctor Rosenthal and his girlfriend Gerda Quernheim aborted pregnant women by force; this was often done using bestial methods.

Due to the rapid advance of the Russian Army, the SS decided to exterminate as many prisoners as possible in order to avoid any testimony about what happened in the camp. At least 130 babies as well as pregnant women were gassed in March 1945. At the end of March, the SS decided to transfer the archives of the camp and the machines of the workshops to a safer place. Mary walked out of the camp on 24 April 1945 in an arranged Red Cross convoy to rescue certain Allied prisoners. On 27 and 28 April 1945, the remaining women still able to walk left the camp on a Death March.

The camp was liberated by the Russian Army on 30 April 1945. The survivors of the Death March were liberated in the following hours by a Russian scout unit. Mary became a key witness in the trial of the Nazi criminals of Ravensbrück.

For very many years after the war, Mary continued to check for her son Oky's name on any list of those returning from Russia; she never gave up hope of finding him. She became the Royal Air Force Escaping Society's representative in France after the war. In the CBS Hallmark Hall of Fame presentation, *One Against the Wind*, Mary the heroine was played by actress Judy Davis.

Even if it had taken forty years for her to be properly recognised by the British Government, she did have the personal affection and enduring love of those she helped which, as far as the author is concerned, is of far greater significance. This extraordinary woman with an extraordinary personality continued after the war to undertake charitable work in France.

One of the things that also should be added is harrowing in its telling, although not reported in any great length or graphic detail. It gives one an idea of how individuals were treated and of the methods used for extracting information by the Gestapo. It is likely that equally sadistic methods were used against any Commandos who were caught; Hitler's decree meant they were to be terminated regardless.

One of Mary's great friends and helper in the Marie-Claire line was a young, dark-skinned monk, in his early thirties, fully committed to God, named Abbé Pean. He was in charge of a 'department' and covered a very wide area of the network. He was not only famous in his parish but throughout the region. He was a great leader and loved and admired by everyone. The Sunday morning mass was more often than not conducted wearing his surplus over his trousers and boots, discarding the same afterwards to become a member of the Resistance. Whilst Abbé Pean was a magnificent worker, he insisted on sending back local information to London, a practice that Mary not only disagreed with but warned him against. The worry was that this would attract attention from the Germans. Unfortunately, this happened and he was arrested one day. His final days on this earth give an impression of the brutality of the Gestapo.

The Gestapo gouged out one of his eyes, he was practically skinned alive and was literally crucified in order to try and make him talk. He was tortured beyond the limits of human endurance, but he never revealed a single name. Despite saving countless airmen, he has never been recognised by the British Government.

It is quite possible that some reading this owe their being to Mary Lindell and Abbé Pean, for without them and others like them, there would not have been any children from those soldiers and airman who escaped through the lines of the indefatigable Marie-Claire; this is indeed a great source of inspiration.

Maurice de Milleville

The eldest of Mary's three children had a normal schooling in both the United Kingdom and France before war broke out in 1939. Until things became 'hot' after the collapse of France, he was involved in 'normal war work' with his mother, the Comtesse, who went into the 'Resistance business'. Maurice assisted his mother in the 'job' and emphasised that 'helping out Maj. Hasler and Marine Sparks was one small part of the job'.

This period was seeded with a few visits to different prisons because of the Gestapo's penchant for arresting those suspected. These included some quite unsavoury and notorious prisons such as Sante near Paris, Fresnes, Fort of Hauterive near Dijon and Fort of Montluc near Lyon.

The Germans requisitioned various prisons throughout France. Thousands of men and women became hostages, or victims of racial persecution. All were packed in for long or short stays in inhumane conditions, awaiting deportation or transfer or death. They were extremely unpleasant places even to have to visit. Maurice also became an inmate.

Most of the war work was done for MI9 until he went to England via Spain and Gibraltar. Postwar, Maurice entered civilian life by finding well-suited employment with United Nations Relief and Rehabilitation Administration (UNRRA) within Germany. This organisation was founded during 1943 to give aid to areas liberated from the Axis powers. Each of the participating countries contributed funds of almost $4 billion. By the time the organisation discontinued its operations in Europe on 30 June 1947, it had provided camps for about 1 million refugees unwilling to be repatriated and returned some 7 million displaced persons to their countries of origin. It also provided various types of emergency aid, including distribution of food, medicine and the restoration of public services, agriculture and industry. Maurice then went to work for the US Army as a Radio Engineer, then with an insurance company, followed by an eight-year stint in the petroleum business before managing an outfit in Spain which produced Scuba equipment as well as managing a scuba-diving school. Maurice then returned to Germany to manage a firm of consultants; then he took over a firm engaged in the aluminium import/export business. He then became employed with Agence Nationale pour l'Emploi as a Charge de Mission in the Rhône-Alpes area.

He himself suffered brutal treatment when he was arrested by the Gestapo, who were trying to find his mother. His longest time in prison was eight months – he seemed to have a similarly good fortune to that of his mother – he survived.

Maurice de Milleville was awarded Legion d'honneur, Croix de Guerre, Médaille de la Résistance and Médaille des Évadés.

CHAPTER 14
The Patellogastropoda Master

When SOE was formed in 1940 from MIR, Section D (of the SIS) and another secret organisation, the technical group of MIR was not included. Instead, the team created by Jefferis and Macrae became a department of the Ministry of Defence (in fact its only department) and was known as MD1. The Minister of Defence was the Prime Minister, thus the organisation became known as Winston Churchill's 'toyshop'. Why they did not combine with the technical division of Section D is not altogether clear, but it is likely that the work on devices for the Auxiliary Units ('the British Resistance organisation') was thought to be too important to be interrupted by a merger. MD1 did work closely with the SOE technical people at Welwyn and Aston House and the altimeter switch is an example of the collaboration. By the latter stages of the war, the department found itself a part of their arch rival organisation – the Armament Development Establishment – and the 'toyshop' was closed down by them soon after the war's end.

'Colonel kept Top Secrets at Home'

The many men who carried out clandestine warfare from their 'insignificant vessels', or the 'Cockles' to give them their proper wartime code name, used a device that became a reliable weapon of war for them. It held such an elevated place in their everyday life, they frequently named an indigenous dog in the area they were serving in after this very device – the Limpet. For the 'Earthworm' Detachment, their 'mascot' was indeed named after Colonel Stuart Macrae's 'little' device.

Without formal qualification in the field of engineering, with his above-average intelligence, Stuart Macrae entered into what was the most famous of all the 'back rooms' of the Second World War. This then is how the Limpet mine, just one of his inventions, was born from the mind of one of the men who worked directly for Winston Churchill in his 'Toyshop', an unorthodox department known as Ministry of Defence 1 (MD1) at the War Office.

The first ship-sinking devices were rudimentary affairs from an experimental department consisting of a bench in the living room of a private house. The device was the project of Stuart and 'Nobby', Captain C. V. Clarke, MC, who went shopping in Bedford town centre to buy some large tin bowls from Woolworths, which were then manufactured into a pseudo-mine with the aid of horseshoe magnets and bitumen, later replaced with Plaster of Paris and porridge.

The 'field trials' were carried out in the deep end of Bedford Public Baths, closed for the purpose. Stuart named it 'The Limpet', in his own words, 'a name which stuck'. Then came the delayed-action initiator, a spring-loaded striker that was maintained in the cocked position by a pellet soluble in water, the idea being that, when the pellet dissolved, this striker

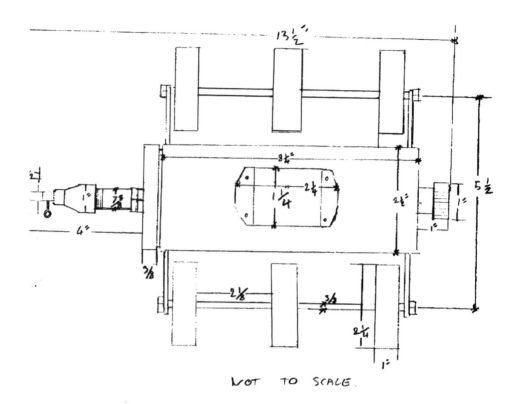

NOT TO SCALE.

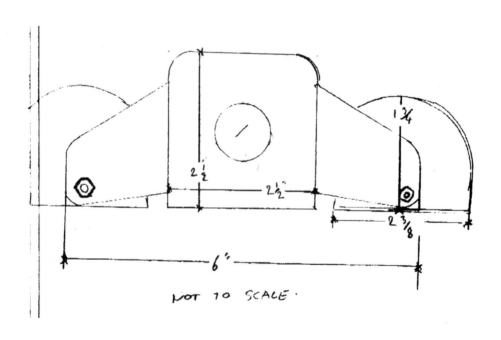

NOT TO SCALE.

would be released to hit a cap, initiating a detonator, exploding a primer, which in turn would explode the main charge.

The difficulty was with the temperature of the water and the variables of the pellets tested. This matter was solved by one of Nobby's children, who was swept into the playpen from the bench one day, sweeties and all. This act resulted in the aniseed sweet bag being knocked onto the floor. Stuart tried one of the said sweets and noticed that it stayed 'with me [for] a long time, getting smaller and smaller with great regularity. After trying a couple himself, Nobby agreed that this might well be the answer, so we commandeered the remainder of the supply and started to experiment.'

Stuart wrote, 'I think I can safely claim to be the first man to drill holes in aniseed balls and devise a fitting to enable this to be done accurately and efficiently.' They found that when they rigged up some of the igniters with the aniseed and tried them out under various conditions 'they behaved perfectly'. The very next day, Stuart and Nobby proceeded to buy up the entire supply of Bedford's aniseed sweet population. The manufacturers[1] explained that the core of the aniseed ball was dropped into vats containing sweetened liquid a specific number of times and for a specified period, thus making each aniseed ball as near identical in the dissolving department as anyone could wish for. The aniseed ball itself was protected from damp, whilst encased in its housing, when stored, by a closed removable rubber seal. This was the birth of the Limpet mine, it was the Mark 1, and half a million were issued for use, made by outside contractors after the initial few hundred were produced at the 'Bedford Establishment'.

The Mark 1 lasted until 1942 when the Mark 2 was introduced and used famously by the Cockleshell Heroes during the *Frankton* Raid. Of the improvements, the horseshoe magnets were replaced with specially designed, flexibly mounted ones for use on uneven surfaces. The aniseed balls were replaced by the same department's 'L' delay fuses.

Limpet mine without AC delay fitted.

The incidents described below in which enemy shipping was damaged or sunk through being attacked with Limpet Mines were selected from a large number of official Admiralty reports on the subject for the appendices of Stuart Macrae's book *Winston Churchill's Toyshop*.

1. On 7 December 1942, a raid against shipping at Bordeaux was carried out under the code-name Operation *Frankton*. The Limpeteers were Royal Marines in five canoes, taken to the Gironde Estuary by Sm *Tuna*. The following enemy vessels were damaged in this raid:

    SS *Alabama* (5,641 tons), SS *Tannenfels* (7,840 tons), SS *Portland* (7,132 tons), and SS *Dresden* (5,567 tons)

2. On 3 January 1943, four Chariots carrying Limpets carried out an attack on Italian shipping in Palermo Harbour. Cruiser *Ulpio Traiano* was sunk and SS *Viminale* was damaged. Limpets laid on *Ciclone*, *Grecale*, and SS *Gimma* were removed by the enemy before they detonated.

3. On 28 April 1943, a number of German steamers was sunk in Oslo Harbour and at Koppernvik in the Haugesund with Limpets. One officer and three ratings in canoes blew up and sank a German mine-locating craft off Koppernvik.

4. On 25 September 1943, a raid against shipping in Singapore Harbour was carried out by British and Australian Navy personnel under the command of Major Ivor Lyon of the Gordon Highlanders. With their canoes, they were carried to the area in an ex-Japanese sailing vessel *Krait*. The following Japanese merchant ships were sunk in this raid:

    Kizanmaru (5,072 tons), *Karusanmaru* (2,197 tons), *Yamagata Maru* (3,807 tons), *Tasyo Maru* (6,000 tons), *Shinkoku Maru* (10,000 tons), and *Nasusan Maru* (4,399 tons).

5. On 18 June 1944, a raid against German shipping in Portolago (Leros) was carried out by Allied sabotage forces commanded by Lt J. F. Richards, RM, under the code-name Operation *Sunbeam*. With the exception of a small water tanker, the ships concerned were all alongside the jetty. In all, five ships were attacked with the following results:

    Patrol Vessel G.D. 91 (Trawler) blew up and sank, Salvage Tug *Titan* sunk, small Water Tanker beached to avoid sinking. Torpedoboat T.A. 14. Two mines blew large holes in her port side forward but the crew succeeded in keeping her afloat. Torpedoboat T.A. 17. Five mines caused extensive damage to the after part of the ship.

6. On 22 June 1944, a raid against shipping at Spezia, on the North West coast of Italy, was carried out by four English and six Italian naval personnel using Limpets. As a result, the *Bolzano* (10,000 tons) capsized.

7. On 31 July 1945, a raid was carried out against Japanese cruisers in Johore Strait by Midget Submarines carrying Limpets. A Japanese craft, the *Takoa* (9,850 tons) was seriously damaged by Limpets placed by Midget Submarine XE 3.

Before the Second World War, a young Stuart Macrae had worked for Odhams Press editing a magazine called *Armchair Science*. An article he had written on high-powered magnets 'attracted' the attention of a military officer named Jefferies, who was in charge of establishing a team to work on sabotage devices for an Intelligence Department of the War Office, known at the time as Military Intelligence Research (MIR). Stuart was offered a job, which he accepted.

As second in command, Stuart became the non-commissioned officer, a captain, under the only other member of the department in 1939, Major (later General) Sir Millis Jefferies, KBE, MC. The department grew in size enormously, and many people were employed who did not follow the normal working day or rules. It was a closed secret society. Later on, the organisation's expertise was in the employment of high explosives and the development of shaped charge and 'squash head' technologies. MD1 produced the PIAT, Hedgehog (with DMWD), Blacker's Bombard, 7.5-inch AVRE, Tank Ploughs, a bridge-laying tank called the Great Eastern, a 4.5-inch naval gun and numerous bombs.

On 21 June 1945, Stuart Macrae's promotion to full colonel came about, and with Sir Millis Jefferies moving on, Stuart became the director of the establishment at the end of the war. It was not until after hostilities and on the arrival of his second child that Stuart Macrae thought it necessary to arm himself with formal qualifications, obtaining entry into the Institute of Mechanical Engineers, and became employed with the British Coal Utilisation & Research Association. He died in 1979. MD1 was responsible for twenty-six new weapons to be accepted by the services, and these were produced in quantity.

Stuart Macrae 'rescued' certain material from his work place when the premises were abandoned. It was during him being called as a witness to a Royal Commission of Awards to Inventors that Stuart disclosed that he had certain documents in his possession. It was then that he was nearly court-martialled. The Crown Counsel 'gruelled me about this and I became a temporary Press sensation under such headlines as "Colonel kept top secrets at home"'.

He was duly ordered to hand over all said documents to a Security Officer, who was supposed to call to collect them. 'But he never did call, so I still have them.'

Without Stuart Macrae having kept his 'diary of events' from 1939 to 1947, along with the 'vast quantity of official files and records', his memory would have let him down and his book *Winston Churchill's Toyshop* would never have been written by him in 1971. If it had never been written then his son, John, would never have been able to give a copy of his father's book to this author. John visited the author after seeing *The Cockleshell Canoes* book mentioned within the local media in our area. It was this meeting that ensured that the 'Toyshop' book was reprinted in early 2010 by Amberley Publishing. *Toyshop* is, as the *Times Literary Supplement* described it, 'a hilarious book'.

A box used by Macrae in his role as travelling salesman is now in a private collection in Europe. 'The box' was used by Macrae to instruct Aux Units and other special groups and, no doubt, to promote the wares and interests of MD1 to senior officials.

Colonel R. S. Macrae, the author of *Winston Churchill's Toyshop*.

3

REMEMBERING

CHAPTER 15
The 'Cockleshell Heroes' Ransom

The world premiere of the film *Cockleshell Heroes* was held at Empire Theatre, Leicester Square, in London on 16 November 1955. The notables who attended were from the political and film world of that era, including Elizabeth Taylor. Of royalty, it was HRH The Duke of Edinburgh who was present.

It was said that 'no ordinary film would command such an audience', but this film premiere was headlined to be no ordinary film. In truth, the film was a pale rendition of the real action and story. The film was based on 'the true life exploits of a group of Royal Marines led by Colonel H. G. Hasler, DSO, OBE'. With any enduring story, tale or event, there is usually a mixture of tragedy, heroism, love, sadness and a sense of fulfilment. These features along with a popularist media link serve to perpetuate the memory of the event. The story in the film of *Cockleshell Heroes* (1955) was produced because it contained all those human emotions, and although inaccurate to the truth and poorly executed, it did serve to continue a memory.

The Most Expensive Royal Marine Premiere Ever Staged

Having spent some years within the film industry, the author is unsurprised to learn of one view that the captain of HMS *Tuna* had on the film *Cockleshell Heroes*. In his most inimitable fashion, he began, 'The script was a mass of bollocks …'

This is borne out to some degree when you learn that producers Messrs Allen and Broccoli might have regretted inviting HRH Duke of Edinburgh to the premiere, for HRH is reported to have said to them, 'I suppose you realise that you've missed out the real point of the raid on Bordeaux?' The two producers are said to have looked startled. HRH continued to inform them that 'the raid was specifically planned in order to destroy four German ships which were about to sail for Japan with radar equipment. There's no mention of that in the picture.' HRH knew this because sitting next to him at the premiere was his uncle, Lord Mountbatten. During the film, Mountbatten was seen several times to lean over to whisper to the Duke. The result of the comments to the producers was, apparently, that they were going to reshoot part of the film.

The extraordinary outcome was that Cubby Broccoli said of the error on the night, 'It will cost us a great deal of money: thousands. But we're honoured that the Duke should take so much interest in the picture.' In fact, all that was done to accommodate this oversight was a rather obvious and awkward 30 second scene in which a German officer explained to his underlings the real reason for the attack.

It should be noted at this juncture that Capt. Dickie Raikes' view was more comprehensive than the author's initial quotation, his complete view was that the script was a mass of bollocks using expressions that just weren't used but the mock-up of the inside of the submarine at Shepherds Bush studio was brilliant and slightly larger than life so that it would look the right size in the film but there was a piece of machinery that I could not identify and as they were paying me £50 to get it right I mentioned this. The director said, 'Ah, you see we had space we couldn't fill and there was something in the store that looked about the right size so we put it in.' The extras had long hair and so I had all that cut off before I drilled them in what they had to do when diving. It was fun.

Dickie Raikes had been asked to act as submarine adviser for the film, and he did comment later on that he had read the proposed script of the submarine sequences, and he had moderated his expressions, saying only that these were 'absolute balderdash – so I rewrote it for them'.

Warwick Films were given a great deal of help from the authorities, providing a submarine, Drill Instructors, SBS canoeists and facilities at Eastney Barracks. For all concerned, it was a bit of a 'jolly'. The then Commandant General of the Royal Marines agreed to supply various bodies at the producers' disposal; and from March 1955, and into the summer, they had fun in Portugal and elsewhere. Hasler and Sparks acted as technical advisors, whilst from the Royal Marines contingent the following were loaned: Captain R. M. (Dickie) Brounger; C/Sgt F. W. (Taff) Evans; Sgt E. (Lofty) Moorhouse; Sgt R. (Reg) Adamson; Sgt E. N. (Bill) Bailey; Sgt D. (Mac) McKerracher; Cpl C. (Clive) Close; Cpl E. (Geordie) Richens; Cpl J. F. (Bubbles) Walters; Mne N. (Taff) Phillips; Mne R. (Darkie) Evans; Mne Lonergan and Mne Howells. Some played small parts in the film from drivers of staff cars, German troops and sailors to sentries, military policemen and the German firing squad. They all dined out to celebrate afterwards. Bubbles Walters thought he had landed well; having just finished training, he now became a 'film star'. Unfortunately, a realisation that filming was not what he had originally signed up for eventually dawned! Regardless, they each were paid ten guineas[1] a week on top of their wages, which for a corporal in 1954 was £5. It does seem that all had immense fun with only one or two serious incidents. Even though they were using Mk 1** canoes, which were far more stable than the Mk 2 type that were actually used on the raid, two actors (one in a leading role) managed to capsize themselves and were saved from drowning by Marines Richens and Close.

The Lisbon Story

This whole event is worthwhile reporting. It was said in official circles that it was wondered how a party of men such as No. 1 SBS were ever to be expected to live in Lisbon without ending up in gaol. After taking Easter leave in February, some eight canoes, twelve breathing sets and clothing were packed up and dispatched under the supervision of Cpl Richens for sea transfer to Lisbon. It took him about a week to get these through the Portuguese Customs due to the fact the officials had never seen such an extraordinary collection of goods. The stores were then stowed in the Lisbon Film Studios. The remainder of the Marine section arrived on 17 March 1955, after being served champagne on the four-hour flight. Three days were spent making up the canoes in a warehouse on location near Lisbon's River Tagus. During the first fortnight of the second unit shoot, they had to complete a scene where five canoes had entered into the uncharted tide race where one canoe capsized and the crew had to swim ashore. This turned out to be the most arduous of the stay. They began at 6 a.m. and finished around twelve hours later on each day. Each little action had to be repeated several times, as control of the canoes was so difficult in the broken sea with waves up to six feet high; the results or 'rushes' were pawed over in the local cinema after processing had taken place. In early May, the main party consisting of around seventy people including some of the actors arrived. In the next four weeks, they began at first light and travelled anywhere from 2 to 25 miles to get to the scenes. They then did short paddles on the river about six times over carrying the canoes through mud or through undergrowth; acting alternately as

German sailors and soldiers; spending a day at launching drill from a Portuguese submarine and diving in Lisbon docks, where a Russian merchant ship had discharged a quantity of fuel oil from her cargo. With the canoes and equipment suffering badly from the lack of maintenance and the fact that the RM crews did not have a day off, tempers became frayed. It was at this time they were told that they were to be staying for a further three weeks, and this was received with less than contentment and was followed by the consumption of great quantities of the local wine and brandy. The main problem was the twelve-hour day working and the night life of Lisbon not beginning until midnight. The words 'burning' and 'candle' spring to mind! It is worthy of report that one marine could actually be quoted as saying, 'Wasn't it wonderful to work normal service hours again?'

A Portuguese Ransom for the 'Cockleshell Heroes'

This film had three working titles: Survivors Two, Canoe Commandos and The Survivors and film posters celebrated the marines as the 'Canoe Commandos'. It is also worth recording that the budget for this film was considered expensive during the era in which it was produced. The British actor Trevor Howard ended up doing the commentary for a documentary about Portugal, which won more awards than the *Cockleshell Heroes* film ever did; Howard went all over the world promoting the documentary. He seemed unimpressed with the actual film he co-starred in. It seems that the Portuguese government had decreed that filming in Portugal would have to stop unless the film company guaranteed to make a documentary about Portugal to be shown with *Cockleshell Heroes*. Rather than argue, it was decided to comply with the ransom request with Trevor Howard volunteering to do the commentary. The schedule was arranged to give Trevor two free days and the unit of three went off to shoot footage of caves and any other points of interest.

In truth, the film was inaccurate to the true story: they used the wrong canoes; they showed the Limpets being placed by frogmen; they showed a Marine going AWOL before they embarked on the submarine, to name but three important mistakes. Blondie himself was not too enamoured with the film on various levels, but his greatest conflict was with the title, and he produced no less that thirty-eight alternatives, none containing the words hero or cockleshell. In the end, Blondie's embarrassment with the fact that his part was 'lionised' was such that he contrived to be out of the country when the film was premiered; he was sat in a French café having taken a cross-channel ferry from Dover.

The accolades of the film came rolling in and further premieres were given in USA and Canada, attended only by Bill Sparks, who thoroughly enjoyed himself. One amusing incident is reported by Bill Sparks, which carried the headline 'Cockleshell Hero captured by German after years of evasion'. The story behind this is that, during the Washington stopover of the film road show, a newspaper ran a competition to 'find the Cockleshell Hero' and the reward was $100. But the Columbia Pictures public relations man had squirrelled Bill Sparks away in a hotel for a week. Unfortunately, at the end of the week, when the PR man came to collect him, Sparks was spotted walking down the street. The gent who made the discovery, and collected the $100, had the surname of 'German'. Hence the nifty line in the newspapers. It turned out that the lucky chap was in fact an Englishman who had just lost his job. Knowing how PR works, it's likely this was all set up for the headline!

CHAPTER 16

The Insignificant Vessel:
The 'Cockle' Mark Two

'Cockle' Mark 2 Semi-Rigid, Two-Seater Collapsible Canoe

For the very first time, a newly formed detachment of Royal Marines undertook a mission with completely new equipment. They ventured out into the night with their own purpose-built craft. The significance was that it was the first time any unit had managed to secure their own type of craft for their own type of clandestine warfare. It was to become a milestone in the development of small craft.

It is quite incredible to learn that of the many drawings, paintings and models depicting the canoe used on the *Frankton* Raid that have been produced since the Second World War, some at great effort and expense, nearly every one has managed to portray the Mk 2 Cockle canoe wrongly to the world. Sadly, even in the *Cockleshell Heroes* film, the later Mk 1** canoe (not produced before mid-1943) was used instead, possibly because the Mk 2 would not have been easy to paddle for the actors.

Due to the depiction in the film and the information within this publication[1], the Cockle Mk 2 is likely to remain the most famous of all canoes. Given the level of security surrounding the code-named 'Cockle' at the time, it is unsurprising to find that misinformation was rife; this continued until the present day until the author's intensive research. Until the publication of the book *The Cockleshell Canoes*, most of the small amount of available information and history concerning the Cockle Mk 2 canoe was inaccurately reported, some wildly so. Regardless, this particular Cockle has its place firmly cemented in history solely due to the *Frankton* Raid. It is therefore extremely important to fully understand the precise details of the actual type of canoe used on that clandestine operation.

The only canoes that were available and that had previously been used for other such operations were those only suited to the warmer waters of the Mediterranean. These canoes, in short, were not robust enough to cope with the kinds of operations that were envisaged. The only type that were available were those that came in bags that needed a considerable amount of time to be erected and themselves posed a hazard to those using them. These canoes could not be dragged over a beach or carried loaded without damage occurring – easily. It has, on more than one occasion, been written that Blondie Hasler designed the canoe that he took on the *Frankton* Raid. For those readers who have always been under this misapprehension, it should be known that the canoe, with its characteristic and unique collapsibility and flat bottom, had already been designed well before Hasler became tasked with finding a small craft for special purposes.

Here then is the correct attribution of the design, designer and history. In short, very few canoe types actually existed at that time, none of which were adequate or purpose-built. When one reads of the waters and distance navigated during the *Frankton* Raid, the five-foot tidal races and so on, you suddenly wonder how this canoe, with its thin three-ply flat bottom and canvas sides, ever made it to its destination. Its robust nature is evident given that even when the commandos slashed and tore into it in order to sink the craft, it refused to do so.

The skill of paddling the Mk 2 canoe for the ordinary man is extraordinarily difficult and tiring, but then again, not only were the men of the RMBPD extraordinary, so too was the designer Fred Goatley. For without him Hasler would have had to rely on a canoe design that was at that time not suitable for the operation in mind.

It was chance that Goatley had designed this flat-bottomed canoe a year before it was needed and chance that someone had remembered him offering it to Fort Blockhouse and subsequently submitting it to the Admiral of Submarines for consideration. The man who designed this canoe and other waterborne craft was forgotten after the war. For him, there was no award, no recognition for the work or the many lives he contributed to saving through his designs. Here, seemingly, is his only celebration.

The full intricacies of the canoes – who, what, when, how and why – can be found in *The Cockleshell Canoes*, but for now, the attention is given to the canoe and its design – with a little reference to the naming as well. Captain T. A. Hussey, RN, was the Commandant of the Combined Operations Development Centre (CODC), previously the Inter-Services Training and Development Centre (ISTDC). This was a small team based at Southsea, Portsmouth, which Hasler, at the age of twenty-eight, had joined in January 1942. Hasler was tasked with the study and development of all methods of attacking enemy ships at harbour by all methods of stealth. On 9 March 1942, a meeting was attended by Maj. Hasler, Maj. Courtney and Capt. Montanaro to discuss the two-man Goatley boat, with regard to the Staff Requirements for an improved type of canoe for commando operations. With a clear understanding of what Hasler required, and with Hussey's advice, a meeting was set up between Fred Goatley, who had, by then, become a consultant contracted to Saro Laminated Woodwork Ltd on the Isle of Wight. This meeting occurred sometime after 14 March 1942.

A sample order was placed with Saro's by Hasler on 14 April 1942. On 22 April 1942, official approval was given 'for the word "Cockle" to be used for all craft of the canoe type for commando operations'. It should be pointed out that the idea of the 'Cockle' nomenclature originated from Fred Goatley, who it is believed came by the name having previously worked on a yacht sporting the name 'Cockleshell'.[2]

It seems that the very first Cockle Mk 2 was launched on 13 May 1942 from Saro's Folly Works (Saunders-Roe) yard into the River Medina for a brief test before being taken to the CODC's very own cordoned-off section of the beach at Eastney. The first testing by Hasler was on 14 May, loaded with ballast.

The Cockle Mk 2 Design

Of all the Marks of canoes that were produced during the war, by far the greatest number manufactured was the Cockle Mk 2. The design drawings by Mr Goatley are the only canoe plans to actually bear the Cockle designation; giving another indication that this was a name borne from Fred Goatley. A sample order was first placed for six pilot models, which required a lot of minor experiments in order to get the simplest method for operation. The estimated cost of design and experiments carried out by Goatley in his own workshop at York Avenue was around £110. The price for the first six delivered Mk 2 canoes for Hasler's *Frankton* Raid was £160 each. It is believed that the additional seventy ordered were at that price, if not a little less. There is no cost indication per canoe for the bulk orders that were subcontracted out.

The six pilot models, the prototype (No. 7) used for the set-up of the production run, and twenty of the first order of seventy Mk 2 canoes were manufactured by Saro Laminated Wood Products Ltd, at their Folly Works in Whippingham on the Isle of Wight. The bulk of the 750 production run for the Mk 2 was undertaken by Parkstone Joinery Co. Ltd, in Parkstone, Dorset. Messrs Tyler's Ltd of Griffin's Mill, Stroud, Gloucestershire, are believed to have supplied the additional 100 canoes at some stage after this time.

Within some PRO documents, different dimensions of the beam and length appear. For some reason, these are different to those in the Goatley papers. The canoe length taken from the Goatley papers could have been disputed except for the fact that all known examples of the Mk 2 are nominally 15 feet long. There are six known Mk 2 canoes: one in private hands and five in museums. Three are in the Royal Marines Museum Collection at Eastney, Portsmouth, and one each at the Imperial War Museum in London and the Combined Military Services Museum in Essex. Indeed, these are very rare beasts.

Private Hands Example, Length 15 feet*, Beam 28½ inches
Royal Marines Museum Canoe (No. 1), Length 15 feet*, Beam 30½ inches
Royal Marines Museum Canoe (No. 2), Length 15 feet*, Beam 28½ inches
Royal Marines Museum Canoe (No. 3), Length 15 feet*, Beam 28½ inches
Combined Military Services Museum, Length 15 feet*, Beam 28½ inches
Imperial War Museum, Length 15 feet*, Beam 30½ inches[3]

*Nominal length (actually *c.* 182 inches)

The actual specifications below relate to those that are found within the Goatley archives, and these are believed to be the figures to rely on. The bracketed figures are those taken from existing examples.

General Specification

(*Indicates alternate figures found from references other than Goatley archives)

Dimensions

Length 15 ft (*c.* 182 and 181.5 in) *15 ft 1 in
Beam over rubbers 2 ft 4⅝ in (*c.* 28½ in) *28 in
Depth (bottom of runner 12½ in – amidships to top of coaming)
Depth (maximum erected) 18 in *16½ in
Depth (collapsed) 6½ in *7 in
Weight 90 lb, hull and fittings only 80 lb
Load capacity (inc. crew) 480 lb (as safe load) *(stores only) 200 lbs

General Description

Double-ended collapsible canoe to carry two men, with sides constructed in canvas with plywood top and bottom strakes. The cockpit arranged approximately amidships of sufficient size to accommodate two men. The deck and bottom made of ⅛-in plywood with the deck beams of laminated material. Runners fitted to the underside of the bottom with four cross members inside. The plywood was of birch/gabon/birch in normal construction, with the grain of the outer plies at right angles to the length of the panel. Any timber other than plywood was seasoned.

The canvas was 18 oz, 36-inch-wide green wax and cupra ammonia treated, with all the joints in canvas waterproofed and all beadings securing canvas to timber close riveted to form a watertight joint. Shrinkage was allowed for during fitting, including for the cockpit cover. Bitmarine was used for adhesive, which did not crack when dry.

The deck, hand-hole cover, compass-corrector fitment and deck reinforcing were of 5/64-inch three-ply. The top and bottom strakes were of 3/16-inch five-ply. The forward and aft breakwaters, paddle blades, cockpit forward, aft, sides and beadings were all of 3/16-inch three-ply. The bottom: cockpit cover coaming and seat top and hand-hole reinforcing rings were of ⅛-inch three-ply. The cockpit cover coaming beading was of 1/16-inch three-ply and the No. 1 deck reinforcing and backrests were of ¼-inch three-ply. The compass chocks, bow struts, mast step, cockpit cover and beam chocks were of 7/16-inch multi-ply. The fitting of the deck ply was fastened damp as was the fitting of the bottom ply.

A rare seaworthy example of the Mark 2 acquired post war. Note to forward and aft circular hand-hole in the deck to allow access to strut for erection. Also note the hinged breakwaters.

Above and below: Photographs showing the split canvas canopy, manhole coaming and the interior mast step, seat and backrest.

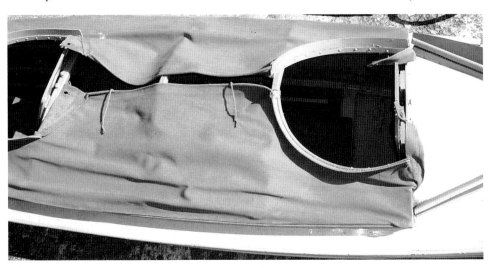

Note the paddle crutches either side of the hinged breakwaters.

Lt-Col. Hasler and Capt. Stewart (No. 2) post *Frankton* Raid off Southsea. Note the low silhouette.

Hasler and Stewart (No. 2) demonstrating the art of launching the Mk 2 when encountering rough sea at Southsea in 1943.

Of the ropes, the painters were 12 feet of fifteen Manilla thread, with the bow ropes being 3 feet by 1½ inches oiled. Hambro line was 14 feet by ⅜ inches and 20 feet, six thread. A canvas cover was fitted over the cockpit for crew protection. Three hinged struts were incorporated to support the gunwale when the canoe was open, and were hinged in a fore and aft direction lying on the bottom when the canoe was collapsed. Two portable gratings with the seat attached and hinged backrests were fitted. Laminate beams to support the canvas cockpit were fitted and were portable. A hinged bow strut was fitted at each end with a hand hole in the deck to allow access to this strut. Two canvas bags, one each side of the cockpit, under the gunwale, were fitted to carry equipment. The hinged breakwaters were fitted on the forward and after decks. There was a hole cut in the forward deck with a mast step fitted for a small mast; this was secured by a cork bung. Three double paddles were supplied, one set as spare, with two separate handles for converting double paddles into singles.

Two portable buoyancy chambers in a rubber material were fitted, one each under forward and aft decks. Four brass cleats were fitted to enable the paddles to rest on the deck of the canoe. The entire canoe was secured when collapsed by two leather straps, one each side buttonholed to a brass stud. The paint used was two coats of dark grey undercoat to specification MSD. It took 8 lb of this to cover one canoe with 4 lb of Admiralty Grey 507 as a single finishing coat, as well as 2 lb of white lead.

Of the timber used, the deck beams, chines, chine blocks and paddle rest blocks were of a hardwood or mahogany. The side struts, bottom bow blocks, bow strut block, chine knees and gunwale bow blocks were of oak. The top and bottom strake rubbers and canvas bag fillets were of ash or elm. The gunwales were pine or spruce laminations. The bottom runner, paddle shafts and paddle bottom blocks were spruce, while the bottom members together with gratings, aft backrest blocks, seat bearers, coaming corner fillets, compass corrector, forward and aft, coaming carlin, carlin block, breakwater and deck fillets, deck beams and cockpit cover beams, were of spruce or pine. The fairlead was of beech. A multitude of brass screws and copper nails were needed. Other materials were metals in brass, iron and stainless steel. Wastage was not allowed for. The paddles were 9 feet long. These were supplied by Morey & Co. Timber Merchants of Newport on the Isle of Wight. Stainless-steel clips used to keep the coaming sections together were supplied by Messrs Robert Riley Ltd. These were to replace the original clips supplied by Combined Operations.

The erecting and folding of the Mk 2 was an easy affair. If the canoe was erected with more than one person, the centre struts on each side were raised together by first releasing the strap that kept the boat folded. The weight was taken by lifting on the gunwale with one hand and raising the first strut with the other hand, with the other struts following. The stretcher at the ends was of the lever type. There was a block fitted at the top and bottom of the boat in which there was a slot into which the bow lever fits. The lever needed to be pulled back, with the lever put into the slots, with the circular end of the strut to the top of the canoe. The lever was then pushed back and secured with a metal link. If the canoe was erected by one person, the bow and stern struts were put into position first. In order to collapse, all the side struts needed to be released first and the bow and stern levers released last.

The Mk 2 behaved very well in rough water and was extremely seaworthy. The crews were comfortable and kept dry under most conditions. The exception was in heavy rain when a lot of water could find its way to the bottom of the canoe, making the legs of the crew very wet. With the warm clothing, no great discomfort was felt from the cold. Although the canoe had buoyancy bags in the bow and stern, which kept it afloat when fully swamped, it was impossible to bail out in rough weather if waves kept washing in. As a consequence, the loaded canoe either had to be abandoned or left for later recovery. Due to its flat bottom, it could not be 'rolled' back after capsizing. It should be said that the low freeboard of the canoe gave no silhouette when viewed from the likes of a harbour launch. From the canoes, distances were deceptive: objects appeared to be much nearer than they were and, on an average dark night, other canoes could not be seen until a few yards away. The canoes were very easy to handle using either double or single paddles. One man in the rear position could maintain a good speed with control while the bowman was able to concentrate on the weaponry. With single paddles the craft could be moved noiselessly.

It is believed very few were in existence by the early 1950s. Six were known of in military circles. In 1951, a Capt. Bruce and Cpl Johnny Litherland used the Mk 2 for the well-known Devizes–Westminster canoe race, due to the fact it was the fastest then available and easy to drag on the many portages. They were the first team to complete the whole trip non-stop. They took just thirty-four hours. The nearest canoe team was six hours behind them.

The demise of the Mk 2 came when it was superseded by the Mk 2 three-man, which was the Mk 2**, also designed by Goatley.

Some Common Misconceptions

It has been written that the Mk 2 was born from the Mk 1**, yet the Mk 1** was designed after the Mk 2. Another commonly held belief was that the Saro works produced all of the Mk 2 Cockle canoes. This is simply incorrect. Of the production model, Saro produced the first few. Some of these were used for the *Frankton* Raid. Whilst it is the case that drawings, pilot models and (seventh) production model were produced from the factory on the Isle of Wight, the only indication that any Mk 2 Cockles may have been manufactured there comes from a document dated 12 September 1942. The document states that 'an order for 70 Cockle Mk 2 [canoes had] been placed recently with Saro Ltd of Cowes, one of which [had] already been delivered to the RMBPD'. This only evidences that an order was placed, not that the seventy were made on the island. Yet it seems illogical that Saro only produced the pilot models and the prototype for the production model. A safe assumption would be that Saro did produce some of these seventy canoes: they had already had a line set up for the preliminary models. It is believed that canoes which incorporated all the modifications for Hasler's party were not received until just before the departure date of the operation – 30 November 1942. Saro did produce these at least.

Anecdotal information from one Mr Robert Porter of Parkstone in Dorset gives an account of his early working years. He relates that in 1942, at the age of fourteen, he began an apprenticeship with Parkstone Joinery, a reputable firm within the woodworking industry. His story goes on to mention that, early on in his training, the normal joinery work became scarce, and the firm took on Admiralty contracts to make small naval craft. They started making 10-foot-long dinghies, then 30-foot-long ambulance landing craft, followed by lifeboats of the airborne variety. The next craft the firm built were canoes used by Commando Forces. Mr Porter remembered his part in making 'all 750 of them, each canoe had a plywood cut-water fore and aft, which was hinged to fold flat on the deck'. He personally fixed several hundred brass butt hinges on the 'cut-waters'. This sort of detail can only be remembered from experience and allows the unquestionable identification of the type of canoe produced. From this account, it is possible to confirm that Mr Porter is talking about the Mk 2 canoes, even though it is not reported by its 'mark'; the 'mark' would not have been known by the industry, let alone a boy of fourteen. The quantity mentioned supports the amounts produced for the Mk 2 as of January 1944 in rough terms, and this two-seater that Porter refers to had collapsible, brass-hinged wave breakers, front and back, a description not matching any other canoe.

It can be shown that various firms subcontracted out orders; Saro's were no different. Saro's had other work such as the assault boats to produce, and they subcontracted the Mk 2 Cockle canoe to other manufacturers. On 6 March 1943, Mr B. F. Miskin of Saro's confirmed to Goatley that they had completed arrangements to subcontract 700 Mk 2 canoes to Parkstone Joinery Co. Ltd, of 255 Bournemouth Road, Parkstone, Dorset, and to Messrs Tyler's Ltd of Griffin's Mill, Stroud, Gloucestershire. As Porter's testimony relates to Parkstone providing 750 Mk 2 Canoes, only two things can be assumed: either the two firms both produced 700 canoes each, or Tyler's could not take the part order for some reason and Parkstone Joinery took the whole order of 700.

The view of the author is that Porter's recollection is accurate and that the entire order for 700 was filled by Parkstone. Of the discrepancy in Porter's account regarding the extra fifty canoes, these seem likely to have been tasked to Parkstone from the remaining part of the original order of seventy given to Saro's. This would mean that Saro's supplied twenty-six Mk 2 canoes, including the six canoes that Hasler took on the *Frankton* Raid. With this rationale, the figure of 776 is accounted for. This would then correspond with the DNC report dated January 1944 in which it states that a total number of 776 Mk 2 canoes had been completed to specified requirements and that 100 were in hand as spares at that time. Of the extra 100, while it cannot be certain who produced these, there is a strong attributable link that Tyler's manufactured some of this type. Confirmation that 876 was the total number produced of the Mk 2 Cockle can then be accurately accounted for within Admiralty documentation.

The 'Cockle' Nomenclature

How the Second World War military canoe became so well known even today is due to two things: the publicised *Frankton* Raid and the code name given to all military canoes. Any aged military canoe seems to be viewed by the general populace as a 'Cockleshell Heroes' canoe. The only contender for this title is the Mark 2 for the simple reasons that this was the only canoe to have the 'Cockle' name on the actual drawing plans and that it was used on the *Frankton* Raid. How this naming came about is one of the least accurately reported historical pieces of information of the Second World War; the story unfolds below.

From the 9 March 1942 meeting, attended by Majors Hasler and Courtney, along with Capt. Montanaro, it was agreed to adopt the name 'Cockle'. Following this meeting, the CODC Commandant, Capt. Hussey, 'propose[d] that the word "Tadpole" be adopted to describe a canoe used for commando operations'. Quite why Hussey should latterly propose an alternative name is unknown; perhaps we can now see Hasler in a different role, as a political animal, not as honest with his feelings toward the 'Cockle' name as the other two officers. During the discussions at another meeting on 13 March 1942, whilst the proposal for the adoption of the word 'Tadpole' was accepted by the DTSD, it was at his (the DTSD's) suggestion that the name 'Cockle' should actually be used as a description for canoes used for commando operations. The DTSD then made the error by proceeding to allocate the 'names' Cockle Mk 3, 4 and 5 to three other types; the eleven-man Folboat, the twelve-man Goatley (river-crossing assault) boat and a submarine punt. This error caused some difficulty in identifying craft, which were unfortunately described as 'of the canoe type'.

Somehow the nomenclature, the code name adopted for military canoes during the Second World War, remained, despite efforts to have 'Cockle' changed to 'Tadpole', even during May 1942. The bivalve cardium had won the day against the amphibian's larva. It seems very likely that the name 'Tadpole' came from Hasler himself. His diary entry of 11 March 1942 reveals the possible source of the use of the 'Tadpole' word for canoes. When referring to explosive motorboats being dropped from an aircraft, he writes, 'Saw Lushington re. Trondheim and studied data. Tried idea of explosive tadpole on Hussey – NOT well received.' Having the Trondheim idea denied, the use of the word 'Tadpole' for the description of this device was still unused. Hasler tended to only refer to canoes as 'boats' – he thought the term 'Cockle' to be contemptuous and derisory. Maybe it was as an off-the-cuff remark to Hussey when asked for an alternative name for 'Cockle' that Hasler suggested the unused 'Tadpole'.

Again, in June 1942, a certain 'entirely necessary action' was undertaken to officially alter the nomenclature. This was an attempt to distinguish between the different types of canoe. It is written that the Cockle Mk 3 became the Mussel Mk 1, the Cockle Mk 4 became the Mussel Mk 2 and the Cockle Mk 5 became the Tadpole Mk 1. The attempt yet again failed entirely because it was then realised, finally, that some of the craft sporting the 'Cockle' code-name had nothing in common with the two-seater canoe. This issue had arisen when the eleven-man Folboat and twelve-man Goatley boat and a submarine punt had been misallocated by the DTSD. Simply put, the Marks 3, 4 and 5, which this June 1942 document was relating to, were not canoes, as evidenced above. The Mark 3 canoe, for instance, was not in existence until a Commander Luard came up with the outrigger concept in early 1943.

Combined Operations began using the 'Cockle' name with the drafting of the Staff Requirements for the two-man type canoe using the nomenclature in brackets at the end of the description. From then on, the term 'Cockle' was constantly used to describe the canoe within documentation. Publications, such as bulletins, that use this word have yet to be found; however, Hasler was openly using the 'Cockle' name by June 1942, calling the craft a 'Two Man Type Cockle'. Strictly speaking, the only plans showing the name 'Cockle' are the early drawings of the Mk 2 canoe by Goatley, prior to April 1942. Since Goatley, the designer, was not in contact with anyone but Hasler (who had disdain for the word), it is almost certain that the use of the 'Cockle' name had originated from Goatley. Despite the turmoil and political manoeuvrings, the name survived to represent our term for a very British military canoe. It would be a little churlish for any individual now, however correct, to term these craft merely as boats. Although Hasler had strong objections to the 'Cockle' name, today, it does not seem either 'contemptuous' or 'derisory', but has reached a part in our history that will always be remembered – warming the valves or 'cockles' of our hearts, you could say.

By 1 April 1943, the DNC politely informed Saro's that they were to refer to the 'Cockle' Mk 2 as 'Canoes' Mk 2. The designation, the code-word, the nomenclature, consigned to history – our very British history of the commando canoe.

CHAPTER 17

The French Affair –
'The English Have Remembered!'

'Avec une profonde gratitude et d'admiration'
'With Deepest Gratitude and Admiration'

You had to be young and foolish; it was my conscience, I knew I would be shot if caught. If I ever thought about the consequences of what I was doing I would have stopped. But I didn't. I know I was very lucky. People were afraid. You did not know who was your friend or your enemy. However, I got to know who the collaborators were.

This is a quote from Jean Mariaud,[1] who played down the role that he undertook and is not untypical of those who 'resisted'. He was just one of those French Patriots who gave assistance to two of ten Royal Marines from Southsea who ventured forth as 'Black-Faced Villains' to serve 'the dull, low, whining note of fear' into the psyche of the German military.

Throughout the world during that time, there were very many more who risked and lost their lives – these are the 'Unknown Warriors' that Winston Churchill talked about. Of the two messages that adorned the interior wall of Jean Mariaud's house in France, one is from the then Earl Mountbatten, who wrote, 'I realised it would be certain death for the gallant men who took part, unless brave men and women of the resistance movement in France came to their rescue.'

Another, showing the gratitude of the Royal Marines, says, 'We in England appreciate your deed, which was in the highest traditions of the French Resistance.' Perhaps the best of appreciation comes from Hasler and Sparks, who were the only two men who survived the raid. Both men knew that they had survived because of the actions of the French people who risked all to help them. At the time of writing, almost all of those who were a part of this one small event of history are now part of the long sleep. This chapter is dedicated to *all* the kind-hearted French people that gave succour to the Allied forces throughout France and risked their lives and those of their loved ones to help the enemies of the Third Reich. Any comment or commendation for any one individual can equally apply to all the brave souls who rendered even the smallest kindness or assistance. Most of the French people avoided the Nazi brutality; a few brave souls did not and were deported, which often meant their death by overwork or in a concentration camp. It is therefore an honour to be able, for the very first time, to highlight each of the individual efforts relating to the *Frankton* Raid, so that the part they played can be known to all, but especially to 'The English'[2], who are happy to be reminded of the sacrifice from an occupied nation.

One lasting sin is to forget what was given when so much was risked. To this end, appreciation must be extended to the families of those who have departed and to those who are left. Gratitude must also be offered on behalf of those who were assisted. When Blondie Hasler wrote to one of these helpers after the war, he did so with 'deepest gratitude and admiration', 'from the bottom of my heart, for risking so much and for helping us so generously'.

Mary Lindell, Comtesse de Milleville, a.k.a. Marie-Claire, was the author of the escape route from the village of Ruffec, an agent of MI9. Even at the age of sixty-five, she was still devoting her life to helping all the French people who endangered their lives and possessions by aiding the airmen and soldiers during the war years. One of the many visits that she made post war in search of the individuals concerned produced an interesting anecdote worth relating to begin our 'French Connection', even though this only relates to Hasler and Sparks' journey during the dates of 15 and 16 December 1942. On 7 February 1961, Mary Lindell typed a letter to Blondie Hasler from her residence at Avenue Emile Acollas in Paris. Within, she describes her efforts. Mary sent Blondie 'the dope on all the people concerned that I know of' and the detailed information of her visit to Saint-Preuil near Barbezieux[3]. Here she was 'lucky enough to catch the Mayor' in session 'so I got all the village … [who] listened coldly to the story, then they thawed and said, "so the story is true! and the *English have remembered*!"' Mary related that the villagers had not forgotten the story of Hasler and Sparks' passage but were not certain if the man in question had done what he really had said; they thought he might be just 'talkative'. The individual concerned was Monsieur Clodomir Pasqueraud, who also involved his wife Irene and his two sons, Yves and Marc. The entire story of the character of Clodomir has been related; here is a snapshot of events played out with Mary. (The reader will remember how the Pasqueraud family played their part by sheltering and feeding our two survivors with Yves and Marc doing the guiding towards the River Charente.) Blondie Hasler was informed that the two sons who had helped them on their way that next morning were subsequently arrested and died in a concentration camp in Germany; Mary highlighted that this was not in connection with his escape.

The story of Mary's visit is related in her words.

> They remember you both to the most acute detail (I have a bottle for you both of fine Champagne, distilled by Pasquereau). I did the search in style so everyone knew about it and for 'public relations', believe me the job was fine, first to the Mayor of Preuil so that the village is talking of nothing else now. 'England has remembered' … then when I got to Pasquereau's farm he was out but one of the daughters told me he was at a pub visiting so off I went to lunch where she suggested he would be.

Mary elicited the help of a traffic officer at the crossroads (near the pub) in order to catch Pasqueraud on his way back saying to the official that she 'was this and that from England'. This then made yet another village agog with interest including the pub where she lunched. Mary reports,

> Later, in comes Pasquereau, very shy, wondering what this was all about. Then I questioned him – he nearly died for joy and drowned me with questions … he was a HAPPY man, I can tell you … insisting I should go to his farm for coffee, cakes and cognac and gave me for you a bottle of his own distilling.
>
> Both he and his wife wept for joy and pride. They are now heroes of the village and I hate to think the drinks he will absorb!! 'Fancy someone from England to see him, to thank him after all these years'. They are happy people, I did not make any promises as to what they may expect. They just asked if you would ever come and see them and I said 'yes one day'.

Pasqueraud told Mary that, as they had the farm now, there was plenty of space for visitors. Mary suggested in her letter that it might be a good idea for the Royal Marines to 'lay on something and invite these people over' saying 'it would be a great affair'. Typically for her, she suggested that Blondie might put this to 'Lord Almighty' (she meant the incumbent RM Commandant General) to see what could be done. Blondie wrote in reply to Mary congratulating her on her 'brilliant detective work' and also reproaching himself: 'in doing something that I should have done myself many years ago'. Blondie also added that he was hoping to visit the CG to see what they were prepared to do. Blondie also wrote to Pasqueraud with great warmth of feeling and this is taken from his penultimate lines: 'from the bottom of my heart, for risking so much and for helping us so generously, on that far off rainy night'. Blondie ended his letter of 9 February 1961 with … 'Le poulet est bon' – 15 December 1942. This was the promised message that Hasler had sent via the BBC when they had returned to England. Hasler, a man of detail, knew well this would create a great stir in the heart of Clodomir.

In June 1961, the Corps did entertain most of these 'good French friends' in London with each being presented a small gilt Corps badge, which was similar or identical to that worn by Hasler on his mess kit. It is known that for many years this was still worn at important times. Such a time of importance came in 1966; they were proud to wear this symbol then.

In 1963, General Pigot had written to Hasler concerning the placing of a memorial plaque in St Nicholas English church in Bordeaux. On 13 January 1966, a Captain Walter of the Portsmouth Group Royal Marines wrote again to Blondie on the same subject and, recalling the 1963 letter, admitted that 'for one reason or another, an opportunity to do this has not presented itself'. It transpired that HMS *Londonderry* was visiting Bordeaux between 31 March and 4 April 1966 and that efforts were being made to arrange a ceremony between the dates in question. At that time, a wooden plaque had already been carved. It was only a question of seeing if Blondie, Sparks and the French Resistance would be available. The call went out, and Mary Lindell was contacted in this regard.

So it was that on 31 March 1966, HMS *Londonderry* left from Portland Bill at 0700 heading for Bordeaux with Lt-Col. P. R. Kay, MBE, (OC of Amphibious Training unit RM) aboard along with an RM detachment consisting of QMS Earle; Sgt Munson and Lynn; Marines Crow, Chiddzoy and Forrest; L/Cpl Cretch and Buglar Trewern; RM Cadets Cpl Christey and Hurley; and Reverend Pope. The wooden plaque was forwarded to HMS *Londonderry* along with 500 copies of the Order of Service and a message from Earl Mountbatten. The next of kin of the Royal Marines who did not return from the *Frankton* Raid had been

Upon meeting during the invitation by the Royal Marines in the UK, another bottle of homemade cognac was presented to Hasler by Clodomir.

contacted and responses for attendance were received. It was duly arranged, with a letter from Hasler to the *Daily Express*, that a 'Heron' plane was chartered for the transportation of all the relatives, Hasler, Pritchard-Gordon[4], Ladbrooke and Sparks to Bordeaux for the ceremony. The British United Airways *Daily Express* charter flight left Gatwick at 1230 on Saturday 2 April for a three-hour flight to Bordeaux along with the *Daily Express* reporters and photographer. The deal was struck that the *Daily Express* got an exclusive interview from Hasler and intended to run a feature of the event in the Monday 4 April issue. The relatives were accommodated at Hôtel Moderne, and the retired Royal Marines were billeted at Hôtel Royal Gascogne.

On Palm Sunday, 3 April 1966, at Saint-Nicolas Eglise d'Angleterre, Bordeaux, the dedication of the memorial to those who died in Operation *Frankton* took place. It was the first such memorial of its kind and took twenty-three years to bring about, but it does show that those who perished were not forgotten. David Mitchell, MBE, Consul at Bordeaux, read from Earl Mountbatten of Burma's message, which ended, 'It is really splendid that this heroic achievement is to be commemorated by a plaque in St Nicholas Church at Bordeaux the scene of their triumph and their sacrifice.' The ceremony was conducted by Bishop The Right Reverend Noel Baring Hudson, DSO, MC, DD, assisted by the Anglican chaplain, Reverend Walter Barnes, and the RN chaplain Reverend R. W. Pope. The lesson was read by Lt-Col. P. R. Kay, MBE, RM; he also unveiled the memorial. The staff carrier, people's warden and British Pro-Consul H. Bernard Shaw – a grandson of George Bernard Shaw – requested the Bishop to bless the memorial.

The following were in attendance from the families of the men lost: Mrs Clabby and Mrs Ward (sisters of Sgt Wallace), Douglas and Isabella MacKinnon, Margaret Simms and Helen MacKinnon (brother, sisters and mother of Lt MacKinnon) and eight individuals from the family of Cpl Sheard. Many French Resistance members were able to attend: Mary Lindell,

Left to right: René Flaud, Robert Pasqueraud (son of Clodomir), Mary Lindell, Blondie Hasler, Madame Rullier, Bill Sparks, Madame Pasqueraud, Jean Mariaud outside the church in 1966.

Clodomir's son and family to left.

Left to right: Flaud, Rullier (Hasler, rear), Sparks, Mariaud.

English church, Bordeaux, 1966. British Pro-Consul H. Bernard Shaw and Hasler following the staff. To the left, standing in the pew, is Douglas MacKinnon, Jack MacKinnon's brother.

Marthe Rullier, René Flaud, Armand and Amelie Dubreuille, Jean Mariaud, Alix, René and Yvonne Mandinaud, Irene Pasqueraud, and son Robert. These were supported by very many other French Nationals with the accompanying flags of reference. The ceremony ended with *La Marseillaise*.

The *Daily Express* reported,

> In the congregation sat Mary Lindell, no longer young but still aristocratically beautiful, Mme. Pasquaraud, her face apple red, weathered by the sun and Atlantic winds – workers in the French Resistance who defied the Gestapo and faced torture and death … Blondie Hasler … no-one could invade the privacy of the thoughts of this quiet spoken, modest man … for a few seconds he looked at [the plaque] intently. Then his head bowed, and the congregation stood in a brief and overpowering silence … these were the names of the young men he had trained for a daring mission involving almost certain death. This was his particular responsibility.

After the lunch that followed the ceremony, the aircraft passengers headed home; this marked a closure for many of the relatives. Mrs Clabby and Ward were able to express their feelings in a letter to Hasler afterward saying that 'they had approached the visit with mixed feelings, fearing it might prove too harrowing, but yourself [Blondie] and your brother officers concerned helped [us] so much to go through the ceremony with a greater feeling of comfort. It was a memorable occasion, a fitting tribute to all who took part in Operation *Frankton* and the fact of your being present is a memory [we] will cherish.'

Within nine months of the ceremony, Blondie had cause to be in contact with the Consul-General Frank Smitherman at Bordeaux, and it was at this time that Blondie wrote, 'My wife and I would like to provide a wreath to be placed annually on about the 7th Dec on the plaque in the English church at Bordeaux dedicated to the casualties of Operation *Frankton*.' Blondie asked if there was 'some way, preferably legal, in which we could write a sterling cheque which could be paid to someone in Bordeaux who would be kind enough to effect the buying and placing of the wreath on our behalf?' Sadly, it is known the church was sold into private ownership and the plaque now resides in the Centre Jean Moulin in Bordeaux within the *Frankton* Exhibition.

Blondie and Sparks Hide Out at Hôtel La Toque Blanche

In August 1969, Blondie wrote to Mary Lindell saying that he had not forgotten he had agreed to take his family to Ruffec sometime towards the end of the year but saying that this idea might require more discussion 'because', he says (happily), 'Bridget [his wife] is now hoping to have another baby around mid-December'. With firm arrangements being made, Mary had written to Armand Dubreuille, who was 'delighted that at long last you are coming over'. Indeed, Mary had also written to the others in order for them 'to fix things up'. And they did fix things … the deal was that on Friday 26 September Blondie and Sparks would return to the Hôtel La Toque Blanche and spend the night there. Hasler writes to Sparks, 'perhaps in the same room in which they sheltered us in 1942 (this time I would hope that we wouldn't have to sleep naked in a double bed together while they washed our clothes!)' On Saturday, they both would go to Armand Dubreuille's farm 'where we had spent 18 days. (I hope he still has that wonderful privy across the yard from our room),' added Hasler. He goes on to say that there would be a formal lunch party in Ruffec, with all the civic dignitaries and as many of our helpers as can be raised. 'They have apparently just discovered the man who actually led us across the fields in the dark to Dubreuille's farm [Monsieur Dumas].' For once, Hasler admits to not knowing 'what can be organised about getting there and back', stating that he needed to return at the latest by midday Monday; he adds 'ring me to confirm [and] I will get cracking on trying to work out how we get there and back'. Given their last jaunt to and through France, it is quite refreshing to hear such a reverse of character in the planning department!

As late as 18 September, Blondie writes to the newly appointed Commandant General of the Royal Marines, Lt-Gen. Hollings, CB, DSC, MC, to seek approval and to inform him that, 'after needling by the indefatigable Mary Lindell', there was a hope that Blondie and Sparks would make the appointment. He relates about the 'hastily contrived brass plate – which Mary dictated to me from Paris' and that he would be carrying it across under his arm. He also informs Hollings that he has suggested to the then MD and Chairman of the *Daily Express*, Johnnie Coote, that they might like to fly them to Bordeaux and back in exchange for some exclusive reporting. It should be noted that the MD had previously arranged the flight in 1966.

Meantime, there is a temporary impasse with Sparks to do with time off work and money but the *Daily Express* rally round and commit to providing the flight with the company of the same reporter who covered the 1966 event, Cyril Aynsley, and a photographer. Penned on the bottom of Coote's letter was, 'PS Don't make a habit of this!' Blondie then writes to Sparks almost pleading for him to try and make the event, even personally guaranteeing that Sparks would not incur any expenses at all. Blondie's exact words used were 'I want to ask you to change you mind, as we need you', also writing 'that there are strong reasons for hoping that you will be there with us!'

Blondie replies to Johnnie Coote's letter, thanking him, adding,

> There is no risk in my making a habit of this sort of thing, which is costing me about a week's work in addition to brass plates and the like, because I really dislike reunions and prefer to look forwards rather than backwards. It was Mary Lindell who persuaded me that it was my duty, which I suppose is true, but I do hope that this is going to be positively my final participation in World War II.

Blondie's frustration with Sparks' apparent implacability was clearly surfacing.

All was not lost, for on 27 September 1969, the duly inscribed brass plaque was presented to the Mayor of Ruffec by Blondie. Mary's words had been faithfully reproduced and listed Hasler and Sparks' *'rescapes du Commando sur Bordeaux en 1942 en temoignage de leur profonde gratitude a'* and goes on to list[5] Mary Lindell, OBE, MI9 ('Marie-Claire'); Armand Dubreuille; Fernand Dumas; René Flaud; Jean Mariaud; Maurice de Milleville (Mary's son); Alix Mandinaud; Yvonne Mandinaud; Clodomir Pasqueraud and Marthe Rullier. It

The presentation of the plaque at Ruffec. Left to right: Flaud (dark glasses), Mayor Ruffec, -?-, Amelie Dubreuille, Alix Mandinaud, René Mandinaud, Yvonne Mandinaud, Hasler, Armand Dubreuille, Mary Lindell.

was acknowledged at the time that Fernand Dumas' name had not appeared on any previous record due to the fact that he had only been found just before the event at Ruffec. It is uncertain why Mary Lindell left René Mandinaud's name from the plague; it is assumed that she believed he had not played a great part in the matter; it is not believed it was an error. Hasler had seen René at the Bistro, and assumed he was married to Alix; he is therefore given credit within.

The hotel Hasler and Sparks walked into in 1942 had changed, and it was one of note featuring in the Michelin Guide. Sparks remarked, 'I would never have known it.' Awaiting them inside were the two sisters Alix and Yvonne Mandinaud, who were recognised instantly. Long had they awaited this momentous occasion. The 1969 meeting at the Bistro was a joyous reunion.

The pair of returning escapees along with Mary Lindell and the newspaper men were driven by Hasler in the hired car to the meeting at the Dubreuille's Farm, and this turned out to be the highlight of the visit.

The jovial Sparks cast his humour over the gathering by putting on and blowing up his twenty-seven-year-old Reliant[6] life-jacket that Armand had preserved since 1942, which Armand's eldest son, Michel[7], (who was a one-year-old baby in 1942) had only recently used for waterskiing! The old dustbin lid that was set up as a signal for warning in the yard during their stay in 1942 was still there. The pride and happiness of Armand and Amelie was clearly evident, and much fun was had by Sparks. In an interview at another time, Sparks said of Armand, 'I owe so much to that farmer.'[8] That whole afternoon was then spent in at the restaurant 'Moulin Enchante' in Condac, where all the Resistance workers and the associated gathering dined with brief speeches by both hosts and guests. All of Ruffec knew of the

27 September 1969. A moment of joy at the Dubreuille farm. Left to right: Monique (daughter), Pierre Vincent, Armand, Remy (son), Amelie's mother, Amelie, Michel (first-born son), Claudette (married to Michel), Blondie Hasler.

The family Dubreuille. All eyes being amused by Sparks off camera.

event, and when Mary Lindell went arm in arm between Hasler and Sparks down the middle of the road for the photographers, many stopped to watch the spectacle from every vantage point. The journey home returned Hasler and co. to Gatwick by 1630 on Sunday. Hasler ensured that Royal Marine Corps badges, which had been given to all those individuals in 1961, were also sent to René Mandinaud and Fernand Dumas at the same time as he sent Mary Lindell her replacement; she had lost hers! Hasler seemed to admit he was wrong in disliking reunions, as he thanked Mary 'for stirring me up to do this, and for organising it so well'.

Following the event at Ruffec, Blondie wrote to thank John Coote for 'his kindness in helping our presentation and reunion with the French Resistance at Ruffec'. It was evident that the French included the *Daily Express* staff in the copious 'hospitality that was being thrown around'. In real terms, the copy was not only relegated to page three but was overwhelmed by the 'Model⁹, 19, mauled by Tiger' article. With the wine flowing, a merry time must have been had by the reporter who omitted the fact that they were Royal Marines. An added bonus was that the photographer, Victor Blackman, put some of the photographs taken at the reunion in his article in the *Amateur Photographer* later that year.

'What I did in 1942 came naturally'

No matter how small the assistance rendered by the many in France the *raison d'être* can be attributed by partly quoting from a letter written by one of the Resistance members, Fernand Dumas, who, following the 1969 ceremony at the English church, replied thanking Hasler, adding, 'Please believe that what I did in 1942 came naturally.'

It was chance that two of these men survived, but it was mostly due to the French people at that time. It is difficult to fully appreciate the environment that existed in which the

French people decided to assist the escaping canoeists. It has been said, and for emphasis it is repeated, 'People were afraid. You did not know who was your friend or your enemy.'

Here then are the names of all those with good hearts who befriended, fed, sheltered, entertained, smiled, laughed, or just simply allowed them to go on their way without reporting the fact. They all felt warmth in their hearts for complete strangers for no other reason than love for fellow man.

The Amazing and Courageous French Folk

Until the research for this work, the names and photographs of individuals had almost been lost. For the very first time and forever more their images remain. In order of date of contact, this covers those who assisted six marines during their escape through France.

Monsieur Yves Ardouin. The French fisherman who was the first to have met and have a conversation with the Commando canoeists at the Pte. Aux Oiseaux and guided canoes *Catfish* and *Crayfish* to a safer lying-up place (LUP) than was originally chosen by Hasler on 8 December 1942. Without this contribution, the team may have been spotted. He shared bread and wine with them on his second visit.

Madame Jeanne Baudray. As a young nineteen-year-old, she helped to maintain secrecy in the village of Saint-Vivien-de-Médoc, Pte Aux Oiseaux, after the initial meeting with the four canoeists. She and others offered the men food and company during daylight hours at the LUP on 8 December. Born in Saint-Vivien-de-Médoc, Jeanne Baudray in later life became Mayor of Saint-Vivien-de-Médoc and holds the French 'Legion d'Honneur'.

Monsieur Alibert Decombes discovered the crews of *Catfish* and *Crayfish* on the bank of the Gironde at lying-up place No. 2 on 10 December. Alibert was the tenant farmer at La Présidente. He was friendly and sincere by nature and Hasler immediately took to him.

Above left: Yves Ardouin. Taken in the 1960s by the first Royal Marines to undertake the paddle following the route of Operation *Frankton*.

Above right: Jeanne Baudray.

Alibert invited, unsuccessfully, all four canoeists to his farmhouse. Alibert's last words of reassurance to Hasler in 1942 were 'I will say nothing, Bonne chance, monsieur!' He kept his word and never mentioned his encounter until after the war. Hasler managed to visit and met his son Robert; Alibert died in 1949.

Monsieur Olivier Bernard as a boy had stumbled upon Laver and Mills hiding in a tool shed on the morning of 12 December 1942. He was asked for food and had then walked to the village in order to provide the same. He enabled food to be brought to the marines and kept quiet about the matter.

Monsieur Pierre Gacis, who brought food to Laver and Mills on 12 December near Fours. Pierre was a clever man who kept this secret even from his wife.

Warrant Officer Georges Rieupeyrout tried his best to warn Laver and Mills by sending someone to the alleged hiding place on 14 December at Montilieu. He hid Laver's escape map and did his best to accommodate them by feeding them and allowing them to wash. If Rieupeyrout had been able, he would not have arrested the marines but assisted in their escape.

Monsieur Gaujean was trusted by Rieupeyrout as a friend enough to be sent to warn the marines that they had been betrayed and to get away from their hideout. He was unsuccessful but attempted to assist in this regard.

Mademoiselle Anne-Marie Bernadet, as a young girl, met MacKinnon on 13 December whilst she was bringing the farm's cows back for the evening milking. She understood that he needed help and obliged by taking him to the family farm near Saint-Médard-d'Eyrans. He was welcomed by all at the farm, fed, had his knee treated, then given shelter in the barn for the night. It is believed her married name is Farre.

Monsieur Edouard Pariente was the twenty-nine-year-old stonemason who had first contact with Marine Conway in the main street of Baigneaux village. He could not accommodate the marine in his house as it was so small; he was married with two children. He spent time trying to secure someone who could understand English and could accommodate and duly asked …

Monsieur Robert Pouget, who was a neighbour and lived with his wife Cecile at 'Chez Loulou'. They sheltered and fed both marines on the evening and night of 15 December. Robert then arranged for the marines to be taken elsewhere.

Monsieur Cheyreau couriered the two marines via roads and a disused railway track to the shelter.

Madame and Monsieur Louise and Louis Jaubert were sheep farmers near the village of Cessac. MacKinnon's problem knee was tended to and both marines were fed and sheltered for three evenings. Louis even tried to help them make contact with the Resistance.

Madame Malichier instructed a youth named **Cadillon** to take Hasler and Sparks to a known place of shelter.

Monsieur Clodomir Pasqueraud and his wife **Madame Irene Pasqueraud** supplied that place of shelter to Hasler and Sparks. In all, they had five children at that time, but they still made room and fed the two marines well. Clodomir also instructed his two sons …

Yves and **Marc Pasqueraud**, to take Hasler and Sparks towards the River Charente; these two boys were deported to Germany and were not to be heard of again. The deportation was not in connection with their actions assisting Hasler and Sparks.

Monsieur Edouard Pariente, 2001.

Above left: Louis and Louise Jaubert.

Above right: Louis Jaubert.

Yves and Marc Pasqueraud, behind, and Robert Pasqueraud as a boy, front left.

Above left: Robert Pasqueraud in 1966.

Above right: Clodomir Pasqueraud and wife *c.* 1950.

Monsieur André Latouche had observed Hasler and Sparks along the road. He welcomed them, fed and sheltered them in a barn for the night. He was subsequently arrested.

Messieurs Lucien Gody, Maurice Rousseau and René Rousseau were three unrelated individuals from Beaunac who fell foul of the occupying forces and were arrested. **Lucien Gody** had warned Hasler and Sparks to leave the area immediately, thus saving the marines' lives. These three Frenchmen were deported. Gody is known to have died in Germany; the others were never heard of again. These three names are recorded on the 2011 Pointe de Grave memorial.

Mademoiselle Alix Mandinaud was the first contact when Hasler and Sparks entered the restaurant La Toque Blanche in Ruffec on 18 December 1942. As the waitress at that time, she served them at the table and with impeccable confidentiality acted on their efforts to illicit assistance. Upon discussions with others, she then set about to close the restaurant and ushered Hasler and Sparks upstairs to hide them in a room. She tended to them and washed their very filthy clothes, fed and cared for them.

Monsieur René Mandinaud's part in the affair is not fully understood, and his name was left out on the commemoration plague by Mary Lindell, but along with ...

Mademoiselle Yvonne Mandinaud, they were part of the trio with Alix. Yvonne was the owner of the Bistro[10]. History does not fully record Yvonne and René's part in the event, but it is without doubt that all these siblings shared in the decision making and efforts to ensure the safe conduct of Hasler and Sparks, who spent one night in the hotel room before being couriered across the Demarcation Line.

Monsieur Jean Mariaud was a man of the revenue, and it was he who had been contacted by, probably, René Mandinaud. He used a friend of his to establish the identity of Hasler and Sparks. He informed Mme Rullier at the Hôtel de France and organised the transfer of Hasler and Sparks to Farm 'B' the next morning.

Monsieur Paillet was a friend of Jean, and a retired professor of English, who was able to confirm after the interview in the room at the hotel without doubt that the fellows were the real thing.

Lucien Gody.

Mandinaud sisters pictured during the first visit by four probationary second lientenants in August 1960.

Above left: Alix.

Above right: Yvonne.

Jean Mariaud.

Monsieur René Flaud was Jean Mariaud's brother-in-law and a baker in Ruffec. He was also cousin to Armand Dubreuille.[11] He was a quiet man but one of extreme courage. He used his baker's van to transport Hasler and Sparks to a spot nearer the Demarcation Line. In 1960, when asked by a couple of probationary Second Lieutenant Royal Marines whether he was frightened of being caught when he conveyed the marines to Armand Dubreuille's farm, he casually remarked that it was 'routine to him'.

Monsieur Fernand Dumas was from Champagne-Mouton; he was picked up en route to the Demarcation Line by René Flaud. Fernand took them across the line to Armand's Farm.

Monsieur Armand Dubreuille and his wife **Madame Amelie Dubreuille** (née Deloume) owned Marvaud Farm near Saint-Coutant. Born in 1916 and 1919 respectively. They had helped around forty escaping airman and soldiers during the war; American, Canadian, British and Indian. Armand Dubreuille received the Legion d'Honneur after the war. They were two quite amazing people who were responsible for sheltering, feeding and trying to entertain Hasler and Sparks for an incredible eighteen days before they were collected by …

Maurice de Milleville, who couriered Hasler and Sparks from Farm 'B' and through to Lyon. Maurice was the eldest son of the Comte and Comtesse de Milleville. He was a French citizen.

Mary Lindell, OBE, by marriage, was Comtesse de Milleville; her nationality was British. She officially started to work for MI9 in 1942; agent 45660. The escape route that bears her name, 'Marie-Claire', was part of the route used by Hasler and Sparks. Her three children, Maurice, Oky and Barbe,[12] also assisted in the work she was involved with. She had the most contact with Hasler and Sparks during their transition.

Above left: René Flaud.

Above right: The only known image of Fernand Dumas.

Flaud with the vehicle used to transport Hasler and Sparks.

Above left: Armand Dubreuille.

Above right: Amelie Dubreuille.

Above left: Marthe Rullier.

Above right: Monsieur and Madame François Rouillon after the war.

Madame Marthe Rullier represented the Marie-Claire line since 1940 and introduced Mary Lindell to the proprietors of Hôtel de France, which was the first HQ of the Marie-Claire escape organisation in Ruffec.

Monsieur and Madame François Rouillon were the owners of the Hôtel de France and were members of the Resistance from 1940–44. Both were deported in May 1944; François returned but his wife died at Ravensbrück Concentration Camp.

Other French people who helped the escapees were those who gave civilian clothes to Hasler and Sparks at Haut Brignac and to MacKinnon and Conway around Macau.

The kindness that was extended to these Royal Marines is easily evidenced, and this is done here for the first time by allowing all to glimpse the moment that these words were written from a kitchen table on a farm in the countryside near Frontenac on 13 March 1945 by a caring French couple. Sometime in the spring of 1945, a letter arrived for James MacKinnon from Cessac. This is the letter that Louis and Louise Jaubert wrote:

> Dear Sir, You will be surprised to receive this letter from France but I write to receive news of your son J. W. Mackinnon. He came here on an expedition to Bordeaux and from there he went on foot. He found himself passing through our region and we were able to give him refuge and hide him for three days and nights in company with another comrade. His comrade was also English (from Jersey[13]). I shall be happy to know if you have had any good news of your son and that he managed to make his journey safely. He promised that he would write to us and that he would come and visit us. Of course we were not able to give him our address as that would have been too dangerous, at that moment it was the 20th December 1942[14]. We have not been able to write sooner as France was occupied by the Germans. I hope that you will be able to give us some news as we have such happy memories of your boy and his friend.

When the film *Cockleshell Heroes* was shown in Bordeaux, Jaubert was rightfully honoured but Edouard Pariente was overlooked. It was not until September 1999 when interest in Operation *Frankton* resurfaced that Edouard found out about events after he had passed Conway on. Edouard never knew what had happened to Conway and had never known about MacKinnon at all.

Whilst this accolade, remembrance and story come too late for almost all those who offered help, it will always remain in the history books for their families and show that indeed the English still remember!

The final words on the matter of the efforts made by those who risked everything are respectfully given over to Blondie Hasler, as he said of them all, 'It is they who are the heroes of nearly all escapes.'

CHAPTER 18

The Cockleshell Heroes Legacy

Over millennia, various individuals have been recorded mainly through their deeds – both good and bad. They have gained their place in history and in turn within the continuing memory of mankind with those related episodes. It would seem that the further one goes back in time, the less known they are to the masses. Only through study or curiosity are the finite details realised. How many know of Sun Tzu[1], Hannibal[2], Xerxes I[3], let alone great scribes and scholars of pre- and ancient history? The 'ordinary' soldier is often forgotten and the interest in the history of the Second World War, which will no doubt wax and wane, cannot be relied upon to save the memory of the efforts of the ordinary soldier. Future generations cannot be expected to remember. Tradition, interest or curriculum will always be tools used with which to focus on these specifics.

Known for his works of modern military history and covert operations, Professor M. R. D. Foot, himself a wartime Intelligence officer attached to Combined Operations, made the comment on the *Frankton* Raid in the context of thousands of men giving up their lives each day, 'against that, what was the loss of another eight men?'

Whilst that may have validity, the important and bigger picture is that, through this particular action being highlighted, it has made it more prominent in 'history'. The death of a soldier, even one who was not formally part of a military organisation, is an event that no one wishes for but will always be an inevitable part of conflict; but there has to be a worth attributed to this sacrifice. In truth, all that ultimately remains is a memory; how long that memory of the effort or person lasts is normally only determined by the relatives through the generations.

It was the suggestion by the military and the decision by the government of the day to allow the story of those men of 'Cockleshell Heroes' fame to be broadcast to the populace. The making and releasing of a film[4], depicting the same operation, secured the interest and place of one heroic action by our special forces during the Second World War in cognitive history. This message was reinforced by words written long before the release of military documents under the then fifty-year rule.[5] It is these things that originally cemented this one story in the memory of the masses. Today, a revival of interest in the Second World War gives an opportunity to ensure that Operation *Frankton* is heralded again; this time much more can be told.

Given the effort and casualties versus the small cost in damage to the German war machine, an analysis of the operation itself could view it as amateurishness redeemed only by courage and the spirit of improvisation. This, however, is an unbalanced viewpoint given from the cosy world we live in today and does not provide the fullest of pictures. The overview is one of a nation mightily heartened at a bleak time; indeed, a communiqué from the Naval Attaché in Stockholm reported[6] that his Vichy colleague had stressed the great effect that raids such as these had on French morale. It was these 'little actions'[7] that served the greater purpose, as has already been explained. So it is that the memory of the daring exploits of a

Bill in canoe.

few has helped to secure the memory of many. If men or women are to lose their lives and are to be remembered, does it really matter the method by which this happens?

The 'jolly'[8] undertaken by ten Royal Marine 'volunteers for hazardous service' during 1942 has served to galvanize and focus the minds of very many different people of differing ages; what a legacy these few have provided for the many during peacetime. For the eight Royal Marines that did not return, the value of their young lives remains unforgotten. If they only could have known how many people have benefitted from their efforts. As long as attention is focused on the remembrance, in any form, future generations should be able to ensure that this kind of worldwide conflict is not repeated, and therefore the sacrifice made was a worthwhile one.

During three weeks in the August of 1960, four probationary second lieutenants decided to undertake the same route paddled during Operation *Frankton* as part of their initiative training. They named the jolly 'Exercise *Formidable*'. Their trip was unsupported, apart from them being loaned two canoes from the stores; in those days, there was no HSE[9] to worry about. They travelled from Southampton to Royan in France and began their trip in the canoes with a paddle across the mouth of the estuary to begin the route paddled by the 1942 Operation *Frankton*. By a stroke of luck an attractive, long-legged girl happened to be walking along the adjacent dyke as the four were trying to find the first LUP[10] of the 1942 raid. A conversation was made with the mademoiselle, who duly learnt the reason why these French-speaking Englishmen were at Pte Aux Oiseaux. This meeting proved fortuitous, as the mademoiselle requested they await her return. She returned with an older man, the very individual that Hasler and co. had met … the fisherman Monsieur Yves Ardouin, the first Frenchman to have contact with the commandos. This fisherman was her father! The ensuing celebration was one reserved for 'friends of Hasler'. The four eventually continued with their journey[11], and once they had reached Bordeaux, due to circumstances, only two continued on the journey to follow Hasler and Sparks' escape route. These two young probationary officers visited the Bistro and through other contacts met Flaud and viewed and photographed him and the very van used for the transport of Hasler and Sparks. It was Flaud who then telephoned the Mandinaud sisters and told them two 'commandos' were on their way to visit them. The Mandinaud sisters, visibly excited, duly showered two young second lieutenants with much affection such was their joy in believing Hasler and Sparks had returned! Although disappointed that Hasler and Sparks had not actually returned, they still happily fed and watered the young men. The young officers also met the wife of Monsieur Gody – one of the individuals who had warned Hasler to leave the hiding place.

These four young men continued in their careers within the Royal Marines. This team recorded for posterity certain aspects of the Cockleshell Heroes raid and escape. For their sterling work and effort, even though the value of it has not been recognised until now, these individuals are named. They are Col. Jake Hensman, OBE, DL; Lt-Col. Peter Cameron, MC; Captain Michael Francis Hodder and Lt Brian Mollan. These individuals were the very first to undertake this kind of effort, and their journey has yielded some invaluable information of great detail which would have been lost with the effluxion of time.

Almost every year, both civilian and military teams as well as individuals test their mettle in France on both the paddle or the walk along the escape route to a lesser or greater degree. This kind of effort is part of the bigger picture that Operation *Frankton* has left for the generations. All ten men of the *Frankton* Raid left a legacy for the future. It has already been said that 'they were not anxious to die – just anxious to matter'. Unfortunately, the intent to succeed in the latter resulted in the premature demise of the eight, and not by normal peril for six of them. All ten men have been held in high esteem over the decades thus far. Through their actions, they continue to encourage, stimulate, and urge us all to strive, to push ourselves further – to accomplish. It *has* encouraged people to undertake a journey or push themselves harder than they thought they could. This is about excelling – being apart from the ordinary. To stand alone when the masses pick you out as something different, to be misunderstood but to carry yourself regardless, and then to succeed. So from a sad story a happier one has emerged that gives a reason to celebrate what these few individuals managed to accomplish. The term the 'Cockleshell Heroes' is known all over the world, and their actions continue to astonish those not familiar with this particular effort undertaken during the Second World War.

It has inspired many individuals even in recent years.

In early 2010, a Commendation from the Commandant General of the Royal Marines, Major General Andy Salmon,[12] CMG, OBE, was presented to François Boisnier, a former French army officer of the elite Régiment Parachutiste. Major General Andy Salmon commented,

> In 1997 François set up the Franco-British support network '*Frankton* Souvenir', to re-kindle awareness of the 'Cockleshell Heroes' operation, and enlisted the support of a French military Old Comrades Association … The 60th anniversary also saw the realisation of another of his aspirations: the *Frankton* Trail, which was opened by the one living survivor, Bill Sparks. This 100-mile trail traces the route taken by the two survivors as they made their way through German-occupied France to their agent RV. He has ensured that every site in France associated with the operation is marked with a plaque and an explanatory panel in French and English, with maps and photographs, explaining the significance of the location … He has provided advice and support to many British parties, including Royal Marines cadets who have undertaken the challenging canoe paddle up the Gironde river to Bordeaux … He has ensured that the bravery and sacrifice of the Royal Marines 'Cockleshell Heroes' is perpetuated as an inspiring example for future generations.

In December 2000, when plans for the *Frankton* Trail were underway, Bill Sparks told *The Times* of London, 'Britain forgets things too quickly, the French are better at remembering. The French people looked after us very well then, and they are looking after us very well now.' While true, Bill Sparks did not live to hear of other developments led by another good-hearted individual.

In the summer of 2008, after Major Malcolm Cavan, OBE, had attended a number of remembrances over a few years, he took mental note that not a single British Memorial existed in the public domain that remembered all ten Cockleshell Heroes. The recognition of the role and the sacrifices made by French people was another glaring omission of outstanding proportions. Recognition was also required for the important and crucial role Lt-Cdr Dickie Raikes and the crew of the *Tuna* played. The existing French concrete memorial on the quay in Bordeaux had been taken away sometime after 2002, and all that remained was a plaque set in the deck close to Hanger 14. Malcolm put his thoughts to François Boisnier, who supported the idea that a British memorial tribute to those concerned would be very well

Hasler and Sparks stand solemnly during the 1983 Poole unveiling.

Poole SBS memorial unveiling in 1983.

This page and next: Artist's impression of the March 2011 memorial at Pointe de Grave in France.

received. The idea was that the memorial would be sited in Aquitaine at a suitable place that the French might decide upon.

Following on from meetings beginning in July 2008, the idea grew, and the project was presented to the RM Corps, the SBSA, and the Submariners Association; the project was agreed and adopted. Patrons were forthcoming, and although it proved difficult going, a major turning point came when the Commandant of the Royal Marines personally backed the project and became the lead for others to follow. The new memorial erected (spring 2011) at La Pointe de Grave with the seascape background of Le Verdon-sur-Mer acknowledges and remembers those who gave as much as they could. It is this narrative and event that has brought many people together, both British and French. Of the French peoples, they were non-combatants, the individuals who did not have to risk their lives to lend assistance, but did so regardless. The phrase 'lest we forget' is often used; this narrative truly lends meaning to that phrase and offers this lasting 'Final Witness'.

Appendix

Below is a small section of the *Frankton* Docket.

From Inter-services Topographical dept. dated 4 October 1942
Special Coast Report on the River Gironde with reference to Small Boat Landings

General

Outside the entrance of the river, which lies between Royan on the north side and Pointe de Grave on the south, the coasts of the estuary are low and sandy, and backed by sand dunes. The beaches are sandy with occasional short stretches of rock.

In the river itself the banks, and the country close behind them, are generally low and bordered by mud and sand, except on the east bank as far as Ortagne where the ground rises steeply to an undulating plateau from 60–160ft in height. On the upper stretches of the river wooded country falls more steeply to the water, particularly on the east bank above Blaye. Between Pauillac and the point where the Gironde divides into the Dordogne and the Garonne there is a series of long narrow islands, which are wooded and in peace time nearly deserted. Bordeaux, on the Garonne, lies about 52 miles by the river from Pointe de Grave.

Coast
East bank

From Royan, where there is a small tidal harbour used mainly by the local pilot boats, the coast trends south-south-east to Blaye, a distance of about 35 miles. As far as Mechers, 5¼ miles from Royan, the coast is unbroken by any inlets and is ordered by a strip of sand, which is 550 yards wide at low water in the bays of Royan and St. Georges-de-Didonne, but merges into a steep -to coastline fronting the small fishing village of Mechers.

Both St. Georges-de-Didonne and Mechers have no harbour facilities but, in common with other small fishing villages on the Gironde, have small ramps and jetties to accommodate local fishing craft.

Between Royan and St. Georges the coast is banked by extensive public gardens. Several roads run between these two places and from St. Georges to Mechers a road runs about 650 yards inland from the coast, and a stretch of undulating ground lies between them. Pointe de Sussac, 1½ miles up river from St. Georges, is 75 feet high, and about half a mile north-east of the point there is a summit of 160 feet. Landing of boats can be effected anywhere, but there is no concealment available for boats along the shore. there is cover on land along pine trees over a considerable area known as Foret de Sussac, between St. Georges and Mechers. At Mechers are the celebrated caves, some of which are near the foot of the cliffs, while the entrance of others are higher up. Up river from Mechers the coastal plateau continues, but it is now bordered by a strip of drying mud which reaches a width of 1,300 yards off the village of mortagne, narrows to 200 yds at Portes de Vitrezay, and finally merges into a steep to river bank at Blaye. Since progress over this mud will be very laborious, and since in places it may be impassable on foot, a low water landing is inadvisable. The river bank is broken by numerous small creeks into which a small boat can proceed at high water. The low bank of the river is covered with reeds, the height of which is not known with certainty but is reported to be about 2 to 3 feet.

Most of these creeks have one or two small hoses or fisherman's huts on their banks and the coast road is about a mile inland between Mortagne and Port Maubert, but closer elsewhere.

Apart from the small fishing communities the countryside is sparsely inhabited and poor. The most remote creeks lie one to the north-west and two to the south-east of Mortagne, but these creeks face the widest part of the drying mud flats and can only be approached or left at high water.

Between Portes de Vitrezay, another fishing village which lies 23 miles from Royan, and Blaye, the bank is no longer constantly broken by small creeks, but Portes de Calonge, Porte Neuve and Chenal Freneau afford appreciable breaks easily entered, as over this stretch the strip of drying mud is very narrow.

From Mortagne upstream to Blaye the land backing the shore is low and flat. A great part of this low-lying ground is reclaimed marshland over which canalised streams run with locks near their junction with the Gironde. This reclaimed area is also intersected by many drainage ditches.

At Blaye, a small riverside town, the land rises and slopes fairly steeply down to the river. The land is wooded, but the bank of the river is exposed and unbroken to the entrance of the Dordogne.

Coast
West bank

Between Pointe de Grave and Pointe de la Chambrette the coast is protected by a sea wall. South-east of Pointe de la Chambrette and the port of Le Verdon as far as Feu de Richard, a distance of 9 miles, the coast is very low and backed by flat marshy fields intersected with creeks and drainage channels. the road, following the higher land, lies well back – in places 2 miles – from the bank and the intervening fields are desolate and seldom frequented. They are liable to inundation in winter. A belt of reeds about 3ft high and 5 yards wide borders the bank and these might afford cover, particularly if cut down and laid over boats. The coast is broken by several creeks with no fishing villages. The principal creek is Chanal de Talais leading to the village of that name on the main road from Le Verdon to Bordeaux just under 1½ miles inland. Extensive drying mud flats, as much as three quarters of a mile wide at low water springs, border the coast and make a high water approach preferable, if not essential. South of Feu de Richard the land rises more quickly and the stretch of flat marsh fields is narrower. Villages lie at short intervals along the road which follows the higher land and is good. The belt of reeds continues and the drying mud flats decrease to 500 yards in width at Feu de Richard and then become narrower still until at Pauillac they are less than 100 yards wide. Many creeks also break this stretch of coast, but in the vicinity of Pauillac-Trompeloup there are the large oil installations of the port and the houses and roads serving them. It is reported that at St. Estephe the reed beds are considerably wider and would afford concealment. Some of Pauillac the coast is steep to but there is still a fringe of reeds at least as far as Lamaroque. This coast is not broken by any appreciable creeks. South of Lamaroque the coast is steeper generally and more thickly populated. Close north of Bordeaux on the left bank of the Garonne there are extensive stretches of marshy fields intersected by drainage channels and lines of trees. this land is under water in winter.

The islands

Between Pauillac and the entrance to the Garonne there is a chain of long, narrow islands. The most northerly islands are Ile de Patiras and Ile St. Louis, which are connected by drying mud flats. Ile de Patrras has few dwellings and a lighthouse. Close south-west of Ile de Patiras is an unnamed island reported to have been completely uninhabited, and the remainder of the islands had only one or two houses used for camping visits in the summer. Photographs provide evidence of modern construction on Ile du Grand Fagnard, south-south-east of Ile de Patiras, and the ships lying close alongside the island give indication the steep-to nature of the shore. Landing at any state of the tide is possible on all the islands except on the north side of Ile de Patiras where the drying mud flats make a high water landing essential. The shores of the islands are reported to be closely wooded and have high grass and reeds affording excellent cover. The larger islands have areas of cultivated and pasture land inside the border line of trees. Although separately named many of the islands are connected by mud flats which only flood under exceptional conditions of weather and tide. The northern tip of Ile Verte is reported to be typical of all the islands.

Note on Boat Landings

While landing is possible at any state of the tide in the Gironde, the mud flats may well prove a very treacherous obstacle and the absence of fishing villages between Le Verdon and Feu de Richard may well be an indication of the impracticability of the flats at low water.

Abbreviations

AS	Able Seaman
BdS	HQ Commander of Security Police in France based in Paris
CCO	Chief of Combined Operations
Ch	Chatham
CIS	Counter Intelligence Section, Paris
CMSM	Combined Military Services Museum (Essex)
CPO	Chief Petty Officer
Dev	Devonport
DNI	Director of Naval Intelligence
DSEA	Davis Submerged Escape Apparatus
DXSR	Director of Experimental Scientific Research
ERA	Engine Room Artificer
FOIC	Flag Officer, Western France; Vice-Admiral Bachmann
LS	Leading Seaman
MFU	mobile flotation unit
MT	motor transport
NOIC	naval officer in charge subordinant to SNOIS
Po	Portsmouth
RMA Eastney	Royal Marines Archives Eastney
RMSA	The Royal Marines Small Arms School, west of Gosport
RNP	Rassemblement National Populaire
RORC	Royal Ocean Racing Club, St James Place, London
(S)3	Submarine 3rd Flotilla
SBS	Special Boat Service/Section
SD	Special Detachment (Sicherheitsdienst). The security service; child of the Gestapo.
SNOIS	Senior Naval Officer Inshore Squadron (
SOG	Special Operations Group, Ceylon
SSRF	Small-scale raiding force
TODT	The Organisation Todt (OT) was a Third Reich civil and military engineering group in Germany eponymously named after its founder, Fritz Todt, from 1942 until the end of the war, when Albert Speer succeeded Todt in office and the Organisation Todt was absorbed into the (renamed and expanded) Ministry for Armaments and War Production (Reichsministerium für Rüstung und Kriegsproduktion). Approximately 1.4 million labourers were in the service of the organisation. Overall, 1 per cent were Germans rejected from military service and 1.5 per cent were concentration camp prisoners; the rest were prisoners of war and compulsory labourers from occupied countries. All were effectively treated as slaves and existed in the complete and arbitrary service of a ruthless totalitarian state. Many did not survive the work or the war.
WCIT	War Crimes Investigation Team
WFSt	Armed Forces Operational Staff, a part of the Führer's HQ dep.

Notes

Author's Note

1. Lieutenant Commander Richard Prendergast Raikes, DSO, RN.
2. Believed to have been Professor D. M. Newitt of 'The Frythe', SOE fame.
3. Foreword of Hasler's unpublished draft manuscript of 'Experimenting with Boats' of Jan 1967.

Introduction

1. Or those accounts that will follow, which will rely on subsequent accounts.
2. Embarked early morning of 30 November, disembarked evening of 7 December.
3. These words are carved into the Purbeck stone block of the publicly subscribed memorial which stands in the SBS HQ at Poole, Dorset.
4. Führer Order Concerning Handling of Commandos, 18 October 1942.
5. COHQ knew of the Hitler Order.
6. Psychiatrist and historian Anthony Storr wrote of Churchill.
7. Britain's Channel Islands were occupied.
8. Mary Lindell's letter to Hasler of 7 February 1961 following her efforts to find M. Clodomir Pasqueraud and family, who fed and sheltered Hasler and Sparks. This exclamation came from the assembled villagers.

1 The *Frankton* Raid

Chapter 1   Of Mice and Men

1. Taken from Robert Burns' poem, 'To a Mouse', in the second-to-last stanza: 'The best laid schemes o'mice and men … Gang aft agley.'
2. DEFE 2/217&218;202/310, ALSO CAB FILES.
3. Without which the port would have quickly become unusable for oceangoing ships due to silting.
4. There was another summary of the outline plan dated 29 October 1942, which shows that special training had commenced on 20 October and included boat practice, handling of Limpets, rehearsal from submarine, full-scale rehearsal on British estuary (if possible), training for escape.
5. The actual Mk 2 canoe could be rigged for a goose-winged sail as a mast stop was provided. There is no evidence to support any such use of assisted travel on the raid itself.
6. Mountbatten said this of the *Frankton* Raid. Source: PRO records.
7. Before decimalisation, there were 20 shillings to a pound and 12 pence to a shilling.
8. The C-in-C, Plymouth, at the time taken from CO 1940–1942.
9. The C-in-C, Plymouth, at the time taken from CO 1940–1942.
10. Commando Order No. 003830/42 g. Kdos. OKW/WFSt.
11. Rifle, wings and superimposed anchor in red thread on a black background.
12. Führer Order Concerning Handling of Commandos, 18 October 1942. The Führer No. 003830/42 g. Kdos. OKW/WFSt. Führer HQ, 18 Oct. 1942, 12 copies, 12th copy.

13. The first victims were seven officers of Op. *Musketoon* on 23 October 1942. In November 1942, British survivors of Op. *Freshman* were executed; then the first executions from Op. *Frankton* occurred from December 1942. Further executions were carried out through the remainder of the war.
14. Deposition from Graf von Seyssel D'Aix 6 June 1945 to American Military HQ, CIC Detachment, Augsberg.
15. Special Detachment (*Sicherheitsdienst*). The security service.
16. From a letter to Philip Zieglar written by Arther Marshall.
17. Micheal Harrison, *Mulberry, The Return in Triumph* (London, 1965), p. 146.
18. Letter to Philip Zieglar from Hasler dated 8 February 1982.
19. Special Coast Report on the River Gironde. The report C/95 of 4 October was preceded by reports C/21 of 3 March 1942 and then C/23 of 8 March, which would confirm that *Frankton* had been in preparation for far longer than would appear at first sight.
20. Report of the mission, dated 7 April 1943. PRO DEFE 218
21. Targeting the Bacalan submarine base many times in 1941 resulted in damage to the town centre and many civilian casualties with little damage to the installation. In March 1942, another raid resulted in the same disastrous results.
22. Despite the fact that as operatives in an escape line they were not supposed to carry information. Marie-Claire agreed to pay 5,000 francs to a harbour pilot who provided them with the exact information regarding the blockade runners' departure (May 1943) out of Bordeaux with vast quantities of rice and other supplies for the Japanese; this was then passed on to London who in turn managed to secure that those same ships were dispatched to the bottom of the sea.
23. See chapters 8 and 10.

Chapter 2   'A Ding-Dong Battle'

1. Royal Ocean Racing Club.
2. Note that the first draft outline plan was completed on 22 September 1942.
3. Hasler Papers.
4. Captain of Flotilla.

Chapter 3   The Thames Fiasco

1. Other authors unfortunately have this timing inaccurately as 2055.
2. Not a happy bunny! Military humour.

Chapter 4   A 'Blanket', a 'Hotel' Bed and the Spirit of 'Polish Grain'

1. Most accounts from those on the *Tuna* were written later in life and some openly admit that part of their account was derived from official sources. Another consideration is the health of the men at the time, e.g., Lt Bull wrote his account in the late 1980s; he died in 1991. Dickie himself had been in poor health before he had written some of his memoirs.
2. All are quoted from the Private Papers of R. P. Raikes.
3. All are quoted from the Private Papers of J. R. H. Bull lodged at IWM ref 67/254/1.
4. All are quoted from the Private Papers of G. J. Rowe.
5. All are quoted from the Private Papers of R. A. W. Quick.
6. Personal Diaries, quotes and notes.
7. From an amalgamation of Private Papers, books and conversations with the author.
8. Postwar private notes of events leading up to Op. *Frankton*.
9. A series of abortive patrols in the northern waters around Norway.
10. It is said that Hasler only told one person about the operation: 'Jock' Stewart. MacKinnon, however, thought he would not be coming back.
11. Colloquial term for Portsmouth.
12. *Larry* subsequently failed her final trials on 4 January 1943 and was replaced by MV *Celtic*, which was then moored at Hayling Island.
13. As a POW.
14. He later became one of Hasler's best friends.
15. It is uncertain whether Hasler joined them, as it is believed that he had his photograph taken elsewhere.

16. The addition of a silencer tube on the end of the muzzle ensured just a very faint click when the trigger was depressed.
17. See Chapter 9, The 'Not Forgotten'.
18. The Fairburn-Sykes double-edged fighting knife seven inches long.
19. See HMS *Tuna* and her Fish section.
20. On the final approach.
21. Full details given in the 'Insignificant Vessel' chapter.
22. See Capt. Raikes' story; *Tuna* and the Trugs chapter.
23. Spies; one French and one English.
24. See diagrams of bags and contents showing storage for passage and during attack phases.
25. IWM 67/254/1 J. R. H. Bull. Unfortunately this account is not as full as it could have been.
26. Batman or Marine Officer's Attendant.
27. Taken from a conversation notes during an interview with Dickie Raikes.
28. Bill Sparks relates 'in small letters on the bows'; normal practice.
29. German military archives, interrogation section, Dulay, Nord Wilhelshaven. Following careful removal of the flexible paint, the names were found. This information must have been related by the men under interrogation.
30. This could have been white paint with the additional paint 'bleeding' into the white making it appear blue.
31. Taken from his post-war anecdotal writing penned towards the end of his years.
32. Interview with Raikes.
33. Built by Ramage & Ferguson, designed by Cox & King. In feet: LOA 318; LWL 275.2; Beam 37.5 Steel/Twin-Screw Schooner.
34. Used by Royal Navy in First and Second World War; Camper and Nicholson, 1920–27, Taylor 1928–39; commercial interests 1947.
35. Postwar account from Gordon J. Rowe (one of *Tuna's* Sub-Lts).
36. The commandos were in pairs carrying one canoe between them.
37. Torpedo room.
38. Dickie Raikes interview. Torpedoes were probably the 1942/3 Mk XV 18-inch, 17 feet 2.75 inches (5.251 m).
39. Equating to 91 nautical miles.
40. A term used affectionately by Ray Quick, but in reality a derogatory term for work-shy sailors.
41. IWM 67/254/1 J. R. H. Bull.
42. Postwar written account from Gordon J. Rowe, RN (one of *Tuna's* Sub-Lts).
43. *ibid.*
44. PRO Adm 173/17677.
45. *Tuna's* log for that date clearly shows, even though there is a spelling mistake, that this is the point where exercises were undertaken.
46. Postwar narrative from Telegraphist Raymond Quick.
47. Written many years after the event, he would not have been familiar with the correct terminology as are most to this day.
48. PRO Adm 173/17677.
49. Appendix C Ref Op. *Frankton* by Hasler.
50. *Tuna's* log.
51. Chicken Rock lies to the south-west of the Calf of Man about three miles (4.5 km) south-west of Spanish Head on the Manx mainland. The rock is home to a 144-foot lighthouse. The southernmost island of the Isle of Man.
52. Hasler's diary entry.
53. Longships is the name given to a group of rocks situated 1.25 miles to the west of Land's End, in Penwith, Cornwall. A lighthouse is situated at Longships.
54. 49° 56'.72 N 05° 48'.50 W. Its name is said to be derived from the unique howl heard when the wind filled the fissures of the rock or because of the assumed shape of the rock to a wolf's head.
55. From written article which appeared in the Marconi magazine during Raikes' time as the company's publicity manager.
56. The author can confirm that the chart track does resemble this format.

57. Similar to a small destroyer.
58. Postwar admission during an interview.
59. Operation *Frankton* – Raikes' official report.
60. These were worn for at least an hour before surfacing at night to acclimatise the eyes for night vision.
61. It could have been that the girder itself had been attached to the 4-inch gun sometime prior to this date.
62. Sparks confirms this, and as owner of an original Mk 2, the author can testify to this claim.
63. The actual operational report (Appendix 1) by Capt. Raikes gives the following timings: commenced Operation at 1937; all boats were out on the upper deck by 1945; last boat water borne 2020; waved goodbye 2022. The author is prone to believe log made at the time as more accurate.
64. An estuarine stretch of water at the point where the tidal River Tamar, Tavy and Lynher meet prior to entering Plymouth Sound; it flows past Devonport Dockyard.
65. Some letters were written on *Al Rawdah* and some on board *Tuna*.
66. At that time, this would have been Saro's on IOW. Full evidenced details are in 'The Insignificant vessel' chapter.

Chapter 5   'It Was A Beastly Clear Night'

1. This is the penultimate sentence from Captain Dickie Raikes' report to Flag Officer Submarines of Operation *Frankton*.
2. This timing is taken from *Tuna's* log made at the time. Hasler's report made 8 April 1943 is believed to have relied upon Raikes' report dated 13 December 1942. It is viewed that the log is accurate and the 2022 timing from Raikes' report is likely to reflect his timing for being clear of the immediate area rather than when the *Frankton* Operatives had been disembarked.
3. It is believed that Hasler's compass was about 20 degrees out.
4. Part of the oral history taken from Norman Colley.
5. He hardly ever referred to the craft as a canoe.
6. The original Navy Rum produced in the British Virgin Islands; highly likely to have been this brand.
7. The Chasseurs were assembled for an inspection that morning.
8. Intentional, an author's indulgence!
9. 26½ land miles.
10. Conversation with F. Boisnier in 2002.
11. Hasler and Sparks did visit and were reunited with the fishermen's families some time in the 1960s.
12. Sparks noted this fact!
13. Just over 25 land miles.
14. NB. Had the Mk 1* type been used, they would have never even managed to get this far. The flat-bottomed design, as with the collapsibility, had been 'invented' not by Hasler but by Fred Goatley a whole year before Hasler came on the scene. This elderly gent was never thanked by award and is largely forgotten.
15. Total length fully extended 58¾; folded up 15½; previously in other publications this had been reported wrongly.
16. Complete process not related here. This was the process to be undertaken in daylight directly before the attack.
17. 1 Cable = 185.2 metres or 202.5 yards
18. Total length fully extended 58¾ inches, 1,465 mm, and size folded up 15½ inches, 395 mm.
19. This minesweeper (No. 5), formally known as *Schwanheim* was a 5,000-tonne cargo vessel crewed by German Navy.
20. Pathfinders were equipped with a VES System, a huge magnetic-field generator which could explode magnetic mines at a safe distance. Used to escort surface ships and U-boats to and from their bases to remove mines. They were equipped with heavy AA armament and often with barrage balloons; mainly former merchant ships with a size of about 5,000 tonnes.
21. From Hasler's report.

22. Killed serving aboard HMS *Naiad*.
23. RMA Eastney.

Chapter 6   The Four Noble Truths

1. e.g., Bungalow instead of single-storey dwelling.
2. Goatley had designed the canoe a year before Hasler had arrived on the scene. Hasler helped with the design of the cockpit canopy and the other deck parts.
3. Bachmann's war diary's for 8/12/42.
4. It should be pointed out that much construction was being undertaken in the area by conscripted TODT workers.
5. Although second-hand, this is from a statement taken from a German sailor, named Karl Tesdordf, when a POW.
6. Head of FOIC western France.
7. At the time of December 1942, the German defence installations were still incomplete in this sector; French civilians lived in their homes around the Pointe de Grave, including employees of the contractor Brousse who worked on the sea defences.
8. There is another report by an assistant staff officer, Wilhelm de Vries, who seems to have confused Wallace and Ewart's capture with that of one of the other pairs of marines. See WO 309/1604.
9. Employees of contractor Brousse were living in the area along with French civilians in their homes. A foreman for Brousse, Monsieur Castets, had contact with the Germans. He was able to relate some details of the capture of Wallace and Ewart.
10. PRO ADM1/18344: Deposition from Graf von Seyssel D'Aix on 6 June 1945 to American Military HQ, CIC Detachement, Augsberg.
11. Deposition from Graf von Seyssel D'Aix 6 June 1945 to American Military HQ, CIC Detachment, Augsberg.
12. According to a worker for the contractor building the defences, Castets, the Flak Division reported that they seemed to have been National Socialists, whose methods were somewhat different to those of the Kriegsmarine.
13. Report made on 9/12/42 at 0352, German archive documentation.
14. From Max Gebauer in March and June 1948; part of the war crimes investigation.
15. Deputy for SNOIS.
16. The maps issued to canoe team had been cut into separate sheets with each sheet covering the section to be completed during one day. After use, each sheet was to be destroyed during the daytime lay-up. This would mean that all the maps would have been collected by the Germans as they were still contained within the map case.
17. An assistant staff officer.
18. Counter Intelligence Section.
19. Sub Section III M Naval Counter Int. Officer (III)M.
20. Sub Section III M Naval Counter Int. Officer (III)M.
21. Liaison officer to C-in-C West.
22. PRO WO 309/1604.
23. It is not clear who provided what information.
24. Wallace said that his training was nine months whilst Ewart's was three to four months.
25. No doubt he probably meant the Welsh, Scottish and Irish as well!
26. 'Specialist Leader'; entry officer without disciplinary powers employed for his technical qualifications, inferior to executive officers holding same rank.
27. Employed at Dulag Nord as interrogator. Previously a tobacconist. He had spent some time in England.
28. Naval HQ for whole of occupied France.
29. Adjutant Bds Paris; HQ Commander of Security Police in France.
30. NOIC, Bordeaux.
31. Adjutant of the Naval Officer in Charge; NOIC, Bordeaux.
32. Statement by Prahm taken on 29 April 1948.
33. A prosecution lawyer, from Frankfurt, well used to interrogating. It is said that Luther was considerably influenced by Dohse, the officer in charge of section 4.

34. This is an intersection, a moderate circle of space where a convoy of vehicles could be parked.
35. Dohse.
36. Naval Officer Inshore Squadron Gascogny; HQ at Royan.
37. Heather died between April and June 1944, before her seventeenth birthday.
38. Viewed by those who knew him as a man of weak character.
39. His profession was that of a Lawyer, a prosecutor.
40. C-in-C Navy Group West.
41. Chief of Staff Navy Group West; possibly the only one with sufficient moral courage to voice his protests; inability to suffer fools.
42. Flag Capt. (AI) Navy Group West; reported to be a hard-bitten man; a strict disciplinarian and efficient at his job.
43. Navy Group West; hard-working if unscrupulous; Intelligence officer.
44. Liaison to Counter Int. Navy group West; an unsuccessful reserve officer a liaison officer; a jack of all trades.
45. Jodl's deputy.
46. Part of WFSt.
47. Section III.
48. Viewed as a 'colourless bank clerk'.
49. Within the author's last publication, *The Cockleshell Canoes*, it was mooted the chateau could have been used for this deed. Deep research of the men's death had not been undertaken at that stage and a reliance was made on the reports by the French. It transpired that although the French had asserted this information as fact, it was later admitted that the chateau was only associated in connection with the executions as a site of remembrance and memorial on the *Frankton* Trail.
50. Security Detachment, the security branch of the SS.
51. Mme Solange Gacis related events during an interview to M. F. Boisnier.
52. A name given by the men of the RMBPD for a special rapid march devised by Sgt Wallace.
53. Interview with F. Boisnier in 2000.
54. The actual date on his report was 17 December, yet all other documentation concerning this gives the 14 December date; it is taken as a typo and duly altered with his reported deposition herein.
55. Of Canton La Garde.
56. Rassemblement National Populaire.
57. Mobilised in 1940, he had been taken prisoner by the British at Saint-Jean d'Acre and was repatriated, immediately joining the Resistance movement.
58. It is up to others to determine the facts behind this matter.
59. Commander of the 18th Legion of the Gironde Gendarmerie, addressed to the Prefect of the Gironde and copied to the colonel commanding the 118th Legion.
60. This was the Feldgendarmarie's next higher authority.
61. After Drey's interrogation.
62. Taken from a deposition by the War Crimes Investigation Team at Wuppertal, Germany, on 23 April 1948. Capt. Lt Drey or Drei, chief of the *Hafenüberwachungsstelle* (the harbour security office).
63. Later described as the municipal prison.
64. Original translation from his deposition.
65. This is either another typographical error, translation mistake or simply an instance of mistaking the corporal stripes to be that of a sergeant.
66. For repetition, it had been established that this place, Château Magnol, was only one of commemoration not the execution site of any Cockleshell Hero.
67. From a testimony by the girl believed to have been recorded by Michel Saint Marc; her married name is Farre.
68. In 1942, she was eight years old.
69. Born in 1913 and moved to the village at the age of thirteen. Taken from an oral history in September 1999 by F. Boisnier.
70. From 'Memories of Edouard Pariente' taken from *A la découverte de l'entre-deux-mers: Baigneaux.*

71. Possibly for black-market trading.
72. Taken from an interview in November 1999 with the Jauberts' daughter-in-law, Mme Roland Jaubert.
73. From a 1956 interview with Jaubert.
74. Letter sent to Mrs MacKinnon (mother) from Louis Jaubert.
75. Statement taken by Capt. R. A. Nightingale on 2 November 1945.
76. Born 26 June 1900 at St Brice, just a couple of miles distant from Cessac.
77. Letter to Mrs MacKinnon, 14 October 1945.
78. 22 Clarendon Street, Glasgow, and 20 Heaton Mersey View, Larkhill Road, Edgeley, Stockport, Cheshire.
79. Possibly S/Lt.
80. Each of the crew were supplied with enough money within the escape box to pay their way.
81. War Crimes Investigation Team; Nightingale was from Intelligence Corps of No. 2 WCIT.
82. Testimony taken by R. A, Nightingale, WCIT, on 2 November 1945.
83. Presumably there were two prosecutors in La Réole.
84. Jaubert had reason to believe this.
85. The (UK) Post Office stamp was marked London 9.45 a.m., 5 March 1943; the date stamp (apparently Censor's) dated 19 January 1943.
86. Addressed Military High Command dated 12 January 1944 reporting action taken against captured men from various raids.
87. Via telegram, hence wording.
88. This from document of the unit of Dulag Nord, Wilhelmshaven, taken from the interrogation of prisoners at GIS Substation in Bordeaux. Dated 28 December 1942.
89. During a conversation with Peter Siddall during the dedication of a memorial plaque to Sheard and Moffatt.
90. Casualty list.
91. It has been found that the surname was easily misspelt in a number of British documents and books including the Lucas Phillips book.
92. Lucas Phillips even relates Moffatt's body as being found elsewhere.
93. PRO ADM 1/18344 Shooting of prisoners/Attack on shipping, Bordeaux.
94. The copy summary of von Runsted's original signal document gives a date of 18 December, yet the information within shows details concerning 28 December. Clearly, it is a typographical error and should read 28 December as is likely on the original German document.
95. From LXXX Army Corps dated 14 December 1942 sent by 1st Lt Willemer.
96. From Dulag Nord, Wilhelmshaven, dated 3/1/43.
97. As recorded by the Germans.
98. They are not keen on changing the date.
99. For some inexplicable reason, Lucas Phillips in 1956 wrote that it was Moffatt's body that was found here.
100. The overriding need was to be seen to be carrying out Hitler's Order save that they might have been 'sent elsewhere'.
101. Heinz Corssen had determined that these interrogations had been carried out 'most ineptly'.

Chapter 7   The Great Escapade

1. Possibly a York but it was deemed more likely a Dakota; there were regular mail runs from Gibraltar.
2. A disputed territory placed under German administration.
3. All timings are from Hasler, who wore his HMG-issued waterproof-covered pocket watch.
4. Clodomir is believed to have been born in Segonzac just after the turn of the twentieth century.
5. No name was available.
6. Hebrew word: said to have come from the heavens and been eaten by the Israelites in the desert; Exodus 16.
7. Said wood still exists and is in place today along with Hasler's DNA.
8. Plural hinting more than one individual was present.
9. Spring/summer 2011: Memorial Commemorative booklet due post event by author.
10. Until May 1943.
11. The obvious reference is made to British situation comedy *'Allo 'Allo!*

12. During a visit by two young Royal Marine Officers undertaking initiative training.
13. For many years, the establishment welcomed many pilgrims. In the 1930s, it was known as Hôtel des Sports.
14. Fortunately, confirmation of events can be taken from a casual interview in 1960 by a group of young officers who were probably the first to have ever undertaken the paddle up the Gironde and followed the escape route.
15. From an informal interview with the sisters in 1960 by two young officers during their initiative training. Exercise *Formidable* Journal 1960.
16. The original account says that they had wine but the 1960 interview with the waitress who served them shows that Hasler ordered coffee.
17. Exercise *Formidable* Journal 1960.
18. Exercise *Formidable* Journal 1960.
19. Exercise *Formidable* Journal 1960.
20. *ibid.*
21. Unevidenced but French research has brought this forward.
22. Exercise *Formidable* Journal 1960.
23. Some of this account contradicts actual evidenced facts, i.e., days spent at Armand's and René Mandinaud's part played.
24. The bells were destroyed in 1941.
25. Hasler's account is quite clear, giving the date they arrived, quoting the number of days spent at the farm and the date they left. This account has to be relied upon. Armand in *c.* 1947 wrote to Hasler asking him to confirm the part Armand played and mentions the length of time Hasler stayed: 'about a month'. Hasler did reply using those same words. It seems that Armand extended the 'about a month' period even further as in some quarters Hasler and Sparks are recorded to have stayed for forty-two days. Clearly, Hasler's 1943 report has to be relied upon; it is thought that Hasler was happy to allow the 'about a month' quote to be used as a kindness. They only stayed at Armand's farm for eighteen days.
26. Seriously injured by a car as she was crossing the Demarcation Line near Loches.
27. His last known address was in Rue Jean Jaurès, and it is believed this was on the crossroads at Rue du Général Leclerc in Ruffec. Corner house.
28. The interview was in the November; Armand's surname was misspelt at the registering of his birth. His parents were Dubreuile with one 'l', but once registered it stayed that way. Source: Amelie, his wife, in a conversation in May 2010.
29. Sauveterre-de-Béarn primarily remained the route for escaping Frenchmen who could afford to pay their own expenses. Marie-Claire had to provide the fare money herself from the money she received from the British Government.
30. Maxim was Marie-Claire's agent. He was twenty-two years old, a big, handsome farmer's son who, being an agricultural worker, had been demobilised from the army. He was responsible for helping several hundred men to escape over the border.
31. This may be an incorrect spelling.
32. As well as Armand's mother, Louise, and one-year-old Michel.
33. Born 5 June 1919.
34. Michel went on to be a talented aircraft technician; Armand and Amelie went on to have ten children.
35. A notable part of the detail was from a telephone interview with Amelie in 2010.
36. Due to Marie-Claire's unconventional ways, the establishment at MI9 sharply forbade the young handler Airey Neave to send her a radio operator.
37. He qualified but remained ignorant of the subject!
38. It now rests at CMSM in Essex.
39. For some reason, this time period is reported, by even the French, as forty-two days, which can be proved to be incorrect. Hasler himself records this time period in at least two different documents as an eighteen-day period.
40. One of the many escape lines this was Pat O'Leary's line.
41. Hasler had pencilled in the margin 'Rich People'.
42. Hasler did actually write this.
43. Young Belgian RAF officer.
44. Meaning that he would be considered past the age of military service.

45. Referring to a visit she would have been told about during the Civil War of 1936.
46. Information care of Norman Colley.
47. RMBPD Diary 31 December 1942.
48. From the cockney rhyming slang pronounced 'brassic', sometimes teamed with '*lint*'; meaning skint or without money.
49. Seemingly the only error in the plan.

Chapter 8   A Repeat of Operation *Frankton*

1. The equivalent now of *c.* £1,550.
2. *Oberleutnant* (*Korvetten Kapitän*) Peter Popp of the Kriegsmarine. He cited the *Frankton* Raid as an example of outstanding merit in all his lectures which he gave whilst employed as an instructor in mines and explosives at a training establishment. He had previously been posted in Bordeaux.
3. *Schwanheim* was a 5,339 ton German motor vessel, owned by Unterweser Reederei AG and built in 1936 by Bremer Vulkan. On 13 August 1944, *Schwanheim* was bombed and sunk by Allied aircraft off Royan at the mouth of the River Gironde (Jürgen Rohwer, *Chronology of the War at Sea, 1939-1945: The Naval History of World War II*).
4. Requisitioned in 1940, seized by the Germans in 1940, assigned to the Kriegsmarine in 1941, renamed *Python*, believed commissioned 25 September 1941, damaged on 11 December 1942 by British Commandos in Bordeaux, converted to Sperrbrecher 122 in February 1943, joined the 2nd Fleet Sperrbrecher, scuttled 25 August 1944 in Saint-Nazaire, refloated and repaired in June 1946, renamed *Cape Hadid* in 1946, renamed *Cap Bon* in 1953 (Roger Jordan, *The World's Merchant Fleet, 1939: The Particulars and Wartime Fates*).
5. There are documents and one drawing that refer to this vessel.
6. The first German supply ship called *Python* was scuttled December 1941. HMS *Dorsetshire* sighted German U-boat supply ship *Python* with submarines UA and U-68 alongside. Submarines departed and made torpedo attack which failed. *Python* scuttled. The 1942 supply ship *Python* damaged at Bordeaux by commando action, ex-*Cap Hadid*, was built in Denmark in 1938 for French owners. If the commissioning date of September 1941 is to be believed (1941 could be a typographical error from original documentation and date could actually be 1942), it would seem that *Python* was a *Tarnschiff* (camouflage ship) being a decoy for the original U-boat supply ship *Python* before she was scuttled in December 1941.
7. Records from the Federal Archives: 61/II RM 129, RM 20/1818, RM 20/1819, RM 20/1820, RM 20/1821. W. Lohmann, *The German Navy 1939-1945*.
8. His activity for the Resistance brought him the award of the Cross of the Legion of Honour in 1945.
9. To date, no files have been found to unquestionably support that the SOE were imminently involved in this matter.
10. Concerning the SOE agents.
11. At the time, the crane equipment was considerable, comprising 177 cranes under 10 tons capacity of which 158 were electric, with six floating cranes (with a maximum capacity of 300 tons) and forty-six other lifting appliances for coal, timber, fruit and grain cargos. There was also a fixed crane of 250 tons capacity. The total length of quays of port of Bordeaux includes the Bassens and Grattequina areas on each side of the bank. The total length of the three quays was 7,225 metres.
12. Full quote from Admiral of the Fleet Lord Fisher: 'The essence of war is violence. Moderation in war is imbecility.'

Chapter 9   The 'Not Forgotten'

1. May they be at God's right Hand – a Gaelic blessing.
2. From the *Introduction to Winning* by Frank Dick, published by Abingdon.
3. The author managed to talk with Bill Sparks in 2002 and Norman Colley in 2009.
4. RMBPD War Diaries.
5. Since 1066 (Norman Conquest) until decimalisation (1971) half a crown was 2*s* and 6*d*. Then there were 20 shillings or 240 pennies to the pound.

6. Blondie's for instructor from Deal, Lt Col. G. W. Ross, RM.
7. Eventually a CSM but at the time a sergeant in No. 2 Troop of Detachment 385, D. B. (Jock) Swan.
8. Report written 26 January 1945 at Hammenheil Camp, Ceylon, by Colonel Tollemache. This report seems unfinished.
9. Lt-Cdr Hornby, SOG's one-time supply officer.
10. From a copy of the diary notes Raikes made during the *Frankton* Patrol.
11. Blondie played the banjo, ukulele, piano and clarinet and apparently the sax!
12. Letter to *Daily Express* editor in September 1969.
13. From a telephone conversation with the author on 6 April 2010.
14. Died in the May.
15. William Benjamin Dean.
16. The registered name on the birth certificate is spelt 'McKinnon'; it is believed that this was an error at that time.
17. The other was Pritchard-Gordon.
18. Interview with Dickie Raikes.
19. Description taken when interrogated; German Archives.
20. Originally thought to be 28 August but during further research this birth date was found in official documents. RMM 3 February 1942 from the Commandant, Plymouth Division.
21. Sparks, Colley, Fisher and Ellery and Hasler.
22. Shore establishment.
23. Page 35 of *Last of the Cockleshell Heroes*.
24. This from document of the unit of Dulag Nord, Wilhelmshaven, taken from the interrogation of prisoners at GIS Substation in Bordeaux. Dated 28 December 1942.
25. At ninety years of age this account was furnished by Elsie, who had kept the letter in her possession since the day it was written.
26. His baptism record shows DOB as 22 November – obviously incorrect.
27. Records confirm baptism and full name as furnished via the Certificate of Baptism Parish of Holy Cross (Ardoyne, Belfast) + Diocese of County Down and Connor.
28. His sister-in-law; she only met him once.
29. Quoted from correspondence sent to the author by Elsie Ambler in 2010.
30. This was a civilian post and required observation from a church tower or some such other high vantage point. Armed with a tin hat and bucket, shovel and stirrup pump, they would watch for incendiary bombs.
31. Phyllis had three sisters and three brothers.
32. Noted from early official documentation; latterly this name is spelt 'Henry'. The former is more likely to be correct.
33. Mr Edward Collett.
34. Evidenced by Phyllis Laver (née Page).
35. Of 'The Profumo Affair' incident, who in later life redeemed himself.
36. As No. 1 of the canoe, it would seem the logical choice as it can be confirmed that Colley was not the 'other rank' alluded to.
37. AWOL.
38. Commanded by Lt J. F. Richards, RM (DSC), with Mne W. S. Stevens, (Ply. X. 105862) RM, as his No. 2.
39. Commanded by Sgt J. M. King, (Ply. X. 1457) RM (DSM), with Mne R. N. Ruff, (Ply. X. 108660) RM (DSM), as the No. 2.
40. Ply. X. 2968.
41. The Mk 1 type was used as the Mk 2 had not yet been produced; see 'Insignificant Vessel' chapter.

Chapter 10　The RMBPD's 'Southsea Stroll'

1. A 1995 letter from Hasler to Lt Tim Wiltshire, RM.
2. 200 yards from the explosion!
3. HQ CODC.
4. From Appendix B to War Diary of July 1942; nominal list of RMBPD.
5. Following *Frankton*, Ellery is reported to have disappeared; source: Norman Colley.
6. Source: Norman Colley.

7. The officers received a daily allowance of 13*s* 4*d* per day.
8. Quoted as said to another officer.
9. For all canoe types refer to *The Cockleshell Canoes*, ISBN 978-1-84868-0654
10. Source: General Anthony Hunter-Choat, OBE, SAS.
11. MV *Celtic* is a former sailing barge that was built by Kievits & Van Reede[2] in Papendrecht, Netherlands, in 1903 for E. & W. Goldsmith Ltd. She is currently undergoing restoration at Sittingbourne, Kent.

2   Timely Lives

Chapter 11   Father 'Cockle'

1. *Blondie* by Ewen Southby-Tailyour; *Cockleshell Heroes* by Lucas-Phillips, 1956 version; dimensions inaccurate; information about Goatley inaccurate.
2. *Blondie* by Ewen Southby-Tailyour, p. 56.
3. Designed and built in 1943 and quite unlike the Mk 2 provided by Goatley.
4. Identified originally as plot no. 524.

Chapter 12   Submarine *Tuna* and the Trugs

1. 12 January 1912 – 5 May 2005
2. Term used by senior officers for midshipmen.
3. A yacht with an overall length of 46.30 metres (152 feet).
4. Il Duce; Mussolini.
5. Known as the glorious bluff, charming, but hopelessly highly strung.
6. Rumour has it the agreement was only to get away from the smelly goats
7. It should be noted that it was not possible at that time to see through the periscope at night.
8. The apostle.
9. The canoes used at this time would have been the very early 'folboat' type (Mk 1).
10. Perisher courses were run twice a year since 1917 and navies throughout the world sent their prospective commanding officers to be tested by the British over six months of tactical training. Possible corruption of the 'Periscope' Course.
11. *One of Our Submarines* by Edward Young.
12. Torpedoes were known as 'fish'; see *Tuna*'s specification.
13. Accredited to Dickie Raikes.
14. 26 August 1942.
15. Captain Submarines as had previously been the case.
16. Reputed to be from a wealthy family owning shipyards on the Tyne. He was a Knight of the Realm.
17. Noted for his ability to cook well for the whole ship, whatever the weather and however much the galley was heaving about. Became PO and gained a DSM. It was noted he was a rogue and a thief, in the nicest way, who stole for the boat's complement not from them.
18. A daily 'magazine' compiled by Raymond Quick.
19. In a letter from the Admiralty dated 5 July 1943 notification was given to Quick that he would be awarded the DSM 'for outstanding coolness, cheerfulness and skill whilst serving on *Tuna* in five arduous patrols and a brilliant and successful attack on a German U-boat on 7 April 1943. He received his award on 24 July 1945.
20. He contrived to get enough news through the radio, providing the sub was not too deep, to type out copies and when unable to get real news would make it up until no one was sure what was true and what was his imagination. Raikes said of this 'it was brilliant' and kept copies of some masterpieces. His pseudonym was 'Kwikus'.
21. Possibly spelt Frite although other documents are spelt as Fright.
22. Borough of Camden in London.
23. All quoted passages within this chapter have been taken from the personal notes and diary amalgamations of Lt Raikes' private papers.
24. An island in the English Channel which marks the north-westernmost point of European France.

25. All radar types for submarines had the 'W' prefix; the experimental predecessor, type 286P, was used in the summer of 1941 with HMS *Proteus*.
26. *We Dive at Dawn* is a 1943 war film directed by Anthony Asquith, starring Eric Portman and John Mills. The British submarine *Sea Tiger* is on a top-secret mission to sink Germany's newest battleship, the *Brandenburg*.
27. X-Craft, the vessels were designed to be towed to their intended area of operations by a full-size submarine , T or S class with a passage crew on board, the operational crew being transferred from the towing submarine to the X-Craft by dingy. These were built during 1943–44.
28. Due for dedication first half 2011.
29. Now National Maritime Museum, Greenwich.
30. Ten shillings was the equivalent to 50p today; it came in note form. Five shillings was coin form.
31. They were married for fifty-eight years before his wife died from a severe stroke in January 1996.
32. After leaving *Tuna*, he lost his arm in an accident.
33. From Royal Naval Submarine Museum Archives (some details of *Tuna*'s spec found elsewhere seem to differ).
34. Information from CPO Raymond Quick, DSM, from oral history interview early 2009.
35. At RN Headquarters, the expression 'to do a Goodeve', which meant 'to do something by hook or by crook', grew to be a popular saying. Goodeve's ability to cut through the red tape and get positive results in very little time earned him notoriety. Through his accomplishments, he was tasked to head up a newly established Department of Miscellaneous Weapons Development (DMWD).
36. Both S and T class were all welded as opposed to previous welded frames and riveted plating, thus saving weight and allowing a thicker plating, which in turn allowed deeper diving depth.
37. Name derived through the work of the Anti-submarine Detection Investigation Committee; the primary underwater detection device used by Allied escorts throughout the war. Known to the Americans as Sonar, it was a transmitter-receiver sending out a highly directional soundwave through the water.
38. It is similar to the board game Ludo and is based on the same principle.
39. After consultation with Ray Quick, DSM.
40. See *London Gazette* of 15 June 1943.
41. See *London Gazette* of 18 April 1944.

Chapter 13   The '*Bébé Anglaise*' from Room 900 – Agent 45660

1. A disputed territory placed under German administration.
2. Air force evaders figures from MI9 show 1,975 from RAF and Commonwealth and 2,962 from USAF.
3. M. R. D. Foot: SOE in France.
4. This is at odds with Airey Neave's (MI9) description.
5. This is the correct spelling; it appears that Armand's surname was recorded with two 'l's by mistake at the registering of birth, hence the difference in spelling. Source: Amelie, his widow.
6. Hasler believed she had blue eyes, but the author is more inclined to believe Neave of MI9, as his observational skills were better.
7. Estuary pilot.
8. Marie Odile ended her days in Ravensbrück.

Chapter 14   The Patellogastropoda Master

1. Barrett.

3   Remembering

Chapter 15   The 'Cockleshell Heroes' Ransom

1. Ten pounds, ten shillings (pre-decimalisation).

Chapter 16   The Insignificant Vessel: The 'Cockle' Mark Two

1. More information in *The Cockleshell Canoes*.
2. *River to Sea* by Wheeler.
3. It should be noted that there is a difference in beam on one of the three examples held at the Royal Marines Museum, as there is in the IWM exhibit, please refer to *The Cockleshell Canoes*, ISBN 978-1-84868-0654, for this information.

Chapter 17   The French Affair – 'The English Have Remembered!'

1. From an article in *The Times* dated 2002 when he was ninety-four.
2. This term is only used for the flow of the narrative. All within the United Kingdom are recognised.
3. Mary found that there were two Saint-Preuils and had gone to the wrong one first.
4. Both 'Jock' Stewart and Dickie Raikes were invited but could not attend. Jock had previous engagements he could not cancel.
5. A notable absence is René Mandinaud, who, although he was invited to the 1966 event, seems to have been forgotten by Mary on the plaque. Given Mary Lindell's penchant for accuracy, it occurred to the author that Mary may have believed that he played no part in the assistance rendered to Hasler and Sparks at the restaurant. The alternative would be that it was an error on either Hasler or Mary's part. Given that Hasler sent René a Corps badge to match that which was given to the others in 1961 and in the absence of any firm documentary evidence to the contrary, the Ruffec story has included René as part of the facts.
6. Surprisingly, Hasler did not know who it had been made by but said they deserved a compliment for the workmanship.
7. Became an aircraft technician.
8. It is believed that Sparks himself visited the Dubruilles in 1999.
9. The name is Marilyn Lamb, who underwent an eight-hour operation to save her right arm.
10. Exercise *Formidable* Journal.
11. *ibid.*
12. Surname for all three is 'De Milleville'.
13. This was Conway, who was born in Stockport; there is no known reason why Louis should think this other than he was mistaken and mistook this for the word Mersey.
14. Since the local Gendarmerie records state that MacKinnon and Conway were arrested on the morning of 18 December, it can only be assumed that his recollection is wrong.

Chapter 18   The Cockleshell Heroes Legacy

1. He wrote about Chinese military strategy and martial arts in *The Art of War*. Sun Tzu was a General in the fifth century BC.
2. Leader of the Carthaginian forces against Rome in the Second Punic War. Hannibal almost overpowered Rome and was considered Rome's greatest enemy.
3. (Xerxes the Great) King of Persia, Pharaoh of Egypt, reigned 485–465 BC.
4. On the basis that cinema was revived, thriving and easily available as a mass media connection.
5. A fifty-year closure period existed until 1967. It was then reduced to thirty years. This applied to papers or records that could be classed as sensitive.
6. PRO Prem 3/376.
7. Attributed to Mountbatten.
8. Far from an easy job or a recreational event, used in an amusing way, a purposeful understatement of the event.
9. Health and Safety Executive.
10. Lying-up place.
11. The wine flowed and so to the tide – they missed it and had to wait until the next day!
12. Until February 2010.

Bibliography

Boisnier, François and Raymond Muelle, *Le Commando de l'Impossible* (Editions du Layeur, 2003).

Colledge, J. J., *Ships of the Royal Navy*, vol. 2 (Greenhill Books, 1970).

Hamilton, Georgia W., *Silent Pilots: Figureheads in Mystic Seaport Museum* (Mystic Seaport Museum, 1984).

Harrison, Michael, *Mulberry: The Return in Triumph* (W. H. Allen, 1965).

Home-Run '94 (Escape Lines Reunion, now the WWII 'Escape Lines Memorial Society', known as ELMS and pioneered by Roger Stanton).

Howse, Derek, *Radar at Sea: The Royal Navy in World War 2* (US Naval Institute Press, 1993).

Jordan, Roger, *The World's Merchant Fleet, 1939: The Particulars and Wartime Fates* (Chatham Publishing, 2003).

Kemp, Paul, *The T-class Submarine* (Weidenfeld & Nicholson military, 1990).

Lavery, Brian, *Churchill's Navy: The Ships, Men and Organisation, 1939-1945* (US Naval Institute Press, 2006).

Macrae, Stuart, *Winston Churchill's Toyshop* (Amberley, 2010).

Morris, R. O., *Charts and Surveys in Peace and War* (HMSO, 1995).

Phillips, C. E. Lucas, *Cockleshell Heroes* (William Heinemann, 1956).

Rees, Quentin, *Cockleshell Canoes* (Amberley, 2009).

Rohwer, Jürgen, *Chronology of the War at Sea, 1939-1945: The Naval History of World War II* (US Naval Institute Press, revised ed., 2005).

Saint-Marc, Michel, *Le Canton de Targon sous l'Occupation 1939–1945* (M. Saint-Marc, 2007).

Southby-Tailyour, Ewen, *Blondie* (Pen & Sword, 2003).

Sparks, Bill, *The Last of the Cockleshell Heroes* (ISIS, 1992).

Unwin, Commander J. H., DSC, RN, 'The Acid Test' (*RUSI Journal*).

Wheeler, Raymond, *From River to Sea: Marine Heritage of Sam Saunders* (Cross Publishing, 1993).

Wynne, Barry, *No Drums, No Trumpets* (Arthur Baker Ltd, 1961).

Young, Edward, *One of Our Submarines* (Rubert Hart-Davis, 1952).

Ziegler, Philip, *Mountbatten* (Collins, 1985).

A la découverte de l'Entre-Deux-Mers: Baigneaux, booklet

Account by Bill Sparks, *John Bull*, December 1951.

Exercise Formidable: Aug 1960. Journal Messers Hensman, Hodder, Cameron and Mollan (Archive documentation, RM Archive)

Richard Mitchell Canvas Kayak Website

References

Fred Goatley Archives
Hasler Family Archives – Bridget Hasler
Henri Gendreau
Laver Family Archives – Gary Bowden
National Maritime Museum Archives, Falmouth – Bartlett Library
Norman Colley Archives – Norman Colley
Raikes Family Archives – Briget Legge
Raymond Quick Family Archives – Raymond Quick
Simms/Archives
Sparks Family Archives

National Archives
IWM Records/Archives

CMSM Records/Archives

PRO ADM1/18344
HS9/75 & 76;WO309/1604; WO232/10b
HS6/418
DEFE2/ 216; 217; 218; 798; 842; 952; 988; 1035;1038
DEFE2/ 1 /173; 1144A
ADM 202/310; 399
ADM 202/310
ADM1/14353; 26411
ADM 334
IWM 67/254/1
CAB 79/24/6; 79/24/27; 79/58/48; 79/25/50
PG 32060/ND
PG 36917; 37729;7730
ADM1/22091
WO 165/39; 170/3962B; 208/3242
WO 309/551 + WO 311/617
ADM 199/1844
ADM 173/17676
ADM 173/17677
ADM 173/17678

Index

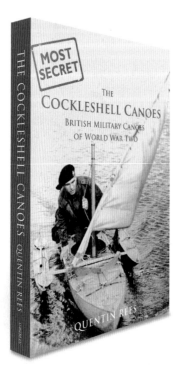